Energy Advice Handbook

JULIA GREEN

sponsored by

Energy Saving Trust

published by

energyINFORM

ENERGY ADVICE HANDBOOK

energyINFORM – **Published by Energy Inform Ltd**

Energy Inform Ltd was established in 1981, and specialises in domestic energy research, energy advice, training, strategy development, project evaluation and the production of publications.

The author, Julia Green, a Director of Energy Inform Ltd, is experienced in the development and tutoring of training courses on domestic energy efficiency, and has been closely involved in researching the effectiveness of energy advice, and the development of standards for advice provision.

Energy Saving Trust – **Sponsored by The Energy Saving Trust**

The Energy Saving Trust is an independent, government funded body that works in partnership with organisations and businesses with the shared goal of promoting energy efficiency. Its goal is to improve the efficient use of all forms of domestic energy in the UK, leading to an overall reduction in its consequential environmental impact – while bringing economic benefits to individual consumers and to the nation as a whole.

The Trust part funds the Energy Efficiency Advice Centres (EEACs) that are local centres of knowledge and experience about energy efficiency. Together they form a UK-wide network giving free, impartial and locally relevant energy efficiency advice to householders. The 52 EEACs around the country work in partnership with local and national bodies to help householders improve the energy efficiency and comfort of their homes.

Whilst every effort has been made to ensure the accuracy and completeness of the information in this Handbook, neither the publisher, Energy Inform Ltd, nor the author can accept any liability for any loss or damage caused as a result of any inaccuracy or omission.

The Energy Advice Handbook should not be used for compliance with planning and Building Regulation issues that can impact upon installations of energy efficiency measures.

1st edition (Heating Advice Handbook) 1987
2nd edition (Heating Advice Handbook) 1993
Energy Advice Handbook 2004

ISBN 0-907800-16-5

Published by Energy Inform Ltd, 5 Hawkyard, Greenfield, Oldham OL3 7NP

Designed by Glynis Edwards, Quest-Designs, Bath
Cover design by Graphite Design, Greenfield, Oldham
Printed by Taylor and Clifton Ltd, Uppermill, Oldham

FOREWORD

The Energy Saving Trust's mission reads, "To inform and transform; to turn good intentions into effective action". I think you will find from this handbook that you are about to read that the author, on behalf of the Trust, has delivered on this aspiration. It is the Trust's intention that all good advice leads to action, and in this particular handbook there are hundreds of very practical suggestions, which will enable practitioners in the field to give good quality advice to consumers so that they can take action to improve the cost effectiveness of their homes; to enhance the comfort of their own environment and, as importantly, to help win the fight against carbon emissions.

The provision of energy advice is fundamentally important if we are to deliver on the overall objectives of the Energy White Paper, published in February 2003, which requires that 50% of the carbon savings need to come from energy efficiency measures. This is clearly a very steep target but, with assistance from handbooks such as these, we will be able to put ourselves in great shape to work with consumers, householders and small businesses to deliver on the promise of the Energy White Paper. This publication will provide a fantastic resource that will enable energy advisors to give very practical information to the customer.

During 2003/04 the fifty-two Energy Efficiency Advice Centres throughout England, Scotland, Wales and Northern Ireland will have made contact with over 750,000 customers. Publications such as these will enable us to ensure those contacts are not just a one-off event, but the beginning of a serious relationship with the customer, leading to installation of energy efficient measures throughout the future.

Finally, our thanks must go to Julia Green, who has great experience in the development of energy advice services for Domestic Energy Efficiency. I think you will agree this handbook sets a new standard in terms of energy advice provision.

Philip Sellwood
Chief Executive
Energy Saving Trust

ACKNOWLEDGEMENTS

For sponsorship

Energy Inform Ltd would like to thank the Energy Saving Trust whose sponsorship and support has made this Handbook possible.

For comments and contributions

The Energy Advice Handbook is a comprehensive guide, and as such has drawn on many other sources of published material.

We are grateful to the many organisations including fuel suppliers, manufacturers, retailers, statutory and voluntary organisations who have provided material for this Handbook.

The Energy Advice Handbook is derived from the Heating Advice Handbook. Of the authors of the first edition of the Heating Advice Handbook, Julia Green is a Director of Energy Inform Ltd and Catrin Maby is the Director of the Severn Wye Energy Agency.

This Handbook could not have been produced without the contributions and comments from many individuals and organisations. We would like to thank the following for their specific contribution and comments on draft sections of the Handbook:

Andrew Amato – EST; Brian Anderson, Ludmilla Kosmina – BRE; Kevin Boniface, Nick Jones - BRE; David Barnes -Ofgem; Roger Critchley – First Report; Brian Daunter – EST; EDF (staff); Gareth Edmunds, Pete Saunders – MVM; Brian Elmer – EST; Malcolm Fletcher, Graham Lauder – Eaga Partnership; Walter French, Phillip Warren - Scottish Power; Peter Guy, David Ross – BRE Rob Howard – NEA; Norman Jones – SALKENT Ltd; Landis & Gyr (staff); Kevin Lane, Jane Palmer - Environmental Change Institute, University of Oxford; Catrin Maby – Severn Wye Energy Agency; Paul Maplethorpe – Rotherham Metropolitan Borough Council; Linn Rafferty – NES Ltd; Ed Reed – energywatch; OFTEC (staff); Simon Roberts, Mark Letcher - Centre for Sustainable Energy (CSE); Jean Morrison - SCARF.

We would particularly like to thank the experienced energy advice staff of SCARF who have commented on most of the content of the Handbook and provided some of the case studies.

Thanks also go to Anne Hughes of Energy Inform Ltd for research, typing and proof reading, and to Glynis Edwards of quest-designs for her design work.

For illustrations / photographs

Many illustrations in the Handbook are reproduced from the 2nd edition of the Heating Advice Handbook. We are grateful for permission to reproduce illustrations and tables from other sources and publications.

A list of credits for illustrations can be found in the back of the Handbook.

CONTENTS

INTRODUCTION ix

1 GIVING GOOD ENERGY ADVICE

1.1 Definition of energy advice 1–1
1.2 Methods of delivering energy advice 1–2
1.3 Energy advice is effective 1–2
1.4 The Code of Practice 1–3

2 HOW TO USE THE ENERGY ADVICE HANDBOOK

2.1 Keeping up to date 2–1
2.2 Reference material 2–2
2.3 Using the action flow charts 2–2
2.4 Using the energy advice home visit checklist 2–2
2.5 Action flowcharts 2–3
2.6 Energy advice home visit checklist 2–7

3 HEALTH RISKS FROM COLD DAMP HOMES

3.1 Excess winter deaths 3–1
3.2 The effects of cold on the body 3–2
3.3 Who is most at risk from the cold? 3–2
3.4 Health risks from damp homes 3–3
3.5 Making homes warmer and drier 3–3
3.6 Partnership projects for warmth 3–3

4 FUEL SUPPLIERS AND CONSUMER ADVICE

4.1 Choosing a fuel supplier 4–1
4.2 How price comparisons are worked out 4–1
4.3 How to change supplier 4–2
4.4 Problems with changing suppliers 4–2
4.5 Services offered by fuel suppliers 4–3
4.6 What is energywatch? 4–4
4.7 What is Ofgem? 4–4
4.8 The Energy Retail Association 4–5
4.9 Solid fuel suppliers 4–5
4.10 Oil suppliers 4–6
4.11 LPG suppliers 4–6

5 METERS, TARIFFS AND FUEL BILLS

5.1 Why read meters? 5–1
5.2 How to read electricity credit meters 5–1
5.3 How to read gas credit meters 5–3
5.4 Electricity prepayment meters 5–3
5.5 Gas prepayment meters 5–4
5.6 Advantages and disadvantages of prepayment meters 5–5
5.7 Tariffs for electricity and gas 5–6
5.8 Understanding fuel bills 5–7
5.9 Information on fuel bills 5–8
5.10 Examples of electricity and gas bills 5–8
5.11 Estimated bills 5–12
5.12 Other information on bills 5–13

6 FUEL PAYMENT METHODS AND DEALING WITH DEBT

6.1 Ways to pay for fuel 6–1
6.2 Choosing a method of paying for fuel 6–2
6.3 Codes of Practice on payment methods 6–3
6.4 Fuel debt 6–4
6.5 Definition of arrears for fuel 6–4
6.6 Ways of paying off arrears for fuel 6–5
6.7 Disconnection of fuel supply 6–6
6.8 Multiple debt 6–7
6.9 Preventing fuel debt 6–7

7 FINANCIAL HELP FOR HEATING AND ENERGY EFFICIENCY

7.1 Government grants to tackle fuel poverty 7–1
7.2 The Energy Efficiency Commitment (EEC) 7–3
7.3 Local authority schemes 7–3
7.4 Health related schemes 7–3
7.5 Benefit take up – 'Benefit health checks' 7–4
7.6 Winter fuel payments/cold weather payments 7–4
7.7 Hardship funds/charitable funds 7–4
7.8 Renewable energy 7–4
7.9 Contacts for up to date grant information 7–5

8 BASICS OF HEATING AND HOT WATER SYSTEMS AND APPLIANCES

8.1 Summary of fuels and heating and hot water systems and appliances 8–1
8.2 Choosing an appropriate heating system 8–4
8.3 Wet central heating systems 8–4
8.4 Warm air central heating 8–11
8.5 Off peak electric storage heaters 8–12
8.6 Electric under floor heating 8–13
8.7 Community heating 8–14
8.8 Individual electric heaters 8–15
8.9 Individual gas heaters 8–15
8.10 Domestic hot water 8–17

9 CONTROLLING HEATING AND HOT WATER SYSTEMS

9.1 Why have controls? 9–1
9.2 Controls on a wet central heating system 9–2
9.3 Controls on solid fuel systems 9–9
9.4 Controls on electric heating systems 9–10
9.5 Controls on warm air central heating systems 9–12

10 COMPARATIVE EFFICIENCIES AND RUNNING COSTS OF HEATING AND HOT WATER SYSTEMS

10.1 Fuel and system efficiency 10–1
10.2 Comparative running costs – published data 10–2
10.3 Predicting fuel costs with energy auditing software 10–5
10.4 Monitoring actual fuel costs 10–6

11 HEAT LOSS FROM DWELLINGS

11.1 How heat is lost from a dwelling 11–1
11.2 Fabric heat loss and U-values 11–2
11.3 Ventilation heat loss 11–4
11.4 Factors affecting the heat loss from buildings 11–5
11.5 Setting limits for heat loss – The Building Regulations 11–6

12 HOME INSULATION

12.1 Why insulate? 12–1
12.2 Which measures? 12–2
12.3 Hot water cylinder insulation 12–2
12.4 Roof insulation 12–4
12.5 Wall insulation 12–6
12.6 Draughtproofing 12–8
12.7 Floor insulation 12–10
12.8 Double glazing 12–11

13 ENERGY RATING OF HOMES

13.1 What is an energy rating? 13–1
13.2 SAP – The Standard Assessment Procedure 13–1
13.3 Who provides SAP Ratings? 13–2
13.4 The National Home Energy Rating Scheme (NHER) 13–3
13.5 What energy rating software is used for 13–4

14 APPLIANCES AND LIGHTING – OPERATION AND ENERGY EFFICIENCY

14.1 Working out running costs of electrical appliances 14–1
14.2 Energy labels 14–3
14.3 Operation of some major electrical appliances 14–4
14.4 Standby 14–8
14.5 Lighting 14–10
14.6 Running costs of gas appliances 14–12

15 RENEWABLE ENERGY

15.1 Renewable energy policy 15–1
15.2 Solar energy 15–1
15.3 Wind power 15–5
15.4 Ground source heat pumps 15–6
15.5 Biofuels 15–6
15.6 Hydroelectricity 15–7
15.7 Green electricity 15–7

16 CONDENSATION AND DAMPNESS

16.1 The causes of dampness 16–1
16.2 Mould growth 16–4
16.3 Understanding condensation 16–4
16.4 Reducing the risk of condensation 16–4
16.5 Procedures for diagnosing and remedying condensation problems 16–6
16.6 Equipment to help reduce condensation and mould growth 16–7
16.7 Legal position of tenants 16–7

17 VENTILATION

17.1 How much ventilation? 17–1
17.2 Different types of ventilation 17–2
17.3 Ventilation requirements for the Building Regulations 17–3
17.4 Ventilation requirements for fuel burning appliances 17–3
17.5 Ventilation and condensation 17–6
17.6 Energy efficient ventilation methods 17–6

APPENDICES

1 Useful Addresses A–1
2 Home Survey Questionnaire A–6
3 How to work out approximate weekly fuel costs from meter readings A–8
4 Units of temperature, energy and CO_2 A–12
5 Basic and Best Practice Specifications for central heating systems (Year 2002) A–13

GLOSSARY G–1

INDEX I–1

INTRODUCTION

The Energy Advice Handbook is written primarily as a reference book for advice workers and people whose occupations bring them into contact with a wide range of domestic energy related issues. It also provides a useful source of advice to any reader requiring comprehensive information on domestic energy use.

Formerly known as the Heating Advice Handbook, this renamed edition has been fully revised, updated and expanded. Action flow charts, checklists and case studies from experienced advisors help to make the contents of this Handbook a practical resource, aiming to answer many of the most common questions asked by the public or by participants on training courses.

Rising to the challenge of both the reduction of carbon emissions and the eradication of fuel poverty will require a comprehensive approach to energy advice. Therefore, this Handbook includes such subjects as understanding fuel bills and monitoring fuel costs as well as energy efficiency in relation to the installation of insulation and fitting energy efficient heating systems, lighting and appliances. Advisors may also be faced with other energy related issues, particularly if they carry out home visits. To deal with this, the Handbook covers subjects such as condensation and the ventilation of homes.

There is a vast and sometimes confusing amount of information available on the Web. During the research for this book, it has been necessary to consider many sources of information. The resulting sections of the Handbook have been written in consultation with experts in the various disciplines. There are references throughout to specialist sources of information.

The Handbook should not be used for specifying installation or building work, or for technical advice, and does not attempt to cover enforcement or legal issues about fuel. Rather it is a comprehensive guide to domestic energy advice, and points the reader to sources of further expertise at a national and local level.

To assist the future development of the material in the Handbook, there is a feedback sheet at the back for readers to make any comments or suggestions on the contents of this edition.

1

GIVING GOOD ENERGY ADVICE

This Handbook is mostly concerned with the subject matter of energy advice. However, there have been many developments in the understanding of how to give the most effective advice, and how to put this knowledge into practice by using quality standards, so it is appropriate to include a brief description of this work here.

Energy advice is provided by diverse organisations. The way in which advice is delivered to the customer varies from dealing with a query over the telephone or sending out a written report, to a detailed consultation between the advisor and the customer in their own home.

Research now shows us what types of advice work best, and what actions customers are likely to take [**1**]. We can also work out the potential energy savings and financial savings that result from installing insulation, using energy efficient heating and appliances and by changing our behaviour to be more energy efficient [**2**].

This section:

- defines domestic energy efficiency advice
- looks at the ways advice is delivered
- looks at the effectiveness of advice
- outlines the Domestic Energy Efficiency Advice Code of Practice.

1.1 DEFINITION OF ENERGY ADVICE

The term 'energy advice' was not commonly understood until recent years. To some it meant advice about grants, to others the demonstration of how heating systems worked; others included fuel debt counselling.

Following a consultation process between energy advice providers in 2001, a definition was agreed. This has been used as a basis for subsequent research and the development of standards.

Domestic energy efficiency advice is defined as:

> **'specific to individuals and their circumstances, and aims to improve energy efficiency and achieve affordable warmth'.**

One of the key points in this definition is that it does not include general information and the provision of leaflets, which are considered to be information but not advice.

The definition does not refer exclusively to energy efficiency, but also refers to the aim of achieving affordable warmth. In this Handbook we look at this definition in its broad sense and cover issues such as choosing fuel suppliers, payment methods for fuel, and the comparative running costs of heating systems.

The aim of advice is to encourage customers to take some action. Advice is no use unless it is acted upon. Types of actions which customers take include:

- Choosing (by buying or accessing grants for) insulation, energy efficient heating and hot water systems or other energy efficient products
- Buying low cost items which will improve energy efficiency
- Using heating and hot water systems, domestic appliances, cookers and lighting in a more efficient manner. This is often called 'behavioural change'.
- Choosing the most appropriate fuel supplier, tariff and payment method. This will not improve energy efficiency but it could improve the affordability of fuel.

Any individual household may act upon a combination of the above.

1.2 METHODS OF DELIVERING ENERGY ADVICE

Energy advice is delivered in a number of ways:

Written advice – Written material is tailored to the customer's needs, for example as a result of them completing a home energy survey form. The information is analysed and a written report sent to the customer. (A leaflet not specific to the customer would not be considered as advice.)

Verbal advice given over the telephone – Advice given over the telephone is usually given when the customer contacts the advice provider.

Verbal advice given face to face – Advice providers may be visited when they are present at an event or have an exhibition stand, for example in a shopping centre. Alternatively customers may visit the advice centre or office.

Verbal advice given face to face in the customer's home – Customers may be unable to get out to speak to an advisor or they may have a problem which can best be discussed in their home, for example a problem with heating controls or fuel meters. They may be receiving an assessment survey for an energy efficiency grant, and at the same time be given other energy advice.

There is often a combination of these types of advice. For example a customer may speak to an advisor on the telephone and also be sent a written report.

1.3 ENERGY ADVICE IS EFFECTIVE

A research project was commissioned by the Energy Advice Providers' Group [**3**] in 2002 to determine the impact of advice, and the relative effectiveness of the different delivery methods. The researchers interviewed almost 2000 people who had received energy advice in the ways described above. The researchers also looked at whether it made any difference if the customer had actually asked for advice (customer led) or whether the advice was given when the customer had not asked for it but there was the opportunity for the advisor to provide advice, for example when a new heating system was fitted (opportunistic advice).

The researchers concluded that:

> **'All types of energy advice can produce useful financial savings and/or improvements in people's comfort, warmth, environmental conditions and even health, when people take note of and follow that advice.'**

Research results show that:

85% of customers remember the advice and what topics it covered

70% of customers who receive advice on measures to install do install some of the recommended measures within 9 – 15 months, sometimes with the aid of grants

75% of all behavioural advice is followed in some way

Of the customers who followed advice:

63% benefited from warmer and more comfortable homes

34% reported lower fuel bills (this rises to 47% of those who received written reports and verbal advice)

23% reported an improvement in health

Researchers recommended that:

- Advice is more likely to be acted upon if customers have asked for it (customer led), than if it is given to them when they are not expecting it (opportunistic). However, customer led advice does rely on people asking for advice. Since there are more situations where opportunistic advice can be provided, so numbers reached are likely to be higher, the researchers recommend an expansion of both types of advice in order to reach as many homes as possible with the energy advice message, and to ensure that the advice is acted upon.
- Two methods of giving advice achieved consistently good results. These were a combination of written and verbal advice and verbal advice given in the home. The costs of the different methods of advice provision need to be weighed up against their effectiveness but there does appear to be a strong case for reinforcing written advice with verbal advice, and vice-versa.
- Behavioural advice is followed more often when given verbally, especially face to face at home, but much less often when given in leaflets. The researchers recommend that energy advice providers should provide home visits for those customers who request them.
- Access to grants is lowest amongst those who receive only written reports or leaflets. There is a need for customers to be supported by their advisor in the process of grant application.
- Written energy advice may not be recognised as such. Professional design, and evaluation of key advice materials should be undertaken.

For full details of the report see reference [**1**].

1.4 THE CODE OF PRACTICE

The development of the Domestic Energy Efficiency Advice Code of Practice [**4**] has been underpinned by the research outlined in Section 1.2, and also extensive consultation with advice providers.

The Code of Practice sets minimum standards for delivering transparent, accurate and relevant domestic energy efficiency advice to customers. It applies to any organisation whose business is the provision of energy efficiency advice (e.g. advice centres) or that gives energy efficiency advice as a part of their main business (e.g. product retailers, energy suppliers etc.).

The standards within the Code of Practice are designed to ensure that an advice organisation or provider is well run and has its own quality control mechanisms in place.

THE STRUCTURE OF THE CODE OF PRACTICE

The Code of Practice consists of a core or the 'Heart of the Code' and five additional sections. The five additional sections provide specific standards for different types of advice delivery. These are based very much on the different methods of advice delivery described in Section 1.2 but are expanded to cover the advice given by retailers and installers.

The Heart of the Code

The Heart of the Code provides the standards that apply to all advice providers. Any organisation wishing to comply with the Code of Practice will be expected to meet the standards in the Heart of the Code and one or more of the additional sections depending on the way in which the advice is provided.

The five additional sections are:

Energy efficiency advice at point of sale – applicable to organisations that give advice about specific products at the point of sale, e.g. retailers and manufacturers.

Advice when installing energy efficiency measures – applicable to installers.

Face-to-face advice, not in the home – applicable to organisations that give advice on their own premises, at exhibitions, trade shows and presentations.

Advice provided in all non face-to-face situations – applicable to organisations that give telephone, written and electronic advice.

Energy efficiency advice in the home – applicable to organisations that provide home visits for the purpose of giving energy efficiency advice.

All sections of the Code of Practice require advice providers to comply with standards relating to:

- Quality of Advice and Information
- Training and Development
- Customer Access
- Quality Assurance and Service Improvements.

APPLICATIONS AND GUIDANCE NOTES

A set of six guidance notes explaining the standards in the different sections of the Code of Practice are available. For more information and application forms to sign up to the Code of Practice, contact:

The Domestic Energy Efficiency Advice (DEEA)
Code of Practice Team
Tel: 08700 667 620
www.goodenergyadvice.org.uk

Contact details for organisations listed here are in Appendix 1.

REFERENCES

1 *Benefits of Energy Advice. Report on a Survey.* March 2002. Prepared for the Energy Advice Providers' Group by New Perspectives in association with BMRB International.

2 Potential energy savings from the energy efficiency measures/behaviour are available from a range of sources. There are references throughout this Handbook in the appropriate sections:
Insulation – Section 12
Energy efficient heating systems – Section 8
Fitting heating controls – Section 9
Energy efficient appliances and lighting – Section 14.

3 The Energy Advice Providers' Group (EAPG) is one of the working groups of the Energy Efficiency Partnership for Homes, which is facilitated by the Energy Saving Trust (EST). It brings together representatives from energy advice centres, energy suppliers, local authorities, and other significant providers of domestic energy efficiency advice.
www.est.co.uk – link to Energy Efficiency Partnership for Homes

4 Domestic Energy Efficiency Code of Practice
Tel 08700 667 620
www.goodenergyadvice.org.uk

FURTHER INFORMATION

Effective Advice. Energy Efficiency and the Disadvantaged. Brenda Boardman and Sarah Darby, Environmental Change Institute, University of Oxford. December 2000.

Advice into Action – An evaluation of the effectiveness of energy advice to low income households. Julia Green, Energy Inform; Sarah Darby, Dr Brenda Boardman, Environmental Change Institute, University of Oxford; Catrin Maby. Eaga Charitable Trust. Report No 5. 1998.

2

HOW TO USE THE ENERGY ADVICE HANDBOOK

The Energy Advice Handbook is divided into seventeen sections plus Appendices. Each section can be used as a stand alone source of information but it is likely that the reader will gain maximum benefit by cross referencing from one section to another, as many of the subjects are closely linked.

Domestic energy problems often have more than one cause and may therefore need more than one solution. Take for example a cold home. The dwelling may be poorly insulated, the heating system may be inadequate or broken, or the householder may not understand how to use it. The householder may not be able to afford their fuel bills, or they may be worried about high bills so leave the heating off. Any one of these problems, or even all of them may apply. Each requires a different course of action and the advisor should have access to the appropriate reference material, and further contacts.

The Energy Advice Handbook contains broad subject matter including case studies and the types of questions commonly asked. It is, however, impossible to cover each subject in depth so the Handbook refers the reader to more specialist sources of information and websites at the end of each section.

This section:

- advises readers on how to keep up to date
- describes how to access further information
- provides flow charts for problem solving
- provides a checklist for use during a home visit.

2.1 KEEPING UP TO DATE

It is important to be able to keep the material up to date in a Handbook such as this.

Some items in the Handbook are subject to periodic change, for example the Building Regulations and grant schemes; others are more unpredictable, for example fuel costs changes, or the development of new energy efficient products.

There are mechanisms throughout the Handbook designed to help the reader keep up to date. They are:

- **Contact details**
  Contact details for up to date material are given both at the end of the appropriate section, and in full in Appendix 1. Phone numbers and website details are provided. Appendix 1 is organised in alphabetical order, not in groups of organisations providing specific services, which would cause duplication.
- **Website references**
  There are many website references in this Handbook. However, websites change, in particular web pages change. If we gave specific web pages as reference and the page had changed, then a search may not work. In this Handbook the majority of website references are the home pages, so readers need to find the appropriate links to the pages they are looking for. Some links are given, but they are not usually difficult to work out – it is often best to follow links to appropriate subjects, for example 'energy efficiency' or 'renewables'.

- **Figures which are easy to update**
  When figures for running costs are given, for example running costs of appliances, or heating systems, the number of kWh is given as well as the cost per kWh. This makes it simple for the reader to substitute the cost with those which are up to date or more locally appropriate. For complex calculations, for example for working out running costs for different house types, reference to appropriate organisations is given.

2.2 REFERENCE MATERIAL

This Handbook has been written using references from many sources. At the end of each section the references and sources of further information are listed. However, we recommend that readers collect their own reference materials, particularly where they relate to local circumstances and to any specialist service which may be provided. There is a great deal of excellent literature, some of which is free.

Many websites provide freely available reports and statistics which may be downloaded. Readers will note that some key websites providing comprehensive information appear in more than one section.

The following groups of literature are useful:

- **Local material**
  For example information on local energy efficiency grant promotions, Codes of Practice for the most commonly used fuel supplier in the area, local debt advice services etc.
- **Good Practice Guides**
  The Energy Efficiency Best Practice in Housing programme produces an excellent range of guides, information leaflets and case studies on energy efficiency, insulation, heating, sustainable housing and other topics. We recommend that readers keep a library of the most appropriate literature.
- **Manufacturers and Trade Associations**
  Manufacturers of appliances, heating controls and systems, insulation and ventilation products provide catalogues and literature which is useful for a more detailed understanding of the nature of the products, and their efficiencies etc.
- **Organisation contact list/referral agencies**
  Maintaining a contact list of other organisations who provide linked advice and services, for example debt advice or home repairs, is essential. It is most helpful to have a named contact at these other organisations.

2.3 USING THE ACTION FLOW CHARTS

On the following pages, there are seven Action Flow Charts. They are designed to help the reader to provide advice of a broader scope. Readers may be faced with straightforward queries which can be answered by looking at the appropriate section of the Handbook. An example may be 'Can I get a grant for a new heating system?' Other situations may be more complex. We suggest the use of the Action Flow Charts when faced with some of the common energy related problems and questions.

The Action Flow Charts begin with a common problem or question and take the reader through the subjects which may need consideration, pointing out the relevant sections of the book to consult.

2.4 USING THE ENERGY ADVICE HOME VISIT CHECKLIST

When energy advice is given in the home, data is usually gathered on a survey form so that the advisor has the basic information upon which to assess the customer's advice needs. We then recommend the use of a checklist so that items of advice are not missed out.

There are various types of home energy surveys regularly in use. The contents and detail of each will depend on the purpose of the survey. For example, surveys are carried out to assess a customer's eligibility for an energy efficiency grant; a customer may complete a survey form themselves to acquire an energy report advising them on appropriate energy efficiency measures. Surveys may be undertaken for a home energy audit to provide the property with an energy rating certificate. A sample survey form is provided in Appendix 2.

This Energy Advice Home Visit Checklist is designed for use in the home. When in the home an advisor has a unique opportunity to tailor their advice to the customer. Comprehensive advice may be provided including the demonstration of heating controls and appliances in the dwelling, and reading fuel meters.

The checklist can be completed by observation and questions addressed to the customer. Not all points on the checklist will be relevant to any one visit. It is written as short notes as reminders and may be modified and photocopied to suit local circumstances.

2.5 ACTION FLOW CHARTS

Vulnerable person found at risk from the cold
IS THERE AN EMERGENCY?
YES
NO
PERSON SUFFERING FROM COLD RELATED ILLNESS
See Section 3
NO HEATING
See Sections 3, 7 and 8
LOOK AT LOCAL PROVISION OF HELP AND SPECIAL PROJECTS
See Section 3
LOOK AT FINANCIAL HELP FOR AFFORDABLE WARMTH
See Section 7
IDENTIFY WHY HOME IS COLD
See next chart

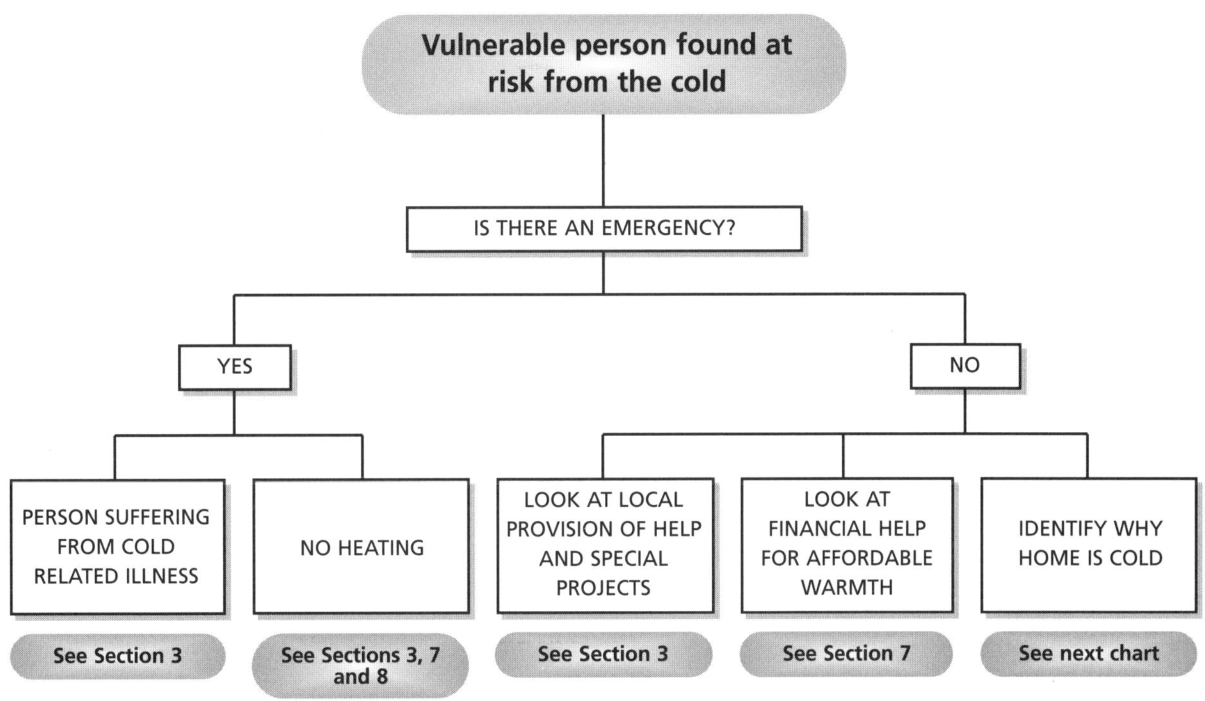

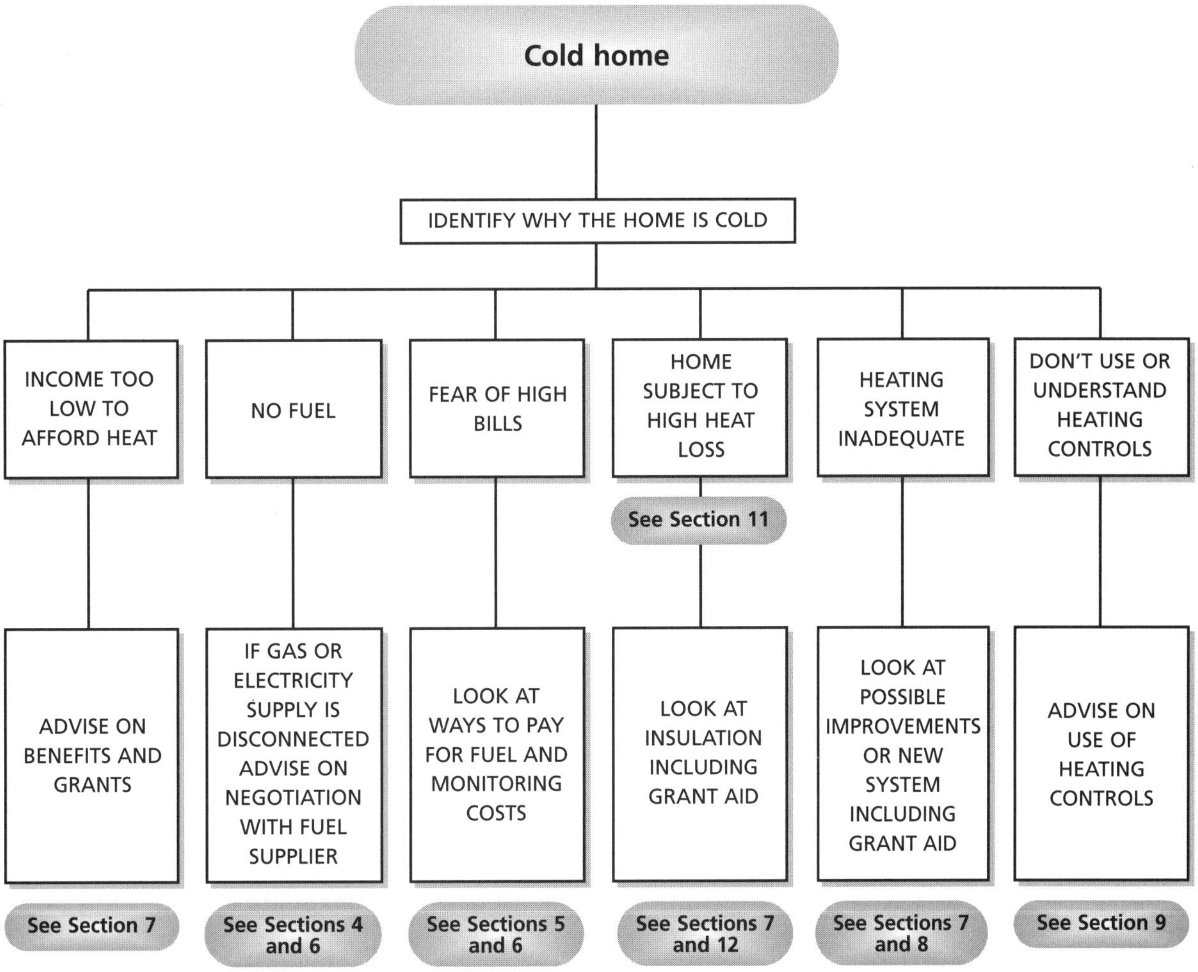

Cold home
IDENTIFY WHY THE HOME IS COLD
INCOME TOO LOW TO AFFORD HEAT
ADVISE ON BENEFITS AND GRANTS
See Section 7
NO FUEL
IF GAS OR ELECTRICITY SUPPLY IS DISCONNECTED ADVISE ON NEGOTIATION WITH FUEL SUPPLIER
See Sections 4 and 6
FEAR OF HIGH BILLS
LOOK AT WAYS TO PAY FOR FUEL AND MONITORING COSTS
See Sections 5 and 6
HOME SUBJECT TO HIGH HEAT LOSS
See Section 11
LOOK AT INSULATION INCLUDING GRANT AID
See Sections 7 and 12
HEATING SYSTEM INADEQUATE
LOOK AT POSSIBLE IMPROVEMENTS OR NEW SYSTEM INCLUDING GRANT AID
See Sections 7 and 8
DON'T USE OR UNDERSTAND HEATING CONTROLS
ADVISE ON USE OF HEATING CONTROLS
See Section 9

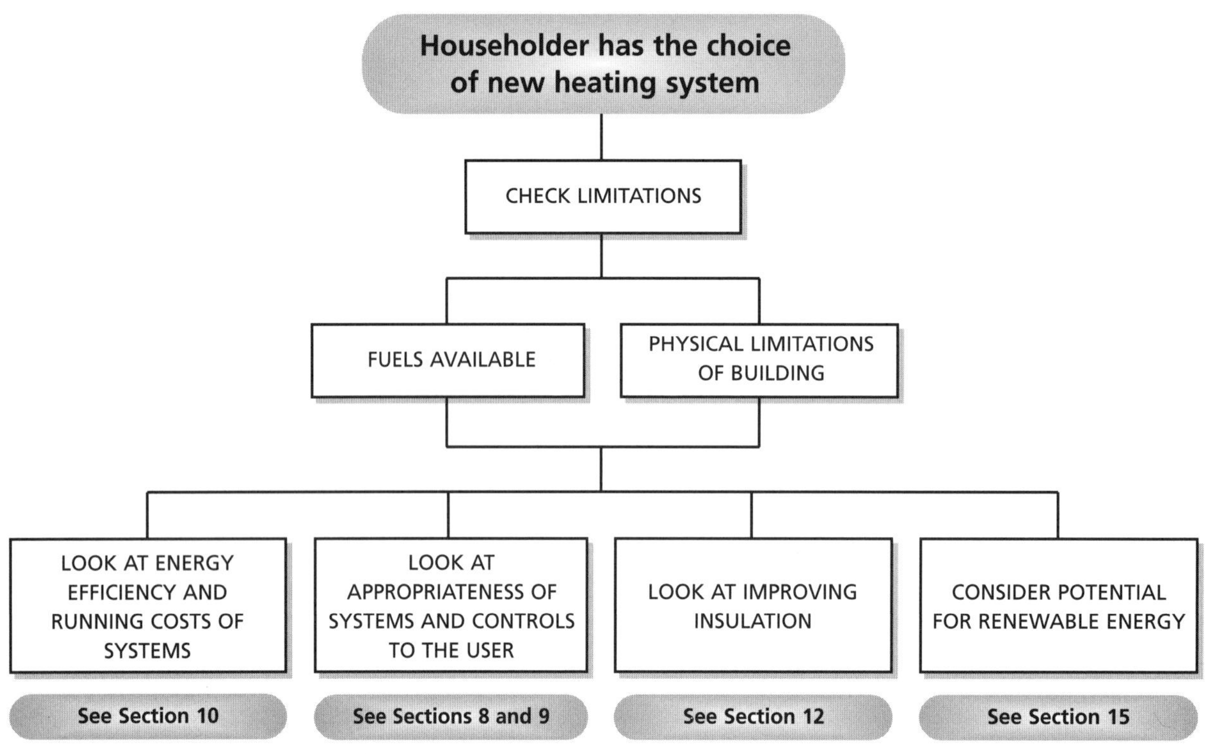
Householder has the choice of new heating system
CHECK LIMITATIONS
FUELS AVAILABLE
PHYSICAL LIMITATIONS OF BUILDING
LOOK AT ENERGY EFFICIENCY AND RUNNING COSTS OF SYSTEMS
See Section 10
LOOK AT APPROPRIATENESS OF SYSTEMS AND CONTROLS TO THE USER
See Sections 8 and 9
LOOK AT IMPROVING INSULATION
See Section 12
CONSIDER POTENTIAL FOR RENEWABLE ENERGY
See Section 15

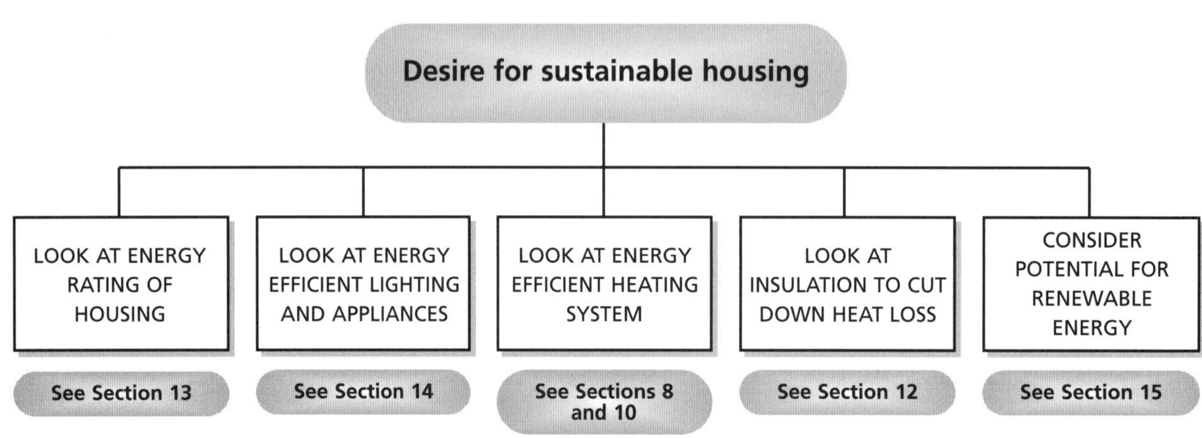
Desire for sustainable housing
LOOK AT ENERGY RATING OF HOUSING
See Section 13
LOOK AT ENERGY EFFICIENT LIGHTING AND APPLIANCES
See Section 14
LOOK AT ENERGY EFFICIENT HEATING SYSTEM
See Sections 8 and 10
LOOK AT INSULATION TO CUT DOWN HEAT LOSS
See Section 12
CONSIDER POTENTIAL FOR RENEWABLE ENERGY
See Section 15

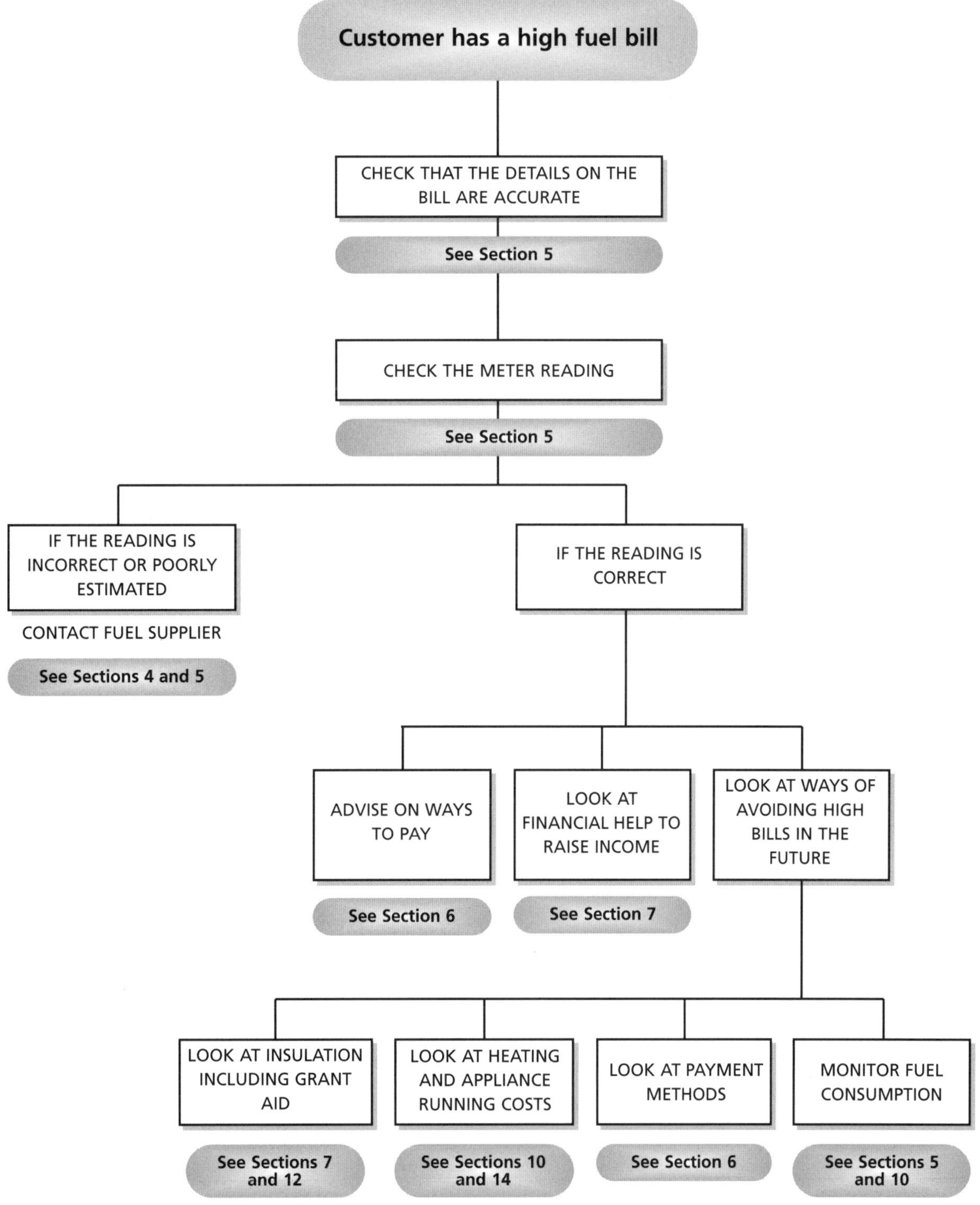
Customer has a high fuel bill
CHECK THAT THE DETAILS ON THE BILL ARE ACCURATE
See Section 5
CHECK THE METER READING
See Section 5
IF THE READING IS INCORRECT OR POORLY ESTIMATED
CONTACT FUEL SUPPLIER
See Sections 4 and 5
IF THE READING IS CORRECT
ADVISE ON WAYS TO PAY
See Section 6
LOOK AT FINANCIAL HELP TO RAISE INCOME
See Section 7
LOOK AT WAYS OF AVOIDING HIGH BILLS IN THE FUTURE
LOOK AT INSULATION INCLUDING GRANT AID
See Sections 7 and 12
LOOK AT HEATING AND APPLIANCE RUNNING COSTS
See Sections 10 and 14
LOOK AT PAYMENT METHODS
See Section 6
MONITOR FUEL CONSUMPTION
See Sections 5 and 10

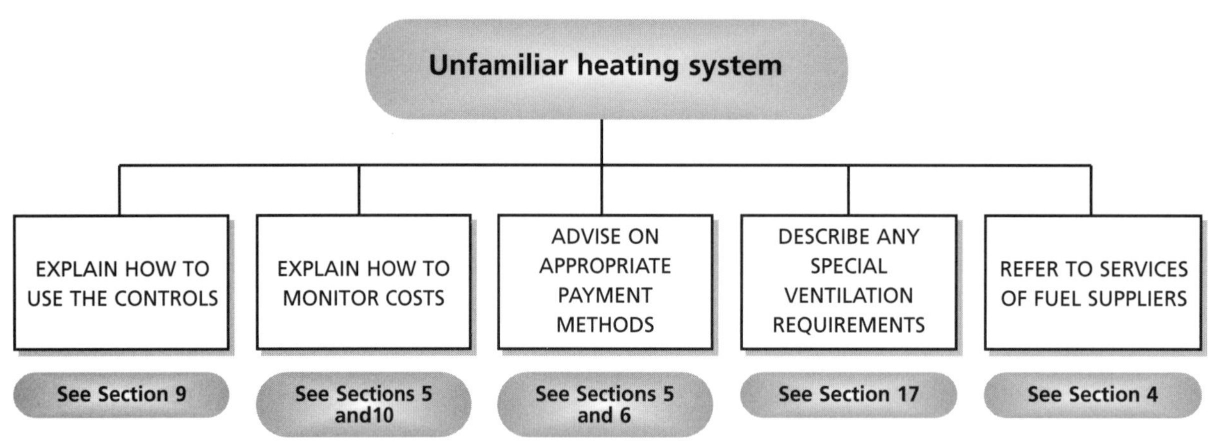
Unfamiliar heating system
EXPLAIN HOW TO USE THE CONTROLS
See Section 9
EXPLAIN HOW TO MONITOR COSTS
See Sections 5 and10
ADVISE ON APPROPRIATE PAYMENT METHODS
See Sections 5 and 6
DESCRIBE ANY SPECIAL VENTILATION REQUIREMENTS
See Section 17
REFER TO SERVICES OF FUEL SUPPLIERS
See Section 4

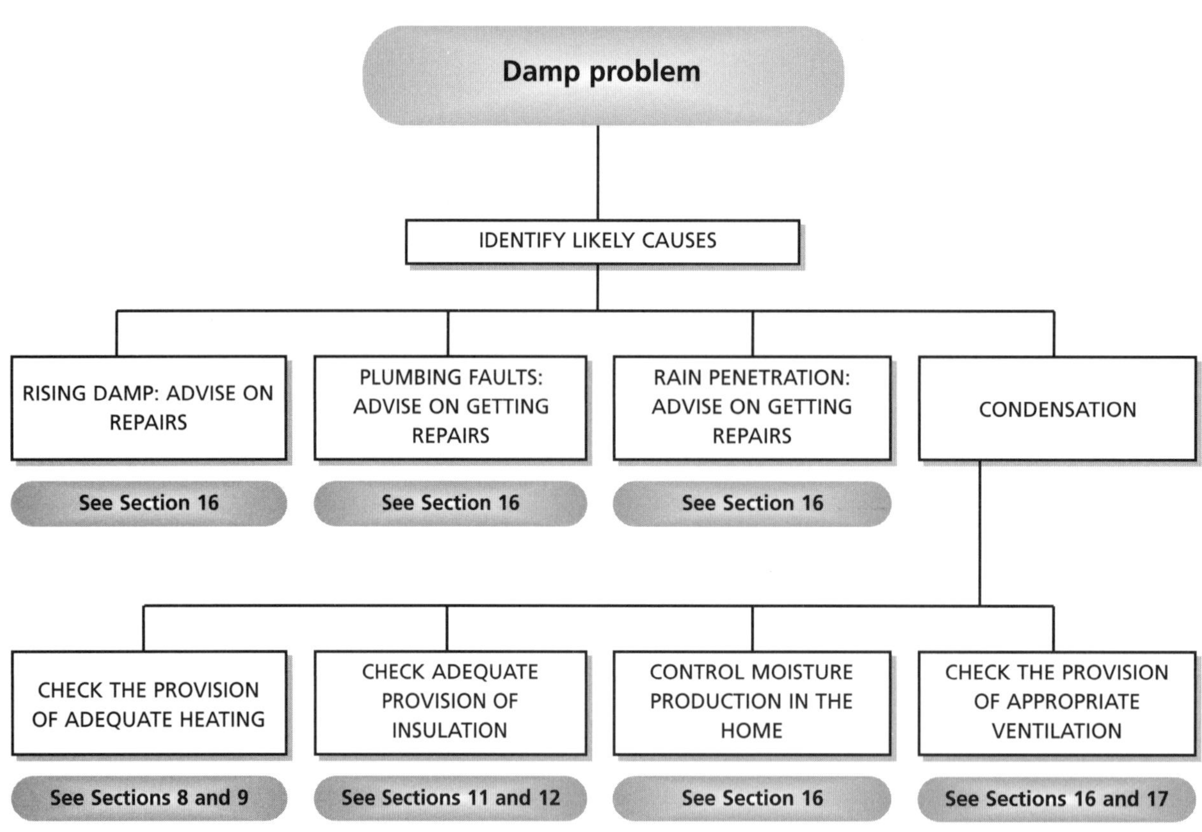
Damp problem
IDENTIFY LIKELY CAUSES
RISING DAMP: ADVISE ON REPAIRS
See Section 16
PLUMBING FAULTS: ADVISE ON GETTING REPAIRS
See Section 16
RAIN PENETRATION: ADVISE ON GETTING REPAIRS
See Section 16
CONDENSATION
CHECK THE PROVISION OF ADEQUATE HEATING
See Sections 8 and 9
CHECK ADEQUATE PROVISION OF INSULATION
See Sections 11 and 12
CONTROL MOISTURE PRODUCTION IN THE HOME
See Section 16
CHECK THE PROVISION OF APPROPRIATE VENTILATION
See Sections 16 and 17

2.6 ENERGY ADVICE HOME VISIT CHECKLIST

SUBJECT	Yes	No	Action Needed	See Section
HEALTH				
Is the home cold enough to put health at risk				3
INSULATION				
Does the dwelling need:				
– loft insulation				12
– draughtproofing				12
– hot water cylinder jacket				12
– pipe and tank lagging				12
– cavity wall insulation				12
If any renovation work is going on, has the householder considered:				
– external solid wall insulation				12
– internal solid wall insulation (or dry lining)				12
– floor insulation				12
– double glazing				12
HEATING AND HOT WATER				
If a new system is planned have all considerations been taken into account for its suitability				8
Is the householder using the most appropriate form of heating currently fitted in their home				8
Is the householder aware of the comparative cost of fuels for heating/hot water				10
If fitted, does the householder know how to use				
– Room thermostat (set to 18°C – 21°C)				9
– Central heating/hot water programmer				9
– Thermostatic radiator valves (TRVs)				9
– Hot water cylinder thermostat (set to 60°C)				9
– Boiler thermostat				9
– Output control on storage heater				9
– Input control on storage heater				9
– Other thermostats				9
If the householder has an electric immersion heater				
– does it have a timer				9
– is it on Economy 7 or other off peak tariff				9
RUNNING COSTS OF APPLIANCES				
Are running costs of electrical appliances understood				14
Are low energy light bulbs used				14
Does the householder understand labels on energy efficient appliances				14
PAYING FOR FUEL				
Does the householder have problems paying for fuel				6
Would an alternative payment method help				6
Are relevant fuel tariffs used, e.g. Economy 7				5
Does the householder understand their fuel bills				5
Are there any problems of fuel debt				6
METERS				
Can the householder read their meter				5
Does the householder monitor their fuel use				5/10
Are the meters appropriate (e.g. prepayment)				5

SUBJECT	Yes	No	Action Needed	See Section
RENEWABLES				
Is any renewable technology appropriate				15
Is the householder aware of grants for renewables				7
DAMPNESS				
Are there any dampness problems: if so is it:				
– rising damp				16
– penetrating damp				16
– dampness due to plumbing defect				16
– condensation				16
VENTILATION				
Does the dwelling have enough ventilation:				
– for fuel burning appliances				17
– to alleviate condensation				17
HELP WITH COSTS				
Is the householder aware of grants and loans for insulation and heating				7
Is financial help for repairs needed				7
Does the household need benefits or debt advice				6, 7

SUMMARY OF RECOMMENDATIONS (Write in)

Advice on insulation measures

Advice on efficient use of space heating and hot water systems

Advice on energy efficient appliances and lighting

Advice on monitoring fuel use / methods of payment / changing fuel supplier

Advice on remedial action for dampness and appropriate ventilation

Advice on grants and financial help

Advice on appropriate renewable energy

Name of agencies householder has been referred to

3

HEALTH RISKS FROM COLD DAMP HOMES

There is increasing recognition that cold damp homes contribute to ill health. One expert in the field said that "Cold damp homes are a major public health problem in the UK ... they impair the quality of life, and cause disease. They aggravate a wide range of medical conditions adding to the burdens on the NHS." [**1**]

There are numerous partnerships being established between local authorities, the health sector, fuel suppliers and energy efficiency organisations to target action to those most at risk from the cold. Organisations which provide energy advice are an important link in these partnerships.

Energy advisors may find it useful to be able to identify the people who are most at risk from cold homes, and to assist health professionals to identify and refer those people to some of the grants and services they are eligible for to make their homes warmer. It is also useful to have some facts and figures to counter arguments occasionally raised that 'it's good for you' to live in a cold home!

This section looks at:

- health risks from the cold
- who is most at risk
- prevention of cold damp homes
- the benefits of partnership working.

3.1 EXCESS WINTER DEATHS

In the UK there is an increase in the number of deaths recorded over the winter months compared to the other times of the year. These 'Excess Winter Deaths' are defined as how many more people die during the four months from December – March than in the average four monthly periods of August – November, and April – July [**2**].

Table 3.1 EXCESS WINTER DEATHS 1997 – 2001 IN ENGLAND AND WALES [**3**]

1997 – 98	23,020
1998 – 99	46,910
1999 – 2000	48,530
2000 – 2001	25,000

Three-quarters of excess winter deaths occur in people over 75, and 92% are people over 65. If this trend stays the same this will become an increasing problem because we have an ageing population.

Age % of total (1997 – 2001)

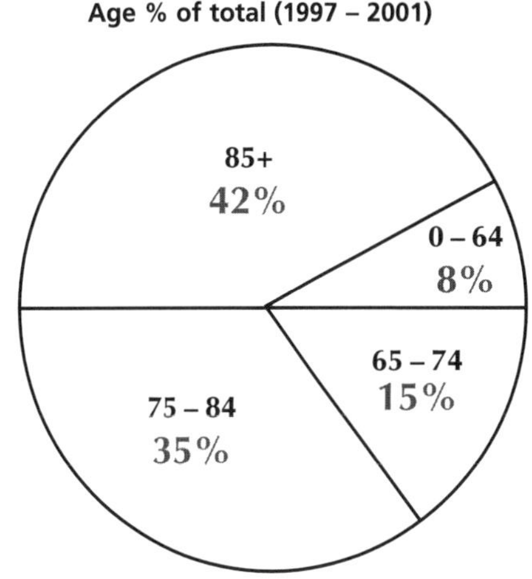

Proportion of age groups which make up excess winter deaths 1997 – 2001 [3]

The underlying cause of most of the deaths (80%) is the cold. There is a greater problem in the UK than in many other colder countries. For example, Finland and Russia have much lower levels of excess winter deaths.

In all age groups over half the excess winter deaths are from cardiovascular (heart, circulatory) disease and a third are from respiratory disease. Deaths can be predicted following a cold day:

- heart attacks after 2 days
- strokes after 5 days
- respiratory disease after 12 days [**4**].

3.2 THE EFFECTS OF COLD ON THE BODY

A living room temperature somewhere between 18°C (64°F) and 21°C (70°F) is generally regarded as a desirable comfort target to aim for. The lower the room temperature and the more inactive the occupant of the dwelling, the more serious will be the effects of the cold. Exposure to lowered temperatures, particularly if prolonged, can have the following physical effects on older people who are fairly sedentary:

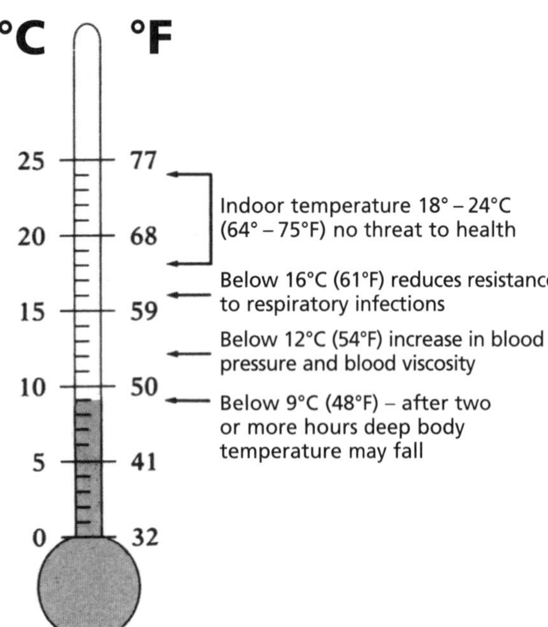

Indoor temperature and its effect on health of older people

Temperatures of 18°C to 24°C (64°F to 75°F) pose little threat to sedentary people.

At temperatures of 16°C (61°F) and below, there may be a marked decrease in the body's ability to stave off respiratory illnesses.

Temperatures of 12°C (54°F) and below result in raised blood pressure which in turn might induce other cardiovascular disorders.

At 9°C (48°F) and below, there may be an increased risk of the onset of low deep inner body temperature – hypothermia itself [**5**].

DESCRIPTION OF COLD RELATED ILLNESSES

Heart and circulatory problems

Blood pressure increases in older people when they are exposed to temperatures below 12°C. This rise in blood pressure can happen within two hours. The risk of heart attacks and strokes increases with increasing blood pressure.

Respiratory disorders

The cold has a direct effect on the respiratory tract, but also can cause other problems. Cold homes are more prone to condensation. Cold damp homes lead to the growth of moulds which can cause asthma and other respiratory infections.

The other effects of the cold on the body include worsening arthritis and increased risk of accidents. In addition people are more socially isolated when they live in cold damp homes and children have more difficulty with schoolwork when only one room is heated [**6**].

Not all cold related deaths are related to being cold in the home. Not wearing adequate clothing when outside, and moving from warm to cold areas are also significant reasons. However, research has looked into the effects of low indoor temperatures. The findings show that [**7**]:

- the older the property, the greater the risk to the residents of winter mortality
- properties which are energy inefficient are linked to increased excess winter deaths
- the indoor temperature of homes is a factor in excess winter deaths.

3.3 WHO IS MOST AT RISK FROM THE COLD?

There are four particularly vulnerable groups who may be at risk from the cold. They are more susceptible to illnesses, and also tend to spend more time at home. They are:

- Older people as a general category. Their ability to sense changes in temperature may not be as effective as it once was, so they could be cold without being aware of it.
- People with long term illnesses, and in particular those who suffer from heart disease, strokes, severe arthritis, paralysis or any other form of physical handicap.
- People with disabilities especially if they have mobility problems. Mobility may be partially or totally restricted and so they will be unable to keep as warm as they would if they were more active.
- Children.

Where these groups of people are living in property which is most likely to be cold, then they may be at risk.

3.4 HEALTH RISKS FROM DAMP HOMES

In addition to the direct effect of low temperatures on the body, condensation, a form of dampness, is most likely to happen in cold homes. It is often accompanied by mould growth. Moulds and their spores are known to be linked with asthma and respiratory problems [**8**].

As well as the association between low temperature and the risk to health, there is considerable evidence of links between dampness and ill health. The presence of moulds and dust mites rises in conditions where there is high relative humidity.

Mould growth is common when a property suffers from condensation problems. Moulds are associated with a range of allergies, infections, toxic reactions, some cancers, and psychological symptoms. Research has shown that mould is less common in homes which have better insulation, cavity walls, good ventilation and air circulation and good heating which is actually used to keep the home warm [**8**].

Dust mites are one of the most common causes of asthma brought on by allergic reaction. The dust mites thrive in higher humidities and it is recognised that a reduction of humidity, particularly in the winter, would help to keep the dust mite population down. Therefore the same measures are needed as those which keep a house warm and dry – heating, adequate ventilation and insulation, all at an affordable cost.

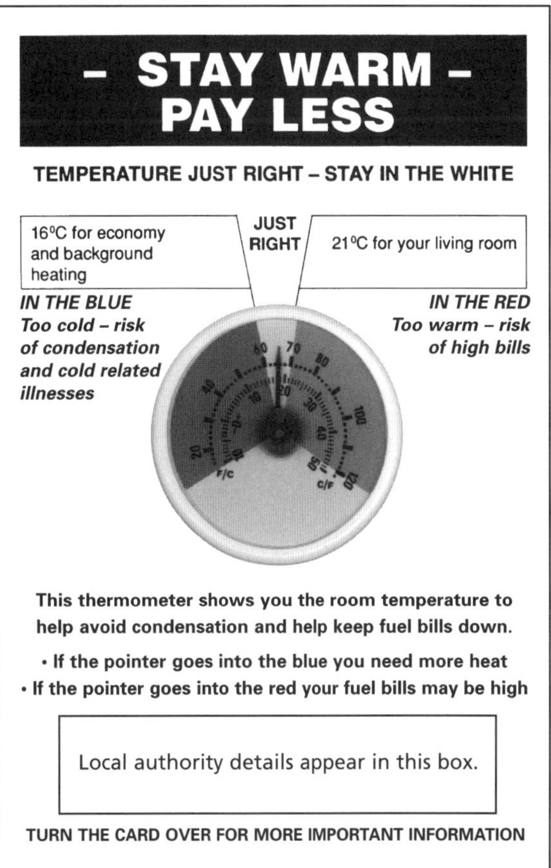

Thermometers can help householders to recognise when temperatures are dropping to low levels

3.5 MAKING HOMES WARMER AND DRIER

Keeping warm at home is one way to help prevent cold and damp related illnesses. There may be many reasons why a home is cold (see chart in Section 2 for reasons and solutions). For vulnerable people there are several areas to look at:

HEATING

Heating must be both affordable and controllable to ensure that the home is kept adequately warm. People on low incomes often have the least adequate and efficient form of heating at their disposal. Existing heating systems may not be working correctly or not understood by the householder. Grants or loans may be available for heating systems. See Section 7.

PAYING FOR FUEL

Worry about high fuel bills often results in heating systems being left unused. Appropriate payment methods and the ability to monitor fuel consumption regularly are both important factors in reducing the anxiety caused by fuel bills. Choosing the most appropriate fuel supplier and payment method can reduce fuel costs. See Sections 4, 5 and 6.

INSULATION

Reducing heat loss from the home will help to keep a house warmer at a lower cost. Grants or loans are available for home insulation through a variety of schemes. See Section 7.

3.6 PARTNERSHIP PROJECTS FOR WARMTH

There has been a growth in the number of partnership projects between health and energy professionals, local authorities, fuel suppliers and the voluntary sector aimed at providing warm homes for groups who may be at risk from the cold. Their main priority is to identify and target help towards people whose health is at risk.

Although all projects have their own characteristics they often have the following in common:

- Initial discussions begin between partners. Health partners are usually from the Primary Care Trusts (PCT).
- Training/briefing of health sector workers is provided to help them to recognise potentially vulnerable clients and to inform them of the services and grants for heating or insulation available.

- A referral system is set up so that health workers refer clients to central point for assistance.
- The client's needs are assessed (eligibility for help).
- Heating systems and/or energy efficiency measures are installed, and repairs or other help provided.
- The project is monitored.

In some cases the health sector contributes either staff time or money towards measures. There have been a number of reviews of schemes, and good practice guidelines have been set up. See Further Contacts for details of projects around the UK.

Contact details for organisations listed here are in Appendix 1.

REFERENCES

1 Statement by Dr. Neil Olsen, consultant advisor to Department of Health, DETR and World Health Organisation, in an article '*Public health and human rights*' in NEA's magazine 'Energy Action' Issue no 79.

2 *Minimising Excess Winter Deaths – A Review of the Research Evidence.* Marcia Darrell. Department of Health. April 2002. Definition of excess winter deaths for the introduction.

3 See reference 2. Table 1.

4 *Fuel poverty and health – a guide for primary care organisations, and public health and care professionals.* Dr Vivienne Press. National Heart Forum. 2003. Facts about cold related deaths.

5 *Low indoor temperatures and morbidity in the elderly.* K.J. Collins. Age and Ageing. 1986, pp212–220.

6 See reference 4. Table 3.

7 *Housing and Excess Winter Death: The Potential Health Impact of Housing Initiatives.* Dr. Paul Wilkinson. Environmental Epidemiology Unit. London School of Hygiene and Tropical Medicine. Presentation at seminar 21.6.01. Health and Fuel Poverty NEA/Eaga CT.

8 *Tackling Condensation: A guide to the causes of and remedies for surface condensation and mould in traditional housing.* J. Garratt and F. Nowak. 1991. BRE.

FURTHER INFORMATION

Affordable Warmth and Health Action Zones – A good practice guide. NEA.

Guidance notes for Primary Care Trusts: PCT Local Plans and Fuel Poverty 2003–2006. NEA.

NEA (National Energy Action)
NEA is involved in a number of health related projects including research programmes which assess the impact of energy efficiency improvements on health.
www.nea.org.uk

Keep Warm Keep Well
This is an annual campaign which runs from October to March. It aims to alert older people and their carers to the help available to keep warm in winter. For information packs and enquiries contact: freephone 0800 085 7000.

Evaluation of HECA Challenge Sector (Health) Schemes.
Energy Saving Trust (EST) and ACE (The Association for the Conservation of Energy) Summary produced in 2002.
www.est.co.uk

4

FUEL SUPPLIERS AND CONSUMER ADVICE

Domestic customers can choose who they buy their gas and electricity from. The choice of fuel supplier can make a significant difference to the size of annual fuel bills; the savings can be enough to lift some households out of fuel poverty.

This section looks at:

- issues to consider when changing electricity and gas supplier
- services offered by suppliers
- the role of the watchdog **energywatch** and the regulator Ofgem
- the work of the trade associations for oil and solid fuel.

This Handbook does not make any comparisons between gas and electricity suppliers because these are subject to change. Up to date information can be obtained from **energywatch** (see 4.3).

4.1 CHOOSING A FUEL SUPPLIER

Domestic customers have been able to choose who they buy their fuel from since 1998 (gas) and since 1999 (electricity). According to Ofgem, 37% of domestic customers are no longer with their original suppliers [**1**].

In May 2003 the National Audit Office reported that 60% of customers were paying too much for their electricity because they had not switched to a cheaper supplier. They said "Domestic customers can ... cut their electricity bills by up to £50. Every customer who has never switched has at least five better deals available" [**2**].

There may be a number of reasons why more customers have not changed their supplier. There have been complaints about fuel suppliers who have misled customers into changing supplier, and cases of suppliers who prevent customers switching. Both of these matters are taken up by the regulator Ofgem (see 4.4).

There are a number of issues to take into account before changing fuel supplier, in addition to the cost of the fuel. **energywatch** and Ofgem both recommend that a number of questions be asked before the fuel supplier is changed, for example:

- How much does the supplier charge for fuel?
- What are the payment methods?
- What is the appropriate tariff?
- Are there any special discounts or incentives?
- Is there a standing charge/does the fuel have a variable rate for the first/subsequent kWhs of fuel used?
- How often are bills sent out?
- Does the supplier have a high rate of complaints?

4.2 HOW PRICE COMPARISONS ARE WORKED OUT

It is difficult for a customer to make price comparisons if a fuel supplier approaches them to encourage them to switch their supplier, particularly if the supplier visits the customer unexpectedly or approaches them on the street. The customer is unlikely to have the necessary information to hand to enable them to make the best decision. In fact research in 2002 showed that customers were not always switching to the cheapest supplier, but possibly switching to the supplier who was the most persuasive [**3**].

An independent source of information on comparative prices is recommended. **energywatch** provides price comparison information, which is updated every two months, and also provide the names of organisations that provide free pricing comparison services. On its Supplier Information sheets, **energywatch** also provides ratings to show how many complaints they have received about accounts, billing, marketing and transfers against each company [**4**].

The cheapest supplier for any particular customer will vary depending upon:

- **where the customer lives** – usually based on postcode. The same supplier will charge different amounts for fuel in different parts of the country
- **how much fuel is used** – see Table 4.1
- **how the fuel is paid for** – comparisons are usually provided for Direct Debit, Standard Credit, or Prepayment
- **if a dual fuel (gas and electricity) account is opened.**

Table 4.1 is an example of how users are defined as low medium or high [**4**]. Most customers will probably be most likely to work this out by how much they pay for each fuel, either annually or monthly. To find out the fuel used (kWh) a customer would need to look at a whole year's bills, which may not be readily to hand.

Table 4.1 DEFINITION OF HIGH MEDIUM AND LOW USERS OF FUEL FOR PRICE COMPARISON [**4**]

Definition of users	Low	Medium	High
Amount of electricity per year (kWh)	1,650	3,300	4,950
Amount of gas per year (kWh)	10,000	19,050	28,000
Cost per month (one fuel)	£10 – £19	£20 – £29	£30 – £39
Cost per year (one fuel)	£120 – £228	£240 – £348	£360 – £468

The price comparison tables show the annual bills for different fuel suppliers depending on the amount of fuel used and the payment method. The area where the customer lives will have been identified by their postcode. This means that a customer can identify their cheapest supplier. The customer is advised to contact their chosen supplier to make sure that the prices have not changed since the comparative tables were published.

After checking the other questions outlined in 4.1 the customer may decide to change supplier.

4.3 HOW TO CHANGE SUPPLIER

energywatch provides advice on how to change gas and electricity suppliers. This is what they say [**4**]:

- Get in touch with the new supplier and agree a contract with them. Once the contract is agreed, the transfer process should take about six weeks to complete. Your new supplier will keep you informed about how your transfer is being progressed.
- Give your old supplier 28 days notice that you are changing to a new supplier. **energywatch** advises that you do this initially by telephone and follow it up with written confirmation. If you do not tell your old supplier that you are changing, this can disrupt or delay your transfer to the new supplier. (This requirement is expected to be dropped.)
- Pay any outstanding bills owing to your existing supplier. If you do not, they may prevent you from transferring.
- Take a meter reading on the day you change supplier. If your old supplier does not use it to work out your final bill, or your new supplier does not use it as the starting point for your first bill, let them know the meter reading you have taken.

4.4 PROBLEMS WITH CHANGING SUPPLIERS

Although many customers would benefit from changing suppliers there have been problems. Here are some of them:

DOORSTEP AND TELEPHONE SELLING

Although most sales representatives act in a proper manner, **energywatch** has received thousands of complaints each year from customers who have been misled or intimidated into signing contracts for new fuel suppliers, or have had their signatures forged onto energy contracts. **energywatch** provides advice on how to avoid these problems and what steps to take if a customer has already experienced them [**5**]. Some key points:

- Sales representatives should be asked for identification.
- Customers should ask for a like for like comparison of price given their use of fuel and the payment method.
- If customers are unsure, they should avoid signing anything – however persuasive the sales representative – it may be a contract.
- The law allows 7 days cooling off period if the customer was approached 'cold'. During this time the contract can be cancelled with no penalty.
- If a customer's signature has been forged it is a criminal offence. The supplier and **energywatch** should be informed. (The suppliers have agreed that if there is a forged signature they should pay £250 compensation.)
- All domestic suppliers are members of the AES (Association of Energy Suppliers) face-to-face marketing code of practice. This is a voluntary code, which governs how sales agents behave during direct selling activity [**6**].

A CUSTOMER IS TOLD THEY'VE CHANGED SUPPLIER BUT THEY HAVE NO RECALL OF THIS

The old or the new company should be contacted as soon as possible to find out why they think they are supplying the customer, and asked for the written contract. The customer may have been misled into signing a contract, by thinking they were signing for something else. If a verbal agreement was made the new company should have followed this up with written information and a contract. (See doorstep and telephone selling.)

NEW TENANTS AND RESIDENTS

When moving home or taking up a new tenancy, it may not be clear which company supplies fuel to the property. The gas supplier can be found by ringing the Transco Meter Helpline on 0870 608 1524. The electricity supplier can be found by ringing the local electricity distribution company and asking for the Meter Point Administration Service (MPAS).

A CUSTOMER IS BEING BILLED BY MORE THAN ONE SUPPLIER

A customer can only be billed by one supplier. See new tenants and residents above – check who is supplying fuel.

A CUSTOMER DOES NOT RECEIVE A BILL

If a customer does not receive a bill from the new supplier, the supplier should be contacted to confirm the date when the supply was switched. Make sure meter readings were taken. The amount owed for fuel should not be allowed to build up.

4.5 SERVICES OFFERED BY FUEL SUPPLIERS

Gas and electricity suppliers produce Codes of Practice. The Codes of Practice are approved by Ofgem and cover the following areas:

- payment of bills and dealing with debt
- using energy efficiently
- priority service register
- prepayment meters
- complaints procedures

ENERGY EFFICIENCY ADVICE

Fuel suppliers provide energy efficiency advice to customers. This may cover general queries, or advice on grants, insulation measures and efficient appliances. Advice is given in a number of ways. Free advice is provided over the telephone. A questionnaire may be sent out to the customer to determine appropriate advice, and in case of best practice, a customer who has high fuel bills or is falling into arrears is targeted for advice. See Appendix 1 (under 'F') for the Energy Efficiency Advice numbers for fuel suppliers. Customer literature is also produced in the form of leaflets and the Code of Practice.

PRIORITY SERVICE REGISTER

The Priority Service Register was set up for vulnerable customers. Those customers are eligible for free services from gas and electricity suppliers if they meet any of the following criteria:

If the customer is of pensionable age, disabled, chronically sick, blind or visually impaired, deaf or hearing impaired, they can apply to join their gas and electricity supplier's Priority Service Register. To register contact the gas and electricity supplier and ask to join. (The supplier's phone number and address are on the back of the householder's bill.) The free services available include:

- **Free safety check of gas appliances and the way they have been fitted.** Customers qualify for a free gas annual safety check if all adults in the home are eligible for the Priority Service Register. The check will show if the gas appliances are safe and whether they are giving out harmful levels of carbon monoxide. In the case of tenants, by law the landlord must make sure a gas safety check is carried out once a year on the landlord's appliances. There is no obligation on an energy supplier to provide a free gas safety check where the landlord has this obligation.
- **Meter reading.** If no one in the household can read the gas and/or electricity meter, the supplier

can arrange for the meter to be read every quarter and bills to be sent to the customer based on these readings.

- **Moving meters.** If it is difficult for the customer to reach or read the gas and/or electricity meter, the supplier will consider moving the meter to a more convenient position – for free.
- **Password scheme.** The customer can ask the gas and electricity supplier to give them a unique password that will be used every time company staff visit their home.
- **Special controls and adaptors.** The supplier can provide special controls to help make gas and electricity appliances and meters easier for the customer to use.
- **Advance notice if the electricity supply has to be interrupted.** If the electricity supply has to be turned off for planned work, the customer will get extra advance notice.
- **Bill nominee scheme.** If the customer would like their bills, or a copy, sent to a friend, relative or carer's address for them to help to read and check the bill, the supplier will arrange this on request.
- **Special help if the gas supply is disrupted.** If the gas supply has been disrupted or turned off for safety reasons, and if all adults living in the house are eligible for the Priority Service Register, the gas transporter will provide the customer with alternative cooking and heating facilities.
- **Services for visually or hearing impaired customers.** The supplier must provide customer information, including meter readings and bills, in a format suitable for the customer, for example Braille, large print or a tape.

4.6 WHAT IS ENERGYWATCH?

energywatch logo

energywatch

your gas and electricity watchdog

energywatch is the independent gas and electricity consumer watchdog.

The organisation was set up by the Utilities Act (2000) to be an advocate for consumers in the gas and electricity markets. **energywatch** receives a grant from the Department of Trade and Industry (DTI), which is derived from the licence fee that energy companies have to pay to the government. This makes **energywatch** accountable to the DTI for the work they do and the money they spend.

energywatch is completely separate from Ofgem, the gas and electricity regulator. However, the two organisations work closely together to promote the interests of consumers.

ENERGYWATCH SERVICES

energywatch acts as a 'One Stop Service' so that consumers need only one point of contact for raising complaints or for obtaining information about gas and electricity suppliers. See the end of this section for contact details.

Complaints

Complaints investigated range from disputed accounts and supplier transfers to problems with connection charges or gas safety and appliance issues.

Enquiries

Enquiries can vary in type from very easy requests for the supply of literature to complex legal matters. They can include competition, industrial and commercial, technical, landlord and tenant, and supplier related issues.

Consumer information

energywatch produces a range of consumer information and advice on issues such as how to change supplier, how to compare prices being offered by different suppliers, and how to use gas and electricity safely. The information is provided in a variety of formats including printed literature in a choice of languages, audiotape, large print and Braille.

4.7 WHAT IS OFGEM?

Ofgem logo

Ofgem is the regulator for Britain's gas and electricity industries. Its role is to promote choice and value for all customers. It is responsible for licensing the companies and ensuring competition is effective. Ofgem is not the first point of contact for customer complaints, which would normally go to **energywatch**. Where **energywatch** is unable to resolve a complaint this will be passed to Ofgem where the issue is relevant to its legal powers.

OFGEM'S WORK

Ofgem protects the interests of consumers by promoting competition where possible, and through regulation only where necessary. Ofgem's annual report describes how work focuses on the following areas [**7**]:

- making gas and electricity markets work effectively

- regulating monopoly businesses intelligently – such as transmission and distribution companies
- securing Britain's gas and electricity supplies
- meeting its increased social and environmental responsibilities.

By a combination of regulation and competition Ofgem aims to keep prices as low as possible and aims to ensure that companies comply with all their obligations.

For domestic consumers, two areas of Ofgem's work are particularly significant. These are the Social Action Plan and the Energy Efficiency Commitment (EEC).

The Social Action Plan is targeted at helping those who have most difficulty paying their energy bills. The plan sets out how Ofgem, working with other relevant groups, fulfils its duties to vulnerable customers. Recent work in 2002 under the Social Action Plan included:

- improving energy efficiency advice
- encouraging older people to take up the benefits of competition
- helping prepayment meter customers
- encouraging best practice in debt prevention and management
- promoting competition.

Full reports on all these areas of research and work are available from Ofgem.

The Energy Efficiency Commitment (EEC) is administered by Ofgem. Working to targets set by the Government for EEC, fuel suppliers help domestic customers improve the energy efficiency of their homes. Under the scheme consumers receive free or discounted measures to improve the energy efficiency of their homes. All suppliers operate telephone advice lines to provide energy efficiency advice to consumers and these can provide information on the help available with installing energy efficiency measures. (See Section 7.)

4.8 THE ENERGY RETAIL ASSOCIATION

The Electricity Association has been the trade association for the UK electricity industry. The Association announced that it would be restructured from 30 September 2003. A separate body will represent the energy network operations, and the Association of Electricity Producers (AEP) will have responsibility for generation. Retail activities will be the responsibility of the Energy Retail Association (ERA) [**8**].

4.9 SOLID FUEL SUPPLIERS

Solid Fuel Association logo

THE SOLID FUEL ASSOCIATION

The Solid Fuel Association is funded by solid fuel producers and distributors and was established to encourage greater awareness of the benefits of domestic solid fuel heating amongst the general public. The Solid Fuel Association operates as an advice centre and provides advice and information on all matters concerning the use of solid fuel to domestic consumers as well as professionals.

The Solid Fuel Association provides guidance and literature on different solid fuels, safety advice, heating appliances, benefits of solid fuel, installers and Approved Coal Merchants [**9**].

THE APPROVED COAL MERCHANTS SCHEME

Coal merchants who join the Approved Coal Merchants Scheme provide the following undertakings to their customers:

- To have their name and address and the Coal Trade Code sign clearly shown on their vehicle.
- To give delivery tickets showing their name and address for each delivery over two bags (100kg or 2cwt).
- To give a clear description of the coal or smokeless coal, so that customers fully understand what they are buying.
- To give trustworthy advice about the most appropriate coal or smokeless coal for the customer's appliance, and to offer help and advice from the Solid Fuel Association.
- To advise of any current summer discounts.
- To investigate promptly and sympathetically any complaint about coal or smokeless coal supplied, or about the service provided.

If customers still have a problem after speaking to the coal merchants, the Approved Coal Merchants Scheme has regional co-ordinators [**10**].

4.10 OIL SUPPLIERS

OFTEC logo

Oil is usually bought by contacting local suppliers for their prices, which include delivery charges. All tankers must meter their delivery by law, so the driver leaves a record of the amount of oil delivered. Many suppliers offer monthly payment plans, automatic tank top up and other services. You can find details of oil suppliers in Yellow Pages or by contacting OFTEC.

OFTEC (the Oil Firing Technical Association) is the technical and marketing body for the oil firing industry. OFTEC looks after the interests of consumers, installers and manufacturers in the oil heating industry. Only OFTEC Registered Technicians are recognised under the Government's 'competent persons' scheme as being qualified (in England and Wales) to self-certify work for which they are registered. For non OFTEC Registered Technicians, building control approval is required on each job they do.

OFTEC Registered Technicians are trained at OFTEC Approved Training Centres, and independently assessed before they can apply for OFTEC Registration. OFTEC Inspectors check their work regularly, and they are re-assessed every five years to maintain their registration. In addition, they all carry identity cards issued by OFTEC confirming the type of oil-heating work for which they are registered, and have appropriate public liability insurance.

An OFTEC Registered Technician will always leave a written statement of the work they have done, any replacement parts fitted and recommendations for work needed in the future. The OFTEC website provides a facility to search for the nearest OFTEC Registered Technician by postcode.

4.11 LIQUID PETROLEUM GAS (LPG) SUPPLIERS

The LPG used for central heating and all other uses associated with natural gas is Propane. The liquid is stored in storage vessels outside a dwelling, which are refilled by local suppliers using road tankers. Alternatively, 46/47kg cylinders, usually in a set of four, are provided and replaced as necessary. Butane in smaller cylinders is provided for portable stoves and heaters. These may either be refilled at local outlets or delivered.

The LP Gas Association is a non profit making organisation representing all major LPG companies in the UK. The Association promotes the benefits of LPG, the safe handling of LPG, and standards in the industry [**12**]. The LPGA provide such information as:

- safe use of LPG
- list of LPG companies and brand names (there are over 300 of these)
- how to contact suppliers.

Contact details for organisations listed here are in Appendix 1.

REFERENCES

1 *Ofgem Key Facts.* **www.ofgem.gov.uk**

2 *Six out of ten could get better deal on electricity bills says NAO.* Ofgem Press Release. Friday 9 May 2003. **www.ofgem.gov.uk**

3 *Competition for the poor: liberalisation of electricity supply and fuel poverty; lessons from Great Britain for Northern Ireland.* Brenda Boardman, Tina Fawcett, Environmental Change Institute, University of Oxford. March 2002. **www.eci.ox.ac.uk**

4 *Comparisons of price and performance.* **energywatch** Supplier Information: **www.energywatch.org.uk**

5 *Frequently asked questions; Doorstep and telephone selling.* **energywatch** Consumer Information: **www.energywatch.org.uk**

6 Association of Energy Suppliers. **www.aes.org.uk**

7 Annual report 2002 – 2003 Ofgem. **www.ofgem.gov.uk**

8 Information from website of the Electricity Association. August 2003.

9 Solid Fuel Association. **www.solidfuel.co.uk**

10 Approved Coal Merchants' Scheme. Helpline 0845 601 4406

11 OFTEC. **www.oftec.org**

12 Liquid Petroleum Gas Association (LPGA) **www.lpga.co.uk**

For gas and electricity suppliers see contact details Appendix 1 – Useful Addresses under 'F' Fuel Suppliers.

5

METERS, TARIFFS AND FUEL BILLS

Gas and electricity meters are fitted to the fuel supply in each home so that the fuel supplier can measure how much fuel has been used, and therefore how much to charge the customer. The meter readings, or in many cases estimated fuel use, appears on the customer's bill.

The most up to date meters can display a large amount of information to customers, allowing the use of a number of different tariffs and in some cases remote reading. However, the majority of meters are based on older technology, and they still have to be read in person.

Gas and electricity bills are not always easy to understand, particularly where there are split tariffs. Gas bills are made more difficult as the fuel is measured in volume but the customer pays for units in kWh.

This section provides information on:

- the different types of meters and how to read them.
- explanation of the operation of prepayment meters and their advantages and disadvantages.
- tariffs for gas and electricity.
- the information on gas and electricity bills.
- how to work out fuel costs from meter readings.

For information on choosing a fuel supplier see Section 4.

5.1 WHY READ METERS?

It is important when providing advice to be able to recognise different electricity and gas meters and be able to read them in order to:

- Check estimated fuel bills – one of the main causes of fuel arrears is previously underestimated bills.
- Check meter readings against any sort of bill.
- Keep a regular check on how much fuel is being used, to aid budgeting.
- Check the amount of fuel used when different heating or hot water use strategies are tried out.
- Have an accurate record of fuel use when moving home or changing fuel supplier.

5.2 HOW TO READ ELECTRICITY CREDIT METERS

These are the most common meters used in domestic property. Most meters simply show a row of figures (referred to below as the digital type) although you may come across older types which have a row of dials or 'clocks'.

DIGITAL TYPE

This meter reads 29897

Read the row of numbers from left to right. Read five numbers only. The sixth number (usually in a box or coloured red) is only a tenth of a unit and should not be read, as it is normally only used for test purposes. Make sure to record the five numbers, even if the first one is a zero, for example – 08456.

DIAL OR 'CLOCK' TYPE

This meter reads 12561

Dial meters have a row of dials with pointers that move in opposite directions from 0 – 9. Only read five dials, from the one marked 10,000 down to the one marked 1. Ignore the one which measures tenths of a unit as this is used for testing. (The way dials are arranged may vary slightly so two different examples are shown.)

This meter reads 10851

When reading each dial, record the lowest number that the pointer has gone past, not necessarily the one it is nearest to. For example, if the pointer is between 6 and 7, record 6. If the pointer is directly on a number, the reading becomes more complicated and you must look at the next dial down to make an accurate reading. In the second example above, on the 10 kWh dial the pointer is exactly on the 5. Look at the 1 kWh dial. The pointer is past the 1 so the reading is 10851. If the pointer on the 1 kWh dial had been between 9 and 0 the reading would have been 10849.

ECONOMY 7 METER (previously White Meter [WM] or Domestic Economy in Scotland)

The Economy 7 meter (or WM) is designed to measure electricity provided through the Economy 7 (or WM) tariff. (See later for full details of whom this tariff is appropriate for.) The Economy 7 (or WM) tariff supplies cheaper electricity for seven hours overnight (can be up to 8.5 hours in Scotland). The meter therefore has two registers, one for the daytime or 'on peak' units, (called 'normal' on the meter), and one for night time or 'off peak' units, (called 'low' on the meter).

In the same way as a normal digital meter, read five numbers from left to right, but make sure that when the numbers are recorded, the low and normal readings do not become confused.

This meter reads low 97666, normal 45338

ALL the electricity supplied to the home for heating, lighting and appliances is measured through the Economy 7 (or WM) meter. The meter is accompanied by a timeswitch, (two examples of timeswitches are illustrated here, although they may vary) which switches the supply between the 'low' and the 'normal' rates at the appropriate time.

(Note: Some of the newer multi rate tariffs developed for customers with electric heating – see later in 5.7 – may either use multiple readouts or may include an extra meter.)

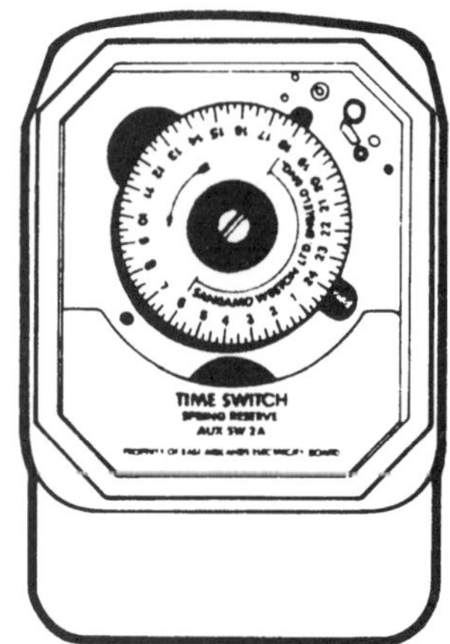

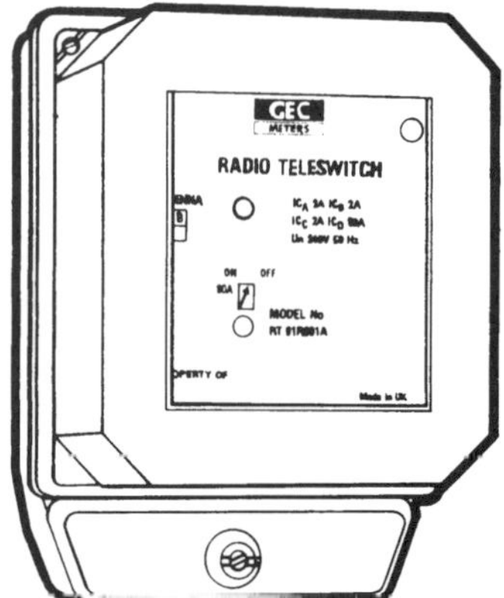

Economy 7 timeswitches

5.3 HOW TO READ GAS CREDIT METERS

Gas meters measure the volume of gas passing into a property. It is measured either in cubic feet or cubic metres, but gas is charged for in kilowatt hours (kWh).

Gas meters show the readings as a single line of numbers, as in the example below.

Cubic feet

Read the row of numbers from left to right, reading only four numbers. Ignore the fifth and the big dial, as these are used for testing purposes.

This meter reads 1668

Cubic metres

Read the row of numbers from left to right reading five numbers.

A single unit on a cubic feet meter is actually measuring one hundred cubic feet which is 2.83 times larger than a cubic metre of gas, as measured on a more modern meter. This can cause problems if the customer and particularly the gas supplier are not sure which meter they have. In October 2002 the Consumers' Association reported that they had uncovered about 4000 cases where various gas suppliers had either undercharged or overcharged customers because the type of meter was mistaken [**1**].

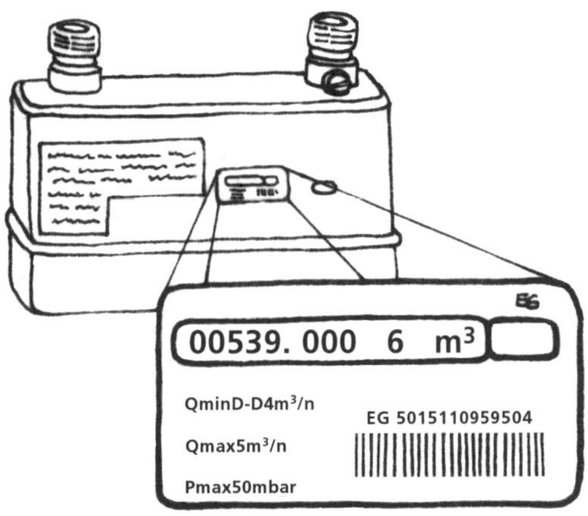

Digital gas meter measuring cubic metres. This meter reads 00539

CASE STUDY

A customer received a gas bill for £168, which she knew was far too high for the time of year. When asked to read her meter she provided the energy advisor with a 5 digit number, which immediately suggested that the meter measured cubic metres not cubic feet. This was checked against the bill and found that the 0 had been left off the beginning and the suppliers had mistaken the meter for one which read cubic feet. The bill was amended to £67.

5.4 ELECTRICITY PREPAYMENT METERS

Prepayment meters are a method of buying electricity as it is used. They may be operated by special keys, Smart Cards or tokens. A special key or Smart Card is 'charged up' or tokens are bought and inserted into the meter. In the South East meters using keys are called Budget Meters. Check for the appropriate name for the meters as they may vary.

In Northern Ireland 'keypad' meters are being introduced where the customer is given a series of numbers to key into their meter rather than inserting a card or token.

The facilities available on the meters also vary between meter manufacturers and electricity suppliers.

There is a brief description below on the operation of the meters, but it is essential that any user has access to the full instruction leaflet. Code of Practice literature, usually booklets, are available from fuel suppliers on the operation of prepayment meters.

TOKEN METERS

Tokens are bought from Post Offices and other outlets. The customer's account is credited when the token is bought. The token is then put into the meter, is cancelled, and can be thrown away.

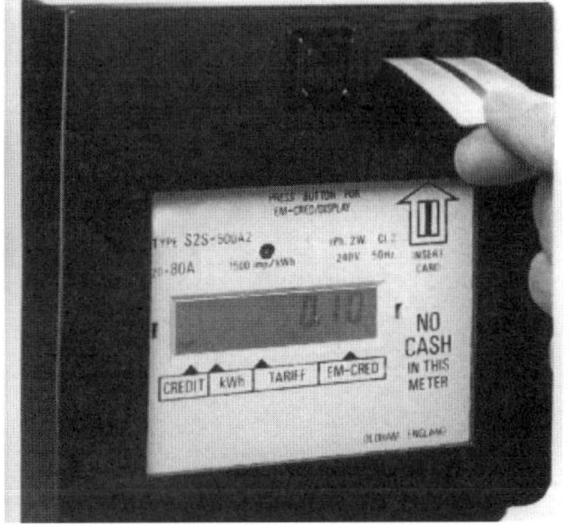

Typical token meter

KEY METERS OR SMART CARD METERS

Key meters or Smart Card meters work in a similar way. The key or Smart Card is rechargeable and is taken to a payment centre, e.g. a Pay Point outlet. When the fuel is paid for the key or Smart Card is electronically 'charged' with that amount of credit. The key or Smart Card is then inserted in the meter, and the account is credited. The key or Smart Card is specific to the meter so is of no interest to thieves.

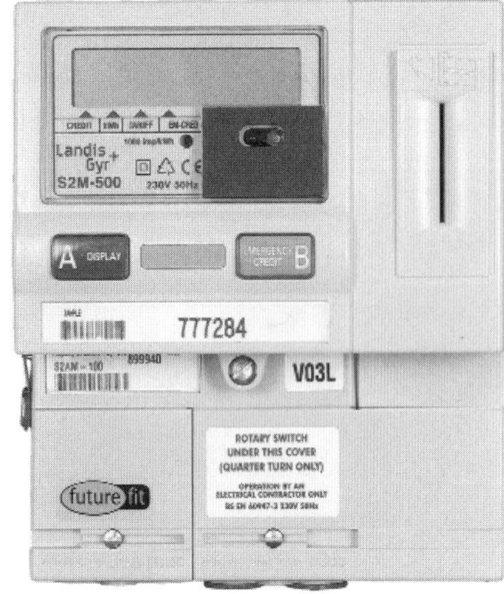

Typical Smart Card meter

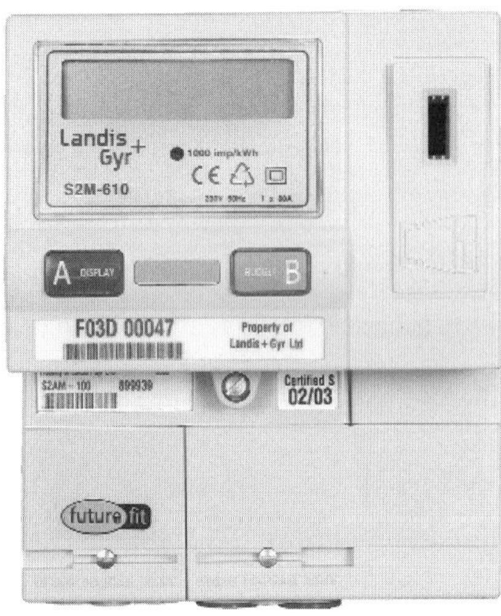

Typical key meter

EMERGENCY CREDIT

All meters have an 'emergency credit' button so that electricity is available even if tokens/keys/cards have not been inserted. The emergency credit is usually limited to £5 – £10 and may have to be paid off before any electricity can be obtained (i.e. put in £6 worth of tokens to get £1 worth of electricity). In some cases if all the emergency credit is used up and £5 is credited to the card, it is split so that some of the money is available for electricity supply. This depends on the policy of the fuel supplier. In some cases the level of emergency credit may be higher, i.e. in Scotland.

5.5 GAS PREPAYMENT METERS

The Quantum Meter is the most common gas pre-payment meter.

THE QUANTUM METER

The Quantum meter uses modern technology which overcomes some of the problems associated with the previously used mechanical token meters. A 'Gascard' is provided with the meter which is unique to the customer's meter. It is recharged every time gas credit is bought. The customer's account is credited with the amount recharged on the Gascard. A statement on the state of the account is sent to the customer – usually on an annual basis. Debt is usually repaid on a weekly basis – on the same day each week the account is debited by the amount taken for debt.

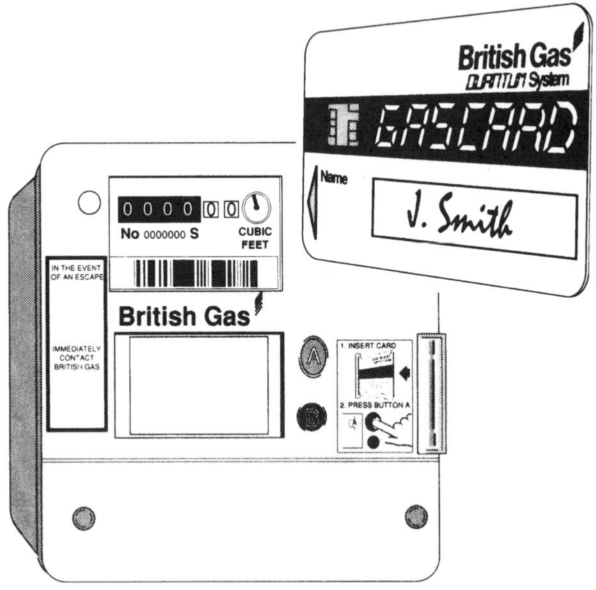

Gas prepayment meter – Quantum meter

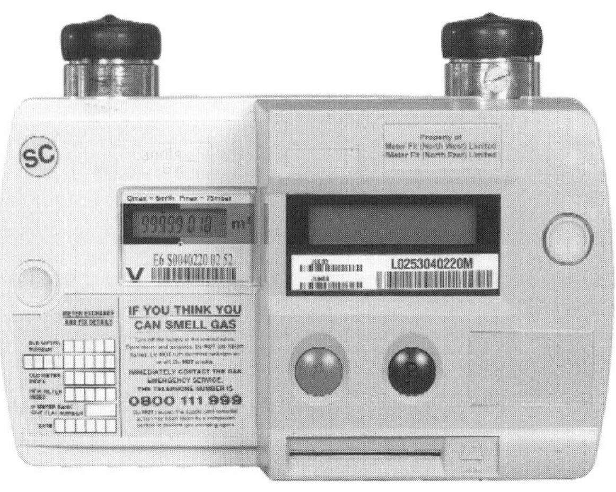

Gas prepayment meter – measuring cubic metres

5.6 ADVANTAGES AND DISADVANTAGES OF PREPAYMENT METERS

Some fuel suppliers promote prepayment meters as a method of providing fuel supply for customers without 'credit worthiness' or payment history and reclaiming arrears (see Section 6). The following issues should be considered:

HELPING CUSTOMERS TO BUDGET

Prepayment meters can help customers to control and reduce expenditure on electricity, and prevent the customer from getting into debt. They show a lot of information and can help customers understand more about electricity and gas usage and consumption.

UNDERSTANDING OF METERS

It is essential that customers understand how the meters work. Written instructions may get lost. Some people will find them difficult to understand and may not be able to ensure that appliances are turned off when the money runs out.

HIGHER COSTS

Make sure that all associated costs of this method of payment are understood, i.e. higher standing charges than credit meters and associated travel costs, e.g. if charging or purchasing facilities are not nearby.

BUYING TOKENS OR CHARGING KEYS/CARDS

Tokens and cards must be bought or the Smart Card or Budget Meter key must be taken to a location where it can be charged up. This may be the local Pay Point outlet or another location. Whichever it is, the customer needs to be able to visit the location. It may be both difficult and expensive (e.g. bus journeys) for some customers to get out. This is likely to be a greater problem for low-income customers who may only be able to pay for their electricity little and often. Prepayment meters may be inappropriate for some disabled and elderly customers.

Customers who cannot easily get out and about need to know how much their weekly consumption of electricity is likely to be, and how much they are paying for standing charges and any debt, so that they will not run out of fuel before they can get out again.

AVOIDING CONFUSION

Using tokens bought for someone else's meter causes problems as one customer is recorded as buying the token and not using it, but the other customer is recorded as using electricity not paid for. Therefore, without realising it, this situation creates a credit on one and a debt on the other. (Not applicable to keys and Smart Cards.)

If a customer uses a key/Smart Card that was provided by a previous supplier, that supplier will receive the payment. Similarly if a new occupier moves in they must not use a key or card used by a previous occupier. It is therefore essential that when a customer either changes supplier or moves home, the fuel supplier is notified immediately and new keys/Smart Cards can be issued.

POSSIBLE 'SELF DISCONNECTION'

Fuel is only available if the customer can afford to pay in advance (except for emergency credit), so it is possible that customers may 'self disconnect' their fuel supply if they do not have enough money to charge their meter.

PAYING OFF DEBT

If a customer is in debt, the meter will be set to reclaim it. In the majority of cases THE DEBT IS COLLECTED OVER TIME WHETHER OR NOT ELECTRICITY IS USED. This means that even if the customer is away, using no fuel, the meter must contain enough credit to pay off debts, or the electricity supply will run out. For customers on Income Support in debt, compare debt repayment levels with Fuel Direct.

DISPLAYS AVAILABLE WITH PREPAYMENT METERS

Visual displays are available usually by pressing a button, the display will 'scroll' through to show:

- units of fuel consumed
- fixed charge per week
- rate per unit of fuel
- credit inserted
- current credit
- outstanding debt
- debt repayments per week
- emergency credit
- weekly fixed charge
- variable calibration
- multiple rates
- on the gas Quantum meter, a message asks if appliances are switched off before the gas supply is back on.

This list is not exhaustive. It is included to illustrate the displays but also to demonstrate the variation in design and operation of the meters. It is essential that the customer leaflet for the specific meter concerned is used for information. Some leaflets are much clearer than others.

5.7 TARIFFS FOR ELECTRICITY AND GAS

Electricity and gas are supplied to the domestic customer under a number of tariffs. To some extent the customer has a choice of tariffs depending on which is most appropriate for their use of fuel, but both the meter in the property and the chosen method of payment are often linked to specific tariffs, for example a prepayment meter or Economy 7.

Tariffs are made up of a number of charges. On fuel bills the charges show as the unit cost of fuel, and standing or fixed charges if appropriate. Both these parts of the tariff may vary. There are an increasing variety of tariffs available as fuel suppliers try to attract more customers. Contact fuel suppliers for details of available tariffs. The most common tariffs are described below with examples. Some indication is also given of the appropriateness of different tariffs.

STANDARD DOMESTIC TARIFF

Sometimes called General Purpose, or simply, Domestic. The unit price does not vary from day to night. Price reductions may be offered for prompt payment.

DIRECT DEBIT

Direct Debit is a method of payment. However, most fuel suppliers offer the incentive of reduced unit costs or a set rebate to the customer paying by Direct Debit, i.e. money deducted (usually monthly) from the customer's bank account.

PREPAYMENT TARIFFS

Prepayment tariffs are almost always more expensive than standard domestic tariffs and Direct Debit. Electricity unit costs are often the same as credit meters but with an additional standing charge to the normal standing charge for a credit meter. Gas prepayment tariffs are often more expensive per unit than Standard Credit tariffs – but this varies from supplier to supplier.

NO STANDING CHARGE?

Fuel suppliers offer accounts with 'No Standing Charge'. However, the fuel consumption is split into two or more price levels. For example a gas tariff offers gas at 2.028p per kWh for the first 12.52 kWh per day (often shown as the first 1142 kWh per quarter). After that threshold the price drops to 1.420p per kWh. This is effectively 7.6p per day (12.52 x the difference between the higher and lower price per unit).

$$2.028p - 1.420p = 0.608p$$
$$0.608p \times 12.52 = 7.6p$$

Look on the bill to see how much split tariffs cost.

SPECIAL TARIFFS FOR OLDER PEOPLE

A number of new tariffs have been designed which are only available for older people, for example paying a flat rate depending on number of people and house size, but not fuel consumption. Contact fuel suppliers for information and the specific details of each.

ECONOMY 7

In England, Wales and Northern Ireland (see the situation for Scotland below) Economy 7 is the second most popular electricity tariff. Economy 7 or 'off peak' electricity is provided for the domestic customer to encourage electricity consumption overnight. (In Scotland the White Meter tariff was similar to Economy 7, giving up to 8.5 hours of cheaper electricity overnight. However, new tariffs have largely overtaken the White Meter tariff. They offer different tariffs for the heating and hot water circuit, either providing these circuits with a cheaper rate 24 hours a day, or providing heating and hot water at a cheaper rate overnight at a marginally cheaper rate than for other appliances. (See other electricity tariffs p5-7.)

On the Economy 7 tariff all the electricity supply to the dwelling for heating, hot water, lighting and appliances switches to a unit cost less than half the unit cost of the remaining 17 hours. The cheap hours are chosen by the fuel supplier and are usually between 10pm and 8am although this may be split e.g. 10pm – midnight, 2am – 7am. The start and end of the cheap rate period may change as the clocks change in spring and autumn. Check with the fuel supplier.

The standing charge, if applicable, is usually more expensive with Economy 7 than that associated with the General Domestic tariff and in most cases the unit cost for the 17 hours is more expensive than the General Domestic tariff as well.

Economy 7 is appropriate for customers who use storage heating systems where heaters and hot water are heated up overnight, but may also be appropriate for other users. An example is shown in Section 5.9.

The following considerations are important for customers thinking of converting their electricity supply to Economy 7.

- The amount of electricity used overnight must be enough to make the extra daytime unit cost and extra standing charge worthwhile. For example, washing machines, tumble dryers and dishwashers can be used overnight, controlled by timers (although safety considerations must be taken into account when using appliances overnight).

- Normal size hot water cylinders or immersion heaters may not be big enough to provide enough hot water overnight for a household's needs. Any extra daytime boost will use the most expensive rate electricity.
- Some electricity suppliers do not increase the unit cost of the daytime electricity for Economy 7 customers to convert to Economy 7 tariff because the only increase is in the standing charge. (For households who run a fridge and freezer, the amount of money saved as these run in the overnight period will save the extra standing charge.)

For all the points above, the Customer Services or Energy Advisor of your fuel supplier should be able to work out whether Economy 7 is an appropriate tariff for any particular household.

PRESERVED ELECTRICITY TARIFFS

Old under floor electric heating and electric warm air heating needed longer periods of charge than the 7 hours on Economy 7, so households with this type of heating may find themselves on the 'preserved tariffs' which operate at a slightly cheaper rate than the general purpose tariff for up to 15 hours a day. These tariffs are no longer available to new customers.

If the supply is on a preserved tariff, it may be tempting to convert to Economy 7. However, it is likely that although the bills may be cheaper, the charge will not be enough for under floor and warm air heating, so the dwelling will be considerably colder.

OTHER ELECTRICITY TARIFFS

A number of new electricity tariffs have been developed providing electricity at varying prices throughout the day and night. The fuel supplier is in control of the times at which electricity is supplied at cheaper rate. There are varying hours during the day and night, often changing at weekends.

Examples in Scotland are Total Heating with Total Control (THTC) and Comfort Plus. These are not considered as an alternative to Economy 7. Storage heating, hot water and other 'direct acting' heaters can all be used on the dedicated circuit. A separately metered circuit provides electricity for other appliances and lighting. Timing over a 24 hour period for the boosts is controlled by the fuel supplier to match the weather forecast.

Most fuel suppliers are developing alternative tariffs so customers with storage heaters, or generally heavy users of electricity should enquire about the appropriateness of the tariffs.

MAXIMUM PRICE FOR THE RESALE OF FUEL

Tenants often find themselves paying seemingly high prices to their landlords for gas and electricity. Ofgem publishes leaflets outlining exactly how much landlords are allowed to charge. Contact Ofgem for information.

5.8 UNDERSTANDING FUEL BILLS

It is the fuel bill that contains all the information about a customer's use of fuel and any amount of money owed to the fuel supplier. It is common practice for bills to be sent to customers even if they have a method of payment which does not require the bill to be paid. In such cases the bill is simply for information as a statement of the account.

On the following pages are examples of electricity bills and gas bills with notes to show what the items on the bill mean, and how the bills are made up. This is particularly important for the gas bill, which involves a fairly complex calculation. Examples of bills reflecting different payment methods and tariffs are shown.

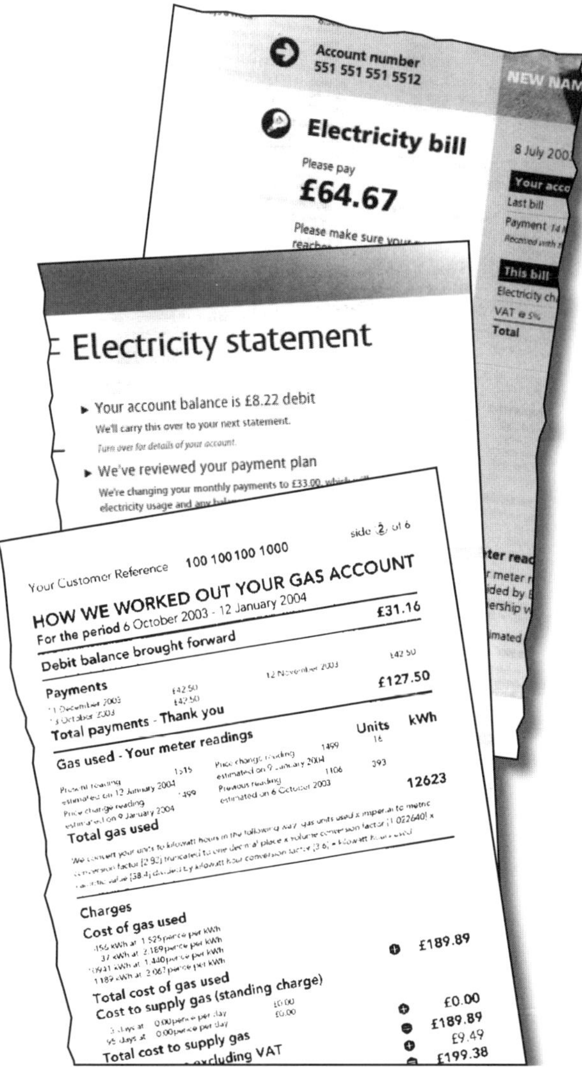

5.9 INFORMATION ON FUEL BILLS

The front of bills and statements now commonly have little information on them – simply the customer reference or account number, supplier's name and the account balance.

■ Name and address

The name and address on the bill does not automatically mean that that person is liable to pay the bill, although in the majority of situations it is the case. Responsibility for payment will be covered in the contract with the energy supplier.

■ The reference number or account number

Each customer has their own reference number, which should always be quoted in correspondence, or over the phone.

■ Date of reading/meter reading date

This is the date on which the meter was read, or the account was estimated. Sometimes this will say 'normal reading date'.

■ Contact telephone number/s

Bills have numbers to contact for queries, reporting power cuts, providing meter readings and for complaints. Website addresses are also provided.

Details of the fuel consumed and cost etc. are shown on the following examples.

5.10 EXAMPLES OF ELECTRICITY AND GAS BILLS

electricity statement

rate	present (1)	previous (2)	units used @ price per unit	VAT%	total charges
Standard	17846 estimated	17037 customer			
			(6) Fixed charges (4)	5.0	£14.36
			(3) 809 @ 4.89 pence	5.0	£39.56 (5)
			(8) VAT @ 5.0% on £53.92		£2.70
			Total charges		**£56.62**

payments

Payment received	(7)	on 28th August 2002	£25.00
Balance adjustmant		on 2nd September 2002	– £50.81
Payment received		on 30th September 2002	£24.00
Payment received		on 28th October 2002	£24.00
		Total payments	**£22.19**
		Previous credit balance	**£50.81**
	(10)	**You are in credit by**	**£16.38**

Labels on an electricity bill to show how the bill is worked out – see key to notes on page 5–9

How the electricity costs are worked out on this bill

	In this example:
Take the previous meter reading from the present reading to give the number of kWh of electricity used.	17846 – 17037 = 809
To find the cost multiply the number of kWh by the cost per kWh.	809 x 4.89p = £39.56
Add the standing (fixed) charge	£14.36
Add VAT @ 5% (on fuel costs plus fixed charge)	£ 2.70
TOTAL	**£56.62**

Summary of formula
kWh x cost per kWh = Total cost. Then add standing charge, if appropriate, and VAT. Payments received and credits from the previous bill will be subtracted from this total.

Notes to the sample bills

(1) Present reading

This is either the latest reading of the meter by a meter reader, or an estimate of the consumption calculated by the fuel supplier. It could also be a reading taken by the customer.

(2) Previous reading

This is the last recorded reading – again it could be an estimate, an actual reading or a customer's reading.

(3) Amount of fuel used

The total amount of fuel used = present reading – previous reading. This is straightforward on electricity bills.

The gas meter records the gas supplied in cubic feet or cubic metres, but the fuel is charged per kilowatt hour.

The formula for converting the meter reading (100s cubic feet or cubic metres) to kilowatt hours is explained in detail below the bill.

(4) Cost per unit

The price per unit may be the same for all units, or set so that a fixed number of units per day are charged at a higher rate and subsequent units charged at a lower rate – this is usually the case where there is no standing charge.

(5) Cost of fuel used

This is the number of units consumed, multiplied by the cost of each unit. (This may be displayed in different bands of costs per unit.)

(6) The standing charge or fixed charge

The standing charge is designed to cover the costs of meter readers among other things. It has been replaced by some fuel suppliers with a variation in the cost of fuel so that a fixed number of kWh per day are charged at a higher rate. (See Cost per unit.)

(7) Credits to the account

Amounts of money paid in – usually on Direct Debit or Budget Schemes or credit from the previous bill.

(8) VAT

VAT at 5% is added to the cost of the fuel and the standing charge where present.

(9) Gas – calculation

The calorific value of the gas supplied to the customer is given on a gas bill. It is the exact quantity of heat produced when a given volume of gas is burned. Because gas is measured in volume we need to be able to work out how much energy is in that volume. It is given in mega joules per cubic metre (MJ/m^3). The calorific value is subject to slight variation from time to time and from area to area, so it is always provided on the bill. The volume conversion factor (1.022640) is also displayed. The other numbers in the calculation are the conversion of cubic feet into cubic metres (2.83) and the conversion of MJ into kWh (3.6).

(10) Total charges/Total bill for this period

The total amount due is the cost of fuel consumed, plus the standing charge, if appropriate. It can also include money owed from previous quarters, or could have amounts deducted which have been paid to the fuel supplier.

If the meter reading is not written in full e.g. 'estimated', there will be a list of abbreviations on the bill:

C or R = customer reading.

E = estimated reading.

X = exchange meter (if a customer's meter has been replaced).

CR = credit (or amount paid in).

EXAMPLE OF A GAS BILL

HOW WE WORKED OUT YOUR GAS BILL

For the period 30 December 2002 – 2 April 2003

Gas used – your meter readings

	(1)		(2)	Units	kWh
Present reading taken on 2 April 2003	8350	Previous reading taken on 30 December 2002	7999	351	10947 (3)
Total gas used					**10947**

(9) *We convert your units to kilowatt hours in the following way: gas units used x imperial to metric conversion factor [2.83] truncated to one decimal place x volume conversion factor [1.022640] x calorific value [38.8] divided by kilowatt hour conversion factor [3.6] = kilowatt hours used.*

Charges

Cost of gas used

(4) 9783 kWh at 1.466 pence per kWh
1164 kWh at 2.594 pence per kWh

(5) **Total cost of gas used**	+	**£173.61**
(6) **Cost to supply gas (standing charge)**		
93 days at 0.00pence per day £0.00		
Total cost to supply gas	+	**£0.00**
Prompt payment reduction	−	**£7.20**
Total charges excluding VAT	=	**£166.41**
(8) **VAT** 5.00% of £166.41	+	**£8.32**
Total charges	=	**£174.73**

(10) **Your gas bill for this period is** **£174.73**

Please pay now.

Labels on a gas bill to show how the bill is worked out – see key to notes on page 5–9

How the gas costs are worked out on this bill

It is a fairly complex procedure to work out gas costs from meter readings. This is because gas is still measured in either cubic feet or cubic metres but is charged for in kilowatt hours – kWh. This step-by-step calculation explains how the information on the bill is derived.

To work out kWh	**In this example:**
Take the previous meter reading from the present reading to give the volume of gas used in 100s cubic feet, or cubic metres.	8350 – 7999 = 351
Multiply this by 2.83 to give the volume in cubic metres (unless already given in cubic metres).	351 x 2.83 = 993.3 cubic metres
To find the number of kWh, multiply the number of cubic metres by the calorific value of the gas shown on the bill then by the volume conversion factor (1.022640) and divide this by 3.6.	993.3 x 38.8 x 1.022640 ÷ 3.6 = 10947 kWh
To work out the costs	
To find the costs multiply the number of kWh by the cost per kWh. In this case there is a split tariff. There are a set number of units per day at a higher cost then all remaining units are at a lower cost. The number of higher cost units is not always the same on every bill as it depends on how many days are in the billing period.	1164 x 2.594p = £30.19 9783 x 1.466p = £143.42 **Added together = £173.61**
Prompt payment reduction is taken off the total.	– £7.20 **= £166.41**
VAT is added at 5%	£166.41 x 5% = £ 8.32 £174.73
TOTAL BILL	**£174.73**

Summary of formula

100s cu ft x 2.83 x calorific value x 1.022640 ÷ 3.6 = kWh x cost per kWh = cost of fuel.

This formula must be used for accurate bill calculation.

Quick method to work out gas costs

The calculation from volume of gas to kWh shown above is not simple.
Here is a simpler but less accurate method.

Meter readings themselves can be used as a rough guide to how many kWh have been used

- 100 cubic feet of gas, (which is the unit on the cubic feet meter) produces around **31 kWh**.
- A cubic metre of gas produces around **11 kWh**.

	In this example:
Take the previous meter reading from the present reading to give the volume of gas used in 100s cubic feet.	8350 – 7999 = 351
Multiply this by 31.	351 x 31 = 10881 kWh

As you can see this is only 66 kWh different to the accurate calculation above. (The reason this quick method works is because 100 cubic feet is roughly the same as a therm – the old unit used for gas measurement – the variation depends on the calorific value of gas which fluctuates from time to time and around the country. 1 therm = 29.3 kWh. Taking into account the volume conversion factor it is reasonable to use 31 as the number to multiply the 100s cubic feet to give kWh.)

5.11 ESTIMATED BILLS

Charges for Gas

Bill Period
26 March 2003 - 25 June 2003

Tariff Type
Standard Domestic

Estimate date
25 June 2003

M number
123456789

Calorific Value
39.0220

Breakdown of charges

	Present	Previous	Units/kWh*	Total
Reading	4361 E	4205 E	156 (100s cu ft) = 4893.74 kWh	
Charges				
268.89 kWh at 1.332p per kWh			(27/03/03 to 31/03/03)	£3.58
1,080.2 kWh at 2.28p per kWh			(01/04/03 to 25/06/03)	£24.63
3,544.65 kWh at 1.38p per kWh			(01/04/03 to 25/06/03)	£48.92
Standing Charge				
5 days at 10.8901p per day			(27/03/03 to 31/03/03)	£0.54
Subtotal (excluding VAT)				£77.67
VAT at 5% on £4.12			(27/03/03 to 31/03/03)	£0.21
VAT at 5% on £73.55			(01/04/03 to 25/06/03)	£3.68
Charges for the period				£81.56

This bill is estimated. Please call the above number to give us your own readings.

Total Charges	**£81.56**

This bill shows that both the previous and present readings have been estimated so it is important that the meter is read. The bill also shows that at the end of March the supplier stopped charging the standing charge and started to provide a split tariff.

An estimated bill is marked by an 'E' or the word 'estimate' next to the reading. If a meter reader has visited but there was nobody in, s/he should leave a card for the customer to take their own reading. If the customer does not do this, an estimate will be made. If they have taken a reading, and have sent it to the fuel supplier this will be shown by a 'C' or the word 'customer' next to the customer's reading. Once an estimated bill has been received the customer still has a certain number of days in which to read the meter and send or phone in the correct reading. (The actual procedure may vary between suppliers.)

Estimated bills if not corrected can cause serious problems. Ofgem and **energywatch** report [**3**] that some of the most frequently reported problems are those that relate to inaccurate estimated bills, or lack of meter readings.

Suppliers are obliged through their licence condition to check the meter at least once every two years but they are encouraged to obtain an actual meter reading at least once a year in the case of customers most at risk of debt.

Research carried out for **energywatch** suggested that 5 million customers had received inaccurate estimated bills and that almost half do not check their estimated energy bills [**4**].

UNDERESTIMATED BILLS

Most suppliers will check estimated bills for accuracy against past consumption but for new customers or those who have changed supplier this may be difficult.

The worst problems are often associated with underestimated bills. If a bill is based on an underestimated reading it may be much lower than usual. Some customers can fall into the trap of being so grateful for a small bill that they do not check to see how inaccurate it is. The problem arises the following quarter when an actual reading is taken and the customer ends up with a bill that they cannot pay. This can lead to fuel debt. It is important therefore to check meter readings to avoid the risk of a debt problem and hardship.

OVERESTIMATED BILLS

If a customer is not aware that the bill is based on an estimated reading, they may believe they have to pay the amount stated. If the bill is based on an overestimate this could lead to anxiety about meeting the bill.

5.12 OTHER INFORMATION ON BILLS

AMOUNTS CREDITED IN

See the bill on page **5–**8 showing amounts credited in.

If a customer pays money in regularly, or in varying amounts, these will be listed on the bill. If the amounts are fixed as with a Direct Debit or Fuel Direct, these amounts are deducted from the total bill, leaving either a balance or a credit. If an amount has been paid in but has not been recorded on the bill, the fuel supplier should be contacted and the receipts for the amount paid in shown as proof.

ECONOMY 7

An electricity customer who has an Economy 7 meter will receive a bill with two sets of readings – one for the 'normal' (daytime) rate and one for the 'low' (night-time) rate. If a meter reader visits an Economy 7 household and there is no one in, two slips will be left to record the readings. They are identical except one has the word 'low' in the top right-hand corner, the other has the word 'normal'. If the customer fills this in it is obviously important to put the normal and low readings in the appropriate boxes.

CASE STUDY

This customer uses appliances overnight but does not have either storage heaters or electric hot water heating. She asked whether it was still appropriate to be on the Economy 7 tariff. The advisor compared the bill with the amount it would have been if the customer paid on a Standard Domestic tariff. Here is the comparison:

Cost on Economy 7	
251 low units at 2.460p	= £6.17
895 normal units at 6.380p	= £57.10
Total cost of units	£63.27
Standing charge	£11.47
Total (before VAT)	**£74.74**

Cost on General Domestic tariff	
All units (1146) at 5.94p	= £68.07
Standing charge	£9.11
Total (before VAT)	**£77.18**

This customer was marginally benefiting from being on Economy 7. With this supplier, the customer needs to use at least 15% of her electricity during the off peak hours. Other suppliers advise up to 20%. By comparing the tariffs as in this case study the cut off point can be worked out.

Economy 7 bill – see case study

Meter readings and charges

Electricity used							£63.27
reading dates	*rate*	*latest*	*previous*	*units*	*cost*	*charges*	
2 Apr – 8 Jul	night rate	*estimate* 14609	*actual* 14358	251	2.460p	£6.17	
	day rate	*estimate* 16626	*actual* 15731	895	6.380p	£57.10	
Standing charge							£11.47
Up to 7 Jul	97 days at 11.82p per day					£11.47	
Total electricity and charges							£74.74
VAT @ 5.0%							£3.74

Contact details for organisations listed here are in Appendix 1

REFERENCES

1 *Which?* Magazine. October 2002.

2 Ofgem.
www.ofgem.gov.uk

3 *Preventing Debt and Disconnection.* Good practice guidelines developed by **energywatch** and Ofgem. **energywatch** and Ofgem. September 2002.

4 **energywatch** News Release 22.07.03.
www.energywatch.org.uk

FURTHER INFORMATION

Fuel Rights Handbook. 12th edition. Catherine Bartholomew. Child Poverty Action Group. 2002.

Tariff information from fuel suppliers.

Instruction booklets from fuel suppliers on the use of prepayment meters, and how to read meters. Most of these are very clear.

6

FUEL PAYMENT METHODS AND DEALING WITH DEBT

There are a variety of ways of paying for gas and electricity. Different methods will suit varying lifestyles, financial arrangements and personal circumstances.

This section:

- describes the payment methods and summarises the suitability of each method for different groups of people.
- outlines briefly the customers' rights to choose a payment method.
- describes fuel debt and defines 'arrears'.
- describes ways to pay off arrears.
- outlines when fuel suppliers may disconnect fuel.

If any advice organisation becomes involved in fuel debt advice we recommend the use of specific sources of information, e.g. The Fuel Rights Handbook [**1**] and contact with specialist debt counselling services – see contacts at the end of this section.

6.1 WAYS TO PAY FOR FUEL

There are essentially two different ways to pay for electricity and gas.

- **Credit.** This is how most people pay for fuel. The amount of fuel used is measured by a meter as it enters the home and the householder receives a bill for it which can be paid in a variety of ways.
- **Prepayment** by means of tokens, Smart Cards or keys. The fuel is paid for as it enters and is used in the home.

The payment methods are outlined below. Table 6.1 summarises the advantages and disadvantages of each method.

CREDIT METHODS

Quarterly/bi-monthly

The customer is usually billed for the consumption of fuel over a previous period (usually 2 or 3 months). The bill they receive can be based on an estimate of consumption or on the actual consumption as recorded on the meter. The bill is either sent by post or in some areas is issued by the meter reader (whether access is gained or not) by the use of a hand-held computer. The customer is expected to pay promptly. Payment can be made by post, at Post Offices, by debit or credit card over the telephone or on the Internet.

Monthly Direct Debit

The fuel suppliers estimate the customer's annual fuel costs based on the previous year's consumption and divide this into 12 equal monthly payments. The customer arranges with the fuel supplier to pay on a monthly basis through a banker's Direct Debit. The fuel supplier can change the amount of the Direct Debit but has to provide 14 days' notice to do so. At the end of the year the customer may be reimbursed if the monthly amounts add up to more than the sum used. They may have to pay an extra amount if they have paid less than their fuel consumption. Suppliers do this in varying ways, for example some reduce or increase the following year's monthly payments, others send the customer a refund or a demand for the amount. Readings of the meter will still be taken (or estimated) and bills received – but they are usually clearly marked 'Direct Debit Statement' or 'For Information Only'.

Direct Debit may also be debited from the bank after the quarterly bill.

Bank standing order

With a standing order the customer sets up the amount to pay. If the amount changes, the customer must inform the bank. There is not usually a price reduction for paying by standing order.

Payment scheme

Customers who do not have a bank account or Post Office account can opt to use a payment scheme card, which is specific to the customer. They can pay either weekly, fortnightly or monthly at a Post Office or Pay Point outlet using cash. The sum is agreed between supplier and customer.

Pay Point logo

Fuel stamps

Fuel stamps can be purchased at some Post Offices, although these are now being phased out. They can be used to pay gas or electricity bills. They are a helpful aid to people on low incomes who can buy them when they have the money and gradually build up towards the bill.

Fuel Direct

Income Support, Job Seekers Allowance and Pension Credit claimants can have their fuel debts (see 6.6) and an amount to cover their weekly consumption of fuel deducted from their Income Support on a weekly basis and paid direct to the fuel suppliers. The current consumption is normally based on the household's bills for the previous year and is reviewed every six months. Fuel Direct is not a payment method as such, but was set up by the (then) DSS as a means of preventing disconnection for claimants in fuel debt.

PREPAYMENT METERS

Budget meter / card / token / key meter

Budget meters or prepayment meters have become very popular with electricity suppliers particularly for low-income customers. The customer buys tokens or charges a Smart Card or key which is inserted in the meter. The fuel is therefore paid for in advance but the meter contains no cash. Full details of this type of meter and the gas prepayment meters are covered in Section 5.

6.2 CHOOSING A METHOD OF PAYING FOR FUEL

How much choice does the customer have when it comes to different ways of paying for fuel?

In practice electricity and gas suppliers are more likely to offer customers with good payment records more flexibility to choose a method of payment which suits them. Those with poor payment records or poor creditworthiness may be asked for money in advance of fuel use – with a prepayment meter.

The degree of choice which a customer has is influenced mostly by their creditworthiness in general and their ability to pay for their fuel. The fuel supplier will make an assessment of both of these. If they doubt a customer's creditworthiness they may ask for some sort of security – which in turn may affect the method of payment for fuel. For example, the customer may not be allowed to choose to pay a quarterly bill in arrears but will be required to pay by budget scheme or prepayment meter.

Probably the most common cases of customers feeling that they are not offered a choice of payment method is when they are in arrears and the supplier tells them they must have a prepayment meter.

Other budgeting and repayment methods may be more appropriate for a customer, so the full range of options should be considered. However, if a customer is in arrears and has not been able to manage any other payment plan, then the prepayment meter may be the only option. For further information or legal provisions for choice or in the case of disputes see the Fuel Rights Handbook [**1**] or contact **energywatch** [**2**].

CASE STUDY

The case of an older man was brought to an energy advisor as he had high electricity bills. In fact he had gas central heating which he did not use because the gas supply was fitted with a prepayment meter which he did not understand. He used electric fires and an electric immersion heater. The prepayment meter was removed, a budget payment method set up and his fuel bills were substantially reduced.

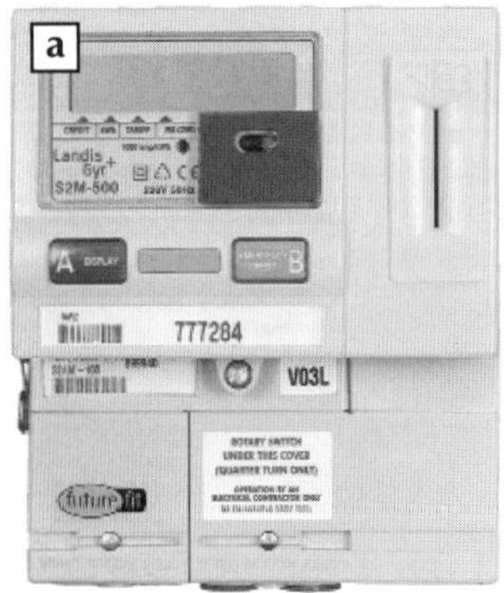

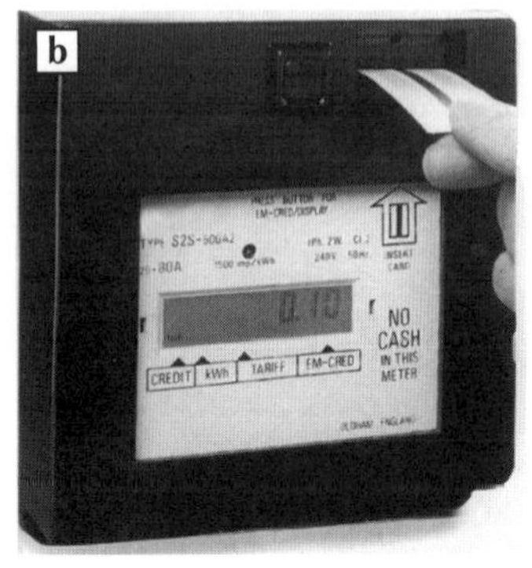

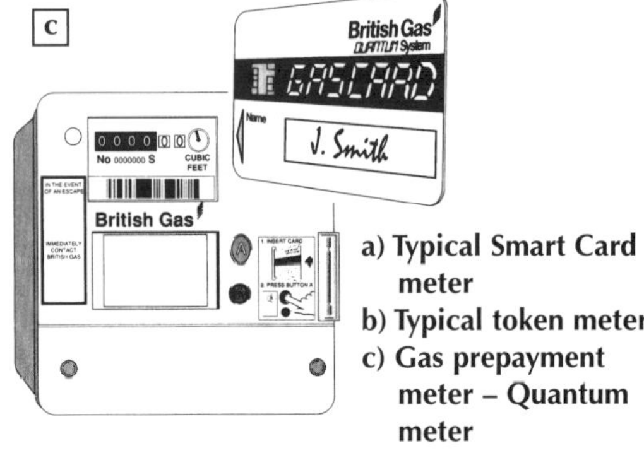

a) Typical Smart Card meter
b) Typical token meter
c) Gas prepayment meter – Quantum meter

Table 6.1 PAYMENT METHODS FOR FUEL

Method of payment	Advantages	Disadvantages	Who would it suit
Quarterly / bimonthly.	• Only have to think about bill when it arrives. • Always paying for fuel after it arrives.	• Difficult to budget because of large differences in winter and summer bills. • Problems can arise with estimated bills.	• Household whose income is stable. • Household whose income easily accommodates fluctuating fuel bills.
Monthly Direct Debit or standing order from bank account.	• Payment the same all year round. • No worry about bills. • Lower unit charges or other discount for Direct Debit.	• Must have a bank account. • Have to make sure consumption doesn't exceed payment. • If there is not enough money in the account to cover the Direct Debit bank charges may apply. • Standing orders do not benefit from lower charges or discounts.	• Households with regular income. • Those who find monthly budgeting easier than quarterly.
Budget schemes or 'cashplan' without bank account.	• Payments on a regular basis. • Can pay at Post Offices or PayPoint outlet.	• Possible inconvenience and travel costs. • Households who want to pay at regular intervals. • Households repaying debts.	• Households without bank account.
Budget meter / Token meter / Card meter.	• No risk of theft from key meter, key specific to one user. • Pay for fuel as it is used. • Can budget according to means. • No large bills to worry about.	• More expensive way to pay for fuel. • Limited number of dispensers for token and key. • Possible inconvenience and high travelling costs. • Essential that people understand their fuel consumption and how standing charges and debt are reclaimed. • If fuel runs out only very limited amount of emergency credit.	• Those who want a prepayment meter and don't find the access to source of keys/tokens a problem. • Those who are in debt – so they can repay debt through meter.
Fuel Direct.	• Payment for current use of fuel and debt taken directly out of benefits so customer doesn't have to think about it. • Fuel expenditure and debt repayment evenly spread. • Usually less expensive for customers in debt than other methods (e.g. prepayment meters).	• Essential to understand that, if current fuel use exceeds amount paid in Fuel Direct, money will still be owed and deductions from benefit will have to be increased. • No flexibility in budgeting.	• ONLY FOR THOSE ON INCOME SUPPORT AND OTHER QUALIFYING BENEFITS WHO ARE IN FUEL DEBT. • Suitable particularly for those with ill health or mobility problems.

Contact your fuel supplier for their fuel payment methods.

6.3 CODES OF PRACTICE ON PAYMENT METHODS

Fuel suppliers to domestic customers produce a series of Codes of Practice, which are approved by Ofgem. There is a Code of Practice on 'Paying your electricity (gas) bills', covering such subjects as:

- how fuel is charged for
- methods of paying for fuel
- security deposits and credit status
- help for people in payment difficulties
- disconnection of fuel supply
- where to get further help.

There is a separate Code of Practice on prepayment meters.

It is important to have to hand the Codes for different fuel suppliers. They can be referred to in discussions with fuel suppliers.

6.4 FUEL DEBT

Fuel debt and the fear of disconnection of the fuel supply can cause a great deal of worry especially to low-income households. Many debts could probably have been avoided or reduced if the customer had received more comprehensive advice before the debt was allowed to build up [**3**].

In 2002 Ofgem reported that [**3**]:

- *Over 1.5 million households were repaying debts to their energy suppliers.*
- *About two thirds were using prepayment meters for repayment.*
- *More than two thirds of households repaying debt were receiving benefits.*
- *The average debt for gas was £160.*
- *The average debt for electricity was £200.*

Ofgem and **energywatch** have produced guidelines for fuel suppliers on the adoption of good practice in the prevention of debt and disconnection, and in the management of debt recovery [**4**].

They identified six key areas:

- Minimising billing errors – customers need regular and accurate bills so they know how much money they owe.
- Using incoming calls to identify customers who would benefit from energy advice or other assistance.
- Using customer records to target energy efficiency – records are held on customers' fuel use so appropriate advice can be targeted to them.
- Demonstrating flexibility in debt recovery – fuel suppliers should be more proactive in helping customers in debt.
- Working with other groups to offer sustainable solutions to customers in difficulty – some customers will need particular help, and those with multiple debts need to get advice from other agencies (see 6.8).
- Helping customers who are unable to manage their affairs – fuel suppliers should have arrangement to help customers who need special help e.g. if they have chronic illnesses.

Details of the good practice guidelines can be found in the report [**4**].

As conditions to their licences, gas and electricity suppliers must anyway adopt methods of dealing with customers in difficulties. Fuel suppliers publish Codes of Practice outlining the procedures for the payment of bills including paying off debt. It is important to get a copy of the Code of Practice for different suppliers as the Codes do vary.

Fuel debt is referred to as 'arrears' in this section as this is the term used by fuel suppliers. We do not attempt to look in depth at the legal issues of fuel debt. Consult reference [**1**] for further information.

6.5 DEFINITION OF ARREARS FOR FUEL

Before trying to solve the problem of fuel debt, there are a number of things to check to make sure there is a genuine debt problem.

IS THE BILL CORRECT?

Check the meter reading to make sure the bill is accurate (remembering that some fuel will have been used since the bill arrived). If the current bill is an overestimate the fuel supplier should be informed and a lower bill should be sent. The bill may be a genuine amount, higher than expected because of previously underestimated accounts. In this case there should be arrangements to pay the bill over a suitable length of time – see payment arrangements on p**6**–5.

WHOSE BILL?

Make sure the bill has come to the right flat or house and that the appropriate meter has been read.

Make sure that the bill is from the fuel suppliers that supply the customer (see Section 4).

There are various legal interpretations of the liability for a fuel bill, particularly if the gas or electricity supply was in someone else's name, if for example someone has left home or died. A customer cannot be held responsible for bills of previous occupiers of property (so it is important to read meters, and get the fuel suppliers to read meters when moving in and out of a house).

CASE STUDY 1

A customer was shocked to find that he owed his fuel supplier £240 as he had been paying for his electricity by Direct Debit and felt comfortable that the bills were being paid.

The electricity consumption had been estimated for the previous three quarters of the year, and had been underestimated. The family had also been using more electricity following the birth of their baby. Following advice, the customer made sure that he checked meter readings.

CASE STUDY 2

A customer changed fuel supplier but did not receive a gas bill from the new supplier for over a year. When the bill finally arrived it was for over £600 which the customer was asked to pay. The amount was correct, but the customer was unable to pay it all at once. Following negotiations, the payment was spread over a year.

6.6 WAYS OF PAYING OFF ARREARS FOR FUEL

Ways of paying off arrears will only work if they are discussed with the customer and are appropriate. Otherwise, there may be examples of customers breaking payment arrangements in which the regular payments were unrealistically high, or self disconnecting from a prepayment meter if they cannot get out to buy tokens or cards.

PAYMENT ARRANGEMENTS

A payment arrangement will include regular (weekly, fortnightly or monthly) payments of an amount to cover the repayment of arrears plus the current consumption of fuel.

Important points to note:

Rate of repayment
Suppliers should agree the repayment of arrears at the rate the customer can afford and should take into consideration advice given by outside money advice agencies. For customers on benefits or low income this is generally understood to be around the rate for Fuel Direct. Suppliers may estimate how much fuel will be used over the next year based on the current consumption (see below), add the sum for arrears and require that the resulting figure is paid at regular intervals. Make sure that this sum is not too high for the customer (especially in cases where the customer has multiple debts, see Section 6.8).

Current fuel consumption
Because repayments include an amount for current fuel consumption, make sure this is as accurate as possible. Note what the consumption has been in the past, and any apparent reasons for changes in fuel use, and keep regular meter readings if possible (see Section 5).

Getting advice
The conditions of the suppliers' licences specifically include the suggestion that advisors help the customer in arrears to work out how much they can afford to pay in a payment arrangement.

Customers in fear of disconnection may agree inappropriate payment methods simply to keep their fuel supply and may not look for future help. It is important that those customers are advised wherever possible, and are made aware of the services of advice agencies.

Broken arrangements
Payment arrangements may break down for a number of reasons. Domestic circumstances may change or the rate of repayment may have been too high in the first place.

The fuel suppliers can be unsympathetic to customers who break arrangements. It should be made clear either by the customer or an advocate if the customer is in multiple debt so that the supplier should not try to collect their debt at a preferential rate to other organisations to which the customer may also owe money.

Most fuel suppliers offer a prepayment meter as an alternative payment method if an arrangement breaks down. However, if the customer wants to keep the credit meter they should provide details of their current financial position, including reasons why the arrangements broke down, and attempt to renegotiate the payment arrangement.

If a debt is a result of previously underestimated bills, resulting in a high bill, Ofgem support the view that the customer should be given at least the length of time to pay off the bill as the time over which the account was underestimated.

PREPAYMENT METERS

Prepayment meters have long been a method of helping customers budget for their fuel.

Prepayment meters set to collect arrears are offered as an alternative to disconnection when a customer has not been able to manage a payment plan as outlined above. It must also be 'safe and practical' to fit a prepayment meter.

Important points to note:

- Although an aid to budgeting for customers who find payment arrangements difficult, there are a number of disadvantages associated with prepayment meters. See Section 5 for details.
- Make sure the level of repayment of arrears is affordable. If it is not, the customer may only be able to afford the arrears repayment but no fuel, and effectively disconnect themselves from the fuel supply. The rate of Fuel Direct deductions (see below) can be used as a guide.

For a description of the advantages and disadvantages of prepayment metres see Section 5.

FUEL DIRECT

Fuel Direct is a method of paying off gas and electricity arrears for customers on Income Support and other qualifying benefits. An amount of money to cover their current consumption of fuel and £2.75 per fuel (£5.50 for gas and electricity) per week towards the arrears may be deducted from their weekly benefit.

The Department of Work and Pensions (DWP) must be contacted and the decision to allow a customer into the Fuel Direct scheme is made by an adjudication officer of the DWP.

The scheme can be useful because the repayment levels are fixed and relatively low compared to some payment arrangements.

Important points to note:

- The fuel supplier must be informed that the scheme is being set up, as there may be delays resulting in disconnection.
- Make sure amounts calculated for the current consumption of fuel are accurate (in the same way as described for payment arrangements above).
- Remember that the current fuel used still has to be paid for. There is a danger of some customers using more fuel because the deductions are being paid automatically. Any consumption in excess of that estimated will have to be paid for.
- Fuel Direct is only available while a customer is on Income Support or other qualifying benefits.
- Some suppliers are keen to use Fuel Direct but others are not. In their published Codes of Practice (see examples below) some suppliers may state that Fuel Direct is only available if the installation of a prepayment meter is not feasible, or they may not mention it at all.
- However, the decision to include a customer on Fuel Direct rests with the DWP not the fuel suppliers. Disputes can ultimately be taken to Ofgem.

6.7 DISCONNECTION OF FUEL SUPPLY

Fuel suppliers claim that disconnection of the fuel supply is a last resort and in practice disconnection happens when there has been no contact between the customer and supplier.

The timing of the procedure if a bill is not paid is outlined in the following example of customer literature provided by a supplier. Each supplier is slightly different, so it is useful to have the different Codes of Practice to hand.

Neither gas nor electricity can be disconnected if the account is 'genuinely in dispute' or the debt is for other charges, e.g. sales of appliances.

NEGOTIATING TO PREVENT DISCONNECTION

Early contact with the fuel supplier is important in the prevention of disconnection. Once contacted, suppliers are obliged to consider various payment options and arrange the repayment of arrears at a rate the customer can cope with. If negotiation is left

Example of suppliers' customer literature describing the timing and procedures if a gas bill has not been paid

We send you your bill

13 working days after the bill we send you a Final Notice.

18 to 20 working days after the bill we telephone you (if we have your telephone number on record) to find out if you are having difficulty paying and offer alternative payment arrangements.

21 working days after the bill we send you a letter explaining what will happen if you do not pay. This letter asks you to contact us if you are having problems paying.

31 working days after the bill we telephone you again to find out why you still have not paid. We will let you know what our follow-up action will be.

At least 33 working days after the bill we will write to you giving a date that a representative will call to collect the amount you owe. If you do not contact us or pay what you owe before that date we will visit your property to collect the debt. If you do not pay on that day (or make a payment arrangement) the representative will leave a letter stating that we will have to begin legal action. (If our representative discovers that you are disabled or have other special needs we may stop follow-up action to give our Special Services staff the chance to offer you advice or support in resolving your payment difficulties.)

At least 60 working days after the bill we will send you a letter saying we will seek legal authority to enter your property. We will then give a date when we will call to disconnect your gas supply or fit a prepayment meter.

until the last minute it is less likely that the customer will negotiate a suitable arrangement but may accept any method (particularly a prepayment meter) to avoid disconnection.

Customers who do not feel able to negotiate with the fuel suppliers should seek the support of an advice agency or other organisation (see 6.8).

Once disconnected, a customer will still have to pay the arrears, and also the cost of both disconnection and reconnection. In some cases the fuel supplier may ask for a security deposit before the supply is reconnected.

There are a number of organisations who can provide free help to produce a financial statement taking into account a household's income, bills and debts, and who will negotiate on behalf of the customer with fuel suppliers, banks, local authorities, etc., for the repayment of debts.

Look for 'Money Advice Centres', Citizens' Advice Bureaux, National Debtline or other independent advice services (see Further Information), but beware of advice from other agencies who may not be impartial and who may charge very high rates of interest.

6.8 MULTIPLE DEBT

Fuel is essential to modern life. It is therefore tempting for customers suffering from hardship to agree to the repayment of fuel arrears at a level they cannot afford in order to keep their supply connected. For customers with a number of debts this can lead to further problems as the household budget is stretched to impossible lengths.

Fuel suppliers are likely to be more sympathetic in agreeing to small regular repayments of arrears if they are aware of other debts of a customer.

6.9 PREVENTING FUEL DEBT

Fuel debts arise because people cannot afford to meet their heating costs. This problem often results in a crisis situation when a debt needs to be paid off. Action must be taken including negotiations with fuel suppliers, and in some cases the DWP and landlords. Once a debt has been dealt with, and in some cases the fuel supply re-connected, the crisis may be over but the problem is not solved.

What this Handbook sets out to do is to look at the reasons for the debt in order to help avert it in the future.

WHY DID THE FUEL DEBT OCCUR? – CHECKLIST	
Was the fuel consumption correctly charged for?	Check bill and meter readings.
Does the bill belong to the customer in question?	Check customer reference number.
Is the bill from the customer's supplier?	Check whether supplier has been changed.
Was the meter reading correct?	Check meter reading.
Was there a history of underestimated bills leading to a high 'correcting' bill when the meter was finally read?	Check past bills if available.
Is the fuel consumption regularly monitored to help budgeting?	Advise on keeping records of meter readings.
Was fuel consumption particularly high?	Check use of appliances/heating for any obvious problems.
Is there something wrong with heating/hot water system causing high fuel use?	Check heating system.

PREVENTION OF FUEL DEBT
Check customer is on the most appropriate tariff and paying in the most appropriate way.
Check insulation/heating grants.
Check whether benefits are being claimed.
Check on use of high consumption appliances.

Contact details for organisations listed here are in Appendix 1.

REFERENCES

1 *Fuel Rights Handbook.* 12th edition. Catherine Bartholomew. Child Poverty Action Group. (CPAG) 2002.

2 **energywatch.** **www.energywatch.org.uk**

3 Ofgem factsheet 20. 11.09.02. **www.ofgem.gov.uk**

4 *Preventing Debt and Disconnection. Good practice guidelines developed by* ***energywatch*** *and Ofgem.* **energywatch** and Ofgem. September 2002. **www.ofgem.gov.uk**

FURTHER INFORMATION

The Debt Advice Handbook. (CPAG).

A Guide to Money Advice (Scotland). The Money Advice Trust in Association with CPAG.

For Multiple Debt:

National Debtline – The National Debtline is a national telephone helpline for people with debt problems in England, Wales and Scotland. The service is free, confidential and independent.
0808 808 4000
www.nationaldebtline.co.uk

Debt advice from an organisation which is a member of Community Legal Services (CLS) Legal Help Scheme.

7

FINANCIAL HELP FOR HEATING AND ENERGY EFFICIENCY

The availability of grants is one of the most commonly requested pieces of information when customers contact an energy advisor. There are a number of different schemes, from local initiatives to major Government grants. They provide grants and discounts for heating and energy efficiency measures as well as renewable energy installations. It is important for energy advisors to keep up to date.

Grant structures change – most undergo a major review at least every five years, and in between, other detailed changes occur, most commonly in the criteria for eligibility and the grant levels. We therefore do not include the details of the grants as they would be out of date very quickly. The basic outlines are included here along with contacts for up to date information.

In addition to the provision of grants and discounts for energy efficiency, other financial issues are important, especially making sure that those people who are eligible for welfare benefits and other allowances are claiming them.

Readers are advised to:

- make sure that the details held of major grant schemes are up to date
- research local information for local schemes, hardship funds etc.
- set up referral systems with other agencies who specialise in benefits advice.

7.1 GOVERNMENT GRANTS TO TACKLE FUEL POVERTY

The grants listed here are the mainstream Government grants for each part of the UK. The UK Fuel Poverty Strategy [1] identified the groups of households most at risk from fuel poverty. The grants are, in general, aimed at those households on income or disability related benefits. Householders aged 60 or over are offered a higher level of help. The grants are aimed at making homes warmer and more energy efficient by providing insulation measures and, in some cases, heating. They are reviewed periodically, but the different countries in the UK are not all reviewed at the same time.

The grants are described briefly here. Some of those in sub-section 7.1 are aimed at owner-occupiers and people who rent their homes from private landlords. They are not available for tenants of local authorities or other registered social landlords. The grants available **only** to owner-occupiers and tenants of private landlords are:

- England – Warm Front and Warm Front Plus
- Scotland – The Central Heating Programme
- Northern Ireland – Warm Homes.

> The term **'qualifying benefit'** is used in this Section. These are the benefits, tax credits or allowances which the householder must receive in order to be eligible for a grant. There are usually additional criteria e.g. having a child under 16. Each grant scheme has slightly different qualifying benefits.

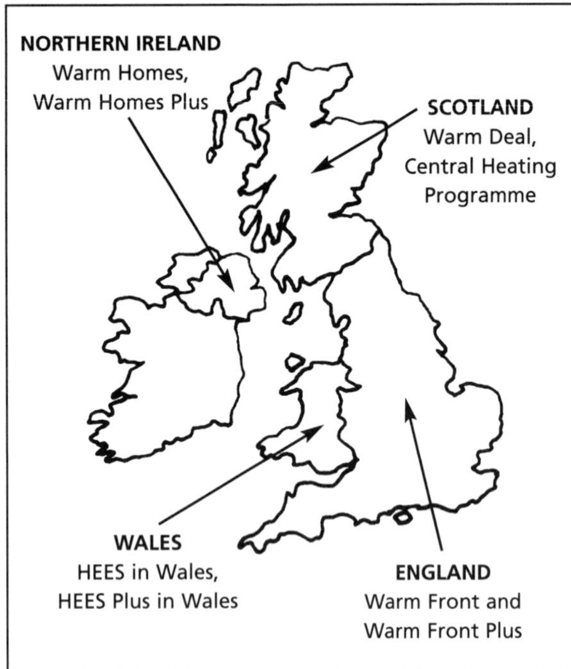

Government grants in England, Wales, Scotland and Northern Ireland

ENGLAND
WARM FRONT AND WARM FRONT PLUS

Warm Front grants are available to householders who receive qualifying benefits, have a child under 16, are pregnant, are disabled or have a long term illness. The grant provides a package of insulation and heating improvements, which is tailored to the property. It also includes energy advice and energy efficient lights.

Warm Front Plus is a higher grant available to people on qualifying benefits aged 60 and over, which includes central heating.

WALES
THE HOME ENERGY EFFICIENCY SCHEME (HEES) IN WALES

HEES in Wales is available to householders who receive qualifying benefits. The grant provides insulation and heating improvements tailored to the property. It also includes energy advice.

HEES Plus in Wales is a higher grant which includes central heating. It is available to householders on a qualifying benefit aged 60 or over, lone parent families with children under 16, or households with a child under 16 who are disabled or have a long term illness.

SCOTLAND
WARM DEAL

Warm Deal is available to householders who receive qualifying benefits. The grant provides insulation measures, energy advice and energy efficient lights. Householders aged 60 or over and not receiving any of the qualifying benefits may be entitled to a percentage of the grant (which is capped at an upper limit).

CENTRAL HEATING PROGRAMME

The Central Heating Programme is available to householders who are aged 60 or over, where the home does not have a central heating system or where the heating system is completely broken and cannot be repaired.

The measures include central heating to the main living areas and insulation measures. Energy advice, energy efficient lights, carbon monoxide detector, smoke detector and cold alarm (which indicates when the home is too cold for the householder's health) are included.

NORTHERN IRELAND
WARM HOMES

Warm Homes is available to householders who are in receipt of qualifying benefits and have a child under 16. The grant provides insulation and some heating measures. Energy advice and low energy lights are also included.

Warm Homes Plus is for householders who are 60 or over and in receipt of qualifying benefits. The grant includes insulation plus a new or repaired central heating system.

APPLYING FOR GOVERNMENT GRANTS

Government grant schemes are run by managing agents. In 2003 all the UK schemes are managed by Eaga Partnership [**2**] except for the Eastern, East Midlands and Yorkshire and Humberside region of England which is managed by Powergen [**3**].

Applications can be made by:

- completing a form in a leaflet (which are widely distributed around a variety of venues and agencies)
- calling a free phone number
- on line at the managing agents' websites
- through networks appointed by a managing agent.

Contact details are in the References and Contacts at the end of this Section.

If the applicant qualifies for a grant an assessor will call at their home to check their benefits details and discuss the appropriate insulation and heating measures. The agreed work will later be carried out. There can be a waiting time before the work is carried out. Both managing agents show the local waiting times on their websites.

7.2 THE ENERGY EFFICIENCY COMMITMENT (EEC)

The Energy Efficiency Commitment (EEC) is a major source of finance for domestic energy efficiency measures. To customers, however, it is not generally visible as a grant, as it is often incorporated into a range of schemes.

The EEC, which is set by the Department of Environment Food and Rural Affairs (DEFRA), requires all major gas and electricity suppliers in Great Britain to improve the energy efficiency of customers' homes. Each company has an energy saving target which it must achieve between 2002 and 2005 by installing energy efficiency measures in homes. The typical types of measures are insulation, lighting, heating and energy efficient appliances. They are provided to the domestic customer either free of charge or at a discount depending on the scheme.

At least 50% of these measures must be targeted at 'priority' customers in receipt of income related benefits or tax credits. Ofgem administers the EEC on behalf of DEFRA by approving energy companies' schemes and monitoring their progress against their targets.

From a domestic customer's point of view they may not be aware of the source of finance for the energy efficiency work, and if they see offers, may sometimes be suspicious of the fuel suppliers' motives. In fact:

- households do not have to be a customer of the fuel supplier from which they receive energy efficiency measures, and do not need to change to that supplier.
- fuel suppliers can provide measures to households heated by gas, electricity, coal, and LPG.

The schemes are delivered in different ways. For example suppliers may work with retailers to discount the price of energy efficient or 'A' rated electrical appliances, they may send information to customers in their bills about discounted insulation offers, and they may work with Social Housing Providers to set up schemes in their housing. Schemes vary and may have different names.

The current EEC scheme ends at the end of March 2005. The future scheme from 2005 – 2008 is likely to be expanded but along similar lines. For up to date information see references [**4**] and [**5**] at the end of this section.

7.3 LOCAL AUTHORITY SCHEMES

Local authorities carry out insulation and heating work in their own housing stock. This is not covered in this section because it is usually part of their programmed work.

Local authorities also have budgets for private sector housing. Private sector housing grants are usually reserved for renovation, repairs and providing facilities for disabled people. Some authorities, though, allocate part of the budget for heating or insulation for those households not eligible for Government grants, or who need works not covered by the grants, for example heating repairs. Such works are usually provided on a discretionary basis, often for older people. Budgets are often very limited. A Housing Improvement Agency may administer private sector housing grants.

There may also be local projects, for example in Neighbourhood Renewal Areas, which incorporate energy efficiency and heating within housing improvement schemes. Interest free loans and equity release schemes are being developed in some areas to pay for energy efficiency measures.

Contact your local authority for further information. The relevant department is likely to be called the Private Sector Housing, Regeneration or Environmental Health Department.

7.4 HEALTH RELATED SCHEMES

There is an increasing recognition that health is adversely affected by cold conditions, particularly for vulnerable groups. This has led to joint working between energy efficiency agencies, local authorities and the health sector, to identify and provide heating and insulation for those vulnerable groups. If clients are judged to be vulnerable to the cold, in some cases if they have specific illnesses, then they receive help from the schemes.

Where such projects exist, there is often an integrated approach to using finance from Government grants, from fuel suppliers' EEC schemes, and from other sources. Funding is sometimes supplemented by the local Primary Care Trust (PCT). Some examples of this are:

- the provision of central heating
- the provision of emergency heating repairs
- the provision of heat recovery fans to improve the air quality.

Contact the local authority, and local energy agency e.g. The Energy Efficiency Advice Centre for more information. (See Section 3 for details of the types of schemes and references to further information about schemes around the country.)

7.5 BENEFIT TAKE UP – 'BENEFIT HEALTH CHECKS'

Most Government grants and some of the EEC grants are restricted to claimants of a range of benefits, most of which are means tested. It is therefore essential to make sure that those people eligible for benefits are receiving them because the benefits act as 'passports' into the energy efficiency grant schemes.

Many organisations including the voluntary sector are involved in benefit take up campaigns and are actively encouraging potential claimants to receive a Benefits Check. The group of potential claimants least likely to claim the benefits they are entitled to are older people.

'Benefits Health Checks' are also carried out by Government grant scheme managing agents, when people apply for grants. The benefits health check is a discussion with potential benefit claimants to establish which benefits they are currently claiming and whether there are any others for which they are eligible.

Make sure you know where to refer clients for a benefits check. This may be a local agency.

7.6 WINTER FUEL PAYMENTS/COLD WEATHER PAYMENTS

WINTER FUEL PAYMENT

The winter fuel payment was designed to help older people to pay their fuel bills. It is paid to people aged 60 and over. In the winter of 2003 – 2004 the amount paid was £200 per household. A person over 80 would receive £300. Even if there is more than one eligible person in the household the sum stays the same i.e. A couple over 60 but not over 80 would still receive £200. (The qualifying period for any individual is usually the third week of September, the payment is usually paid as a lump sum in December.)

Although the payment is normally paid automatically through either the State pension or through the Benefits Agency for those on benefit, it is always worth checking, for example for people who have not retired or who have deferred their pension.

COLD WEATHER PAYMENTS

Cold Weather payments are paid to households on qualifying benefits during periods of very cold weather. (The average temperature at a specified weather station is recorded at, or forecast to be, 0°C or below for seven consecutive days.) The payments are paid automatically.

7.7 HARDSHIP FUNDS/CHARITABLE FUNDS

Because of the limits on eligibility for Government grants, local hardship funds may sometimes fill the gap to pay for heating or insulation. These are particularly helpful in cases of pensioners whose small private pensions put them over the income limit to claim benefits. Hardship funds may also be used if there is an emergency.

Local hardship funds may be available to provide financial help for households not eligible for Government grants. Typically they may be limited to groups of people, for example ex servicemen. Some fuel suppliers have charitable trusts who may also be able to help their customers [**6**].

7.8 RENEWABLE ENERGY

Grants for renewable energy are available throughout the UK.

PHOTOVOLTAICS (SOLAR PV)

Solar PV uses energy from the sun to generate electricity (see Section 15).

For domestic applications, grants are available from the Department of Trade and Industry. From 2002 – 2005 the £20 million demonstration programme offers 50% grants (which are capped) for installations including domestic installations. For further information see the Solar PV website [**7**].

CLEAR SKIES

The Clear Skies Initiative provides grants and advice for community organisations and householders. Grants for a part of the cost of installation are available for householders for:

- solar hot water heating
- wind turbines
- small scale hydro turbines
- ground source heat pumps
- room heaters/stoves with automated wood feed
- wood fuelled boiler systems.

Clear Skies supports projects in England, Wales and Northern Ireland. For further information see the Clear Skies website [**8**].

THE SCOTTISH COMMUNITIES AND HOMES RENEWABLES INITIATIVE (SCHRI)

This applies in Scotland for both homeowners and community groups. A proportion of the capital cost of measures is provided. For further information see reference [**9**].

7.9 CONTACTS FOR UP TO DATE GRANT INFORMATION

THE GRANTS INFORMATION DATABASE (GID)

The Grants Information Database (GID) is a computer based central database of current grants and discounts for energy efficiency and heating. The database is updated monthly, and is available on-line. The illustration here shows the web page where an individual's details are inserted so that all available grants are displayed. The categories requested are:

- postcode
- specific measure required
- energy supplier (gas and electricity)
- tenure of housing
- age (whether they are over 60)
- whether they are on any benefits

When these personal details are inserted, the database will show the schemes available for that category of householder. The accuracy and scope of GID, particularly for local schemes, is reliant on the regular inputting of schemes into the database.

How to access the Grants Information Database (GID)

Find the GID on:
www.saveenergy.co.uk
link to 'find out about grants' or 'Grants and Information Database'
or
www.est.co.uk
link to 'Energy Efficiency' which takes you through to the above site.

Example of web page on the Grants Information Database

GRANT INFORMATION BY TELEPHONE

For information on a range of national and local grants contact the local Energy Efficiency Advice Centre on 0800 512 012.

FOR INFORMATION ON GOVERNMENT GRANTS

England
All regions except Eastern, East Midlands and Yorkshire and Humberside

Eaga Partnership Ltd
Freepost NEA 12054
Newcastle upon Tyne
NE2 1BR
freephone 0800 316 2808

Eastern, East Midlands, Yorkshire and Humberside

Powergen Warmfront
Freepost ANG 20756
Milton Keynes
MK9 1BR
freephone 0800 952 0600

Wales

Eaga Partnership Ltd
Unit 4
Ty Nant Court
Ty Nant Rd
Morganstown
Cardiff
CF15 8LW
freephone 0800 316 2815

Scotland

Eaga Partnership Ltd
Freepost SCO4421
Edinburgh
EH6 OBR
freephone 0800 072 0150

Northern Ireland

Eaga Partnership Ltd
Freepost BE2107
Dungannon
County Tyrone
BT70 5BR
freephone 0800 181 667

Contact details for organisations listed here are in Appendix 1.

REFERENCES AND CONTACTS

1 *The UK Fuel Poverty Strategy. 2001.* Department of Trade and Industry(DTI), Department of the Environment, Food and Rural Affairs (DEFRA).

2 Eaga Partnership Ltd – for information on all UK Government grants except Eastern, East Midlands, Yorkshire and Humberside regions.
www.eaga.co.uk

3 Powergen – for information on Government grant schemes in Eastern, East Midlands, Yorkshire and Humberside regions.
www.powergen-warmfront.co.uk

4 Ofgem – for description and details of EEC schemes.
www.ofgem.gov.uk – link to energy efficiency.

5 Consultation document for the future of EEC to be published by DTI in Spring 2004. Department of Trade and Industry.
www.dti.gov.uk

6 For an example of a supplier's charitable trust: EDF Energy Trust – for details see
www.edfenergytrust.org.uk

7 DTI solar PV for grants for solar photovoltaic panels.
www.solarpvgrants.co.uk

8 Clear Skies programme for grants on renewable technologies
www.clear-skies.org

9 The Scottish Communities and Homes Renewables Initiative (SCHRI)
www.est.co.uk – link to Scotland, link to grants.
SCHRI Hotline 0800 138 8858

8

BASICS OF HEATING AND HOT WATER SYSTEMS AND APPLIANCES

This section describes the types of heating and hot water systems and appliances found in homes. Although modern central heating systems are the most efficient and cheapest to run, there are still many homes with inadequate and expensive heating systems.

From an energy advisor's point of view it is important to be able to recognise a heating and hot water system or appliance, and broadly understand its operation. Heating controls are covered in Section 9.

In England, Wales and Scotland the Building Regulations [**1**], [**2**], require that new boilers or hot water storage systems must meet new energy efficiency requirements. These requirements will impact on the choice of new heating systems and are described briefly here, but because the majority of heating systems encountered will be existing ones, the majority of descriptions are for older systems and appliances.

This section covers:

- a summary of systems and appliances depending on fuels used
- choosing an appropriate heating system or appliance
- descriptions of the operation of heating and hot water systems and appliances.

8.1 SUMMARY OF FUELS AND HEATING AND HOT WATER SYSTEMS AND APPLIANCES

By far the most commonly installed new heating systems are 'wet' central heating systems using mains gas. Mains gas is not, however, available throughout the UK so the other fuels listed below may be used. Personal preference may also determine the fuel used. Households without central heating will often use a variety of room heating appliances and may rely on electricity for water heating. Households with central heating are also likely to use other room heating appliances.

The table on this page shows the proportion of different types of heating systems used in housing in England [**3**]. In Scotland the figures are broadly similar (68% of dwellings have full gas central heating) although the numbers are not directly comparable as they are split into 'full', 'partial' and 'no central heating'. In some areas the proportion of different types of heating will vary, for example in rural areas where there is no gas network, or in areas where coal had been mined, there may still be a significant use of solid fuel.

In order to provide appropriate advice in local areas it is useful to be aware of the most common types of heating systems. The local authority may have conducted its own Local House Condition Survey for private sector housing and should have statistics for heating types in social housing.

Types of domestic heating in all dwellings in England in 2001 [3]

	% of total
Gas central heating (including back boiler)	78.2
Oil central heating	3.3
Electric central heating	1.0
Solid fuel central heating	1.6
Communal central heating	1.8
Electric storage heaters	7.5
Room heaters only	6.6
	Total 100%

NATURAL GAS

Advantages:
- piped direct to homes
- no fuel storage
- easily turned on and off manually or automatically (quick response)
- one of the least expensive fuels
- relatively low CO_2 emissions

Disadvantages:
- not available everywhere

Heating and hot water systems
- Boiler (regular or condensing) with radiators and hot water cylinder
- Combination or combi boiler (regular or condensing) with radiators and instantaneous hot water
- Combined Primary Storage Unit (CPSU). A combi with a large water store to buffer the heating and hot water supply
- Warm air heating, and hot water supply
- 'Wet' under floor heating
- Gas fires – variety of styles and efficiencies
- Wall mounted convector heaters

Hot water only
- Multipoint hot water heaters
- Circulator – small boiler for hot water only

OIL

Advantages:
- price known on ordering – no retrospective bills
- can be widely obtained
- has been one of the least expensive fuels
- easily turned on and off manually or automatically (quick response)

Disadvantages:
- need storage space for tank
- needs to be delivered
- prices may fluctuate depending on world oil prices

Heating and hot water systems
- Boiler (regular or condensing) with radiators and hot water cylinder
- Combi boiler (regular or condensing) with radiators and instantaneous hot water
- Combined Primary Storage Unit (CPSU). A combi with a large water store to buffer the heating and hot water supply
- Warm air heating and hot water supply

LIQUID PETROLEUM GAS (LPG)

Advantages:
- price known on ordering – no retrospective bill
- easily turned on and off manually or automatically (quick response)

Disadvantages:
- needs to be delivered (except cylinders for mobile heaters)
- portable butane room heaters are unflued, which can lead to condensation because water vapour is produced
- explosive but has safety controls
- large cylinders for central heating require storage space
- one of the most expensive fuels

Heating and hot water systems
- Same as natural gas
- Plus mobile bottled gas heaters

ELECTRICITY

Advantages:
- available almost everywhere
- easily turned on and off manually or automatically (not storage heaters)
- needs little maintenance
- needs no flue or storage area

Disadvantages:
- no immediate control for storage heating systems
- one of the most expensive fuels (except off peak rate)
- usually the highest CO_2 emissions (due to fuel burnt in power stations)

Heating and hot water systems
- Storage heaters – variety of models
- Electric boilers with radiators, and hot water cylinder – dry core, water storage, direct acting, CPSU
- Warm air heating
- Under floor heating
- Ceiling heating
- Direct acting heaters – fires, panel heaters, convector heaters, fan heaters

Hot water only
- Immersion heater – standard cylinder, large cylinder for 'off peak' heating
- Instantaneous shower

SOLID FUEL – COAL AND COAL PRODUCTS

Advantages:
- price known on ordering – no retrospective bill
- delivered everywhere
- depending on the system and fuel, can be one of the least expensive fuels

Disadvantages:
- storage space needed
- extra work associated with fuel and ash handling, may be difficult for older or infirm people
- needs to be delivered
- relatively difficult to control (slow response)
- most forms need daily attention
- relatively high CO_2 emissions

Heating and hot water systems
- Automatic or manual feed boilers with radiators and hot water cylinder
- Closed fire with back boiler with radiators and hot water cylinder
- Open fire with back boiler with radiators and hot water cylinder
- Stoves with radiators, hot water cylinders and cooking
- Closed room heaters
- Open fires

SOLID FUEL – WOOD AND WOOD PRODUCTS

Advantages:
- price known on ordering – no retrospective bill
- wood may be free
- low CO_2 emissions (almost carbon 'neutral' as wood is regrown)

Disadvantages:
- storage space needed, large amount of fuel needed
- extra work associated with fuel and ash handling, may be difficult for older or infirm people
- needs to be delivered or collected
- relatively difficult to control (slow response)
- needs daily attention

Heating and hot water systems
- Stoves with radiators and hot water cylinders (some may be automatic feed when using wood chip or wood pellets).
- Stoves with radiators, hot water cylinders and cooking
- Closed room heaters
- Open fire

8.2 CHOOSING AN APPROPRIATE HEATING SYSTEM

Here are the main factors to take into account when choosing a heating system or appliance:

- the fuels available (see above).
- the efficiency of the system and its compliance with Building Regulations [**1**].
- the construction of a building and its insulation levels.
- the appropriateness of the system for the user.
- the cost to buy and install the system (grants may be available).
- the cost to run.

THE EFFICIENCY OF THE SYSTEM AND ITS COMPLIANCE WITH BUILDING REGULATIONS

Recent changes to the Building Regulations in the UK except Northern Ireland have meant that heating systems and hot water storage have to meet certain minimum energy efficiency standards. The regulations apply to new and existing homes in England and Wales but only new homes in Scotland. A full description of the implications of the Building Regulation requirements can be found in a guide produced by the Energy Efficiency Partnership for Homes [**4**].

THE CONSTRUCTION OF A BUILDING AND ITS INSULATION LEVELS

The construction of a building may prohibit some forms of heating. For example, flues are needed for gas, oil and solid fuel. Some system built tower blocks cannot have gas because of risks of explosion. Warm air needs ducts so warm air systems are rarely fitted to existing dwellings. Adequate insulation levels are important for all types of heating systems, but essential for all electric storage systems. Storage systems work by storing heat overnight and releasing it the following day. If the dwelling is poorly insulated the heat will be lost in the early part of the day.

THE APPROPRIATENESS OF THE SYSTEM FOR THE USER

If an individual is in a position to choose a system, or if a tenants' group is being presented with a choice of systems, it is useful to make a checklist of the needs of the users.

Checklist of user's needs

- The need for timed, controllable heat and hot water at specific times of day for energy efficiency and convenience.
- The need for affordable heat. If the system is too expensive to run it will probably not be used.
- The need for constant warmth, e.g. in the prevention of cold related illnesses in vulnerable people. Important considerations would be insulation of the building (to keep the heat in) and running costs.
- The needs for safety and convenience for older and infirm people, i.e. easy controls, no need to carry solid fuel, lower surface temperatures on heat emitters.
- The need for flexibility in different rooms in a dwelling.

THE COST TO BUY AND INSTALL THE SYSTEM

This is sometimes the factor which determines the heating type provided. Appliances which are cheap to buy are often the most expensive to run, for example an on peak electric room heater is relatively inexpensive to buy but expensive to use. Whereas an efficient gas fire would cost more to buy but approximately one third of the cost of an electric heater to run for the same amount of heat. There are grants, discounts and low cost loans available to encourage householders to install efficient heating systems. (See section 7.)

DESCRIPTIONS OF HEATING SYSTEMS AND APPLIANCES

8.3 WET CENTRAL HEATING SYSTEMS

Wet central heating is the most popular system currently installed. In a 'wet' central heating system the heat is circulated around the dwelling by hot water. Typically, a boiler heats up the water which is driven by a pump around pipes and radiators. As the radiators lose their heat into the rooms the cooled water returns to the boiler where it is heated up again. The same water continues around the system.

In systems with a hot water cylinder, the water from the boiler passes through a coil of pipe inside the hot water cylinder (a heat exchanger) so warming up the water in the cylinder which in turn is drawn off the hot taps. In combi boiler systems a secondary heat exchanger in the boiler heats water directly from the cold mains.

Many variations may be found in wet central heating systems depending on their design and in some cases modifications made to existing systems.

The controls which may be fitted to a wet central heating system are covered in detail in Section 9.

The main parts of a wet system are:

- the boiler
- the circulation of the hot water in the system
- the radiators or convectors
- the provision of domestic hot water.

THE BOILER

The boiler is the appliance which heats the water. The fuel is burned in a combustion chamber, and the heat passes to a heat exchanger or around a water jacket. A flue pipe for the exhaust gases leads from the boiler to the outside air. The fuel may be natural gas, liquid petroleum gas (LPG), oil or solid fuel.

Boilers are usually described by their heat output. This is the amount of useful heat extracted from the fuel, which depends on the efficiency of the burner and the rest of the boiler. For example a 13kW (or 45000 Btu/h) boiler is capable of producing 13kW from the fuel which it burns. On some gas appliances, input is also quoted.

There are different types of boilers:

- **Floor mounted regular boiler (open flued)**

  As the name implies a boiler of this kind stands on the floor and is usually made out of cast iron. Floor mounted boilers may burn gas, LPG, oil or solid fuel. They are open flued so require fixed ventilation for fuel combustion.

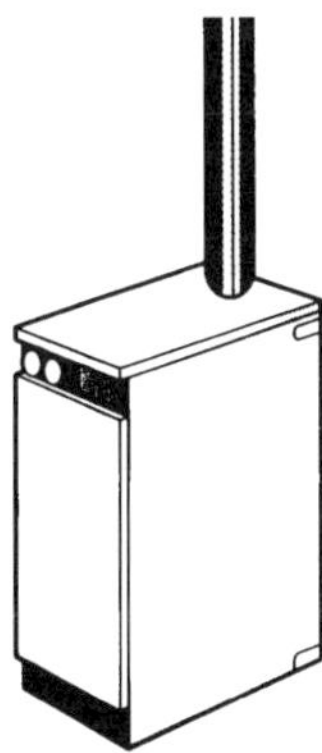

Oil fired floor mounted boiler

- **Wall mounted (room sealed)**

  These are lightweight and compact. Wall mounted boilers can be fitted on any suitable outside wall or inside wall with a longer fanned flue. They burn gas LPG or oil. Because they are room sealed they do not require fixed ventilation for fuel combustion.

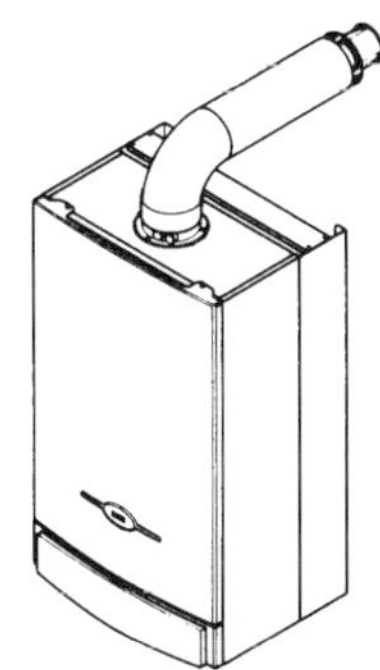

Gas fired wall mounted boiler

- **Back boiler**

  A solid fuel back boiler includes a small steel or cast iron water container which fits behind an open fire or as part of a solid fuel room heater or central heating system. Gas back boilers are something of a misnomer in the traditional sense, because the boiler works independently of the gas fire and is specially designed to fit in the fireplace. Oil back boilers are generally fitted behind an electric fire. Back boilers require fixed ventilation for fuel combustion.

- **Combination systems – combis**

  A combi is the common name for a combination boiler. Central heating is provided in the usual way, but the inclusion of an extra heat exchanger in the boiler means that cold water directly from the mains can pass through the unit to provide instantaneous domestic hot water without the need for a hot water cylinder or a cold water tank (in a similar way to gas multipoint instantaneous water heaters).

  Some models contain an internal hot water store. The boilers can be fuelled by gas LPG or oil. Because combi boilers do not have expansion tanks (which allow for the hot water in the system to expand as it heats up) the systems are pressurised and sealed. In addition to the controls on the boiler is a pressure gauge. If the system loses pressure because of water loss (e.g. a leaking joint) the boiler will stop working so the pressure gauge should be checked. In modern combis it is a simple matter to reintroduce water into the systemalthough the reason for any pressure drop should be investigated.

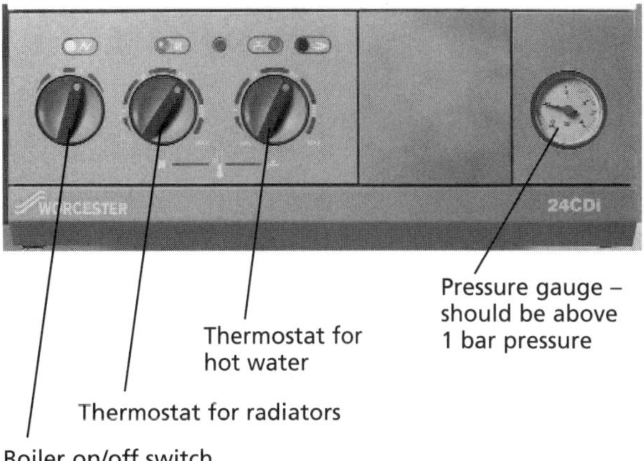

Front panel of a combi boiler

- **Combined Primary Storage Unit (CPSU)**

  This is a boiler with a burner that heats a thermal store directly so that there is always a small store of hot water.

- **Condensing boilers**

  Condensing boilers run at higher efficiencies than conventional boilers and are therefore cheaper to run. The higher efficiency is due to the extra surface area of the heat exchanger (or the presence of a second heat exchanger) and because the boiler extracts heat from the flue gases which would otherwise have been lost out of the flue. Condensing boilers can run on gas, LPG or oil. They may be regular boilers with a hot water cylinder or a combi.

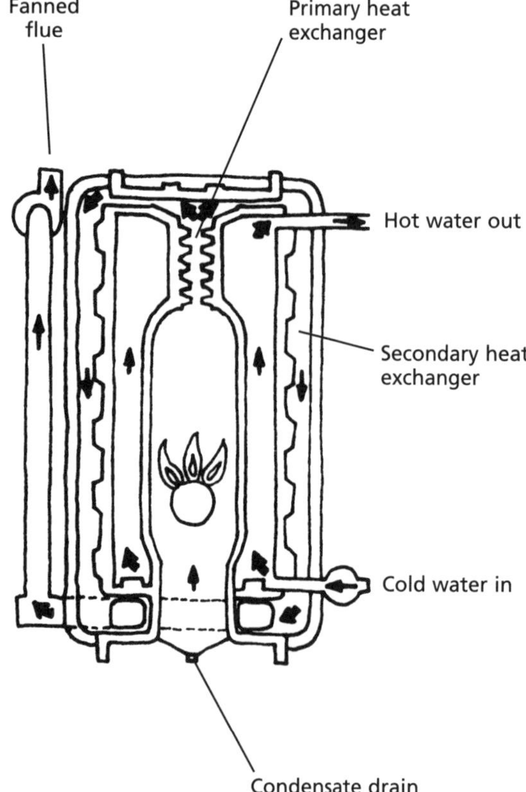

A condensing boiler

Condensing boilers do not always work in condensing 'mode' but even if they do not, they are still always more efficient than non-condensing boilers because of their larger heat exchanger.

The temperature of the flue gases from a condensing boiler is typically 50–60°C compared to 120–180°C in a non-condensing boiler. As the flue gases in a condensing boiler condense, a liquid is produced so a plastic drain is usually fitted to remove this condensate. The flue gases, because they emerge at a lower temperature, can be seen as a 'plume'.

There has been considerable promotion of condensing boilers as they have an impact on domestic energy efficiency. Replacing an old boiler with a condensing boiler will often improve the SAP rating of a dwelling more than adding insulation (see Section 13). In the past there has been some resistance to the installation of condensing boilers.

Energy Efficiency Best Practice in Housing has produced a leaflet on condensing boilers [**5**] which aims to provide information on the benefits of condensing boilers and to help dispel the popular myths surrounding them. The leaflet explains why condensing boilers:

- are efficient even when not fully condensing
- are not necessarily more expensive to buy
- do not need larger radiators
- are not less reliable than non condensing boilers
- are not more difficult to install
- are not harder to maintain
- can be fitted to existing system
- do not have limited availability
- do not cause a nuisance by the plume of flue gases if located properly
- do not cause a problem with the condensate.

Seasonal Efficiency of Domestic Boilers in the UK (SEDBUK)

SEDBUK is the average annual efficiency achieved by boilers in typical domestic conditions in the UK, making reasonable assumptions about pattern of usage, climate control and other influences. It is calculated from the results of standard laboratory tests together with other important factors such as boiler type, ignition arrangement, internal store size, fuel used. The method provides a basis for comparison of different models and was developed with the co-operation of boiler manufacturers.

SEDBUK figures are used in Standard Assessment Procedure (SAP) assessments and the Building Regulations. The SEDBUK efficiency of most current and obsolete boilers can be found on the website [**6**]. SEDBUK is expressed as a percentage, but an A to G scale of percentage bands has also been defined:

SEDBUK efficiency range	band
90% and above	A
86 – 90%	B
82 – 86%	C
78 – 82%	D
74 – 78%	E
70 – 74%	F
Below 70%	G

ENERGY EFFICIENCY BEST PRACTICE IN HOUSING SPECIFICATION FOR HEATING SYSTEMS

Energy Efficiency Best Practice in Housing has also produced a specification for the components of domestic wet central heating systems that are critical to energy efficiency.

CHeSS

The Central Heating System Specification in 2002 provides basic and best practice specifications.

Basic

Basic means sufficient to comply with the Building Regulations in England, Wales and Scotland [**1**] [**2**] that came into effect in 2002.

Best practice

Best practice means the 'adoption of products and techniques that are already established in the market, cost effective and able to save energy without incurring undue risks'. For full details of the specification see the CHeSS leaflet [**7**].

The factors of the specification which affect the system efficiencies are:

- the efficiency of the boiler (either natural gas, LPG or oil)
- the efficiency of the hot water store (in systems that are not combis)
- the controls fitted to the system
- the correct installation.

RECOMMENDED BEST PRACTICE (CHeSS – HR4 2002) (see Appendix 5)

The recommended Best Practice (CHeSS – HR4 2002) is an improvement on the above by increasing the SEDBUK efficiency of the boilers, using high performance hot water cylinders and storage systems and improved controls (programmable room thermostat with additional timing capability for hot water).

> For dwellings with gas boilers, using the recommended Best Practice specification can save 23% – 32% of the energy used in a typical dwelling [**7**].

Basic Central Heating Specification (Year 2002) (This is the Basic specification for a regular boiler. For Best Practice and combi boilers see the specifications in Appendix 5)

Reference	CHeSS – HR3 (2002)
Description	Domestic wet central heating system with regular boiler and separate hot water store.
Boiler	A regular boiler (not a combi) which has a SEDBUK efficiency of at least: 78% (natural gas) 80% (LPG) 85% (oil)
Hot water store	EITHER Hot water cylinder, whose heat exchanger and insulation properties both meet or exceed those of the relevant British Standards OR Thermal (primary) storage system, whose insulation properties meet or exceed those specified by Water Heater Manufacturers Association Specification for thermal stores.
Controls (see Section 9)	Systems with regular boilers must have separately controlled circuits to the hot water cylinder and radiators, and both circuits must have pumped circulation. Large properties must be divided into zones not exceeding 150 m^2 floor area, so that the operation of the heating in each zone can be timed and temperature controlled independently. Full programmer. Room thermostat. Cylinder thermostat. Boiler interlock. TRVs on all radiators, except in rooms with a room thermostat. Automatic bypass valve.
Installation	The design and installation of the system must be in accordance with relevant specifications and regulations.

SOLID FUEL BOILERS

Solid fuel boilers are treated separately here because the nature of the fuel means they are slower to respond to control than oil or gas as the burning fuel cannot be 'turned on and off' completely. They always have hot water cylinders. The boilers fall into four main categories:

- open fire with back boiler
- closed room heater with backboiler
- free standing manually fed boiler
- free standing automatically fed boiler.

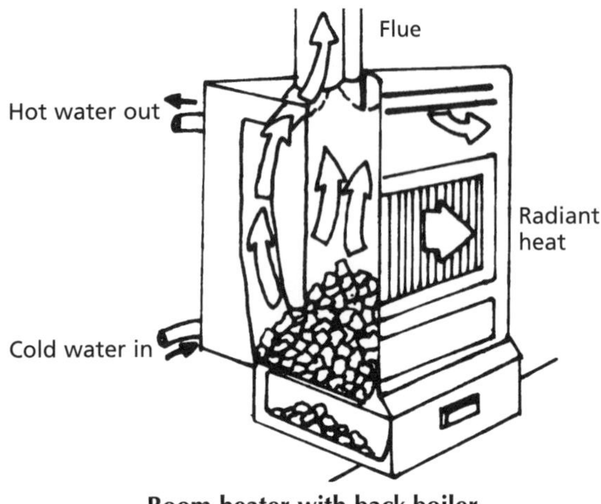

Room heater with back boiler

There are different fuels best suited to the design of the fireplace/room heater or boiler, and whose use may be determined by 'smoke control' areas.

House coal is a smoky fuel and must generally not be burnt in smoke control areas. Manufactured smokeless fuels or anthracite, which is a naturally occurring slow burning fuel, are used. The Solid Fuel Association will be able to advise on the most appropriate fuel to use [**8**].

With a hand fed boiler, fuel is shovelled through the refuelling door to the fire and in cold weather this may need to be done 3 or 4 times a day. With a gravity fed boiler a large amount of fuel is stored in a hopper in the boiler so it may only need refuelling once per day in winter.

With solid fuel boilers the rate of burning may be controlled either thermostatically or manually via a damper. Some models have a fan and time switch so that the fire can be fanned to give out more heat when it is most needed.

All solid fuels produce relatively high carbon emissions.

ELECTRIC BOILERS

These are unusual, but again may be found in areas where electricity is the only practical fuel to use.

The boiler is a large free standing storage heater (the storage medium may be thermal blocks, 'drycore' or water) which is heated up overnight on the Economy 7 or other off peak tariff. Water flows through and is circulated around the dwelling in the conventional way. The boiler is larger than for other fuels. Separate hot water heating is necessary, usually with a large hot water tank heated up overnight on the Economy 7 or other off peak tariff, controlled by a timeswitch.

Another form of electric boiler uses a large water tank (usually under the floor) which is heated directly by immersion heaters on the overnight tariff. The tank must be very well insulated.

FLUES

All fuel burning appliances (e.g. gas, oil, solid fuel) need ventilation and must have some sort of flue. This is an 'exhaust pipe' through which the products of combustion can escape to the outside.

There are different types of flues:

Open flued

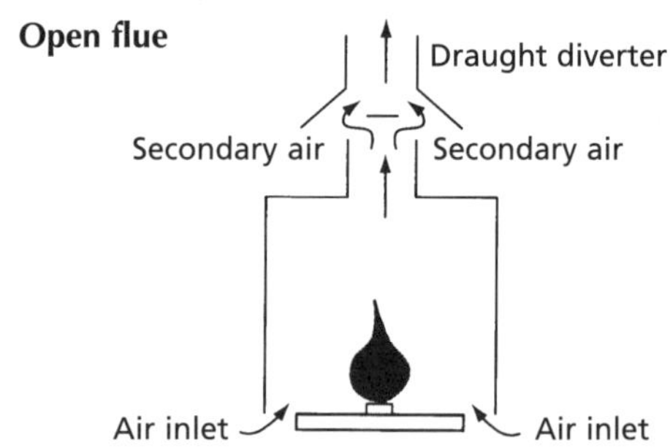

Open flued appliances take their air to burn the fuel from inside the room where the boiler is fitted. This may be a boiler fitted into a chimney, or a floor mounted boiler.

If using an existing chimney it must be big enough to take the flue gases, fumes or smoke and must be in reasonable condition. There are regulations governing the provision of ventilation for appliances with open flues, as fixed ventilation must be fitted (see Section 17).

If a chimney or flue becomes blocked fumes may come back into the room. They are particularly dangerous because they may be invisible. One of these gases, carbon monoxide, is very poisonous and cannot be detected by smell. Chimneys are usually lined, as dictated by current Building Regulations, often with a stainless steel liner. There are also factory made insulated chimneys which can be installed internally where no existing chimney is available.

Room sealed

Room sealed boilers take their air for the fuel to burn from the outside. They are generally considered safer than open flued.

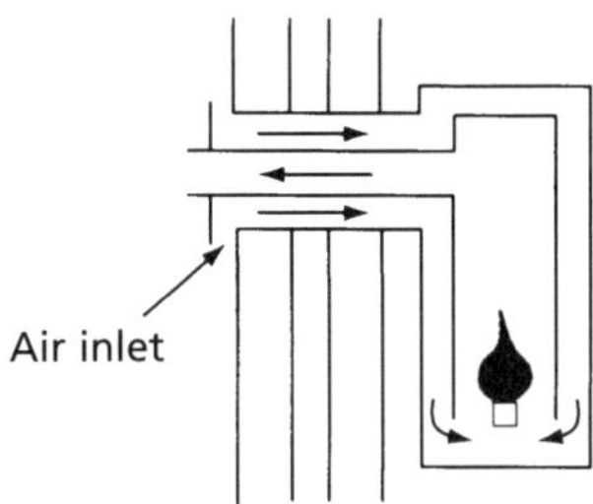

Room sealed flue

A room sealed flue consists of a metal duct which links the boiler with the outside air. The duct is made in two parts: there are two tubes, one through which the flue gases go out, and the other through which the air is drawn in for combustion. (A balanced flue is so named because whatever the external wind pressure is on the flue terminal, the inlet and outlet have the same, or balanced pressures.) The boiler is fitted onto an outside wall, or it can be fitted with an extended fan assisted flue. Room sealed boilers may be gas, LPG or oil fired.

Fanned flue

Some room sealed flues have a fan which assists air circulation. Condensing boilers always have fan assisted flues.

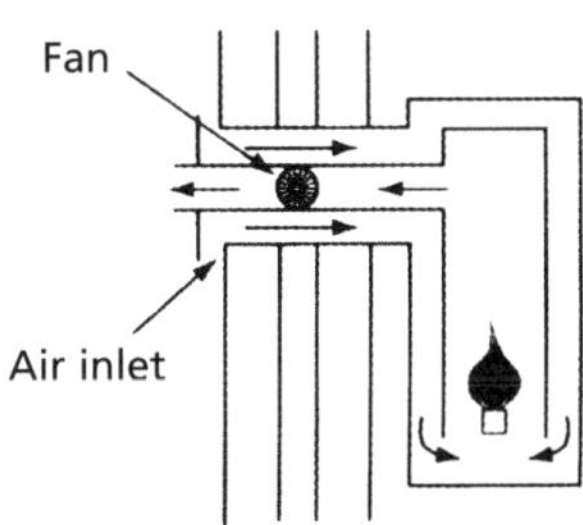

Fanned flue

There are regulations governing the placing of flues, and appliance manufacturers' installation instructions must be followed. Boilers with fan assisted flues are likely to have the least restrictions on where they are situated.

Special consideration should be given to the siting of flue terminals for condensing boilers because the boiler will 'plume' (give off visible steam) most of the time it is on.

For further details of flues see reference [**9**].

CIRCULATION OF HOT WATER IN A WET SYSTEM

Fully pumped system

This is the most common type of system. It incorporates a pump to force water through the pipework which means the pipework can be smaller than gravity fed systems, usually 15–22 millimetres in diameter (modern systems use even smaller pipes

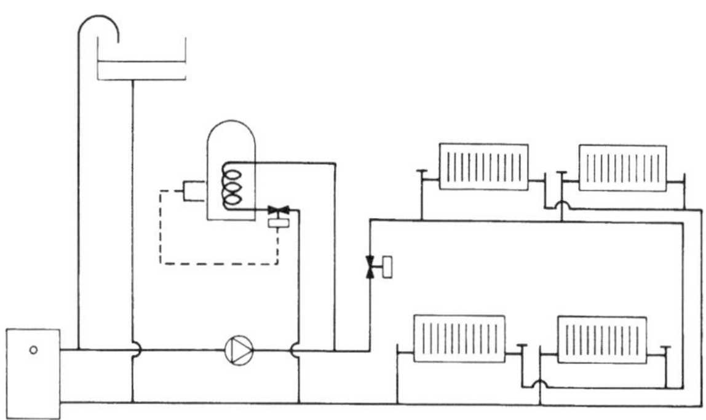

Fully pumped system

6 – 12 mm diameter known as microbore). The system heats up quickly and is responsive to controls.

Hot water by gravity/heating system pumped

This is still fairly common as the hot water rises by gravity from the boiler to the hot water cylinder, but is pumped around the radiators. In this type of system there is rarely a boiler interlock (see Section 9 on controls) so the boiler will keep firing to keep itself hot enough even when there is no demand for hot water.

Gravity system

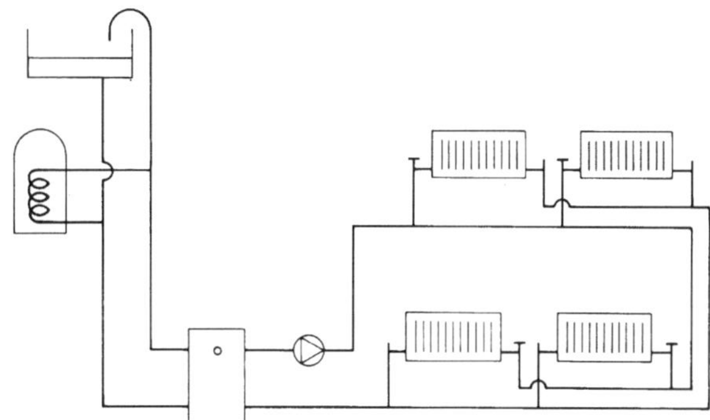

Layout for system with gravity fed hot water

This type of piping circuit is rare nowadays for heating systems. Water circulates through the pipework and radiators with nothing driving it except gravity. The system is based on the principle that the warmer water is, the lighter it is, therefore warm water goes up and cold water comes down, eliminating the need for a pump. To be reasonably successful, the boiler must be sited as low as possible in the house and preferably close to the hot water tank. The slight advantage of not having to run a pump is far outweighed by the disadvantages. The system will not respond quickly to heating requirements, larger pipes are needed which are expensive and often radiators at the ends of the system do not get hot.

When boilers are replaced, the systems should always be upgraded to fully pumped systems, and new controls attached. This has a significant impact on the efficiency of the system.

RADIATORS AND CONVECTORS

In a wet central heating system the most common type of 'heat emitters' which give out heat into rooms are radiators. A few systems have convectors.

What is radiant heat and convected heat?

- **Radiant heat** is heat which travels in straight lines directly from the heat source. It warms up whatever is in its path. An example is the heat given out by an electric bar fire.
- **Convected heat** is heat which travels by the movement of a heated substance, such as air or water, as warm air or water is lighter than when it is cold. An example is the heat rising from a convector heater which can be felt if the hand is held above the heater.

Radiators

Radiators (despite their name) give out both radiant heat and convected heat. The older types of radiators were made from cast iron, but the modern type is made from pressed steel. Inside the metal skin of the radiator are channels through which hot water circulates.

The most common radiators can be obtained in standard heights (30 to 75 cm) and lengths (up to 4 metres) and their size is related to the amount of heat they can give out. Extra heat output may be obtained from double or triple panel radiators which are radiators sandwiched together with a gap in between. [**10**]

High efficiency radiators have metal fins between the panels so that there is a larger area of hot metal surface. These are often called 'convector' radiators. These are useful where space is at a premium. Radiators of a vertical 'ladder' design and also radiators designed to mimic old cast iron models are also available.

Examples

Examples of heat outputs of radiators:

Single panel 1 m long x 70 cm high 1.4 kW output

Double panel 1 m long x 70 cm high 2.5 kW output

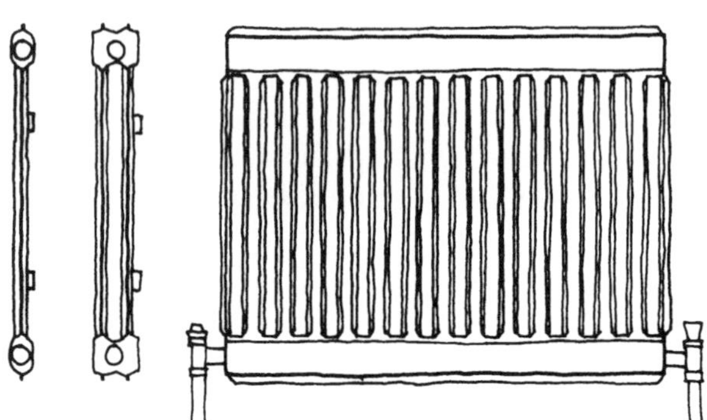

Example of single panel and double panel radiator

Whatever the type of radiator chosen, the heat output should be chosen appropriate to its situation.

When a contractor designs a heating system, measurements are taken of the size of rooms, and the fabric of the building to determine the heat demand of a house before the radiator sizes are chosen (see Section 13).

Questions about radiators [**10**]

Why are radiators usually put under windows?

They are usually put under windows to counteract the cold down-draught from windows. This is not necessarily a draught caused by incoming air but because the glass is cold and cold air sinks. Radiators can be placed on internal walls, particularly if the rooms are not where the occupants sit for long periods.

Why do radiators need 'bleeding'?

Radiators need to be bled to let trapped air or gas out when the bottom part of the radiator is hot but the top is cold. A small key should be used at the special tap at the top of the radiator, taking care not to let any water out. Brand new systems will give off a lot of air when they are first installed but should settle down. If they don't then advice should be sought because there may be problems with the pipework and vents. If the water is black then the gas may be hydrogen – which suggests corrosion in the system and the build up of sludge. A special de-sludging agent can be used to clear this.

Why shouldn't curtains and furniture be placed in front of radiators?

Radiators warm the room by losing the heat within them into the room. If the radiator is 'insulated' from the room by covering it then it cannot warm the room effectively.

Are radiators affected if they are boxed in?

Yes, in the same way as above. Boxing in a radiator can reduce its output by up to 40%.

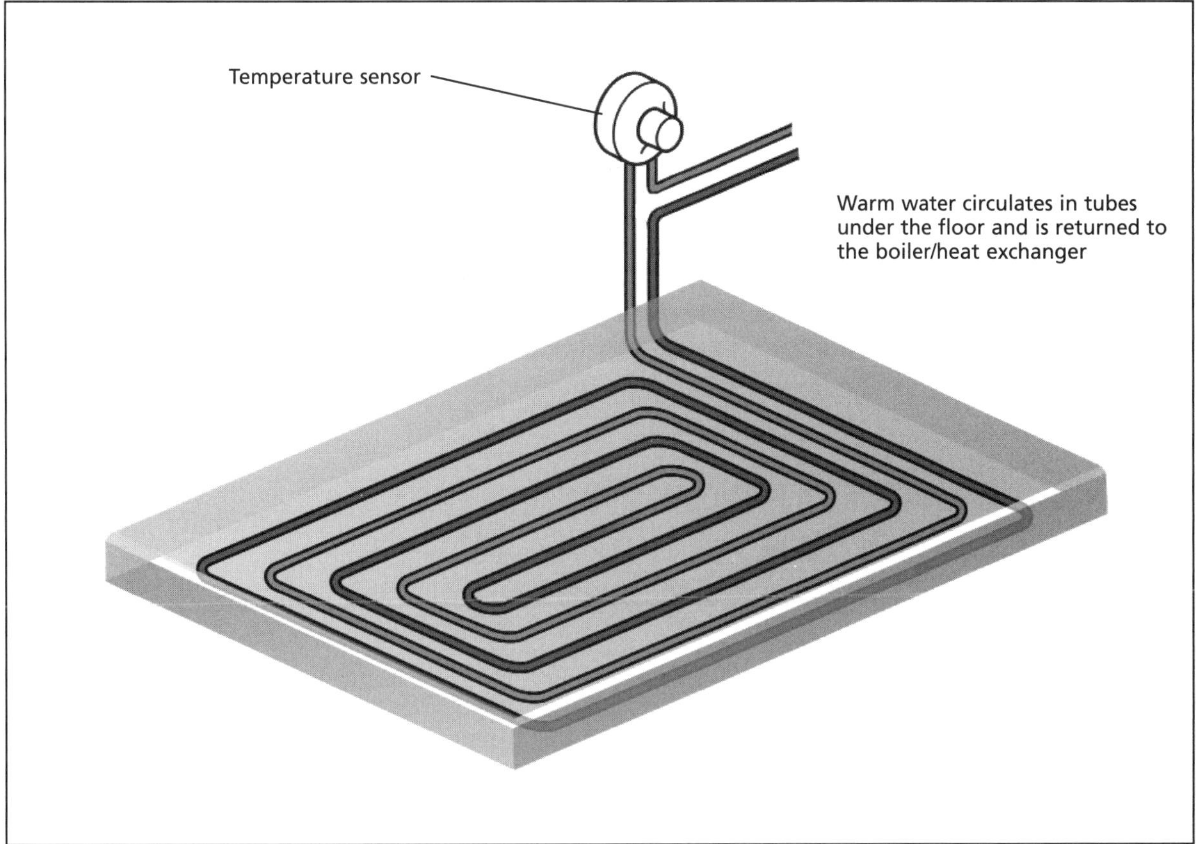

Wet system under floor heating

Convectors

Natural convectors (as opposed to fan-assisted) consist of tubing, through which hot water flows, inside a metal casing. Convectors are not as popular as radiators on wet systems. The tube is usually finned, to increase surface area and therefore give out more heat. Air enters at the bottom of the casing, passes over the tube and rises out through a grille in the top of the casing. Some models have a damper on the outlet grille which can be opened or closed to control the heat output.

Wet system under floor heating

There is increasing interest in under floor 'wet' central heating. Instead of the hot water from a domestic boiler being distributed through radiators it is run through a series of plastic pipes under the floor. The temperature of the water typically circulates at flow and return temperatures of 45°C/35°C. The benefits include an even distribution of heat, but the system is slow to respond to required changes in temperature.

Controls are very important and the floor zones are usually controlled by locally based accurate temperature sensors. The floor must be well insulated at the edges and underneath. Information from SAP calculations (see Section 13) suggests that under floor wet heating runs more efficiently than other forms of wet systems and can achieve over 90% efficiency with condensing boilers [**11**].

8.4 WARM AIR CENTRAL HEATING

In this system air is used to distribute the heat around the house, rather than water. The air is heated up in a centrally located unit. It then passes through ducts and enters the rooms through grilles.

THE WARM AIR UNIT

The unit may run on electricity, gas or oil. It is usually a self-contained heater with timing controls, a thermostat and a fan to drive the air through the ducting. An air filter cleans the air before it passes over the heater unit. It is very important that this filter is kept clean and dust free so it must be cleaned regularly. An electric unit will usually run on a night storage tariff; the core will heat up overnight and give out its heat during the day. Less common today 'Electricaire' systems were found in local authority housing. Gas or oil warm air systems (gas is the most common) need flues or chimneys similar to a boiler.

DUCTS

There are two main ducting systems:

- The short duct system uses a fan to drive the warm air through the grilles near the central unit. These are more likely in well-insulated small dwellings.
- The perimeter duct system also has a fan which drives the warm air through ducts to outlets situated at the perimeter of the dwelling.

Ducting is usually concealed under floors, and sometimes in the roof space. The same air is re-heated and distributed around the house. This can be a disadvantage, for example it can carry smells or moist air from the kitchen around the house, so air should not be re-circulated from the kitchen or bathroom. Care needs to be taken with the distribution and placing of ducts, so the transmission of noise from room to room is minimised.

Because of the need for ducting around the house it is not usually practical to install warm air heating after a house has been built, except in cases where major renovation work is being carried out.

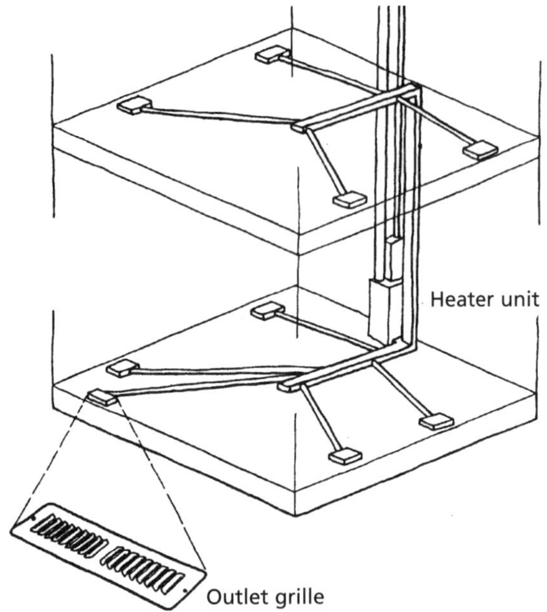

Layout of perimeter ducting in a warm air system

GRILLES

The warm air enters rooms via grilles. As warm air naturally rises, the grilles are best placed at a low level. If they are at ceiling height much of the warm air will stay at that height. Nothing must be placed over or in front of the grilles.

It is usually possible to open or close grilles by means of sliding 'dampers' and sometimes to angle the airflow in a chosen direction. This is, however, the only form of room by room control.

Air is dried out after passing through a warm air unit so some people find warm air heating uncomfortable, especially if they have respiratory complaints.

HOT WATER IN WARM AIR SYSTEMS

In a warm air system, domestic hot water can also be provided. Depending on the system used, a hot water heating system may be incorporated either by a small gas boiler called a circulator or an electric immersion heater. Instantaneous hot water from a multipoint is often built into the package in a gas warm air system.

8.5 OFF PEAK ELECTRIC STORAGE HEATERS

The most popular form of electric central heating is usually a combination of storage heaters in downstairs rooms and 'on peak' or 'direct acting' heaters in bedrooms and bathroom. A typical layout would include:

Lounge	–	storage heater and focal point fire
Dining room	–	storage heater and panel heater
Kitchen	–	plinth (or fan) heater
Hall	–	storage heater
Bedrooms	–	wall mounted panel heaters
Bathroom	–	heated towel rail and downflow heater (wall mounted fan heater)

The storage heaters provide background heat to upstairs and the 'on peak' heaters are used for short periods only.

Electric storage heaters use electricity at off peak times. Inside the heaters are electric elements which heat a very dense 'thermal block' (usually feolite) at specified hours overnight. These blocks cool down thus releasing heat during the following day.

Modern storage heaters charge up for a period of up to seven hours, on the Economy 7 tariff, (the cheaper tariff period is longer – up to 8.5 hours – in Scotland). Electricity during these hours is usually less than half the cost of normal price 'on peak' electricity. Other tariff structures are also available which allow the heaters to be charged up for set hours during the afternoon and early evening, or to be automatically controlled depending on weather conditions.

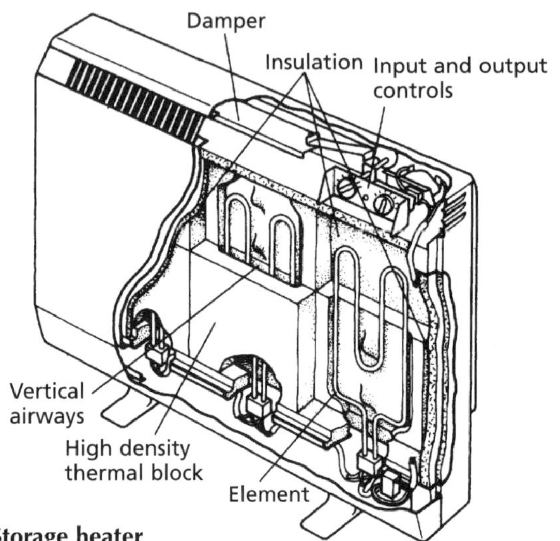

Storage heater

Storage heaters are fitted with a damper that opens to allow air to flow through the heater by convection, and although this will use the available heat up even faster, it offers some control over output. The output controls may be manual or automatic (see Section 9).

Some models have a built-in fan. When the fan is off the unit gives out very little heat. The fan is usually

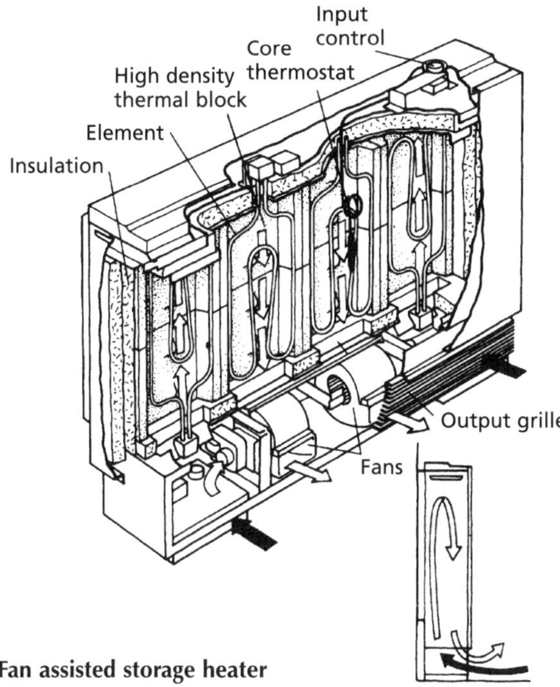

Fan assisted storage heater

operated by a thermostat to achieve a constant temperature in the room. In this way, more heat is available at the end of the day. These types of heaters are larger than slimline versions due to the amount of insulation in the body of the heater so they are not as common as slimline heaters for domestic use. They should not be confused with storage heaters incorporating a fan heater at the bottom or an additional convector heater for boosts of heat on 'on peak' electricity.

Storage heaters can be fitted with charge or input controls which measure the room temperature, and in some cases the outdoor temperature, and adjust the amount of time the heater charges up during the night. Hence, when it is warm outside, the heater will have a shorter charge up period.

As storage heaters are fitted and wired individually, a number of different models can be put in a dwelling, providing individual room or central heating.

POINTS TO REMEMBER FOR STORAGE HEATING SYSTEMS:

For any storage heating system, the dwelling must be well insulated otherwise the rooms will need supplementary heating when the storage heaters cool down before the next charge period.

When on Economy 7 or White Meter all the electricity supply to the dwelling switches to night rate for seven or eight hours overnight. Therefore hot water is heated overnight and it is possible to use other electrical appliances at this time. It would be worthwhile to time high electricity consuming appliances, e.g. tumble dryers, dishwashers and washing machines, to come on at night, but this may not always be practical.

8.6 ELECTRIC UNDER FLOOR HEATING

Electric elements are embedded in concrete floor slabs and run on 'off peak' or special tariff electricity as the slabs store the heat. It is not possible to control the rate at which the heat is given out. Putting carpets on the floor reduces the amount of heat given out during the day.

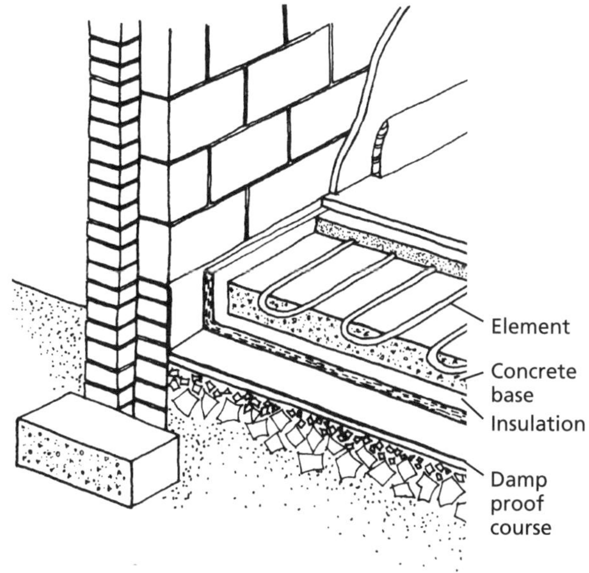

Electric under floor heating

This was a common system fitted into blocks of flats in the 1960s and 70s when it was considered that electricity would always be a cheap form of fuel. This type of system needs to be heated up for a longer period than modern storage heaters so is usually operated on 'preserved' electricity tariffs. Under floor heating often proves too expensive to run, especially in poorly insulated homes. Householders are then only able to use 'on peak' electricity, or other types of portable heaters are available as an alternative.

Some householders have been tempted to convert their under floor 'preserved' tariff to Economy 7, but have found that the 7 hours does not provide enough heat for the floor – especially during the day.

Some developers are fitting a combination of under floor heating and ceiling heating into new well-insulated properties to maximise floor space.

TILE WARMING

Not to be confused with under floor heating, low temperature electrically heated pads or mats are available to lay under tiles where they would otherwise be cold, e.g. in a bathroom. They typically provide approximately 400W – 800W of heat for a small area.

8.7 COMMUNITY HEATING

Community heating schemes are large heating systems where, instead of having a small boiler for every dwelling (as with central heating), there is one large one serving a block of flats, a row of houses, or several blocks. On a larger scale, whole town centres or large parts of suburbs can be served by one system.

Community heating is much less popular in the UK than in other Northern European countries. For example in the UK it forms less than 2% of the domestic heating needed compared to 40% in Denmark [**12**].

In community heating the boiler may be located on the roof or basement of a block of flats or in a separate boiler house sited centrally or adjacent to the buildings it is serving. The pipes taking the hot water round the building or round the whole complex need to be heavily insulated to keep the heat in.

In a domestic central heating system the water is circulated using a single pump at a relatively low pressure and temperature because it doesn't have far to go. In community heating systems water can be pumped over very long distances by installing pumps at regular intervals.

In the past, community heating in Britain had a very poor track record. Some of the common complaints are listed below:

- Poor quality installation. In some schemes, insulation around the pipes leading to homes failed so that much of the heat produced by the boiler was wasted before it reached the houses and flats. Distribution of heat between dwellings was often poor.
- Inadequate system controls. This was another common problem. Sometimes the only control that a tenant had over the temperature of the home was to open the window to cool it down.
- Inaccurate metering. The actual flow of heat to a particular property may be measured by a device known as a heat meter. Most of the meters in use in the 1970s were inaccurate and tenants were unhappy with the bills they received based on meter readings.

Modern community heating schemes have been improved so that:

- controls are similar to those for individual central heating
- electronic heat meters with prepayment facilities are available
- heat distribution problems have been overcome
- heat mains have fault detection systems and are factory insulated
- contractor and equipment supplier have recognised the need for high quality. Long warranties and maintenance contracts are more common.

Operation of community heating

In a modern community heating scheme, the dwelling will contain a Consumer Interface Unit (CIU) which contains the incoming and outgoing heat mains, control valves and metering where required.

Hot water may be provided in a storage cylinder or instantaneously in a similar way to a combi boiler.

Residents pay for their heat either by a 'heat with rent' arrangement where fuel consumption is not measured or pay for the metered fuel. Heat meters can directly measure the heat consumed by an individual dwelling, customers are charged per kWh for heat used.

COMBINED HEAT AND POWER (CHP)

CHP is a means of generating electricity locally to where it is needed, and using the waste heat to contribute to the heating of the dwelling, which usually has top up boilers. Electricity may be sold to the national grid when surpluses are produced.

Because of past problems outlined above, many local authorities have replaced district heating with individual heating systems. However, there is now growing support for the development of small combined heat and power schemes in which fuel (usually gas) is used to generate electricity locally, which is sold locally (any excess being sold off to the electricity supplier). The heat produced during the generation of electricity is also used for local heating purposes and is ideal for the group or district heating of blocks of flats.

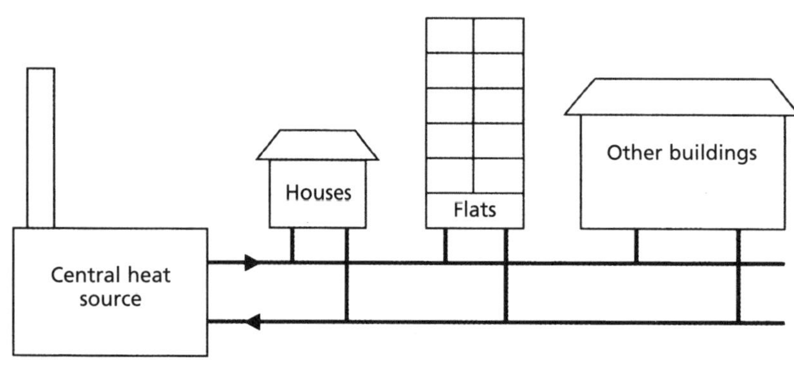

Community heating. Hot water is distributed from the central heat source to local houses, flats and other buildings

8.8 INDIVIDUAL ELECTRIC HEATERS

There are a variety of electric heaters which are plugged into sockets. As such they generally use daytime or 'on peak' electricity which is one of the most expensive fuels. For people connected to the Economy 7 tariff the heaters will operate on the cheaper tariff if used during the cheaper hours. This does not apply to some of the special tariffs for which the cheaper rate is available for the storage heating and/or hot water, which are wired in to a special circuit and metered separately.

ELECTRIC FIRES

These have an electric element set in front of a curved reflective metal surface. Some electric fires are also fitted with convector heaters so they provide both radiant and convected heat. Their portability and low capital cost makes them a popular heat source for those without central heating. The output typically varies from 1 kW to 3 kW. Many new electric fires have flame effects and may look like stoves incorporating a fan heater in the base. They are used as a focal point and do not usually exceed 2 kW.

electric fire

ELECTRIC OIL FILLED RADIATORS

These have an electric element which heats up oil inside the radiator. They may look similar to wet central heating radiators. Or they may have wheels for portability. Output sizes vary from 0.75 kW to 3 kW and they are thermostatically controlled. Some models have timers.

oil filled radiator

FAN HEATERS

These small portable heaters contain a fan which forces air over electrically heated coils. It is possible to vary the number of coils being heated and hence the output of the heater, usually 1 to 3 kW. Fan heaters usually have thermostatic controls.

CONVECTOR HEATERS

Portable electric convector heaters contain an electric element in a metal casing. The heat rises out of the top of the convector. Nothing should be placed over the top, or there may be a danger of overheating.

PANEL HEATERS

Slimline wall mounted panel heaters including timers and thermostatic controls are often used in bedrooms when storage heaters are fitted in other parts of the dwelling. They are usually rated at about 750 W to 2 kW and are fitted with thermostatic and timing controls.

8.9 INDIVIDUAL GAS HEATERS

Modern gas fires provide both radiant and convected heat. Most recent models simulate solid fuel fires. A suitable flue must be provided to remove the products of combustion and these units are often installed in a suitable fireplace. If there is no fireplace, various flue methods are available.

As these fires are popular and may be chosen for aesthetic reasons it is important to understand that they vary in efficiency – and probably equally important to the customer, they vary in their heat output. In addition decorative fires all need fixed ventilation, which will increase heat loss and may cause discomfort. (See Section 10 for more on efficiencies and running costs.)

The more open a fire is to a chimney the less efficient it is likely to be, and the more encased, including a glass front and heat exchangers, the more efficient it will be. The main types of gas fire (although the terminology may be slightly different from one manufacturer to another) are:

- flame effect, radiant convector
- inset flame effect
- decorative flame effect.

EXAMPLE

Gas fires vary enormously in their efficiencies, fuel used, and cost to run. In one manufacturer's brochure one balanced flue flame effect gas fire was 77% efficient (input 3.6 kW, output 2.8 kW) whereas an inglenook fireplace containing a decorative fire was 13% efficient (input 11.9 kW output 1.5 kW). The decorative fire would cost three times the amount of the balanced flue fire to run for around half the amount of heat.

RADIANT CONVECTOR OR FLAME EFFECT GAS FIRE

Radiant convector gas fires have a panel that heats up and glows when hot. Most older type gas fires were of this type before flame effects became popular. They also provide convected air. Flame effect gas fires have imitation fuel behind glass, and flames flicker through this. A heat exchanger on most models provides convected air. Both these fires may sit in front of a plate fitted on an original fireplace, or they may have a balanced flue if on an outside wall. These fires are typically around 60% to 75% efficient.

Flue system the same as Flame effect gas fire below

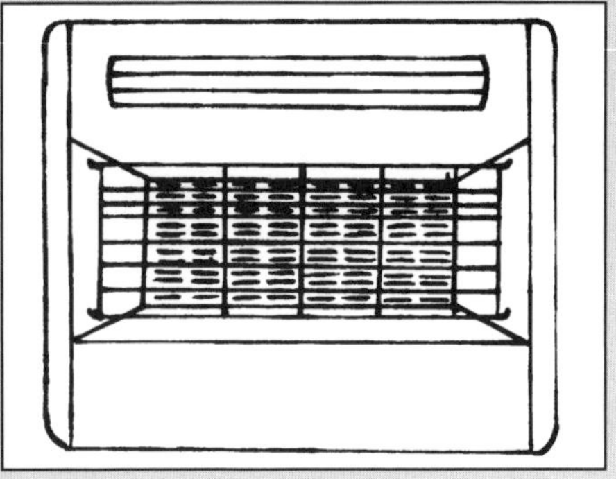

Radiant convector gas fire

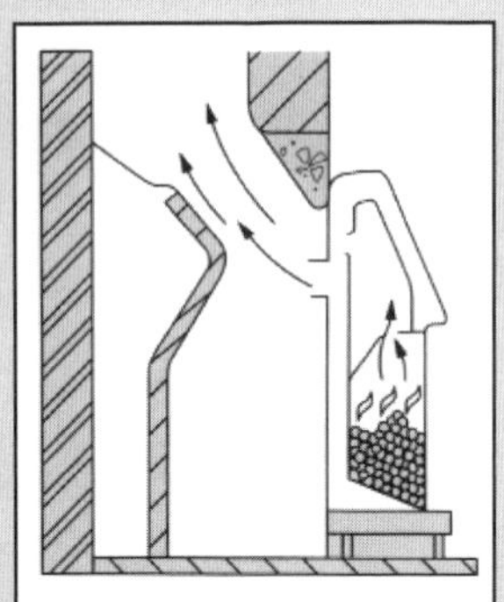

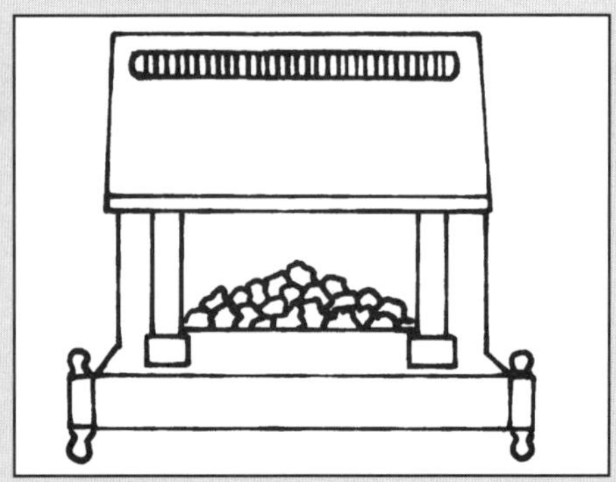

Flame effect gas fire

INSET LIVE FLAME EFFECT GAS FIRE

This type of fire is fully or partially inset within the fireplace opening. The flames are usually open. In addition to radiated heat, heat exchangers provide convected air. These fires are typically around 45% to 60% efficient.

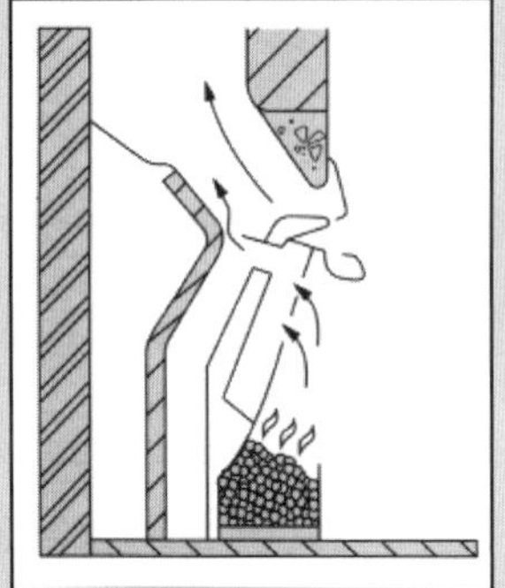

Inset live fuel effect gas fire

DECORATIVE FUEL EFFECT GAS FIRE

This type of fire is totally inset within the fireplace opening. A simple fire basket with an open flame provides very little heat and is normally intended for decoration only. These fires are not normally considered as heating appliances and may be from 0% to 25% efficient.

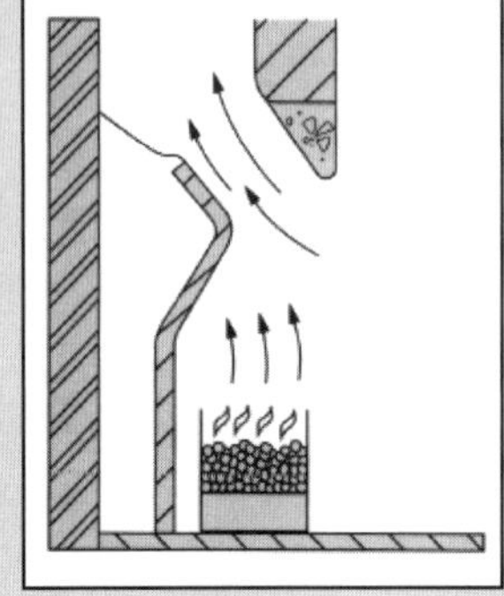

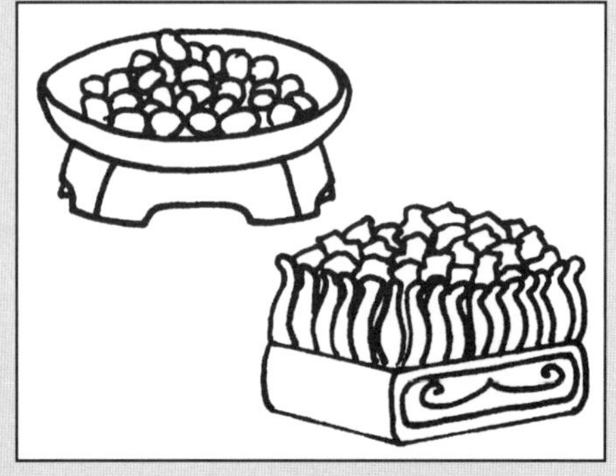

Decorative fuel effect gas fire

WALL MOUNTED GAS HEATERS

The wall mounted convector heater is a balanced flue appliance. This provides convected heat and is sometimes fan assisted. Air enters the base of the unit, is heated indirectly and exits through a grill at the top. Because they have a balanced flue the heaters can be fitted onto any suitable outside wall, and are suitable for rooms where the open flame of a gas fire would be undesirable.

Gas wall heater

Wall heaters are more efficient than many gas fires fitted into fireplaces and can have thermostatic and timeclock control. Installing wall heaters room by room can be built up to form a 'modular' system, i.e. gas fire, wall heaters and instantaneous hot water from a multipoint.

BOTTLED GAS HEATERS

Bottled gas heaters are free standing and are fuelled by refillable cylinders of pressurised gas (LPG). The most common types have radiant panels at the front, although much of the heat given out is convected heat from the top of the unit.

This type of heater is frequently used where there is no central heating. One reason is that the fuel is paid for in advance, so avoiding bills.

The heaters are fitted with castors so they can be rolled from one room to another. The disadvantages are their high running cost, approximately the same as 'on peak' electricity, and their production of water vapour. For every kilogram of the liquid gas burned a kilogram of water is produced, so increasing the risk of condensation. As they have no flues, care must be taken that adequate ventilation is provided.

Bottled gas heater

Many local authorities have banned the use of bottled gas heaters in some types of system built tower blocks where fire or explosion could lead to the collapse of the block.

8.10 DOMESTIC HOT WATER

Domestic hot water may be provided from a central heating boiler, or a separate heating system may be used.

HOT WATER CYLINDER LINKED WITH CENTRAL HEATING

When there is a wet central heating system in a dwelling, it is usual to obtain hot water from the same boiler. The outlet pipe from the boiler generally splits two ways to the radiators and to a heat exchanger in a hot water storage cylinder. A valve diverts the water to one circuit or the other, or shares the water from the boiler between the two.

Domestic hot water cylinders are usually made of copper or sometimes galvanised steel. The most usual size is 120 litres. Too small a cylinder can be a serious defect in the system, as there may not be enough hot water.

The cylinder has a heat exchanger inside (usually a copper coil) through which very hot water (approx. 80°C) flows from the boiler. This heat exchanger heats up the water in the cylinder, which is the water that comes out of the taps. The cylinder is known as an 'indirect' cylinder. A cylinder thermostat controls the temperature of the water coming out of the taps. Using a high performance hot water cylinder, a cylinder of water should be reheated within 20 minutes.

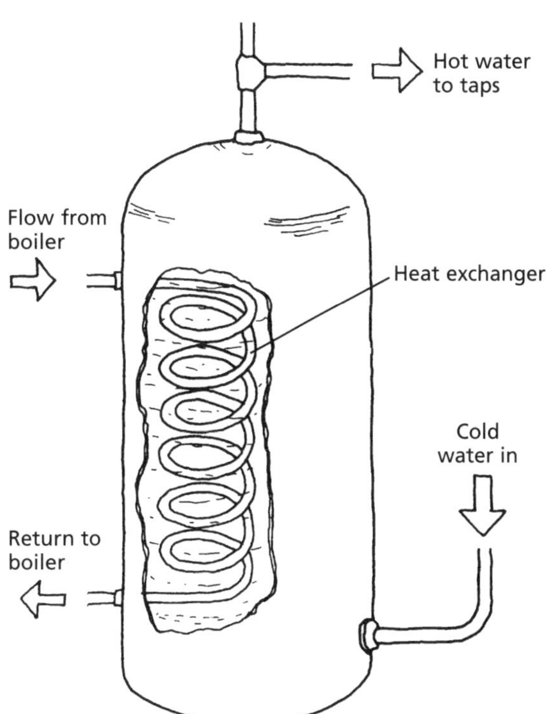

Hot water cylinder with heat exchanger

A storage cylinder should always be well insulated. During the winter some of the heat loss from cylinders will contribute to the heating of the house, but in summer it is a direct heat loss.

HOT WATER FROM COMBI BOILERS

Most combi boilers provide instantaneous hot water as well as central heating. There is no hot water cylinder or cold water tank needed. Features of hot water from a combi boiler:

- The water is heated up as it is required so does not run out, and is always available irrespective of the time of day or any controls on the heating system.
- There needs to be adequate mains water pressure for this type of water system to work effectively. Low pressure may lead to very slow flow rate (e.g. baths taking a long time to fill).
- When one hot tap or shower is being run the water will often be 'robbed' if another tap is turned on – that is one tap will slow down or stop running. Usually only one shower could be used at a time. The size (power) of the boiler will affect the delivery of hot water.
- Showers can run at mains pressure. It is important to choose showers compatible with combi boilers.

Combi boilers with an internal hot water store work on the same principle as described above, but depending on the size of the store will provide hot water more quickly when the taps are turned on. These hot water stores vary in volume – the bigger the store the more hot water is available immediately.

SEPARATE HOT WATER SYSTEMS

Gas

There are three main types of gas water heaters:

- **An integral heater unit and storage cylinder (circulator).** This is effectively a small boiler with its own storage cylinder, totally separate from any central heating system. It is not very common to find this type of arrangement in single domestic premises, but it may be found where water is supplied to a number of outlets such as in a block of flats. Small gas circulators may be provided alongside warm air heating systems.
- **Instantaneous single point gas water heater.** Instantaneous water heaters are connected directly to the cold water system and supply hot water instantly when taps are turned on. Single point heaters provide water to one basin only.
- **'Multipoint' gas water heaters.** These instantaneous water heaters provide hot water to a number of outlets through hot taps (the burner lights up when the taps are turned on). The characteristics of multipoint water heaters are similar to those described above for combi boilers.

Electric immersion heater

An immersion heater is an electric heating element located inside a water storage cylinder. If the immersion heater runs on the general domestic electricity tariff, then hot water will prove expensive. A timer should be fitted to the immersion heater to control it so that it is only used when needed and not left on. It is not recommended to leave an immersion heater on all the time as some people believe. The heat loss from the cylinder means that the thermostat regularly brings the immersion heater into operation, so wasting energy and money.

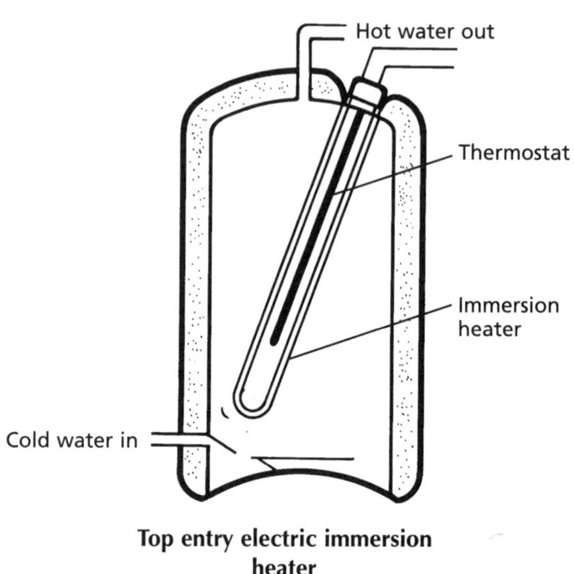

Top entry electric immersion heater

Economy 7 or other 'off peak' tariff for water heating

If hot water is to be heated by electricity it is advisable to use one of the 'off peak' tariffs such as Economy 7 to heat the water overnight in the cheaper periods. The aim is to heat as much hot water as possible on the cheaper rate to minimise the use of the more expensive daytime tariff for top up quantities of water. There are different ways of achieving this:

Separate immersion heaters for day and night operation (dual immersion heaters). The night element is situated at the bottom of the tank and operates during the hours of cheaper electricity to provide a full tank of hot water. The day element heats a smaller quantity of hot water, at the top of the tank for 'top up' during the day when electricity is more expensive.

The best arrangement for immersion heaters is found on the specially designed Economy 7 cylinders, where the immersion heaters enter the cylinder at the side and are controlled by an Economy 7 controller. The cylinder is larger than the standard size, holding around 46 gallons (210 litres) so that enough water is heated overnight for the household's needs.

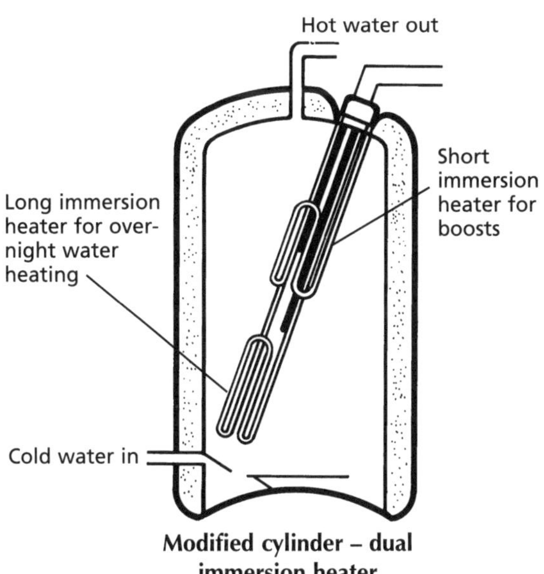

Modified cylinder – dual immersion heater

The top entry single immersion heater (the most common existing arrangement) is not recommended for Economy 7 water heating as it is unlikely to give enough hot water overnight. (The immersion heater itself may be fairly short so not projecting deep enough into the cylinder.)

Modification of existing cylinder for dual immersion heater – Dual immersion heater modifications can be fitted to replace existing single ones. There is a longer element which operates on cheap rate electricity and a shorter one operating on day rate electricity. These work on the same principle as the side entry immersion heaters.

In a modified existing cylinder, remember that there is a limit to how much water can be heated overnight depending on the size of the cylinder. If a standard cylinder of 25 gallons (110 litres) is retained there may not be enough stored water for household needs, so the daytime boost may be used regularly and may prove expensive. Some electricity tariffs may mean that cheap rate boosts are also available during the afternoon. Contact your electricity supplier for details of its tariffs.

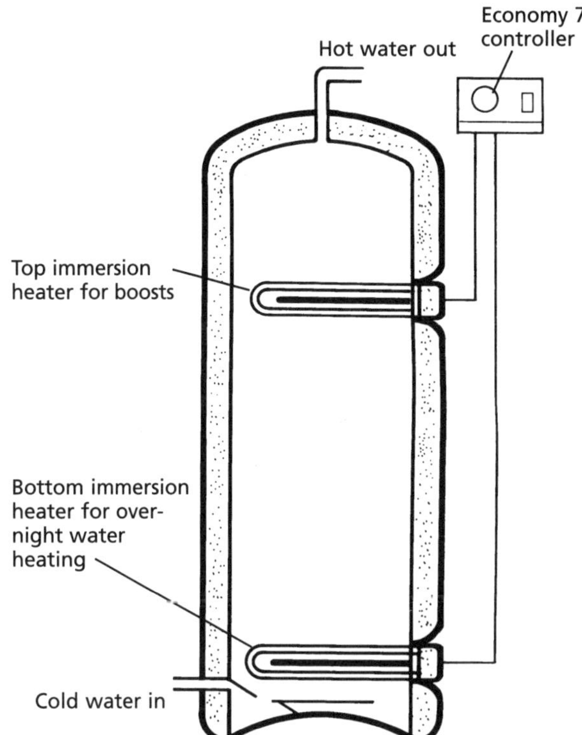

Economy 7 large cylinder with 2 side entry immersion heaters

Instantaneous electric line heaters

These are similar to the individual gas water heaters already described but the water is heated from an electric element. As it is necessary to operate them during the day, it is not possible to take advantage of the 'off peak' tariffs and hence the operation of these units is more expensive. There is no electric equivalent of the gas multipoint water heater.

Electric showers

A shower only normally uses about one fifth of the water of a bath. Instantaneous shower heaters are available for electricity although sufficient water pressure must be available to provide a satisfactory shower. Electric showers use cold water which is heated instantaneously by the unit which may be rated up to 11 kW. Electric showers are more expensive to run than showers fed by hot water from a gas or oil heated hot water supply.

Contact details for organisations listed here are in Appendix 1.

REFERENCES

1 *The Building Regulations 2000 (England and Wales). Approved Document L1, Conservation of fuel and power in dwellings,* 2002 edition.

2 *The Building Standards (Scotland) Regulations 1990, 6th amendment (September 2001), Technical standards to Part J, Conservation of fuel and power.*

3 English House Condition Survey 2001. Table A8.19 *Whole stock by central heating system.* **www.odpm.gov.uk**

4 *The Domestic Heating & Hot Water Guide to the Building Regulations 2001* – Part L1, Energy Efficiency Partnership for Homes.

5 *Domestic Condensing Boilers – 'The benefits and the myths'*: GIL 74. Energy Efficiency Best Practice in Housing. November 2002. **www.est.org.uk/best practice**

6 *The Little Blue Book of Boilers 10th Edition March 2003.* Energy Saving Trust. **www.sedbuk.com**

7 *Central Heating System Specifications (CHeSS) Year 2002.* GIL 59. Energy Efficiency Best Practice in Housing. July 2002. **www.est.org.uk/best practice**

8 *'Getting the best out of ...' Choosing the right fuel* – set of leaflets on getting the best out of various appliances produced by the Solid Fuel Association.

9 *Domestic central heating and hot water: systems with gas and oil-fired boilers.* GPG 284. Energy Efficiency Best Practice in Housing. March 2000. **www.est.org.uk/best practice**

10 *'Frequently asked questions',* Heating and Hot Water Information Council. **www.centralheating.co.uk**

11 *The Government's Standard Assessment Procedure for Energy Rating of Dwellings, 2001 edition.* **www.bre.co.uk/sap2001**

12 *Community heating – a guide for housing professionals.* GPG 240. Energy Efficiency Best Practice in Housing. February 1999. **www.est.org.uk/best practice**

FURTHER INFORMATION

The material in this section is derived largely from the second edition of the Heating Advice Handbook. In addition the following documents and a range of manufacturers' literature were referred to.

Domestic heating and hot water – choice of fuel and system type. GPG 301. Energy Efficiency Best Practice in Housing. February 2002

Controls for domestic central heating and hot water. GPG 302. Energy Efficiency Best Practice in Housing. September 2001.

Domestic heating by electricity. GPG 345. Energy Efficiency Best Practice in Housing. March 2003.

Heating and Hot Water Information Council for *Frequently asked general questions about radiators/ boilers/flues/water treatment.* **www.centralheating.co.uk**

Manufacturers' brochures and a variety of leaflets for consumers.

Manufacturers' literature is very useful for recognition of different types of heating systems and heaters. Their technical specifications also give heat outputs, efficiencies, etc. Contact manufacturers, or visit their websites.

9

CONTROLLING HEATING AND HOT WATER SYSTEMS

This section looks at the control of central heating systems. It is not intended to be used to specify controls, but to describe the minimum recommended controls required for optimum energy efficiency, and to explain how they work.

Modern central heating systems, although providing greater energy efficiency and controllability, often cause confusion as the range of controls on the system are not understood by the householder. Studies have shown that in some cases householders do not use the controls on their systems at all, or that they are commonly used ineffectively.

Helping householders to understand the operation of heating controls can:

- improve comfort in the home
- reduce energy use and therefore fuel bills and CO_2 emissions
- ensure adequate room temperatures for elderly people and infants
- avoid the risk of condensation.

Here we describe the operation of a range of heating controls found on domestic systems. Some of the problems associated with the use of controls are illustrated by case studies.

We concentrate on the controls found on wet systems, as they are by far the most commonly installed central heating systems today. Controls on storage heaters are also described.

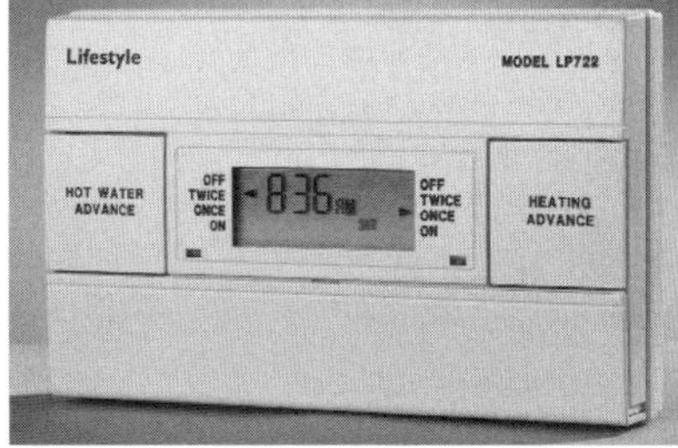

9.1 WHY HAVE CONTROLS?

For a central heating system to run efficiently it must be controlled so that heating and hot water are only provided when and where they are required at a temperature they are required.

The latest revision to the Building Regulations [**1**] for England and Wales includes requirements for minimum efficiency standards for boilers and hot water cylinders in new build and replacement heating systems. The heating systems would be unable to achieve this efficiency rating without the presence of a minimum set of controls. The householder's understanding and use of these controls is therefore important.

For energy savings to be achieved when thermal insulation is installed in a dwelling, it is important that heating controls can respond to the reduction in heat loss, otherwise the dwelling may simply be overheated. Average fuel savings by fitting controls to existing systems can be found later in this section.

9.2 CONTROLS ON A WET CENTRAL HEATING SYSTEM

The controls found on any one system will depend on the age, design and installation of the system. At the most unsophisticated, a wet system may only have a boiler thermostat, with a gravity fed hot water cylinder and a hand switched pump to circulate the water around radiators.

The most modern systems are fully pumped with automatically switched electronic controls. Between these two extremes is a wide range, and the only accurate way to understand how any one system works and so to be able to advise the householder, is to look for and identify the controls fitted, and to experiment with their operation.

The controls on a heating system should ideally be able to sense and respond quickly to changing conditions, then adjust the temperature in smooth stages. In addition, the system needs to be switched on only when required. To manage a system effectively and to keep running costs low, controls are needed for the following:

- **Temperature** – requirements may vary from room to room.
- **Time** – requirements may vary from day to day.
- **Area** – may vary from whole house to individual rooms.
- **Hot water** – to be provided at the times required, and at a suitable temperature.

BASIC AND BEST PRACTICE SPECIFICATION OF HEATING CONTROLS

The Government's Housing Energy Efficiency Best Practice programme produes a leaflet on basic and best practice specifications for the components of domestic wet central heating systems that are critical to energy efficiency [**2**]. The 'Basic specification' for heating controls means sufficient to comply with the Building Regulations Part I [**1**] and Building Standards Regulations Part J (Scotland) [**3**]. 'Best practice' means the adoption of products and techniques that are already established in the market, cost effective and are able to save energy without incurring undue risks.' [**2**]

The individual controls which are fitted to achieve the specifications are described, including examples of the way they work in the systems. They are:

Boiler thermostat

This thermostat controls the temperature of the water leaving the boiler to flow around the radiators and the indirect coil in the hot water cylinder. It is normally fitted inside the boiler jacket or on a pipe next to the boiler. On back boilers it is normally at the base of the fire. It is an essential feature of all oil and gas boilers as one of its purposes is to prevent the boiler overheating.

The boiler thermostat alone cannot effectively control the space temperature of the house, although in some homes it is the only thermostat present.

The fuel supply advisory bodies recommend that where there are room thermostats and hot water cylinder thermostats, the boiler thermostat is set on maximum and the other thermostats used to set comfortable room and hot water temperatures. If the boiler thermostat is the only temperature control, it is recommended that in winter it is set to maximum (or High on some boilers) representing a temperature of 82°C, and in summer to between minimum and maximum (or Low on some boilers) representing a temperature of approximately 70°C.

CASE STUDY 1

A householder complained that her new central heating system did not keep her house warm on a cold winter's day. Despite turning the room thermostat up to 25°C the house still felt cold. On examination it was found that another occupant in the house had turned the boiler thermostat down to minimum. The temperature of the water circulating in the radiators was not hot enough to bring the house up to the desired temperature. The boiler thermostat was turned up.

Room thermostat

A room thermostat on a central heating system reacts to the temperature of air around it. It is usually connected to control the whole heating installation in a dwelling. The thermostat should be placed in a position which is representative of the whole house. It must not be in a position where:

- it is too close to a heat source such as a radiator, TV set, lamp, fridge, flue, etc.
- air cannot circulate freely around it such as in an alcove or behind curtains
- direct sunshine can fall on it
- it is particularly cold, e.g. near a regularly opened door.

In a wet system the room thermostat acts by switching the circulating pump on and off in a system which has gravity fed hot water or by opening and closing a motorised valve in the pipe work of a fully pumped system. In this way, the circulation of hot water from the boiler to the radiators (and hence the flow of heat) is stopped and started.

A room thermostat is usually set between 18°C and 21°C depending on the requirements of the occupants. For energy efficiency it should be set to as low a level as possible to achieve satisfactory comfort levels. Electronic thermostats are more accurate than the mechanical models. Indicator lights show when the temperature has been reached.

> *A 1°C reduction in the setting of a room thermostat can save between 6% and 10% of the annual heating cost* [**4**].

Programmable room thermostats

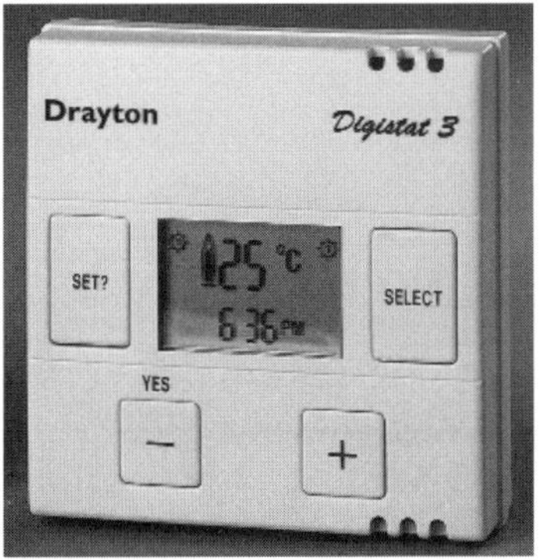

Programmable room thermostat. This example shows that the current time is 6.36 pm and the actual room temperature is 25°C

A programmable room thermostat enables different room temperatures to be set for different times of the day usually in a daily or weekly cycle. Programmable room thermostats are part of the Best Practice controls in the Central Heating System Specification (CheSS).

Thermostatic radiator valves (TRVs)

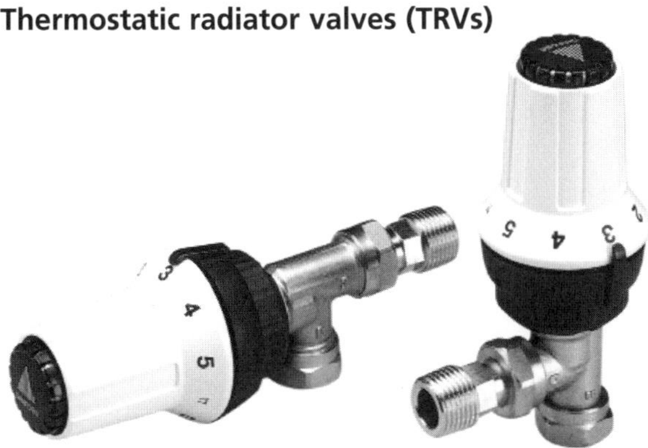

Thermostatic radiator valves are fitted onto radiators and are designed so that different rooms can be kept at individual temperatures. They are fitted to radiators in the place of the ordinary radiator valves. Each TRV has its own temperature sensitive unit which enables it to open and close automatically to vary the amount of hot water that flows through the radiator. In this way the amount of heat the radiator gives out is varied according to the temperature of the room. There are other sources of heat in the house apart from the central heating, including sunshine, cooking and body heat. TRVs take all of these into account and keep each room at the required temperature. Remember TRVs cannot bring the heating on if it is switched off by the room thermostat or the timer/programmer.

CONTROLLING THE TEMPERATURE OF HOT WATER

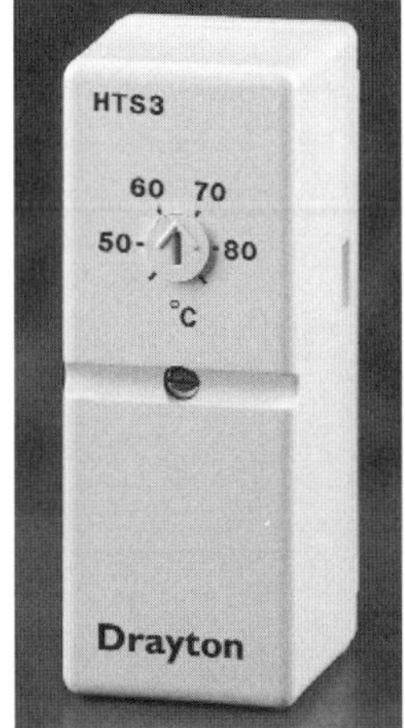

The hot water cylinder thermostat controls the temperature of water in the domestic hot water cylinder and therefore the water that comes out of the taps. The thermostat acts by sensing the temperature of the water and sending a signal to open and close a valve between the boiler and the cylinder.

Hot water cylinder thermostat. This should be set at 60°C

The most common type of thermostat on the hot water cylinder is clamped on to the outside of the cylinder about two-thirds of the way down. (In foam covered cylinders a hole is cut out of the foam in the appropriate position so the thermostat touches the copper cylinder.)

The recommended temperature for hot water is 60°C. Remember that the temperature of the hot water cannot be hotter than the water circulating around the system from the boiler – it can only be the same temperature or cooler.

Another type of thermostat is sometimes fitted to do the same job, is similar to the TRV described above, and is fitted to the hot water pipe between the boiler and the hot water cylinder to slow down the flow of hot water into the cylinder. It can be used on gravity fed systems.

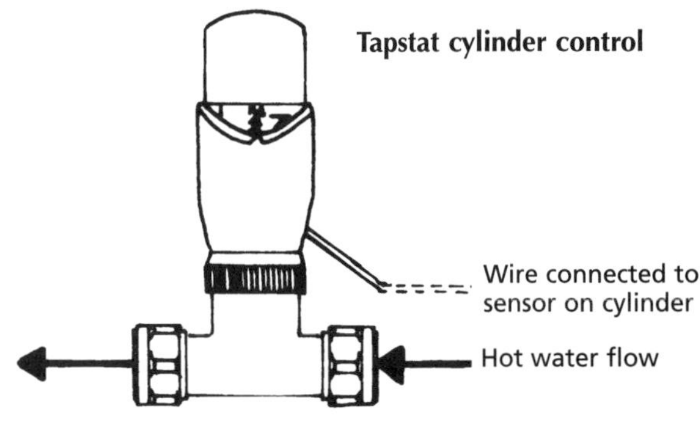

Tapstat cylinder control

Controls required for Central Heating System Specification (CHeSS) – Year 2002 [2]

BASIC
Regular boiler and separate hot water store

- Full programmer
- Room thermostat
- Cylinder thermostat
- Boiler interlock
- TRVs on all radiators except rooms with a room thermostat
- Automatic bypass valve.

BEST PRACTICE
Regular boiler with separate hot water store

- Programmable room thermostat with additional timing capability for hot water
- Cylinder thermostat
- Boiler interlock
- TRVs on all radiators except rooms with a room thermostat
- Automatic bypass valve.

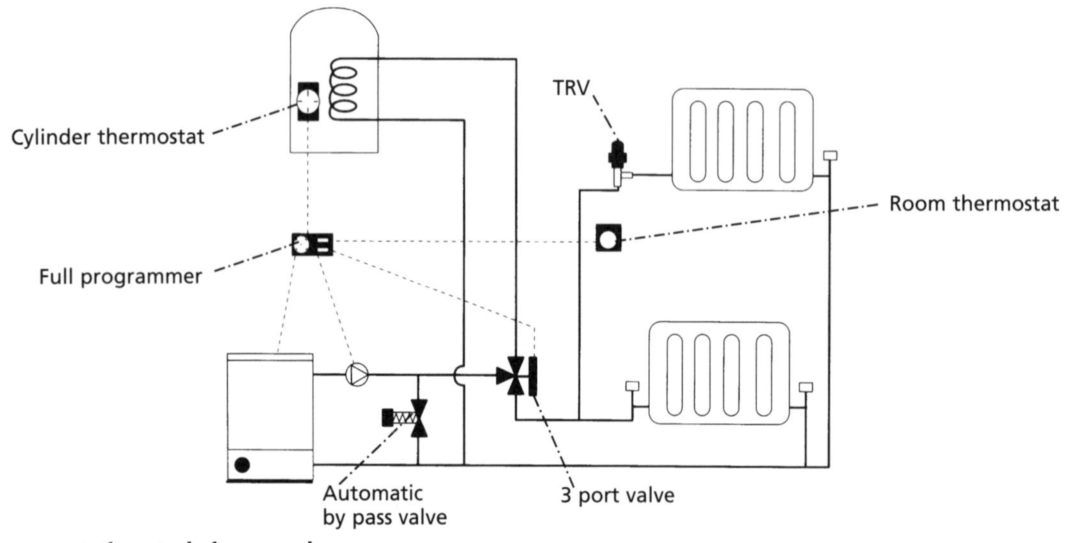

Minimum set of controls for a regular boiler with a hot water store

BASIC
Combi or CPSU boiler

- Time switch
- Room thermostat
- Boiler interlock
- TRVs on all radiators except rooms with a room thermostat
- Automatic bypass valve.

BEST PRACTICE
Combi or CPSU boiler

- Programmable room thermostat
- Boiler interlock
- TRVs on all radiators except in rooms with a room thermostat
- Automatic bypass valve.

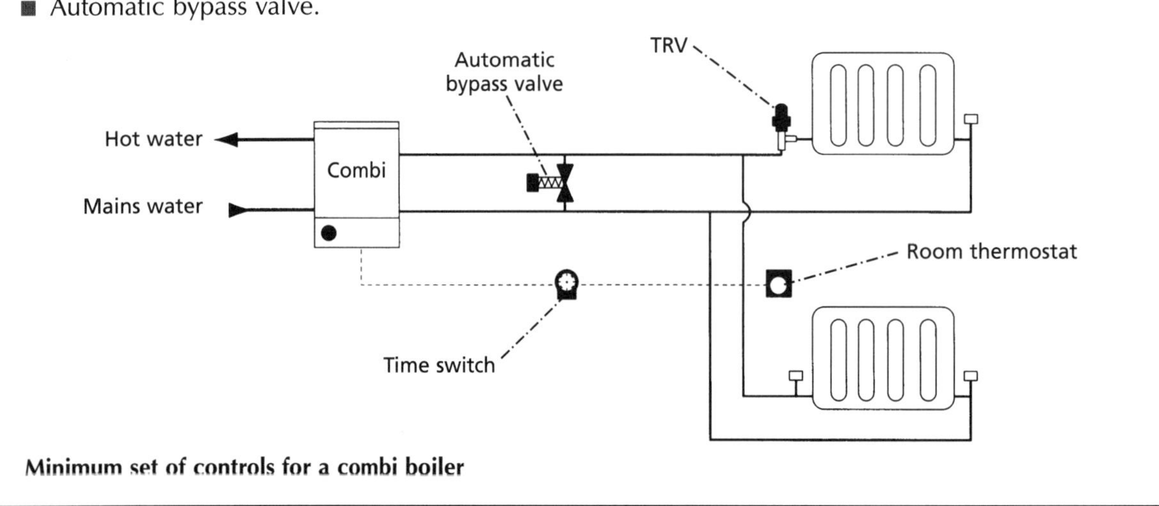

Minimum set of controls for a combi boiler

Illustrations on p9–4 reproduced from GPG 302with permission [4]

Case Study 2

A householder told an advisor that she never had enough hot water to fill the bath so always topped it up by using the kettle. The water from the gas central heating system was hot but there was not enough of it. On inspection it was apparent that the hot water cylinder thermostat was only one quarter of the way down the cylinder instead of three-quarters of the way down, so the cylinder thermostat was turning the hot water off when only a small quantity of water at the top of the cylinder had been heated. The thermostat was moved lower down the cylinder.

Hot water from combi boilers

Because there is no hot water cylinder in a combi system, a thermostat for the hot water temperature is found on the boiler itself.

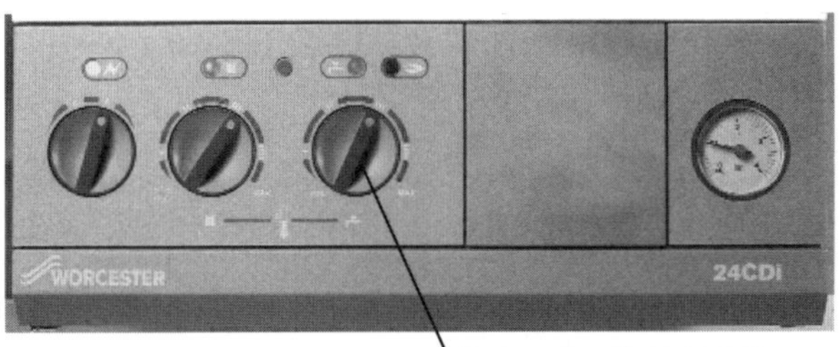

Controls on a combi boiler

Boiler interlock

This is not an actual device but it is an arrangement of controls which makes sure that the boiler does not fire when there is no demand for heat. In a system with a combi boiler this can be achieved with a room thermostat. In a system with a regular boiler it can be achieved by making sure that the wiring is correct between the cylinder thermostat, the room thermostat and the motorised valves. A boiler interlock may also be achieved by a boiler energy manager.

SHARING THE HEAT BETWEEN THE HEATING AND HOT WATER SYSTEMS

In older wet heating systems and solid fuel systems the hot water is gravity fed, that is the water rises from the boiler to the cylinder by gravity – it is not pumped.

In modern fully pumped systems, however, the water from the boiler is pumped to both the hot water cylinder and the radiators.

Motorised valves share the flow of hot water from the boiler between the heating and hot water circuits on demand. Thus, the hot water may be channelled to the radiators or the hot water cylinder or both. Generally, separate room thermostats and hot water cylinder thermostats operate two separate motorised two port valves in the system. This means that in the summer the valve to the heating system pipework can be closed down.

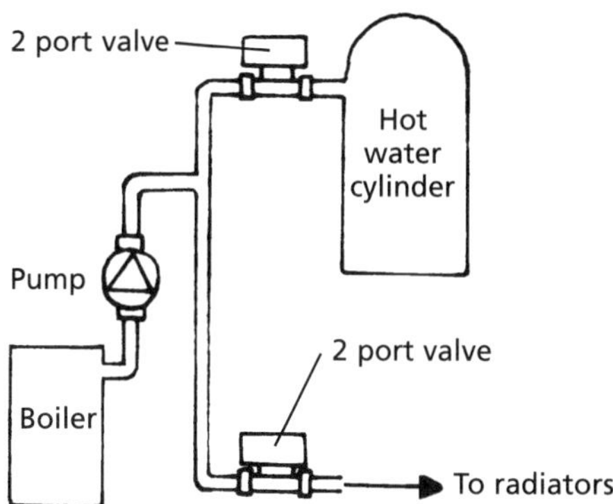

Two port motorised valves – separately controlled for heating and hot water

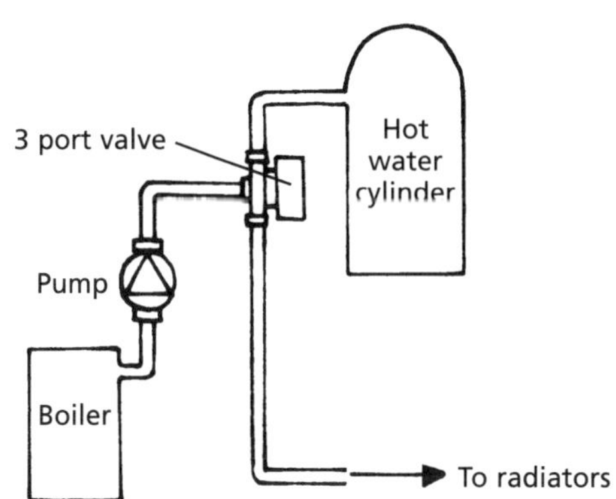

Three port or 'flow share' valve – allows hot water to circulate to heating, hot water or both

An alternative method is a three port valve which either distributes domestic hot water to the heating or hot water circuit (divert valve) or shares it between them (flow share valve).

Flow share valves mean that both the heating and hot water can demand heat at the same time, so that, for example, the heating system does not go cold when a bath has been run.

TIMING AND PROGRAMMING CONTROLS

The aim of timers and programmers is to provide heating and hot water only at the times they are needed. They are probably the element of the central heating system which cause most confusion, so they will be dealt with in some detail here.

> Reducing the heating 'on' time by 2 hours can reduce consumption by 6% [**4**].

Timeclocks

Timeclocks are the simplest form of automatic time control as they consist of a clock only, which is commonly used to switch systems on and off twice a day. Seven day timers are available. No facility is available for separating heating and hot water circuits. Timeclocks are appropriate for the heating circuits on combi boilers because the hot water is permanently available.

Programmers

A programmer is a more complex form of timeclock which is capable of providing different programmes for heating and hot water. It operates motorised valves, thus diverting heat from the boiler to either the heating circuit or to the hot water supply, or both, as required. The programmer usually also operates the pump or boiler to switch the heating and/or hot water on and off.

The programmes required will depend on the living patterns of the house occupants, for example, whether people are at home all day, or just in the mornings and evenings, and the time of year, e.g. the heating will not be required in the summer.

Most modern programmers are now electronic and have digital time displays rather than a circular time-clock.

There is a very wide range of programmes available so it is important to choose one which suits the needs of the householder (taking into account the range of functions that are possible on the system to which it is fitted).

Here are some common considerations:

- For people out most of the weekday and in at weekends a 7 day programmer (allowing different times to be set for each day) would be useful.
- Programmers with very stiff or small tappets (to set the clock) are not appropriate for people with limited dexterity, e.g. arthritis.
- Complex programmers with several possible 'on'/'off' positions each day and 7 day facility may only cause confusion unless those functions are required.
- Studies have shown that many elderly people prefer 'on' and 'off' switches to control heating and they often do not use the programmers. Programmers providing an easily understood on/off booster or override switch would be more suitable than complex models.

> ***Turn on and off or leave on all day?***
>
> As long as the temperature inside a dwelling is higher than it is outside, the dwelling will lose heat to the outside (see Section 11). It is therefore not advisable to leave heating on during the day (or night) when it is not needed [**5**].

Setting programmers

There is such a variety of models available that specific details cannot be given here. Manufacturers' literature does provide setting instructions, but they are not always easy to follow. Face to face instruction and experimentation is the best way to learn how to use any particular programmer, but here are some important points to remember when setting up either an older type mechanical programmer or an electronic programmer.

Set the time of day

- Make sure the clock on the timer/programmer is telling the correct time (the clock may be a 24 hour clock, i.e. 13.00 is 1 pm, etc., or it may say 'am' or 'pm' after the time).
- Remember when the clocks change in March and October you will need to reset the clock. Most electronic models have battery back up to keep them going during a power cut but you may need to reset the clock.
- If someone turns the heating system off at the electrical isolating switch, the timer may stop.

Set the times required for 'ON' and 'OFF' periods

- For the simplest timers there are usually 2 on and off periods a day. For example on at 7 am, off at 9 am, on at 5 pm, off at 10 pm. Set these by sliding the knobs or 'tappets' around the face of a clock face timer, or pressing the buttons on a digital or electronic timer.
- If the programmer has a number of setting periods (some have more than 6) set all these.
- If the programmer allows for different settings each day either copy from the previous day set, or change the setting each day.

Select the programme required

Depending on the rest of the control system (thermostats and valves) various programmes may be selected. If the system is fully pumped it may be possible to programme the heating and hot water separately from each other. If the system is gravity fed for hot water, it is often not possible to have central heating without hot water. You should find that the programmer will not let you select a facility which the system cannot cope with. (For example the hot water will come on automatically with the heating.)

The labelling on programmers can be confusing. Below is an explanation of some of the terminology used to describe the programmes selected.

Labelling found on programmers

- **on / constant / continuous / 24 hrs** – means that the function is on all the time.
- **auto / timed / twice / all** – means that the programmer is following the automatic times set.
- **all day / once** – means the programmer will switch on at the first 'on' time set, and off at the last 'off' time set, ignoring the times set in between.
- **hot water only** – means the heating circuit will not operate (it is only possible to get central heating on its own on a fully pumped system. Hot water is usually provided at the same time as central heating).

- **override / advance** – means the current phase or situation can be overridden, usually bringing the next 'on' or 'off' phase in earlier. The programmer then reverts back to its automatic operation.
- **1 hour / 2 hours / 3 hours** – means that the current phase can be interrupted by a one, two or three hour change e.g. bringing the heating on when it would otherwise be off. It can also be used to extend the programmed phase, e.g. when a householder is staying up later but doesn't want the heating to stay on all night.

There follow below some examples of programmers with a brief description of the functions of each. For full instructions on how to set up programmers, contact the manufacturers or fuel suppliers.

Boiler energy management systems

There is no set definition for this, but it is typically a device intended to improve boiler control by weather compensation, load compensation, optimum start control, night setback frost protection, anti-cycling control and hot water override [**4**].

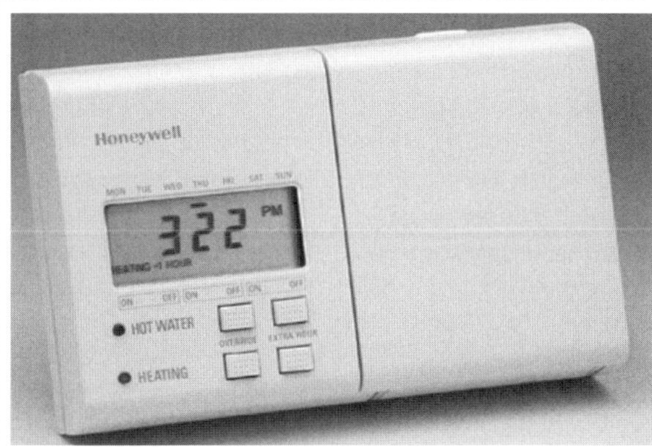

This is a 7 day programmer with the facility to over-ride programmes and also provide an extra hour of heating or hot water.

It is now 3.22 pm on Thursday.

The heating has been put on for 1 hour.

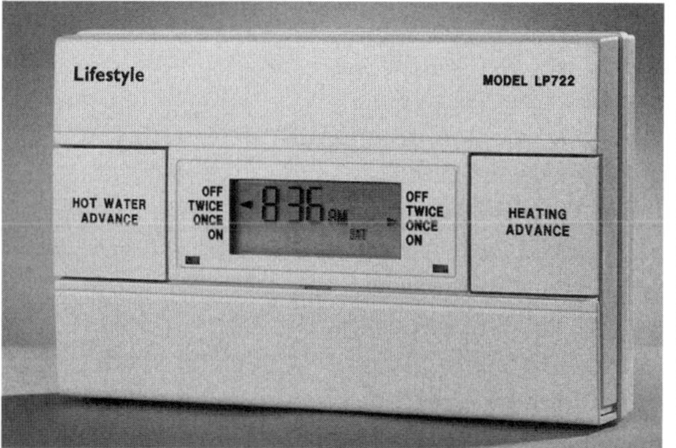

This is a 7 day programmer with the facility to advance the heating or the hot water programme.

It is now 8.36 am on Saturday.

The hot water is programmed to be on twice a day. The heating is programmed to be on once – that is from the first time set to the last – ignoring any times set in between.

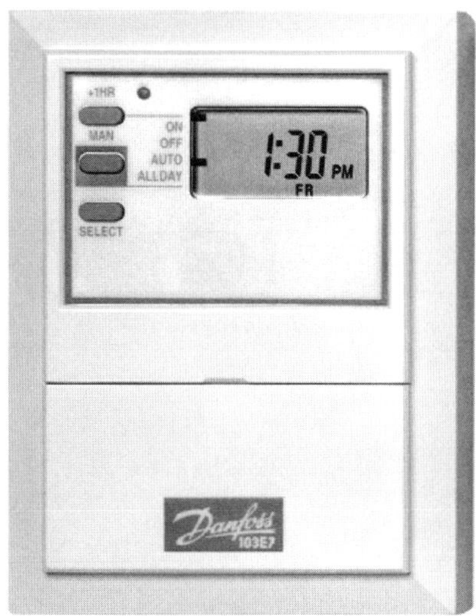

This is a 7 day timer with the facility to override the times set and also provide an extra hour. There is no differentiation between heating and hot water. This type of timer is used with a combi boiler.

It is now 1.30 pm on Friday.

The timer is on automatic but the 1 hr button has been pressed.

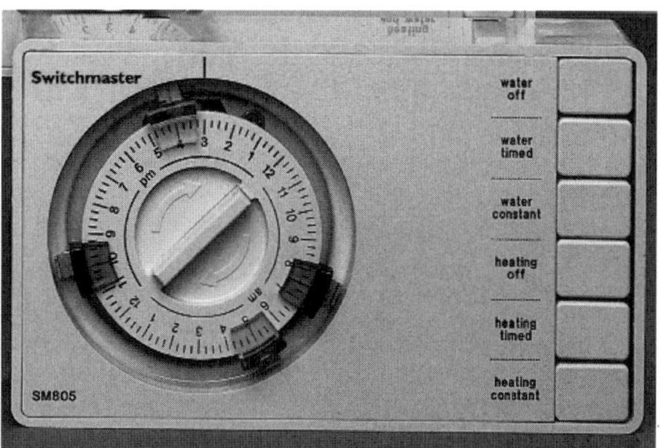

This is a mechanical programmer. Times set for heating and hot water are the same.

It is now 3 pm.

The heating and hot water have been timed to come on at 5 am until 7.30 am, then on again from 4 pm until 10 pm.

For this programmer to operate, two of the buttons on the right need to be pressed.

Checks to make if a wet system does not appear to be working

There are a number of checks that a non-technical person can make if a central heating system is not working properly before technical assistance is called out.

No heating or insufficient heating

- Is the fuel source turned on?
- If your boiler has a pilot light, is it working?
- Is the electricity supply to the system switched on?
- If you have a room thermostat, is it set to the temperature you require? (If the room has reached the temperature set on the thermostat, the radiators will cool.)
- Is the programmer showing the right time, and in an 'on' period?
- Is the selected programme calling for heat?
- Is the pump running – you can usually hear or feel a pump working.
- Is the boiler thermostat turned down too low?
- If you have thermostatic radiator valves, are they at the settings that you require?
- If a radiator is hot only at the bottom, you may need to release trapped air, or 'bleed' it.

No hot water

- Is the fuel source turned on?
- If your boiler has a pilot light, is it working?
- Is the electricity supply to the system switched on?
- Is the clock showing the right time, and in an 'on' period?
- Has the clock been 'on' long enough for the boiler to heat the water? If you run water off whilst the clock is in an 'off' period, the hot water is not replaced.
- If you have a cylinder thermostat, or thermostatic valve on the cylinder, is it set at the temperature you require?
- Is the boiler thermostat turned down too low?

Energy savings by improving control systems

Existing system has the following controls	Improved system: add the following[1] for the 'minimum set'	Approximate average savings[2] (% of the existing fuel consumption)
	Typical boiler with gravity DHW	
	Room thermostat, Cylinder thermostat, Motorised valve(s), Boiler interlock, TVRs on most radiators	17%
Room thermostat	Cylinder thermostat, Motorised valve(s), Boiler interlock, TVRs on most radiators	12%
Room thermostat, Cylinder thermostat, Boiler interlock[3]	Motorised valve(s), Boiler interlock, TVRs on most radiators	11%
Room thermostat, Cylinder thermostat, Motorised valve(s), Boiler interlock	TVRs on most radiators	4%
TVRs on most radiators	Room thermostat, Cylinder thermostat, Motorised valve(s), Boiler interlock	9%
	Typical boiler – fully pumped[4]	
	Room thermostat, Cylinder thermostat, Motorised valve(s), Boiler interlock, TVRs on most radiators	17%
Room thermostat, Cylinder thermostat, Motorised valve(s)	Boiler interlock, TVRs on most radiators	10%
Room thermostat, Cylinder thermostat, Motorised valve(s), Boiler interlock	TVRs on most radiators	4%
TVRs on most radiators	Room thermostat, Cylinder thermostat, Motorised valve(s), Boiler interlock	9%
	Typical combi boiler[4]	
	Room thermostat, Boiler interlock, TVRs on most radiators	15%
TVRs on most radiators	Room thermostat, Boiler interlock	7%
Room thermostat, Boiler interlock	TVRs on most radiators	4%

NOTES

1 All improved systems should include a programmer (regular boiler) or timeswitch (combi boiler).
2 These are average savings assuming normal controls, systems and user behaviour. Actual savings in individual systems may be significantly different. It is assumed that the SEDBUK is 68% (i.e. with the minimum set of controls fitted).
3 This option provides only a partial boiler interlock (hot water only).
4 Improved systems should include an automatic bypass valve if a bypass curcuit is necessary.

KEY

Room thermostat; Boiler interlock; Cylinder thermostat; TVRs on most radiators; Motorised valve(s)

This table is reproduced from GPG 302 with permission [4]

9.3 CONTROLS ON SOLID FUEL SYSTEMS

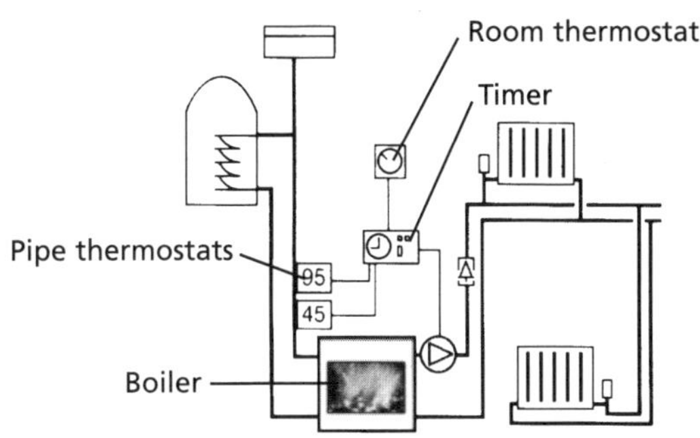

Layout of controls on a solid fuel central heating system

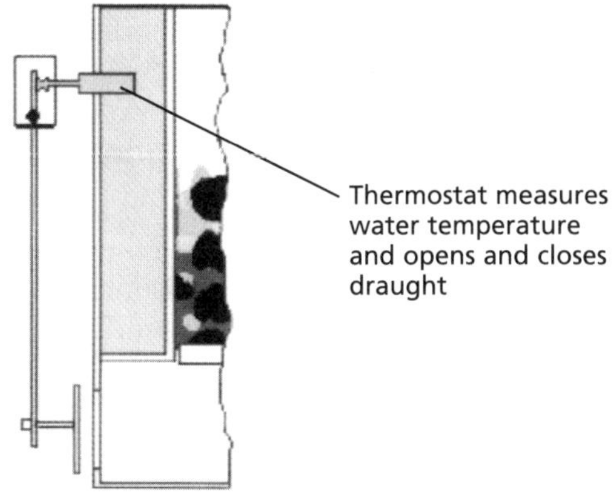

Operation of the thermostat on the back boiler of a solid fuel room heater

Although a number of controls are found on solid fuel wet systems, solid fuel is by nature more difficult to control because it cannot easily be turned on and off.

Basically, thermostats on solid fuel room heaters (with hot water and/or central heating provision) operate by opening and closing a damper to let in air which will cause the fire to burn more fiercely.

Solid fuel systems do not generally have a hot water cylinder thermostat because the hot water is gravity fed and acts as a safety escape for hot water as the solid fuel room heater cannot actually be switched off. Hot water is sometimes diverted into a radiator or towel rail used for the purposes of any extra 'heat leak'.

Two pipe thermostats may be fitted. One stops the water circulating if it is below 45°C. The other turns the pump on to dissipate the heat if the water reaches 95°C. A room thermostat fitted to a solid fuel system will switch the pump on to circulate hot water from the boiler around the radiators. As the cooled water returns to the boiler, the boiler thermostat comes into operation either opening a damper letting air in for the fuel, or an electric fan is switched on. A timeclock may also be fitted which controls the pump.

The checks that follow are there for problems commonly found with solid fuel room heaters with or without associated radiator systems.

Checks to make if a solid fuel room heater is causing problems

Excessive fuel consumption

Associated problems: water boiling, unable to control fire.
Caused by: uncontrolled air entering appliance below grate level.

Check that:

- The thermostat is closing correctly.
- The thermostat flap is not distorted or wedged open by fuel or cinders.
- The ashpit door is sealing properly.
- There is no air leak along the base of appliance.

Fumes to room – warning: fire must NOT be used

Check that:

- The throat plate is not clogged with fly ash (clean at least once per month).
- The chimney has been swept.
- The chimney is not obstructed or in need of repair.
- There is sufficient ventilation.

NOTE: downdraught can be caused by a variety of external factors.

Fire bars burning out

Associated problems: firebricks burned, distortion to front bars and throat plate. Excess clinker.
Caused by: overheating or not clearing ashes.

Check that:

- Ash is not allowed to build up in ashcan to touch fire bars.
- The fire is not being allowed to get too hot by removing ashpit door for periods whilst fire door is closed.
- Unauthorised fuel such as petroleum coke with zero % ash is not being used. (Fuel blends which include petroleum coke must not be used either.)
- The cause is not one of those listed above under 'Excessive fuel consumption'.

Fire will not stay alight

Check that:

- The thermostat setting is correct.
- The combustion air bypass needs opening.
- There is excess ash on grate.
- The riddle mechanism is jammed.
- There is sufficient fuel. A 6″ – 8″ deep fire bed is recommended for maximum efficiency.

NOTE: some fuels, e.g. Sunbright, require more air.

9.4 CONTROLS ON ELECTRIC HEATING SYSTEMS

ELECTRIC STORAGE HEATERS

Electric storage heating systems have, generally, been associated with a lack of controllability. Automatic sensing devices have improved both the amount of heat stored in the heater overnight and the rate at which the heat is given out into the room the following day. In addition a combination of storage heaters and controllable panel heaters in bedrooms has improved the controllability of the whole house. It is still essential, however, that a dwelling is well insulated if storage heating systems are used. If the heat is lost from the storage heaters during the day expensive day rate electricity will be needed to boost heating.

The control of a storage heater is achieved by:

- controlling the input of the charge of electricity into the heater overnight.
- controlling the output of the stored heat the following day. (The heat from a storage heater is radiated from the case by the heater itself, but most rises by convection out of the grille in the top of the heater. A simple metal damper opens and closes to allow this heat to escape.)

Input or charge control

With an older conventional storage heater, the input has to be adjusted manually to ensure that an appropriate amount of heat is stored overnight. Automatic input controls include thermostatic sensors – either in the heater itself or better still on a remote sensor so that the temperature of the room overnight determines how much heat is stored up for the following day. This form of thermostatic sensor should not be located in rooms where there may be another source of heat overnight, for example a solid fuel fire which would still be warm for some time into the night. Manufacturers claim cost savings of up to 15% by using automatic controls compared to non-automatic storage heaters [**6**].

Output control

On older storage heaters a damper is lifted manually by turning a knob marked 'boost' or 'output'. This allows the warm air to rise over the heated blocks and out through the grilles at the top of the heater. If this damper is left open (i.e. 'output' on max.) the heat will escape from the storage heater early in the day.

Automatic output control is achieved by a thermostatic sensor or a timer delaying the opening of the damper so that although the case of the heater will be losing some heat, the air flow over the blocks is not boosted until needed.

Fan assisted storage heaters

These contain more insulation than standard models so lose their heat more slowly. When the heat is required a fan draws the air through the thermal bricks.

Choosing storage heaters

The Building Regulations state that new storage heaters installed should be fitted with automatic charge (input) and output (boost) controls.

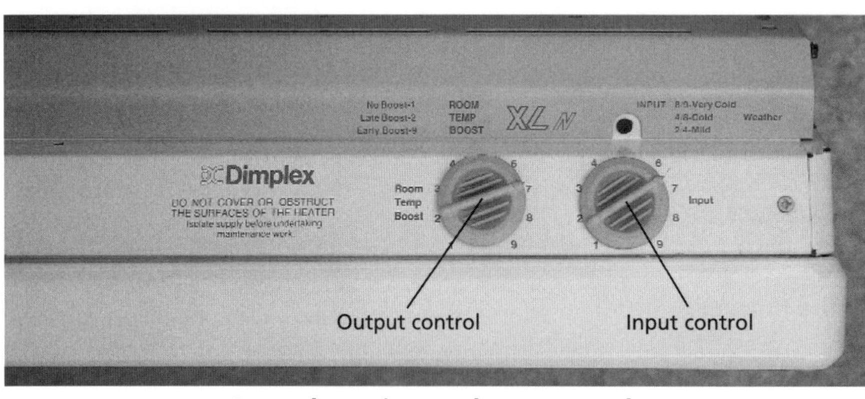

Storage heater input and output controls

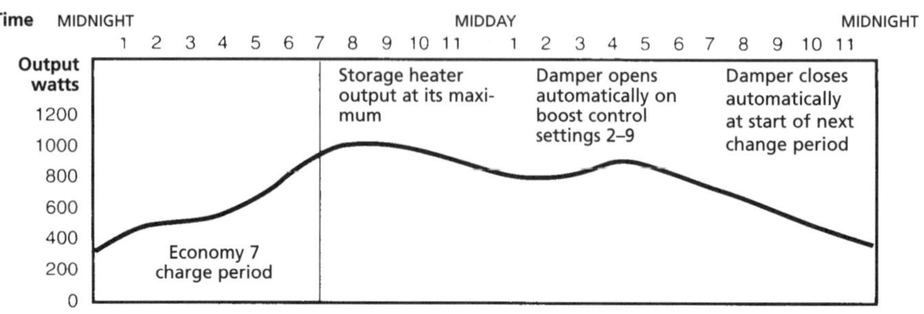

Typical profile of the heat output of a storage heater

A range of models of storage heaters can be used in different rooms depending on requirements for the room (e.g. background heating to reduce condensation risk) and on the other sources of heat (e.g. sunshine, cookers, etc.) in the room.

Assuming the decision has been taken to choose storage heaters in preference to other forms of heating, make sure that the storage heaters/panel heaters fit the needs of the householder in terms of the controllability of the system.

Contact the manufacturers for the range of models available.

CONTROLLING 'ON PEAK' ELECTRIC HEATERS

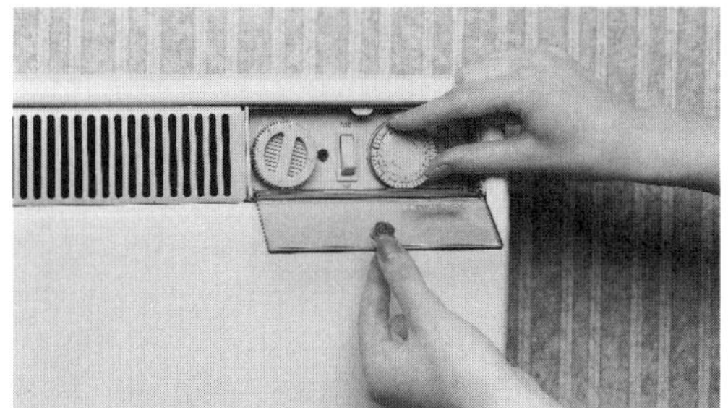

Controls on panel heater

Most models of panel heaters, fan heaters, convector heaters and electric radiators are fitted with thermostatic controls and many with timers. Those without integral timers can be plugged into plugs which incorporate timers.

CONTROLLING HOT WATER HEATED BY ECONOMY 7

When the dual immersion heater system for Economy 7 water heating is fitted, an Economy 7 controller should also be fitted. This includes a timer which brings the lower immersion heater into operation overnight so the whole cylinder is heated up. The controllers also include a 'boost' switch to enable the householder to turn the smaller (or higher) immersion heater on for short boosts when needed. The earlier versions of the controller incorporate a spring loaded switch which allows for a one hour boost. More modern electronic models allow a number of boosts to be programmed in if hot water runs out. It must be remembered that all these daytime boosts are the most expensive method of heating hot water unless the water is heated as part of a new off peak tariff.

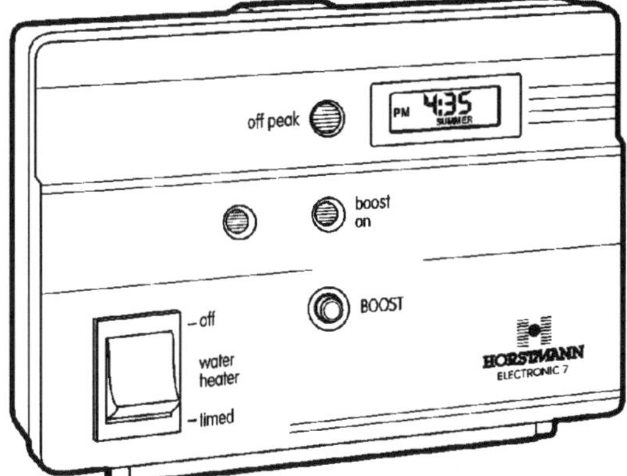

Economy 7 hot water controller – digital

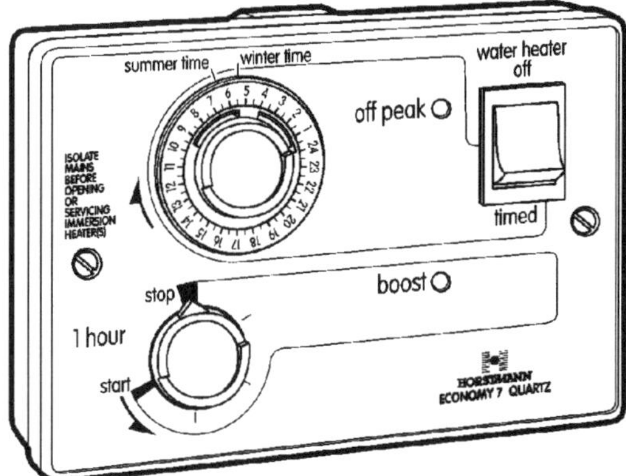

Economy 7 hot water controller – mechanical

Checks to make if a storage heating/hot water system does not appear to be working

There are a number of checks that a non-technical person can make if a storage heating system is not working properly before technical assistance is called out.

No heating or insufficient heating in the morning

- Is the electricity switched on?
- Has there been a power cut overnight causing the heaters to be undercharged?
- Was the 'input' or 'charge' control turned down too low overnight?
- For models with automatic input or charge control, was there some heating on in the room overnight, causing the automatic control not to operate the overnight charge?

No heating or insufficient heating in the afternoon/evening

Same points as above, but more commonly the output or boost control has been left on high so that all the heat is lost before the afternoon/evening.

No hot water or water too cool

- Is the electricity switched on?
- Has there been a power cut overnight causing the immersion heater to be undercharged?
- Is the Economy 7 controller set at the wrong times?
- Has the hot water been used up (if so use the one-hour boost)? If the hot water cylinder is too small the hot water may be used up before the next night-time charge period.
- Is the immersion heater thermostat set too low – it should be on 60°C.

9.5 CONTROLS ON WARM AIR CENTRAL HEATING SYSTEMS

Modern warm air systems use room thermostats and timers in the same way as described in wet systems. Modern systems are an improvement on older systems because a delay mechanism prevents the circulation of air until it reaches the desired temperature. In some models a 'modulating control' enables the fan speed and the burner firing to be variably controlled so that temperature variation and fan noise is decreased, and comfort improved.

Temperatures in each room cannot be controlled individually as they can with TRVs on a wet system, but the grilles can be opened or closed in each room until the heat distribution is satisfactory.

Controls on electric warm air systems

Electric warm air systems operate by air being drawn over a core which has been heated overnight. Thermostatic control operates the fan so that as the room cools down the fan draws air through the core of the heater and not through the grilles into the room's heater.

Contact details for organisations listed here are in Appendix 1.

REFERENCES

1 *The Building Regulations 2000 (England and Wales). Approved Document L1. Conservation of fuel and power in dwellings.* 2002 edition

2 General Information Leaflet 59. *Central Heating System Specification (CheSS) Year 2002. Basic and best practice specification for the components of domestic wet central heating systems that are critical to energy efficiency.* 2002. Housing Energy Efficiency Best Practice Programme. **www.est.org.uk/bestpractice**

3 *The Building Standards (Scotland) Regulations 1990, 6th amendment (September 2001), Technical Standards to Part J. Conservation of fuel and power.*

4 *Controls for domestic central heating and hot water – guidance for specifiers and installers.* GPG 302. Housing Energy Efficiency Best Practice Programme. **www.est.org.uk/bestpractice**

5 Based on information in NHER Plan Assessor Training Manual Version 3.7; Issue1, Revision A.

6 'Dimplex' product brochure 2002.

FURTHER INFORMATION

Manufacturers' literature

Trade Association for Heating Controls Manufacturers
For lists of members etc.
TACMA 020 7793 3008
www.heatingcontrols.org.uk

See also Further Information in Section 8 for further publications covering heating systems and controls.

10

COMPARATIVE EFFICIENCIES AND RUNNING COSTS OF HEATING AND HOT WATER SYSTEMS

The type of fuel used and the efficiency of the heating and hot water system are critical to its running cost, and also to the amount of CO_2 produced by the system. The cost and availability of fuels will also affect a customer's choice of a heating system. The levels of insulation in a dwelling and the way in which systems are used are dealt with elsewhere in this Handbook. Here we concentrate on the impact which the type of fuels used and the efficiency of the heating system have on the running costs of those systems. This material should assist energy advisors to have a broad understanding of comparative costs to help householders to make choices, and also to enable readers to access up to date and accurate information.

This section looks at:

- the difference between primary, delivered and useful energy
- published material to illustrate the comparative running costs and efficiencies of heating and hot water appliances
- how to work out the efficiency of a gas fire from manufacturer's literature
- calculating specific running costs more accurately from energy auditing software
- monitoring actual domestic fuel costs from meter readings.

10.1 FUEL AND SYSTEM EFFICIENCY

To understand the impact which a fuel has on the environment, particularly in terms of its CO_2 emissions, it is important to understand what happens in the whole process of changing energy from **primary** to **delivered** to **useful** energy.

Primary energy

Primary energy is the energy value available at the very beginning of any process, for example in a coal fired power station generating electricity, the primary energy is in the coal.

Delivered energy

Delivered energy is that which reaches the customer and is measured through a meter in the case of gas and electricity.

Useful energy

Useful energy provides the warmth. The difference between delivered and useful energy is determined by the efficiency of the heating and hot water system.

Before fuel even reaches the domestic customer there are large differences in the energy losses as the energy is extracted, transported and converted.

When we look at the comparative cost tables which follow, for example, electricity is shown as 100% efficient. This is true once it has entered the home, but in the generation of electricity the conversion of primary to delivered energy is only around 35% – 45% efficient, so much of the primary fuel is wasted (unless that waste heat is used, for example, in combined heat and power systems). Fuels vary in their efficiency, see Appendix 4 for a list of the CO_2 emissions per unit of energy for a range of fuels.

In this section we are concerned with how the fuel is used once it is in the home. The same fuel can be used, but the system may use it in an efficient way or it may be wasteful. The most common reason for a system to be inefficient is its age – older systems are generally less efficient.

10.2 COMPARATIVE RUNNING COSTS – PUBLISHED DATA

The running costs of a heating and hot water system are determined by:

- the heat demand of the dwelling
- the fuel used and its cost
- the efficiency in the way that fuel is burnt.

This section of the Handbook is not concerned with the heat demand of the dwelling. Standard sized houses and rooms are used so that the only variables are the fuel and the heating system.

The more efficient a heating system is, the less fuel is wasted when the system is used. The current emphasis on installation of condensing boilers is due to the high efficiency of these boilers. The householder receives more heat for their money, and the system produces less of the polluting gas CO_2.

During the research for this material, a number of sources of information were found on comparative running costs. They vary because they use different assumptions. The Good Practice Guides which describe the operation of heating systems [**1**], use data from SAP 2001 (i.e. the basis of the SAP calculations), but it was felt that these costs were out of date. The decision was made to use SALKENT Comparative Domestic Heating Costs tables [**2**] which are produced on a six monthly basis, for six areas of the UK and Ireland. The main purpose of the tables is not to predict actual running costs of any one system but to compare different fuels when used under similar conditions.

Clearly, any information on running costs can only provide a snapshot, and will become out of date, but by using this source of information our intention is for the reader not only to understand it but also be able to update or substitute information if required. The source publication [**2**] describes how the figures are derived, so the reader will be able to substitute the unit fuel costs on the tables with those which are known locally to be accurate and up to date if required.

Two tables are reproduced here as an illustration. Table 10.1 is the Comparative running costs for space heating and hot water. Table 10.2 is the Comparative heating costs for space heating for an average size room. We have taken the Midlands as an example for the month of October 2003.

The tables deal with the variety of prices and tariffs available for gas and electricity from competing suppliers. The annual running costs take into account standing charges where applicable and maintenance costs to give the full cost for heating and hot water.

Notes are provided here to help readers interpret the contents of the tables. They refer to the letters across the top of each table.

NOTES ON TABLES 10.1 AND 10.2

A Fuel sold in units of:
This is how you buy this fuel, e.g. a sack of anthracite grains weighs 50 kg; electricity is sold in units of 1 kWh.

B Unit cost in pence (including VAT at 5%):
The cost of a unit, e.g. a 50 kg sack of anthracite grains costs 864p or £8.64 and a unit of electricity on a standard tariff costs 6.08p/kWh

This column also shows the day and night rates for electricity costs when on Economy 7. The night rate is used for 90% of the time and day rate for boosts only – 10% of the time. This column also shows the split tariff used by suppliers who do not charge a standing charge.

C Type of heating system:
A brief description of the actual system which provides the heating and hot water system, or in the case of room heating, the type of heater. Read both lines together (DHW or dhw means domestic hot water).

D Average % system efficiency:
Although not always consistent with other efficiency tables (see Section 9) SALKENT provide different system efficiency figures for heating and hot water. These figures relate to the overall efficiency of a system, not just the boiler. The use of a system for heating is more efficient than the use of the same system to heat hot water. The less efficient a system is the more it will cost to run. This shows clearly in the examples of gas room heaters. Using the same fuel and the same tariff, it costs more than twice as much to provide the same amount of heat to the room using a decorative effect fire than it does using a wall heater.

E Cost per useful kWh in pence:
This column is the most useful for comparative purposes. It is the cost in pence for the SAME amount of output in heat. (1 kWh is the amount of heat you get from a one bar electric fire in one hour.) Note that on the gas fire costs there is no standing charge included in the annual running costs but the unit cost of the fuel is high because two assumptions are made.

- The customer is paying cash or a cheque (more expensive than Direct Debit).
- The customer does not use enough gas to take advantage of the lower rate of the split tariff. The amount of gas used for room heating is 3100 kWh. If the customer only uses gas for the gas fire, they would not use the 4572 kWh necessary to move them into the lower unit cost.

[Notes continue on page **10**–5]

Table 10.1 COMPARATIVE RUNNING COSTS FOR SPACE HEATING AND HOT WATER

COMPARATIVE HEATING COSTS – THE MIDLANDS – OCTOBER 2003
SPACE AND WATER HEATING FOR HOUSES

	A		B	C	D		E	F	G	H		
FUEL			Unit cost pence (inc VAT)	Type of heating system	Average system efficiency % space htg	dhw htg	Cost per useful kWh pence	Annual standing charges (Inc VAT) £	Cost of service & running circulating pump £	Annual cost of space & water heating for average size houses 2 Bed (1)	3 Bed (2)	4 Bed (3)
SOLID FUEL	Housecoal-Grade A		701	Open fire with back boiler	60	-	2.80					
	50 kg			Radiators & DHW cylinder	-	25	6.73	-	35	446	582	818
	Anthracite Nuts		934	Room heater with back boiler	70	-	2.76					
	50 kg			Radiators & DHW cylinder	-	25	7.73	-	35	462	601	840
	Man.Ovoids (Phurnacite)		1191	Room heater with back boiler	70	-	3.75					
	50 kg			Radiators & DHW cylinder	-	25	10.49	-	35	614	803	1127
	Anthracite Grains		864	Gravity feed boiler	70	-	2.73					
	50 kg			Radiators & DHW cylinder	-	30	6.37	-	35	431	563	792
ELECTRICITY	Representative Supplier (Powergen)											
	Price / unit		6.08	Electric radiators	100	-	6.08	35.44	-	808	1073	1558
				Immersion water htr	-	70	8.69					
	Economy 7 Domestic Tariff (DD)											
	First No of Day Units/Annum		1100									
	Price per Unit	a)	11.99	Storage htrs, living rooms	90	-	3.06					
	Price of balance of day units	b)	6.24	Electric rads, bedrooms	100	-	2.75					
	Night Units	c)	2.75	Immersion water htr, night	-	70	3.93					
	Night Use = 90%			Immersion water htr, day	-	70	17.13 (4)		-	484	629	896
NATURAL GAS	British Gas	a)	2.170		70	-	*					
	Direct Debit Tariff			Gas fired boiler	-	35	*		55	384	485	663
		b)	1.512	Radiators & DHW cylinder	70	-	*					
	a) First 4,572 kWh/p.a.				-	35	*					
	b) After 4,572 kWh/p.a.											
		a)	2.170		85	-	*					
				Gas fired condensing boiler	-	45	*		55	327	409	555
		b)	1.512	Radiators & DHW cylinder	85	-	*					
					-	45	*					
	Alternative Supplier			Gas fired boiler								
			1.420	Radiators & DHW cylinder	70	-	2.03	40.00	55	376	470	638
	Powergen				-	35	4.06					
	Direct Debit Tariff											
			1.420	Gas fired condensing boiler	85	-	1.67	40.00	55	323	399	536
				Radiators & DHW cylinder	-	45	3.16					
LPG			25.09	LPG fired boiler	70	-	5.04					
	Propane	(5)		Radiators & DHW cylinder	-	35	10.08	69.56	55	822	1057	1473
	1 Litre											
			25.09	LPG fired condensing boiler	85	-	4.15					
		(5)		Radiators & DHW cylinder	-	45	7.84	69.56	55	690	881	1221
OIL			17.50	Oil fired boiler	70	-	2.42					
	Heating oil	(6)		Radiators and DHW cylinder	-	35	4.83	-	55	390	502	701
	28. sec viscosity											
	1 Litre		17.50	Oil fired condensing boiler	85	-	1.99					
		(6)		Radiators and DHW cylinder	-	45	3.76	-	55	326	417	580

Notes
(1) Terraced 2 bedroom house, 9850 kWh space heating & 2000 kWh DHW heating.
(2) Semi-detached 3 bedroom house, 13500 kWh space heating & 2500 kWh DHW heating.
(3) Detached 4 bedroom house, 20750 kWh space heating & 3000 kWh DHW heating.
(4) These costs/useful kWh are indicative only and may not be used in the calculation process.
(5) Fuel delivered to 1200 litre storage tank. Rental shown in standing charge column.
(6) Fuel delivered in 1000 litre drop.

* Because of the split tariff, it is difficult to include an accurate figure here as cost depends on amount of fuel used.

Table 10.2 COMPARATIVE HEATING COSTS FOR SPACE HEATING IN AN AVERAGE SIZE ROOM

COMPARATIVE HEATING COSTS – THE MIDLANDS – OCTOBER 2003
SPACE HEATING FOR AN AVERAGE SIZE ROOM

	A	B	C	D	E	F	G	H
FUEL		Unit cost pence (Inc VAT)	Type of heating system	Average efficiency %	Cost per useful kWh in pence	Annual standing charge (Inc VAT)	Cost of maintenance £	Cost of 3100 kWh for room heating (1) £
SOLID FUEL	Housecoal-Grade A 50 kg	701	Open fire	28	6.01	–	25	211
SOLID FUEL	Coalite 50 kg	1161	Open fire	37	7.06	–	25	244
SOLID FUEL	Anthracite Nuts 50 kg	934	Closed room heater	60	3.22	–	25	125
ELECTRICITY	Typical provider – Powergen Standard Domestic Tariff (Cash or Cheque) 1 Unit a)	6.080	Electric fire	100	6.08	24.92	–	213
ELECTRICITY	Economy 7 Tariff Night a)	2.57	Single storage heater	90	2.86	6.60 (2)	–	106
ELECTRICITY	Day rate for 10% of use b) Night rate for 90% of use	6.24	Electric fire	100	6.24			
GAS	Cash or Cheque Payment 1 kWh	2.470	Radiant/convector fire	60	4.12		30	158
GAS		2.470	Wall heater	73	3.38		30	135
GAS		2.470	Decorative effect open fire	28	8.82		30	303
GAS	(3)	1.420	Decorative effect open fire	28	5.07		30	187
LPG	Propane 47 kg Cylinder (4)	2561	Radiant/convector fire	60	6.54	–	30	233
LPG		2561	Decorative effect closed front fire	60	6.54	–	30	233
LPG		2561	Decorative effect open fire	28	14.01	–	30	464
LPG	Propane 1 Litre (5)	25.09	Decorative effect open fire	28	12.60	6.11	30	427
LPG	Butane 15 kg Cylinder	1725	Butane heater	92	9.15	–	–	284

Notes

(1) Annual heating requirement of an average room.
(2) Difference between Economy 7 and Standard Domestic Tariff annual standing charge.
(3) Used in conjunction with central heating system.
(4) 47kg Cylinder at heating pack price from May 1995.
(5) Illustrated as 1200 Litre tank supply. Used in conjunction with central heating system. 10% of tank rental included.

EXAMPLES OF HOW TO INTERPRET THE TABLES

EXAMPLE 1

A customer who lived in 3 bedroom house who had a conventional gas boiler and bought their gas from Powergen wanted to know how much they would save if they had installed a condensing boiler. From Table 10.1 (middle column under H), they would have saved £71 per year (£470 – £399).

EXAMPLE 2

A householder was surprised when they changed their room heater from an open coal fire to a closed room heater using Anthracite nuts, that they were not spending so much on solid fuel even though the fuel was more expensive per bag. (The annual cost of the coal fire was £211 and the room heater £125.) The answer is because they are getting more heat for their money as less of it is wasted. The coal fire was only 28% efficient, but the closed room heater is 60% efficient.

F Annual sStanding charge:
Annual charges, where they apply, are added on to the cost of fuel to give running costs. It is conventional to include the full annual standing charge for gas, but only the difference between the Economy 7 (or other off peak in Scotland) and the Standard Domestic Tariff for electricity. This is because it is assumed that all households already have electricity irrespective of the heating fuel.

G Cost of maintenance and running a circulating pump:
Annual costs to be added to the cost of fuel and standing charges to give full costs.

H Annual costs of space and water heating for average size houses:
Taking all the given costs into consideration, annual running costs are given for three different sizes of house (or for one room in the case of a single room). The energy demand for the houses is based on properties built before the current Building Regulations. They are intended to represent 'average' housing stock in the UK. The energy demand varies depending on climatic conditions in different parts of the country. The example shown here is for the Midlands.

CHECKING THE EFFICIENCY OF GAS FIRES

The efficiency of gas fires varies widely (see Section 8). To check the efficiency look at the manufacturer's, or retailer's literature to find the input and output of the fire.

EXAMPLE

Two gas fires look very similar to the customer. She asks how much they cost to run. The retailer looks at the specification. Gas fire A has a maximum input of 6.8 kW, and output of 2.7 kW.

To work out the efficiency:

Energy output ÷ Energy input x 100 = % efficiency
Therefore 2.7 ÷ 6.8 x 100 = 39.7% efficient

Gas fire B has a maximum input of 6.9 kW and a maximum output of 4 kW

4 ÷ 6.9 x 100 = 60% efficient

Fire B is much more efficient. Apart from the fact that the customer is getting less value for money from Fire A, she may also find that the amount of heat (Max 2.7 kW) is not warm enough for her needs.

Some manufacturers' literature shows the comparative running costs as actual money, i.e. compare a fire which has 4 kW output for 8.7p per hour to a fire which has a 1.5 kW output for 8.7p per hour [5].

10.3 PREDICTING FUEL COSTS WITH ENERGY AUDITING SOFTWARE

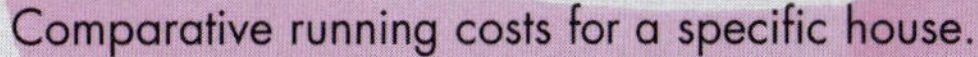

The information used in the SALKENT data is based on average dwellings and patterns of occupancy. A more accurate assessment of any particular dwelling can be achieved by using energy auditing software (see Section13). This can be used to compare running costs of different options in the same dwelling. A case study here illustrates how the choice of fuel and heating system makes a difference.

CASE STUDY

Comparative running costs for a specific house.

A householder lives in a terraced house with solid stone walls in West Yorkshire. The house is in an exposed position. It has two storeys, 6 rooms, 100 mm of loft insulation and is double glazed. The house has a coal fire with a back boiler but the householder is finding it inconvenient.

There is no mains gas nearby and the fuels being considered are oil or bulk LPG. Storage of either is not a problem. The householder still wants to use either a coal fire or a 'coal effect' fire in his lounge.

The energy advisor used a software programme NHER Surveyor [5], to produce the following comparison.

	Oil £ per year	LPG £ per year
Main heating and hot water – new boiler	£241	£477
Secondary heating – fire in lounge		
Oil – open fire with smokeless fuel	£107	
LPG – inset live effect fire		£123
Standing charges	–	£57
Total for heating and hot water	**£348**	**£657**
Cooking	£45	£45
Lighting and appliances	£100	£100
Total annual fuel costs	**£493**	**£802**

Analysis of fuel use and costs – NHER Surveyor Nov 2003

This comparison shows that LPG would be considerably more expensive than oil. Because the software programme used is BREDEM 12, the cost of cooking, lighting and appliances is also included.

10.4 MONITORING ACTUAL FUEL COSTS

The only certain way to monitor actual fuel costs is to read meters, record fuel consumption and work out the running costs. Section 5 of this Handbook explains how to do this.

In Appendix 3 there is a template for the weekly monitoring of gas and electricity meter readings.

Fuel Monitoring Charts
Electricity and gas tariffs can be complicated, making it difficult to work out running costs from meter readings in a simple way. The two charts here cut out some of the steps needed for accurate bill calculations, but should still provide an adequate guide to likely fuel costs. These are examples so up to date local costs should be used. In Appendix 3 these examples are repeated with blank templates which can be copied to produce weekly monitoring sheets. Monitoring can be carried out for a whole quarter on the charts.

Fuel Monitoring Chart – Electricity – Example

Wk No	**METER READING**	**UNITS in kWh** Subtract previous week from current week's reading	**COST** (6.6p per unit)	**Other costs to add in** (Either add the weekly standing charge, or a similar amount if there is a split tariff instead of a standing charge. VAT also needs to be added. These costs are not likely to be more than 15p per day.)	**Approx Weekly Cost**
1	21602				
2	21802	200	£13.20	Add 7x15p = £1.05	£14.25
3	22014	212	£13.99	Add 7x15p = £1.05	£15.04

Fuel Monitoring Chart – Gas (with a meter reading cubic feet) – Example

Wk No	**METER READING**	**100s of cubic feet** Subtract previous week from current week's reading	**UNITS in kWh** (100s cu ft x 31)	**COST** (1.5p per unit)	**Other costs to add in** (Either add the weekly standing charge, or a similar amount if there is a split tariff instead of a standing charge. VAT also needs to be added. These costs are not likely to be more than 15p per day.)	**Approx Weekly Cost**
1	3211					
2	3229	18	558	£8.37	Add 7x15p = £1.05	£9.42
3	3252	23	713	£10.69	Add 7x15p = £1.05	£11.74

See Appendix 3 for a Fuel Monitoring Chart for Gas with a meter reading cubic metres.
For Economy 7 or other off peak tariff, both types of unit will need to be recorded.

Contact details for organisations listed here are in Appendix 1.

REFERENCES

1 *Domestic heating by electricity.* GPG 345 Housing Energy Best Practice Programme. March 2003. **www.est.org.uk/bestpractice**

2 *Comparative Domestic Heating Costs.* October 2003. SALKENT Ltd. **www.salkent.co.uk**

3 *NHER surveyor analysis of heating costs* provided by Rotherham MBC.

4 Figures taken from retailers specifications in brochure, November 2003.

5 For information about NHER contact: **www.nher.co.uk**

11

HEAT LOSS FROM DWELLINGS

It is important to know about heat loss from buildings for a number of reasons:

- So that technical terms such as U-values are understood in discussions about insulation, renovation, and the planning of a new heating system.
- So that Energy Rating schemes and the requirements for the Building Regulations are understood.
- So that the relevance of good thermal insulation and draughtproofing becomes clear.
- So that areas of high heat loss from buildings can be identified as a possible cause of condensation.

This section describes how heat is lost from buildings and explains how U-values are used by builders, energy efficiency professionals and heating engineers.

It outlines the current Building Regulations, and how they determine the standards of heat loss allowed from dwellings. The factors which affect heat loss from existing buildings are described with examples.

11.1 HOW HEAT IS LOST FROM A DWELLING

Heat travels from heated areas to colder areas. Therefore in cold weather, when buildings are warmed up by their heating systems, other 'incidental' gains such as appliances and machinery and even the people inside, the heat is continually being lost to the outside environment as long as it is warmer inside than out.

The heat lost from a dwelling can be divided into two categories:

- **Fabric heat loss** – heat lost as it is transmitted through the fabric of the building.
- **Ventilation heat loss** – heat lost through ventilation or draughts.

Therefore, total heat loss is a combination:

Fabric Heat Loss + Ventilation Heat Loss = Total Heat Loss

In other words the specific measure of heat lost, in watts, per degree centigrade temperature difference between the inside and the outside of the dwelling.

(Heat is also lost through flue gases from heaters and heating systems. This is discussed in Section 10.)

Heat loss calculations are an important element of energy auditing programmes and energy rating schemes (see Section 13). The characteristics of dwellings – the materials they are made out of, the size and layout of the building – are used to calculate heat losses and therefore to prioritise insulation methods. The calculations are almost always carried out using dedicated computer software. To a large extent the age of a dwelling will indicate its construction but energy efficiency improvements may have been undertaken and will need to be taken into account.

Heat loss calculations are also used to determine heating system requirements. The heating system needs to be sized correctly so that the dwelling is maintained at approximately 21°C in the living room, and 18°C elsewhere. Heating contractors measure the external surfaces of the dwelling/extension, and as accurately as possible determine the construction of the building. They will also make some assessment of how draughty the dwelling is. Together this information will indicate size (and hence heat output) of the radiator or other heater for each room.

11.2 FABRIC HEAT LOSS AND U-VALUES

This is heat loss through the fabric of the dwelling (walls, roofs, floors) including that lost through the fabric (glass, timber, etc.) of the windows and doors.

The fabric heat loss from any particular dwelling depends on:

- the different fabrics which make up the building and their U-values
- the area of each of the fabrics
- the temperature difference between inside and outside the building.

THE FABRIC OF THE BUILDING

Heat loss characteristics of building fabrics vary. As a general rule, metal, very thin materials e.g. glass, and dense materials e.g. concrete, conduct heat well so lose heat easily, and materials which trap air e.g. mineral wool, special blocks, expanded polyurethane, slow down heat loss considerably.

The term used in relation to fabric heat loss from dwellings is 'U-value'. This is known as 'thermal transmittance'. It is a measure of the rate at which heat passes through the fabric of the building. The higher the U-value, the greater the rate of heat loss.

The U-value is the rate at which heat passes through one square metre of area of the material if a temperature difference of one degree Centigrade is maintained between the two sides. It is measured in Watts per square metre, per degree Kelvin (K) (degrees Centigrade may be used here). This is symbolised by:

$$U = W/m^2\,K$$

The U-value of a structure is dependent upon each of the materials used and the construction. Each material in the structure (e.g. a wall may include brick, insulation, blocks, internal plaster etc.) adds to the structure's insulating properties – i.e. more layers, or thicker layers, add more resistance to the loss of heat from the dwelling.

There are generic U-values available in documents [**1**] which may be used. However, in most cases these are not specific enough for builders and architects working to strict budgets and specifications. A calculated U-value for each of the fabric components of the building is always preferable.

By knowing the different U-values for a building's fabric the overall heat loss can be calculated. A simple illustration of heat loss through a window is shown in the box in the previous column.

A single glazed metal framed window has an area of 3 square metres
The U-value of the window is 5.7
The temperature difference between inside and outside is 20°C

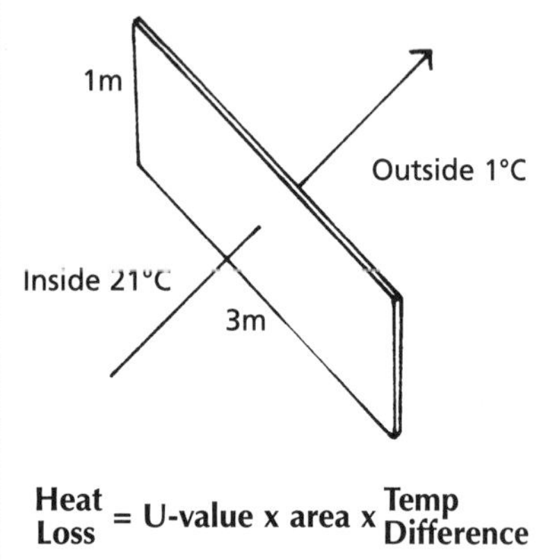

Heat Loss = U-value x area x Temp Difference

Heat Loss = 5.7 x 3 x 20 = 342 Watt

Simple example of heat loss

Table 11.1 EXAMPLES OF TYPICAL U-VALUES (Note, this table is intended to give an illustration of some U-values. It is not intended for heat loss calculation purposes, for which accurate values are needed.)

Walls	**U-value in W/m²K**
Wall built to 2002 Building Regulation Standard [1]	0.35
Solid brick wall, insulated from the inside	1.0
Solid sandstone wall (380mm)	2.0
Uninsulated cavity wall	1.4
Solid brick wall	2.1
Concrete panel	3.5
Windows	
Double-glazed, (Low E glass 12 mm gap)	2.2
Double-glazed, wood or upvc frame (6mm gap)	3.1
Single-glazed, wood frame	4.8
Single-glazed, metal frame	5.7
Roofs	
Pitched, with 250mm loft insulation	0.20
Flat, insulated	0.40
Flat, uninsulated	2.5
Pitched uninsulated	2.6
Floors	
U-values for floors depend on the ratio of their area to their exposed perimeter, so they depend on the shape of the floor. For example, for the same floor size, a detached house is worse than a semi which is worse than a mid terrace. Hence it's not possible to give a value in a table like this.	

These are examples, and are included to give an idea of U-values. There are a great variety of types of construction, and so of U-values. For accurate values for the components of a particular building, consult the appropriate CIBSE (Chartered Institution of Building Services) Guide [**2**], the BS EN 12524 [**3**] or the manufacturer's details.

> *A dwelling with concrete panels (U-value 3.5) would lose heat through the walls ten times faster than a dwelling with the same area of insulated cavity walls built to standards in place in 2002 (U-value 0.35).*

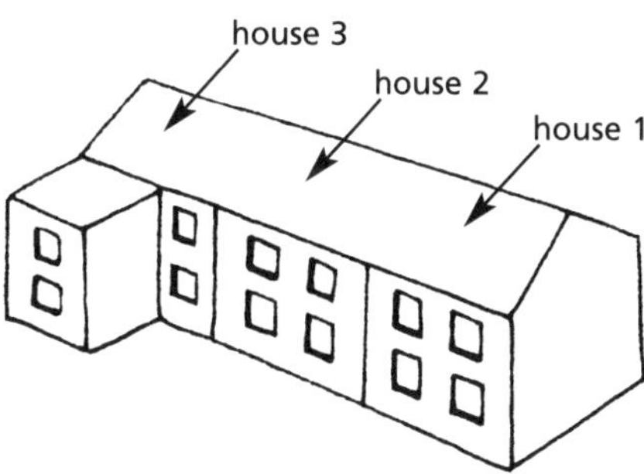

House 1 has more external wall area than house 2, but house 3 has more than either of the others because of the extension

AREA OF EACH BUILDING FABRIC

As each different type of building fabric loses heat at a different rate, the area of each fabric is worked out and the heat losses added up. Heat loss will be increased by:

Large areas of building fabrics with high U-values

For example large areas of glazing (particularly single glazing) will contribute to high heat loss, as heat is lost faster through glass than most other building materials.

Other building fabrics, whether walls or roofs, may have high U-values. Examples are solid brick or stone walls without cavities, and prefabricated concrete panels built in the 1960s–70s with no, or very little, insulation added.

A high proportion of external surfaces

Heat is lost through external surfaces, so large areas of external surfaces will result in high heat loss. The proportion of external surfaces will depend on the plan (or layout) of the dwelling, and whether it is at the end or in the middle of a block. A detached house will have a higher heat loss than a semi-detached, and a semi-detached higher than a mid terraced house. A middle floor flat will lose less heat than a top or ground floor flat. A top floor flat will lose heat through the roof, and a ground floor flat will lose heat through the floor.

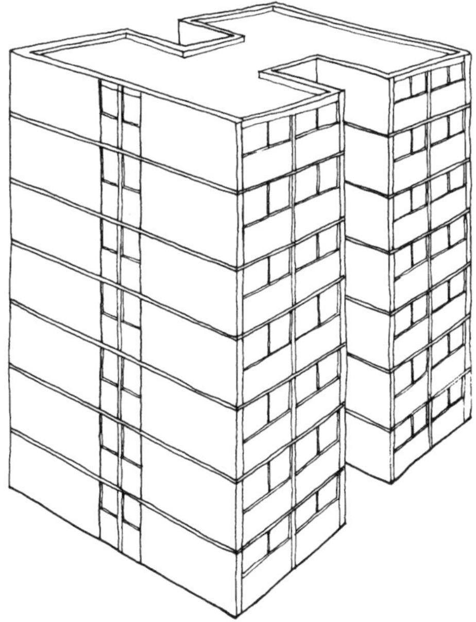

Each flat in this block has three external walls and one internal wall

A floor that is exposed to the outside will be a source of heat loss. Examples of this are rooms situated above walkways, or overhanging.

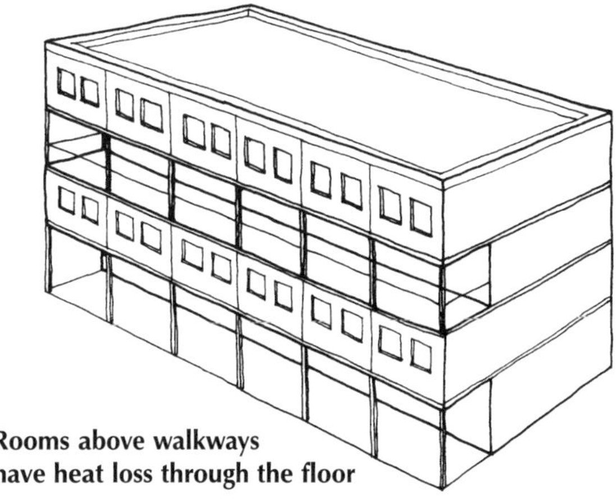

Rooms above walkways have heat loss through the floor

A wall to an unheated space, such as a stairwell, a lift shaft, an empty building, or a garage, will also lose heat, although not as quickly as through an external wall, because the temperature inside the unheated space is likely to be higher than the external temperature.

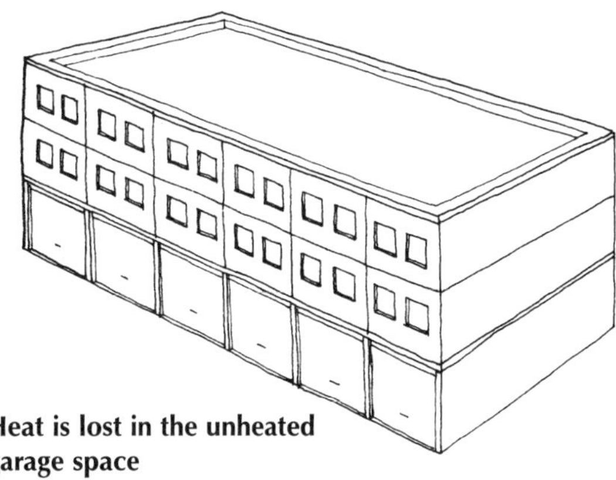

Heat is lost in the unheated garage space

11.3 VENTILATION HEAT LOSS

This is heat lost as air leaves a building and is replaced by cooler air, such as through deliberate ventilation, draughts, and opening and closing of doors. As cold air from outside enters a building, the same amount of warmer air leaves. The rate at which heat is lost because of this depends on the rate at which these air changes are happening and the difference in temperature between the air coming in and the air going out. (For the way in which ventilation is measured see Section 17.)

Some ventilation is essential to maintain air quality and to remove moist air so that the risk of condensation is reduced. It is specifically needed if open flued fuel burning appliances are used (see Section 8 and Section 17). However, excessive ventilation leads to heat loss and can lead to uncomfortable draughts. Ventilation accounts for approximately a third of the heat loss from an older dwelling and up to a half the heat loss from an energy efficient dwelling [**4**].

Traditionally UK dwellings were ventilated by 'natural air infiltration' and much of the ventilation happens by accident rather than design. The illustration below shows the routes of essential ventilation as well as the sources of draughts or 'air infiltration'.

During tests the BRE have found that only 16% of air leakage routes in dwellings is through doors and windows [**5**]. The rest is through:

- plasterboard dry lining on dabs or battens
- cracks, gaps and joints in the building structure
- timber floors – skirting and between boards
- holes where pipes and wiring are fitted
- areas of unplastered wall.

(Chimneys were not included in these tests – unused chimneys are also a significant source of heat loss as warm air rises up chimneys creating the 'stack effect' and thus added ventilation heat loss.)

When looking at any particular building there will be other factors which affect the heat loss from that building.

Diagram of unwanted air leakage and essential ventilation

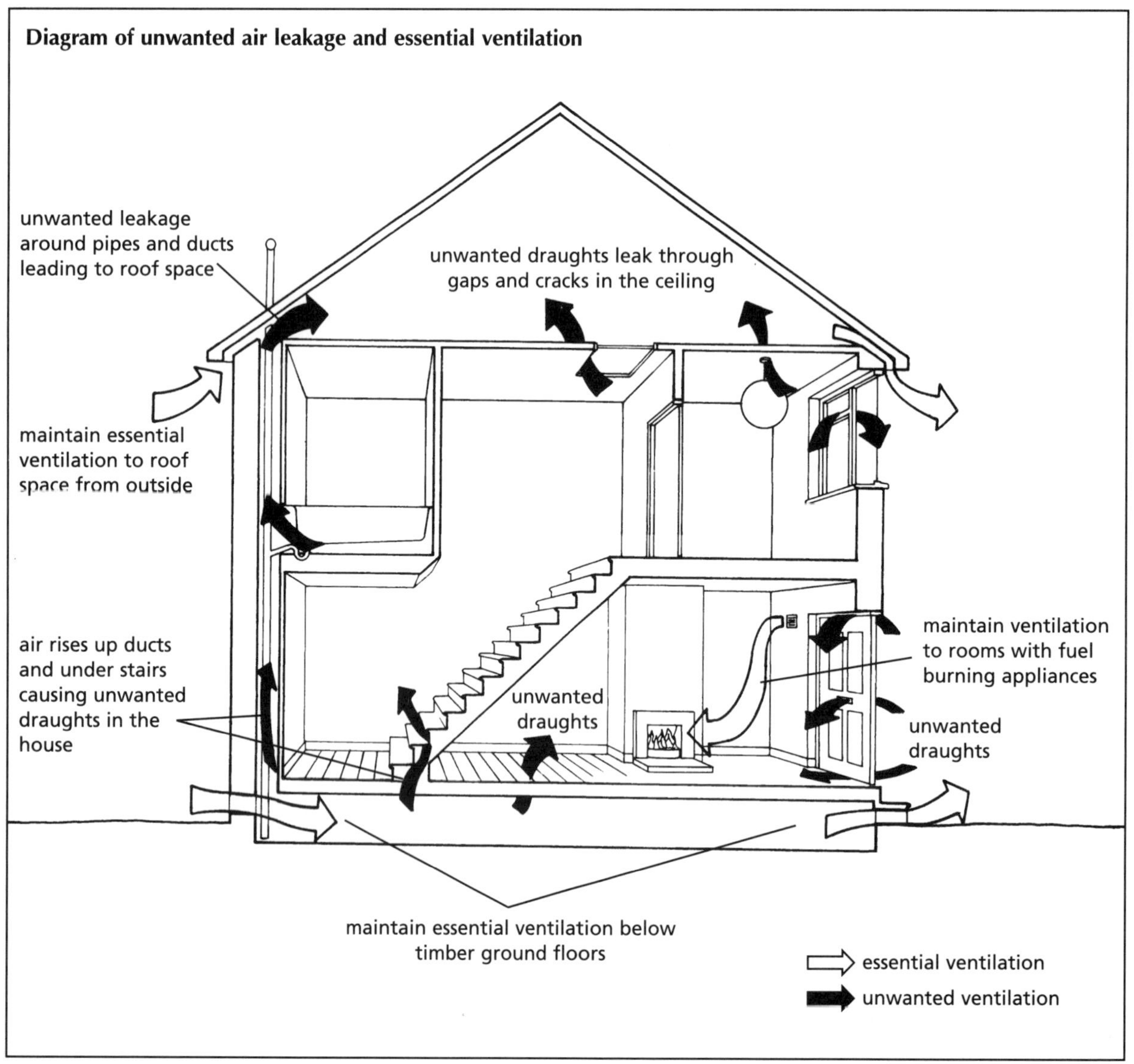

11.4 FACTORS AFFECTING THE HEAT LOSS FROM BUILDINGS

The examples below describe what to look for when trying to identify some of the reasons for high heat loss from dwellings other than the building materials and the obvious causes of draughts.

EXPOSURE

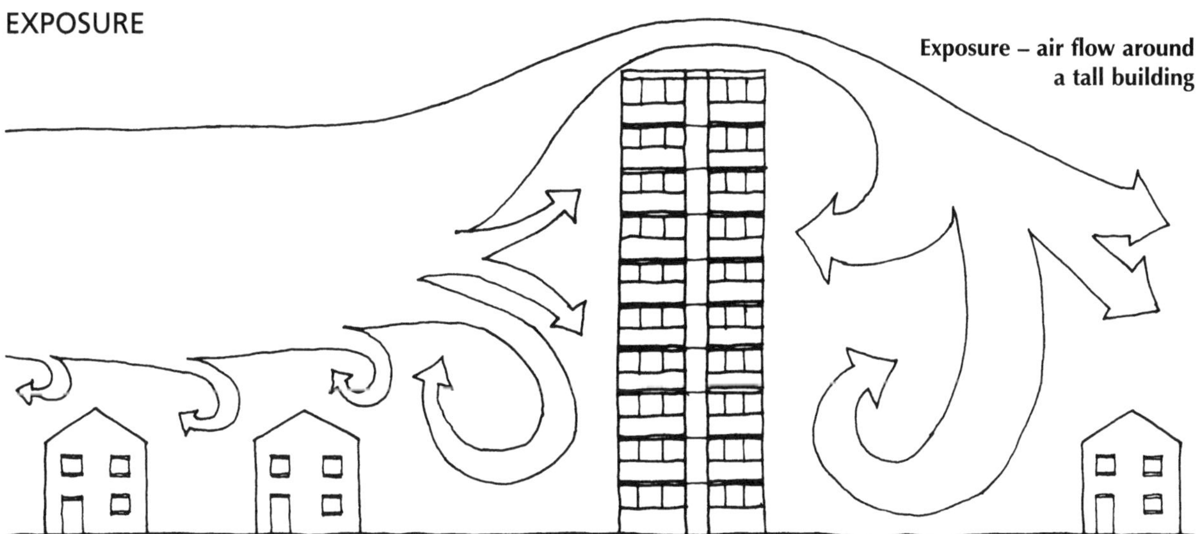

Exposure – air flow around a tall building

An exposed dwelling will lose more heat than a sheltered one in two ways:

- the draughts will be worse
- the fabric of the building will be cooled down by the wind (this is known as the 'chill factor').

Examples of exposed homes are those in windy positions such as on coasts or exposed hillsides, and flats high up in a tower block. Flats low down in a tower block and other homes nearby may also be affected, because of the air turbulence caused by the presence of high buildings.

Other factors, including the siting of a building in relation to the ground features, the direction in which it faces, whether it is overshadowed e.g. whether it receives much sunshine or 'solar gain' and local climate all have an effect. For these reasons, identical buildings in different locations may have different heat loss characteristics.

DAMPNESS

Dampness increases the problem of heat loss, as damp materials conduct heat better than dry materials. An insulating material is no longer a good insulator when it is wet through.

'COLD BRIDGING'

A 'cold bridge' is a continuous path for heat loss, from the inside to the outside of the building. It is provided by a material that conducts heat relatively well (such as steel or dense concrete) bridging a material which conducts heat less well (such as a brick cavity wall).

Examples of this are steel or concrete structural members which are exposed, concrete dividing floors with exposed edges (or continuous to balconies or walkways) and concrete lintels and sills.

Cold bridges are often associated with condensation, and mould growth on the inside of the cold bridge is the coldest spot in the room.

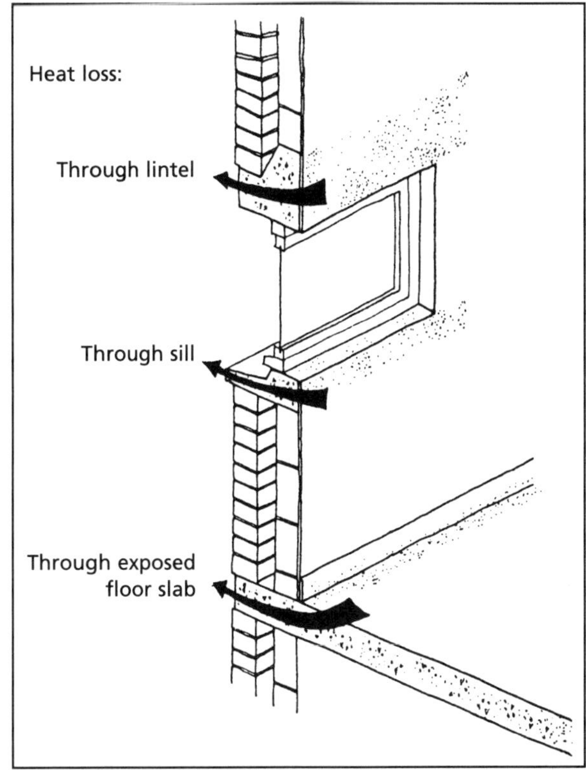

Examples of 'cold bridging'

11.5 SETTING LIMITS FOR HEAT LOSS – THE BUILDING REGULATIONS

The Building Regulations for new buildings and new extensions to existing buildings set upper limits for the U-values of building elements, and for the proportion of external walling that may be glazed. These limits have been lowered in stages since they were first introduced in 1965. This, together with changes in construction methods, means that the age of a building can give some indication of the likely construction and level of insulation of a building, as can be seen from Table 11.2.

Table 11.2 ROOF AND EXTERNAL WALL U-VALUES TYPICAL OF UNIMPROVED DWELLINGS IN THE UK HOUSING STOCK (W/M²C) [**6**] + 2002 UPDATE

Date of Construction	Roofs	U-value	External Walls	Typical U-value
Pre-1919	Pitched roof (unfelted)	2.5	Solid brick wall	2.1
1919 – 1939	Pitched roof (unfelted)	2.5	Solid brick wall	2.1
1939 – 1965	Pitched roof (with felt)	2.0	Brick-to-brick cavity wall (unfilled)	1.7
1965 – 1975	Maximum established by 1965 Building Regs	1.0	Maximum established by 1965 Building Regs	1.5
1975 – 1982	Maximum established by 1975 amendment to Building Regs	0.6	Maximum established by 1975 amendment to Building Regs	1.0
1982 – 1985	Maximum established by 1982 amendment to Building Regs	0.4	Maximum established by 1982 amendment to Building Regs	0.6
1985 – 1990	Maximum established by 1985 Building Regs	0.35	Maximum established by 1985 Building Regs	0.6
1990 – 2002	Maximum established by 1990 Building Regs	0.25	Maximum established by 1990 Building Regs (includes ground floors and floors exposed to external air)	0.45/0.6 if d/glazed
2002 –	Maximum established by 2002 Building Regs (elemental) Insulation between joists Insulation between rafters Flat roof construction	 0.16 0.20 0.25	Maximum established by 2002 Building Regs (elemental) (includes basement walls)	0.35
Revisions to the Building Regulations came into force in 2002. Requirements of Part L1 in England and Wales, Part J in Scotland and Part F In Northern Ireland serve to conserve fuel. [1]				

Table 11.3 COMPARISON BETWEEN U-VALUES IN THE 2002 REGULATIONS AND THOSE REQUIRED UNDER THE 1990 AND 1985 BUILDING REGULATIONS

Maximum U-Values (W/m²K) – Dwellings	1985	1990	2002
Roofs	0.35	0.25	0.2 (between rafters) / 0.16 (between joists)
Exposed walls	0.6	0.45/0.6	0.35
Ground floors	None	0.45	0.25
Floors exposed to external air	0.6	0.45	0.25
Semi-exposed walls, roofs and floors	Not categorised	0.6	N/A
In 1990, the higher U-value for walls applied if double glazing was installed. In 2002 Regulations, semi exposed walls are no longer recognised (this is because the U-value calculation now takes account of the effect of the shelter provided by the structure that provides the shelter).			

There are three alternative ways of demonstrating compliance with the Building Regulations for new dwellings: [7]

Method 1 – Elemental

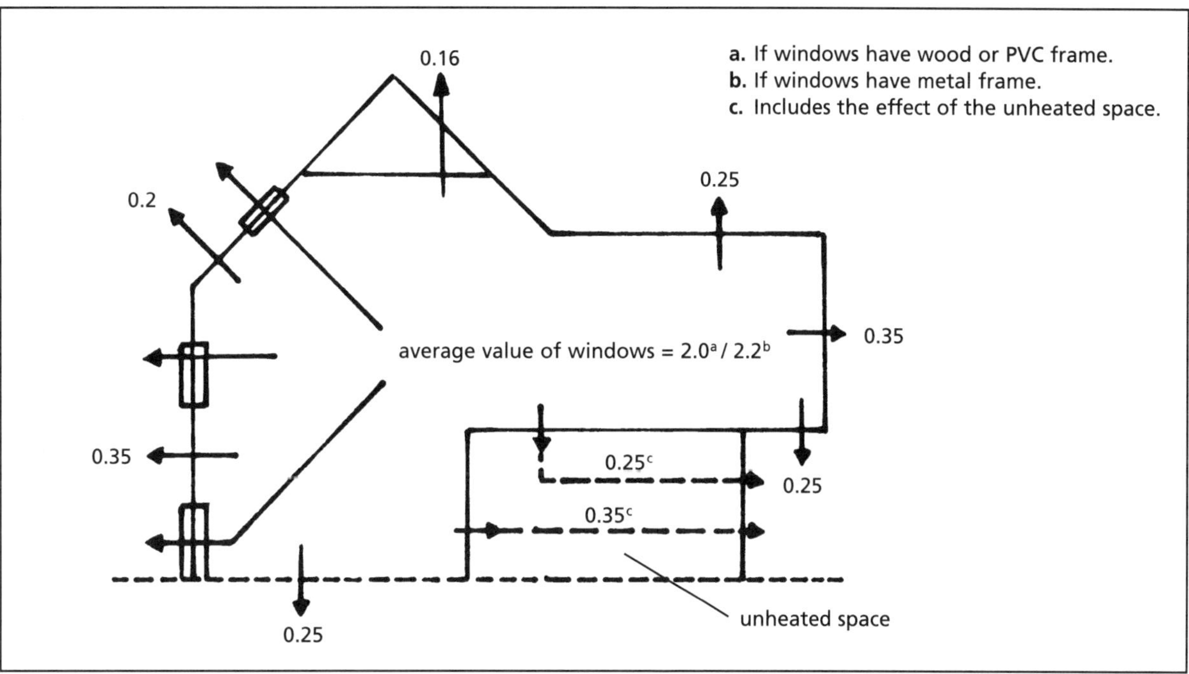

Summary of Elemental Method for compliance with the Building Regulations 2000

From April 2002 in England and Wales, this method can only be used if the heating is by gas or oil boiler, heat pump or community heating with CHP, biogas or biomass fuel (i.e. not for electric heating).

This is a requirement for the U-value of each element of the building not to exceed a prescribed maximum. The elements are walls, roofs, floors and windows, doors and rooflights. There is also a limit on the area of windows, doors and rooflights allowed and minimum efficiencies for gas and oil boilers. The requirements are summarised above.

In the case of windows, doors and rooflights, an area weighted U-value can be used. The higher U-value for metal framed windows allows for the additional solar gain due to the greater glazed proportion.

Method 2 – Target U-Value

This method can be used for any type of heating. This is equivalent to a method of averaging out the U-values of the major building elements. The whole house target U-value must not exceed a prescribed maximum. To avoid excessively poor performance in any one element, U-values for roof elements must be no poorer than 0.35 and U-values for wall or floor elements must be no poorer than 0.7. The target U-value is calculated from a formula that includes an adjustment to allow for the efficiency of the heating system i.e. more relaxed if the heating system is above minimum efficiency levels, and if applicable, a factor to make it more demanding for a heating system or fuel with high carbon emissions. (In Scotland, however, there is no relaxation for better heating efficiency.) There is also a means of addressing and obtaining credit for passive solar gains. This method is more flexible than the elemental method since it allows more insulation in one place to be traded off against less insulation elsewhere (or greater opening area, or less efficient heating).

Method 3 – Carbon Index

The dwelling can pass the requirement simply by meeting the prescribed minimum Carbon Index of 8.0 (see Section13) provided U-values for roof elements are no poorer than 0.35 and U-values for wall or floor elements are no poorer than 0.7.

In all methods of compliance with the Building Regulations further requirements also need to be satisfied:

- limiting thermal bridging at junctions and around openings
- limiting air leakage
- commissioning of heating and hot water systems (ensuring systems are in working order)
- provision of operating and maintenance instructions for heating and hot water systems
- insulation of space and water heating pipes and warm air heating ducts
- reasonable provision of lighting outlets for efficient lighting.

Contact details for organisations listed here are in Appendix 1.

REFERENCES

1 *Building Regulations 2002 Approved Document L1 (England and Wales). Conservation of Fuel and Power.* The Stationery Office.

2 CIBSE Guide Section A3. *Environmental Design: thermal properties of building structures,* Chartered Institution of Building Services, Engineers. London 1999. For thermal conductivity values of common building materials. (For specific insulation products contact the manufacturers.)

3 BS EN 12524: 2000 *Building materials and products. Hygrothermal properties* – Tabulated design values.

4 *Energy efficient ventilation in housing. A guide for specifiers on the requirements and options for ventilation.* GPG 268. Energy Efficiency Best Practice in Housing. 1999.

5 *Airtightness in UK dwellings.* Roger Stephen BSc. BRE Information Paper IP1/00 January 2000.

6 *Public sector investment in energy conservation versus investment in Sizewell 'B',* Moorcroft and Hodgkinson, Proof of Evidence GLC/P/3 (revised) to the Sizewell 'B' Power Station Public Inquiry, undated.

7 Description of Building Regulation requirements adapted from *NHER (National Home Energy Rating) Plan Assessor Training Manual, Version 3.7, Issue 1, Revision A,* July 2002.

12

HOME INSULATION

Standards of insulation in new housing are considerably higher than they were in older housing. However, properties built before current standards make up by far the largest proportion of the UK housing stock. In order to improve energy efficiency, reduce heating and hot water costs, and to reduce CO_2 emissions, the fitting of insulation into existing housing is essential.

This section aims to provide an understanding of the insulation methods and materials used in different parts of buildings, and their appropriateness to house types. It does not cover the building of new dwellings. In terms of prioritising measures, a brief indication of the costs and payback times is provided. There are grants and discounts available for some of the more effective insulation measures. See Section 7 for details.

This is not an installation guide and should not be treated as such. Good Practice Guidance is referred to at the end of this section and industry guidelines should also be followed.

This section includes:

- hot water cylinder insulation
- roof insulation, including insulating a room in the roof
- wall insulation, both cavity and solid wall
- draughtproofing
- floor insulation
- double and secondary glazing.

12.1 WHY INSULATE?

All heat which is produced in a dwelling will eventually escape to the outside if the outside temperature is colder. (See Section 11.) Insulation slows down the rate at which the heat escapes. Since this means that the heat will stay in the dwelling longer, it should be possible to turn the heating off, either manually or automatically, when it would otherwise have been needed. This is why heating bills are usually reduced after insulation is installed.

However, heating bills are not always reduced as households who have been cold at home are known to take some or all of the benefit of their new insulation as extra warmth. This is often called the 'comfort factor'.

A lack of adequate insulation can also have other side effects:

- cold walls and window areas tend to make the whole room feel colder
- warm air inside a room cools quickly when it hits cold walls or windows, creating uncomfortable 'downdraughts'
- as warm air cools on cold surfaces, it can lead to condensation problems and mould growth.

As well as cutting down on the overall heat loss, insulation will counteract these 'cold surface' problems, by helping raise the temperature of internal surfaces, thus making the living spaces more comfortable and reducing the risk of condensation.

12.2 WHICH MEASURES ?

The type of insulation measures which can be fitted into any particular property are likely to be determined by:

- The technical feasibility of the measure – for example not all houses are suitable for cavity wall insulation.
- The cost effectiveness of the measure – some measures pay for themselves in savings in energy costs very quickly. Others have very long 'payback' periods.
- Whether or not refurbishment work is being undertaken. Some measures are only feasible if they are incorporated into other work.
- The availability of grant aid or subsidy for the measure. This will encourage householders who may not otherwise have been able to afford, or not considered, the measure before.
- The requirements of the Building Regulations.

For a useful guide to the opportunities for measures in different house types, and cost effectiveness see Good Practice Guide 171 – The Domestic Energy Efficiency Primer [**1**]. For detailed guidance on energy and CO_2 saving attributable to measures, it is useful to refer to the Technical Guidance manual used for calculating the savings for the Energy Efficiency Commitment Programme (EEC)[**2**].

Table 12.1 illustrates the various types of insulation to be described, their average costs, and how long each measure should take to pay for itself through savings in fuel (this is referred to in the table, and further on in the text, as the 'payback' period).

12.3 HOT WATER CYLINDER INSULATION

Insulating the hot water cylinder is important because it is cheap, simple and will save energy quickly. It is particularly cost effective if the hot water is heated by electricity.

If a cylinder is completely unlagged, or has one of the older insulation jackets with a thickness of less than 80mm, then a modern jacket should be fitted. These 'segmented' jackets come in various lengths and widths to cover most sizes of cylinder, but should comply with the current British Standard Specification BS5615 [**5**]. The jacket should be tied to the top and strapped round the sides of the cylinder, making sure that the segments fit closely together.

New hot water cylinders are ready-insulated with factory-applied foam insulation. This will keep the heat in more efficiently than a cylinder insulated with a jacket, and it will also be less bulky, so the tank will fit in a smaller space.

The Building Regulations

The Building Regulations vary between England and Wales, Scotland and Northern Ireland. But there are now for the first time in England and Wales regulations for the insulation levels of not only new buildings and extensions but also for the insulation levels of roofs, walls and floors when home alterations are made, and for replacement windows in all homes. See reference [**4**] for details.

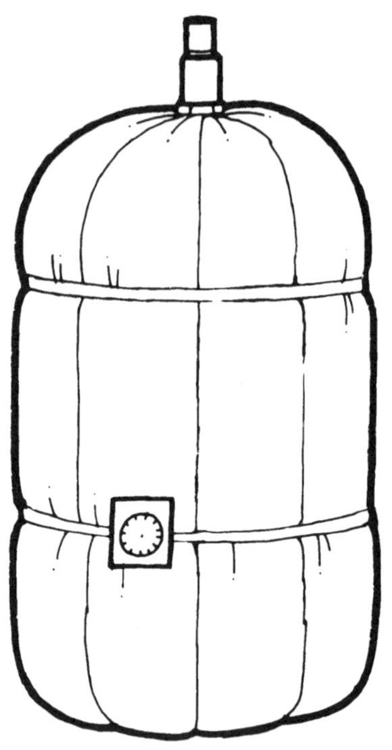

Hot water cylinder with fitted jacket

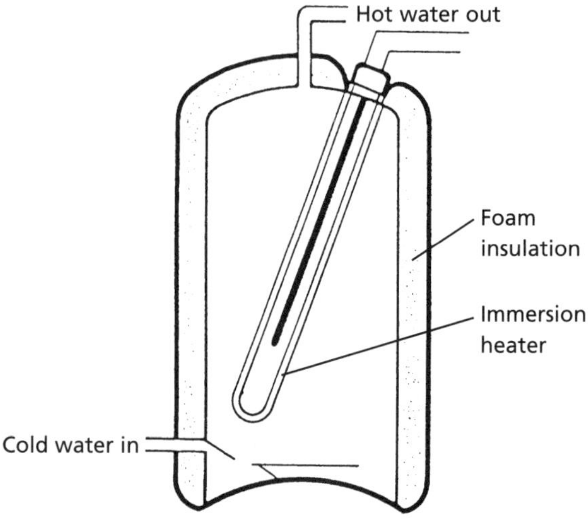

Hot water cylinder with foam insulation

Square hot water tanks, though rare, are still occasionally found. They are the wrong shape for ordinary cylinder jackets and should instead be insulated by attaching rigid polystyrene blocks around the sides and taping the edges to prevent damage.

Table 12.1 ENERGY SAVINGS ACHIEVED – TYPICAL COSTS AND PAYBACK PERIODS
(These figures are for a semi detached house with gas heating and standard occupancy. The costs and savings will vary according to the size of the house, its location, the measures, fuel and heating system used.)

Measure	Average U-Value reduction (W/m²K)	Typical Cost	Typical Savings (annual)	Typical Payback Period
Hot water insulation package (cylinder and pipes)		From £20	£10 – £20	1– 2 years
Draughtproofing windows and external doors	(reduces ventilation)	From £40 (DIY) £85 – £110 (Installer)	£10 – £15	3 – 4 years 6 – 11 years
Fill gaps between skirting and floor boards	(reduces ventilation)	Around £25 (DIY)	£5 – £10	3 – 5 years
Loft Insulation Adding 200 mm to existing 50 mm of loft insulation		From £140 (DIY) £200 – £230 (Installer)	£20 – £30	5 – 7 years 7 – 12 years
250 mm loft insulation where none at present	1.9 – 0.016	From £170 (DIY) £220 – £250 (Installer)	£80 – £100	Around 2 years 2 – 3 years
Cavity wall insulation using: Mineral wool fibre Polystyrene/polyurethane beads or granules	1.5 – 0.55	£260 – £380 (Installer)	£70 – £100	3 – 5 years

Some of the insulation techniques listed below involve extensive work and considerable cost. They would generally only be carried out either to remedy severe heating problems or where other repair work is necessary. In the latter case, it is always worthwhile to install the appropriate insulation measure at the same time. The table below gives either the total cost or the extra cost of installing insulation when repair or replacement work is being carried out.

Measure	Average U-Value reduction (W/m²K)	Typical Cost	Typical Savings (annual)	Typical Payback Period
Solid Wall Insulation Adding 50 mm external insulation to a solid wall	2.1 – 0.55	From £1500 (if walls are being repaired anyway)	£140 – £170	9 – 11 years
Insulating wall internally using 50 mm plasterboard laminates, or using batten method and 60 mm mineral fibre quilt	2.1 – 0.64	From £900	£140 – £170	5 – 6 years
Floor Insulation Insulate timber ground floor with 60 mm mineral fibre quilt or 50 mm polystyrene board	0.85 – 0.4	From £100 (DIY)	£15 – £25	4 – 7 years
Double Glazing Install sealed unit double glazing with low emissivity glass	(wood frame) 4.3 – 2.0 (metal frame) 5.6 – 2.2	varies*	£30 – £40	20+ years (new windows)

* (Costs and payback times depend on type of windows)

Source: Cost Benefit Tables GPG 171 CE 2003 [**1**] with additional material from EEAC consumer literature – 'It's Criminal to Waste Energy!' 2003 [**3**].

For costs and savings for specific house types, one of the software packages for energy auditing will provide more accurate results. See Section 13.

12.4 ROOF INSULATION

Types of roof insulation are split into three categories:

- **Loft insulation** – where the insulation is fitted above the ceiling in the loft space. The loft area is one of the easiest and cheapest parts of the structure to insulate. Loft insulation is the most common type of roof insulation, and is included in most insulation grant schemes.
- **'Room in the roof' insulation** – where the loft space has been converted to a room so the insulation is fitted to the sloping ceiling.
- **Flat roof insulation** – insulation fitted onto an existing flat roof.

LOFT INSULATION

Many householders will know that they have some loft insulation, but they may be unaware of the current recommended standards. For example, there may only be 2″ or 50 mm of insulation in their loft so a 'top up' should be installed. In order to achieve the current recommended standards, insulating a loft involves placing an insulating material between the ceiling joists, and also over the joists to achieve a depth of 250 mm of insulation.

The most commonly used material is mineral fibre quilt which can be installed either on a DIY basis or by a contractor. The material is sold in rolls of various lengths, widths and thicknesses and is laid between and over the ceiling joists.

Loose fill materials such as granules of cellulose fibre or blown in mineral fibre can also be used. A contractor would blow it into place mechanically. This is useful if movement in the loft is restricted or if the loft is of irregular design or has awkward corners or obstructions. With some types of loose fill materials, a greater depth of material is needed to provide the same level of insulation as a roll of mineral fibre quilt. The depth of material necessary to give the required U-value should be stated on the container.

All materials used for loft insulation should comply with BS 5803, Parts 1, 2, 3, or 5. See reference [**6**] for details. Loft insulation is possible as a DIY job but as the materials can be an irritant, householders should use face masks, gloves and goggles to undertake the work. See reference [**7**] for further information.

Tank and pipe insulation in the loft

One result of laying insulation in the loft is that the roof space itself will then be colder, so that any tanks and pipes in the loft will be more liable to freeze over in cold weather. For this reason they too must be insulated.

The material used for insulating cold water tanks in the loft usually consists of mineral fibre covered with polythene, and is cut to size and strapped around the tank. No loft insulation should be laid under a cold water tank to allow the heat from the room to reach the tank, but if the tank is raised 300mm or more above the ceiling, then the whole tank should be insulated.

Pipes in the roof space should be insulated, hot water pipes so that heat loss is reduced, and cold water pipes so that they are protected from freezing. The material used is polyethylene foam or synthetic rubber moulded sheaths which clip around the pipes and should be carefully joined and taped to fully cover the pipes.

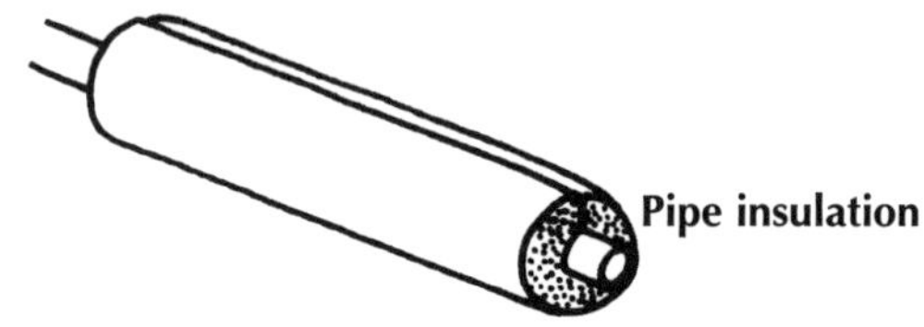

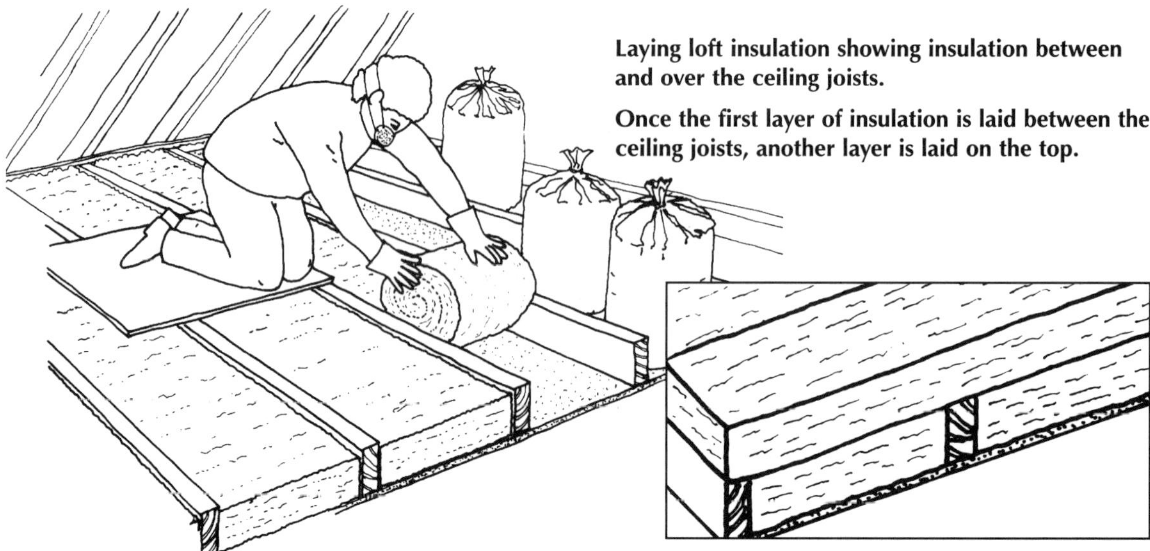

Laying loft insulation showing insulation between and over the ceiling joists.

Once the first layer of insulation is laid between the ceiling joists, another layer is laid on the top.

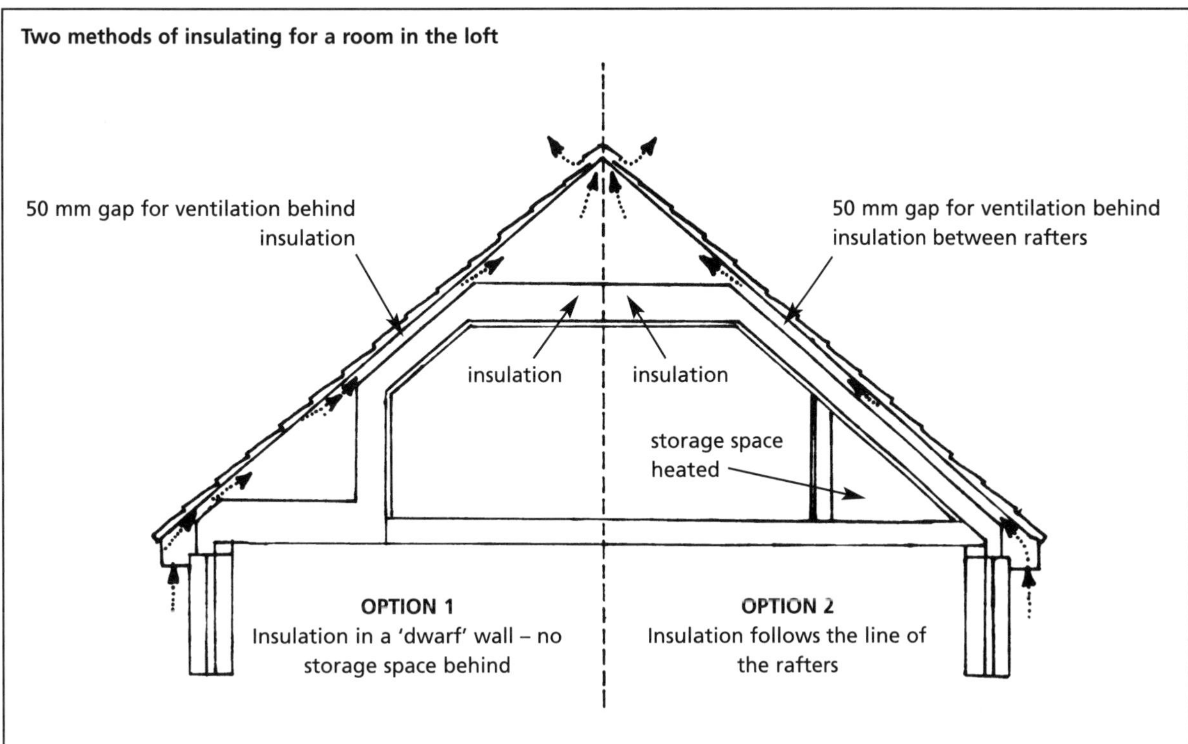

Options for insulating a roof when there is a room in the loft

'ROOM IN THE ROOF' INSULATION

If there is a room in the loft, the room can be insulated. The target U-values should be the same as insulating a loft, but it can be more difficult to achieve, particularly on the sloping surfaces. The insulation can be a combination of mineral fibre batts on the vertical stud or 'dwarf' walls and quilt on the horizontal areas. The sloping ceiling may be fitted with mineral wool between the rafters and then covered in insulated plasterboard. It could alternatively be covered in thicker insulated plasterboard to give the same U-value. Whichever method is used, it is essential that a 50 mm air space is maintained behind the insulation to the sloping ceiling to allow for air movement or the roof timbers may rot. See reference [**1**].

Ventilation in the loft

When a loft is insulated the roofspace becomes colder. Therefore the loft area must be well ventilated, to avoid condensation forming which could rot the roof timbers. When installing insulation, it is essential that gaps are left at the eaves to allow the free flow of air into and out of the loft.

In older buildings no provision was originally made to ventilate lofts, and some roofs have been re-tiled and left no provision for ventilation. Ventilation tiles are available but installation guidance must be followed. See BS 5803 [**6**].

Ill fitting loft hatches and gaps and holes in the ceiling allow extra moisture up into the loft, so these should be sealed to avoid condensation. This is especially important above the bathroom and kitchen where a lot of moist air is produced.

FLAT ROOF INSULATION

Flat roofs are often found on new extensions to older properties, single storey flats, or on blocks of flats. Insulating this kind of roof is more complicated and expensive than insulating pitched or butterfly roofs which have lofts.

The best place for insulation is on top of a flat roof, as this helps keep the structure of the roof warm and lessens the risk of condensation within the roof itself. Flat roof coverings only have a life of about 20 years, so when re-roofing it is often best to replace the outer waterproof surface, adding insulation at the same time. If the roof is in good condition, or has recently had a new finish, then the insulation can be placed on top of the waterproof layer as long as it is held firmly in place.

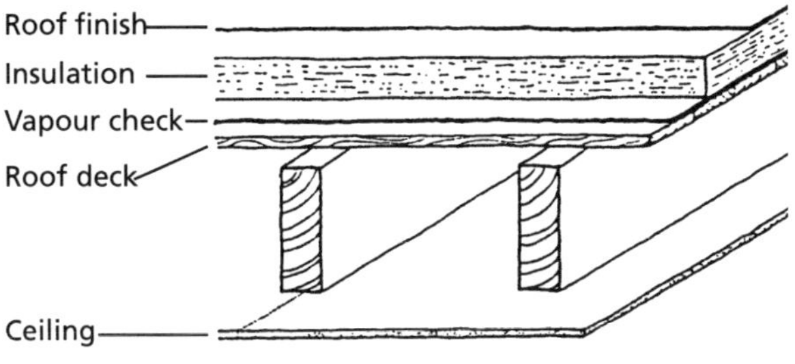

Flat roof insulation 'warm roof'

12.5 WALL INSULATION

RECOGNISING WALL TYPES

There are two main types of wall construction to be found in houses in the UK – cavity walls and solid walls. Most homes built since 1930 will have some type of cavity wall; this means that the wall itself actually consists of two layers of brick or brick and block, with a gap in between. The two walls are connected by 'wall ties' which hold the outer and inner faces together. Most homes built before 1930 have solid walls. These can be made of brick or stone blocks.

Recognising what kind of wall a house has is not always easy. Building construction in the country did not begin to be standardised until the 1940s, so older houses display a variety of different types of construction. However, in brick-built houses, if the bricks in the wall have all been laid side-on, and the wall is about 300 mm (12") thick, the house probably has a cavity wall. If there is a systematic arrangement of side-on and end-on bricks, and the wall is about 225 mm (9") wide this will usually indicate a solid wall. Solid stone walls are usually wider than solid brick walls.

Cavity wall brickwork

Solid wall brickwork

CAVITY WALL INSULATION

In an average semi detached house with unfilled cavities, approximately 35% of the heat loss is lost through the walls.

Cavity wall insulation makes an important contribution to energy efficiency. After loft insulation it is the most cost effective single insulation measure [**8**]. It is therefore a major component of most energy efficiency grant and discount schemes.

Insulating a cavity wall involves filling the cavity between the inner and the outer walls with an insulating material. A series of holes is drilled in the mortar on the outer skin of the wall and the insulation material is pumped or blown into the cavity.

The installer should check that no air vents, ducts, flues etc. have been blocked by the insulation material. When the cavity is full, the holes are filled with mortar matching in colour as closely as possible to the original. The work usually takes a few hours and, because insulation is installed from outside, should not cause disruption or mess inside the dwelling.

The materials used for cavity wall insulation are:

- **Mineral wool** – this includes glass wool (or fibreglass), and rock wool. It is blown into the cavity using compressed air. It is probably the most popular material.
- **Beads and granules** – these include expanded polystyrene beads or granules, or polyurethane granules. Beads flow easily, and have been known to flow out of the wall through any gaps if not sealed, so they are sometimes installed with an adhesive. Granules have a rougher surface so are not likely to flow so much.
- **Urea Formaldehyde (UF) foam** – pumped in as chemicals which create a foam in the cavity. The foam then hardens and dries. Formaldehyde vapour, produced as the foam hardens, can cause irritation of the eyes, nose and throat in some people, although ventilation of the dwelling should get rid of any vapour. UF foam is normally only permitted for walls that have relatively sheltered exposure unless they have external cladding [**8**].
- **Polyurethane foam** may also be used. It is more expensive than other methods, but has slightly better insulation properties.

Installation of cavity wall insulation

Cavity wall insulation is a specialist job and can only be carried out by a contractor registered by the British Board of Agrement (BBA). The insulation materials themselves and their installation are also subject to BBA certification and British Standards. See reference [**8**]. The contractor is normally responsible for deciding whether the walls are suitable for cavity fill, and is also responsible for making sure that the work is completed properly.

Are all cavity walls suitable for cavity fill?

Although most dwellings with cavity walls are suitable for cavity wall insulation, some are not, or the choice of insulating material is affected. Here are some of the reasons:

- **The width of the cavity** – The cavity must be at least 50mm wide to be considered for filling.
- **Blocked cavities** – If the cavity has mortar or other materials blocking it, the blockages should be cleared before the cavity is filled.
- **Building defects** – The external wall must be in good condition, and any necessary repairs carried out before the cavity can be filled.
- **Exposure** – The height of a building and its exposure to wind driven rain will determine which material can be used for cavity wall insulation.

SOLID WALL INSULATION

Solid walls lose heat more quickly than cavity walls, but because they are solid there is no easy way to insulate them. Both the insulation methods detailed here involve disruption to the existing building, and can involve considerable cost.

There are two main ways of insulating solid walls:

- Internally, by adding an insulated lining to the inside of an external wall.
- Externally, by adding insulation to the outer surface of the wall and then covering it with some form of protective layer, or render.

Internal wall insulation

This method, often referred to as 'dry lining', involves insulating the inside of the wall by one of two methods, each using different materials:

Insulation/plasterboard laminates With this method, ready-made insulation boards are fixed directly to the wall. The boards usually consist of plasterboard backed with up to 50 mm of insulation material, and include a built-in vapour barrier to reduce any risk of condensation. The thicker the board the better the insulation. Plasterboard tape is used to fill the groove where the boards meet, before replacing mouldings and electrical fittings.

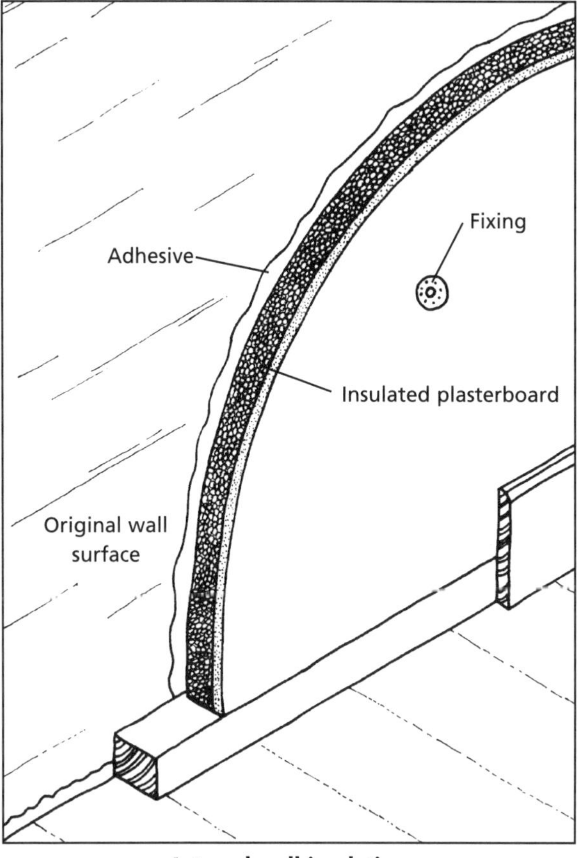

Internal wall insulation

Timber battens filled with insulation Here a framework of wooden battens is attached to the wall, and the spaces between the battens infilled with some form of insulation – for example mineral fibre quilt – and then covered over with a plasterboard finish. A polythene sheet stapled to the battens behind the plasterboard will provide a vapour barrier, although extra care must be taken to seal round any breaks in the vapour barrier where fittings and wiring pass through.

Important points – internal wall insulation:

- Internal insulation means a substantial degree of disruption to the household, as it involves the removal and re-siting of all the internal fittings, such as door and window mouldings, skirting boards and electrical fittings.
- Because of the extra layer of insulation, the size of the insulated room will be slightly reduced.
- If the vapour barrier within the wall is broken in any way, there may also be a risk of 'interstitial' condensation occurring behind the new wall as warm moist air from the room hits the original wall, which will now be colder. This is a form of condensation which can occur within the fabric of a building, and it is particularly difficult to deal with as it cannot be seen, and, if left unchecked, can damage building materials.
- The new wall surface will not be as robust as the original wall, and so may not be strong enough to support shelving and other fittings.

External wall insulation

To insulate a solid wall from the outside, an insulation material is fixed to the external surface of the wall by mechanical means, and then given a protective, water-repellent finish such as tiles or render. The insulation itself can consist of mineral fibre batts, or rigid insulation boards, with an insulation thickness of 12 mm upwards. This is the most expensive form of wall insulation, and is usually only carried out where there are severe heating problems or if the exterior of the building requires some other form of repair work which provides the opportunity of adding insulation. It is carried out by a contractor.

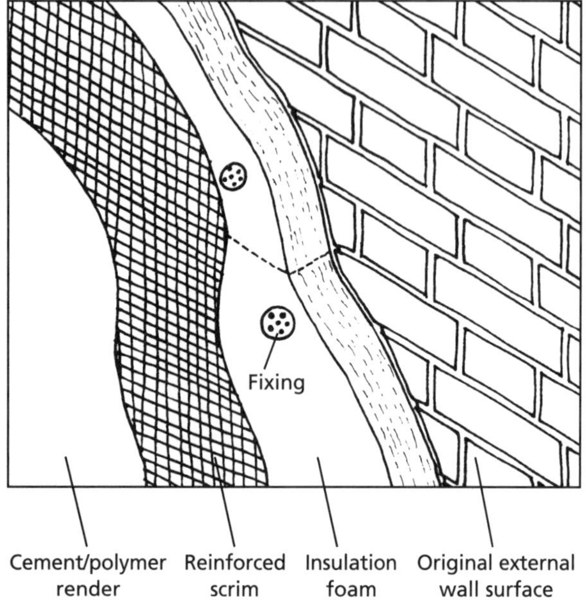

External wall insulation

Important points – external wall insulation:

- Because external insulation will mean the outer fabric of the building will be warmer, any problems of 'cold bridging' will be reduced.
- The new outer 'skin' of the building will reduce the risk of water penetration.
- Any surface condensation within the house will be reduced.
- Because of the new outer finish, the appearance of the house will be affected, so in certain areas planning permission may be needed.

See reference [**9**] for further information on solid wall insulation.

REFLECTIVE RADIATOR PANELS

Reflective radiator panels are fitted behind radiators, most commonly on an outside wall. They are a light-weight panel which can be fitted behind existing radiators designed in a louvred fashion, and have a reflective surface, usually silver. The panels reduce the heat loss through the wall by reflecting the heat and pushing it back into the room. Energy savings from reflective radiator panels are recognised as an energy saving measure by the Energy Efficiency Commitment scheme. Energy savings are worked out on a panel basis, and for the types mentioned here the savings are 134 kWh/m^2 (for homes heated by gas, LPG and oil). For example, a panel with a surface area of 0.3 square metres would achieve an energy saving of 134 kWh x 0.3 = 40.2 kWh [**2**].

Some grant schemes include reflective radiator panels fitted to solid walls as one of their measures.

12.6 DRAUGHTPROOFING

Figures for the amount of heat loss that can be accounted for as a result of draughts in a building can range from 15% to as much as 50% depending on the structure and exposure of the building [**10**].

Before draughtproofing, check that there is adequate ventilation for any fuel burning appliances in the home, and to ensure condensation problems do not arise. (See Section 17.)

There is an assortment of draughtproofing materials available from high street shops or DIY stores, although some of the better quality materials may not generally be available through retail outlets. Durable materials should be used in preference to cheap flimsy materials. The British Standard BS 7386 sets down standards for materials used for draughtproofing [**11**].

Compression seals

With these, the door or window is pushed firmly against the draughtstrip when closed, forming a seal. The material which is compressed is usually fixed to a metal or plastic carrier, and can consist of, for example, a rubber or plastic blade, a silicon covered foam strip or a rubber tube.

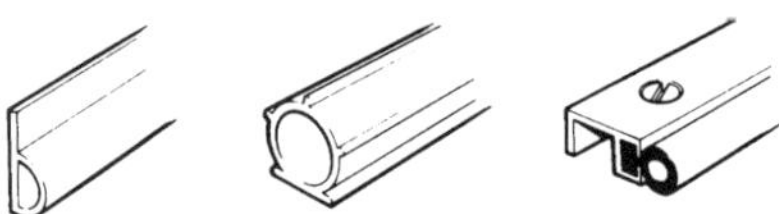

Draughtproofing – compression seals

Low friction or wiper seals

With draughtstrips of this type, the strip rubs against the closing edge of the window or door, pinching it to form a seal as it does so. A typical example of a friction seal is a fine brush pile which is fixed into a metal or plastic carrier.

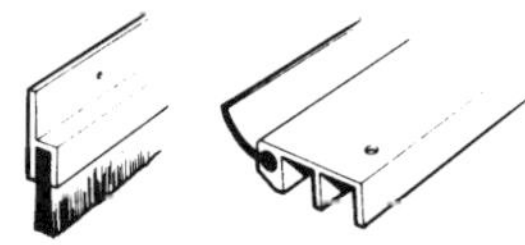

Draughtproofing – low friction seals

Gap filling seals

'Gap filling' involves filling any spaces in the structure of the house (for example the space between a window frame and the wall) with a product which will take up the exact shape of the gap, including any distortion. Silicone sealants are often used for this purpose indoors, and are applied from a 'gun'.

Gap filling sealant

Draughtproofing a sash window

Sash windows tend to be very draughty, and older types are often ill-fitting. Best results can be achieved by fitting 'wiper' seals along the edges where the window and the frame meet. The brush-type seal or the silicon covered foam seal are suitable, as they allow the sash to slide easily up and down without catching. The meeting rail is also draughtproofed using a special draughtstrip on an angled carrier.

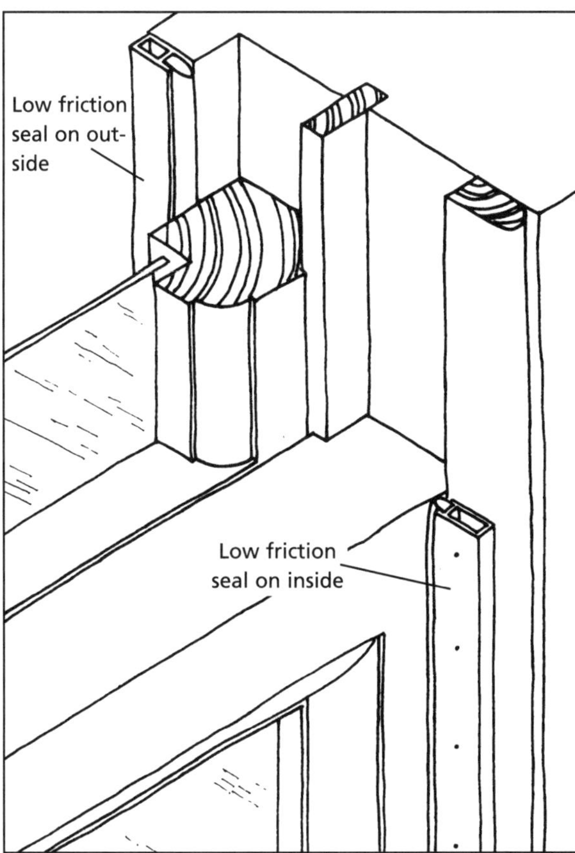

Draughtproofing a sash window

Wooden hinged windows

For this type of window a 'compression' seal should be used. The seal should fit the size of the gap between the window and frame and be fitted on the inside of the frame to protect it from the effects of bad weather. If the gap between the window and the frame varies, then self adhesive silicone rubber tubing or a wiper seal can give better results, and should also be able to accommodate changes in gap size which might occur during bad weather.

Draughtproofing doors

For doors it is important to choose draughtstrips which can accommodate changes in gap size between the door and the frame. Doors are constantly being opened and closed, so strong, long lasting materials should always be used.

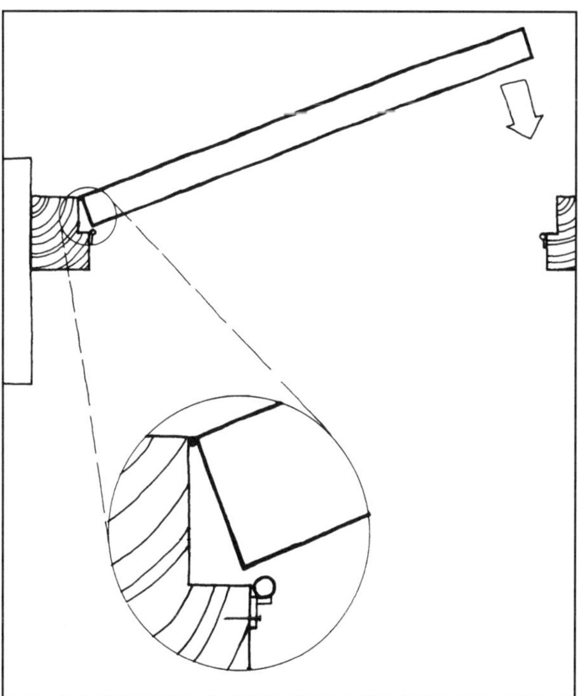

Draughtproofing a door

A variety of types of compression seal may be fitted along the doorframe from the outside, so that when the door is closed a firm seal is formed. A threshold excluder should be attached to the bottom of the door. Bottom-of-the-door excluders are made of very robust materials and come in various lengths and widths to fit even very large gaps.

Letterbox covers and keyhole covers are also available for further protection from draughts.

Draughtproofing a suspended timber floor

In timber floors, gaps between floorboards, below skirting boards and around cables or pipes cause unnecessary draughts. These should be filled using mastic, sealants or (along skirting boards) rounded lengths of timber beading.

Laying flooring grade hardboard over the whole floor is another way to eliminate draughts between boards in a timber floor.

12.7 FLOOR INSULATION

Heat loss through floors is relatively slow compared to the other areas of an average house. Heat loss is greatest at the edges of floors so the floor of an end of terrace house will lose heat more quickly than the floor of a mid terraced house. Opportunities for reducing heat loss through the floor will depend on what the floor is made of.

There are two main types of floor construction to be found:

- suspended timber floors
- solid floors, usually made of concrete.

It should be noted that not all floors with a timber finish are suspended. They may be timber or laminated floors fixed to a solid floor.

SUSPENDED TIMBER FLOORS

Suspended timber floors can be found in both ground and upper floors of houses and can be insulated from above or from below (e.g. in the case of a ground floor, from the cellar).

Because of the time and effort involved, this type of insulation is rarely installed from above unless the floor requires some other form of attention which involves raising the floorboards. Once the floorboards are raised, a netting or mesh is draped over the joists and firmly stapled into place, and the insulation roll placed within it.

Access to underfloor areas from a cellar would make the installation of the insulation easier. If insulating from below, rigid insulation boards can be bought to size and fitted between the joists and held in place with battens.

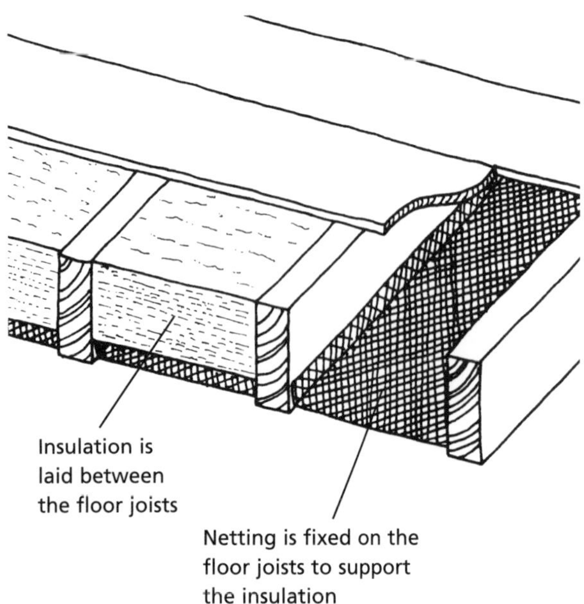

Floor insulation – suspended timber floor

Important points – insulating floors:

- When insulating a ground floor, it is essential to ensure there will be adequate cross-ventilation beneath the floorboards in the subfloor void, to avoid any risk of condensation.
- Central heating and water pipes should always run above the insulation, and should themselves be insulated; if left bare the extra heat in the confined area could warp the floorboards above.

SOLID FLOORS

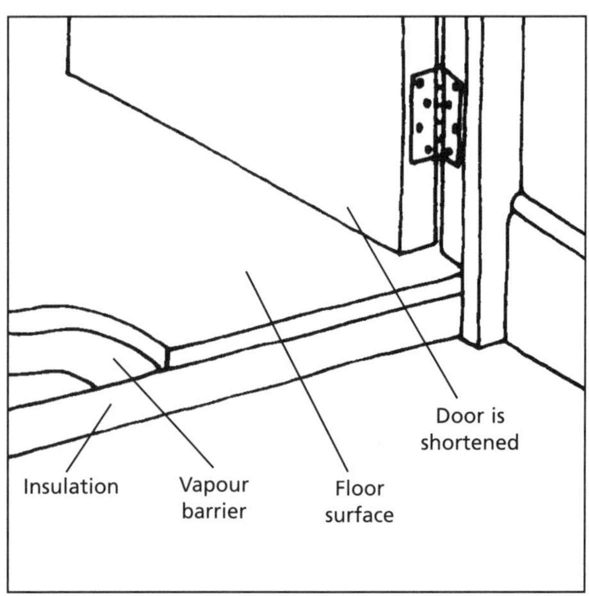

Solid floor insulation

In traditional housing, solid floors are usually only found in ground floors, with upper floors being made of timber. Modern multi-storey blocks. however. often consist of solid floors on all storeys. So there are a number of cases where an upper solid floor might require to be insulated – for example:

- if there is an empty unheated space below
- if the underside of an upper floor is exposed to the outside or to very cold air – for example a walkway or a built-in garage (see Section 11)
- where there is a serious problem of cold bridging (see Section 11) from balconies or from other external parts of the building.

The opportunities for insulating a solid floor are limited, but the most common method is to lay a new insulated floor on the original solid floor. This is made up of a layer of rigid insulation, usually polystyrene, overlaid with hardboard or chipboard to provide a smooth surface. The fitting of the insulation will, in most cases, cause the floor level to rise so the skirting boards, doors, thresholds etc. will need to be raised. This may cause other problems which may outweigh the value of the insulation.

See ref [**12**] for further information on floor insulation.

12.8 DOUBLE GLAZING

'DOUBLE GLAZING' AND 'SECONDARY GLAZING' – WHAT THEY MEAN

Double glazing systems tend to fall into two main categories:

- ready made double glazed window units for new or replacement windows
- 'secondary' glazing systems involve the addition of a second pane to an existing window.

Single glazed windows lose heat very quickly as they have high U-values. The addition of a second pane of glass will reduce the heat loss because the air between is, in effect, 'trapped'. This trapped air slows down the rate at which the heat escapes outside, and at the same time increases the temperature of the internal pane. The gap may instead be filled with an inert gas – usually argon – which provides a higher level of insulation.

There is a wide selection of double glazing and secondary glazing systems to choose from, from professionally installed double glazing to DIY kits for secondary glazing.

DOUBLE OR TRIPLE GLAZING UNITS FOR REPLACEMENT WINDOWS

Double and triple glazed windows are manufactured and sealed in factory conditions and require careful handling and installation. The panes are fixed within the unit at a set distance apart. Frames are made of aluminium, wood or pvcu (rigid, weather-resistant plastic).

The Building Regulations in England, Wales and Scotland now require all replacement windows in any dwelling to comply with minimum standard U-values for windows doors and rooflights.

This means that no single glazed window will satisfy this standard, and most units will need at least a 16 mm gap between the panes. There is a variety of double and triple glazing units on the market. They vary in terms of:

- whether they are double or triple glazed
- the gap between the panes of glass (usually 6 mm, 12 mm or 16 mm)
- the gas in the unit – either air or an inert gas
- whether or not the glass is covered with a 'low emissivity' coating – a thin coating designed to reflect heat back into the room.

Reference [**4**] provides a table of types of windows indicating which of them comply with the Building Regulations.

Energy rating for windows

An energy rating scheme for windows has recently been developed by the British Fenestration Rating Council and European partners. It is known in the UK as the BFRC Rating. It is more complex than U-values and takes into account the heat loss and solar heat gain. The ratings are classified into bands A to G so that the system is more consumer friendly. It is anticipated that the BFRC will eventually replace U–values for specifying windows. For full details, and for details of best practice when fitting new windows see reference [**13**], which also looks at high performance windows and new glazing technologies.

SECONDARY GLAZING SYSTEMS

Although secondary glazing systems are unlikely to achieve the thermal standards described for sealed units, there will be situations where householders are likely to install secondary glazing, for example single glazing is in good condition, or where the window is a difficult shape or the building is governed by conservation rules which prohibit the installation of new windows.

Hinged or sliding systems can be fitted on the inside of the original window.

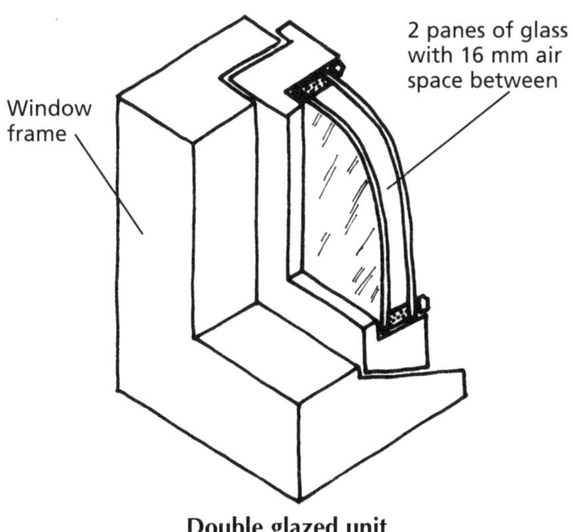

Double glazed unit

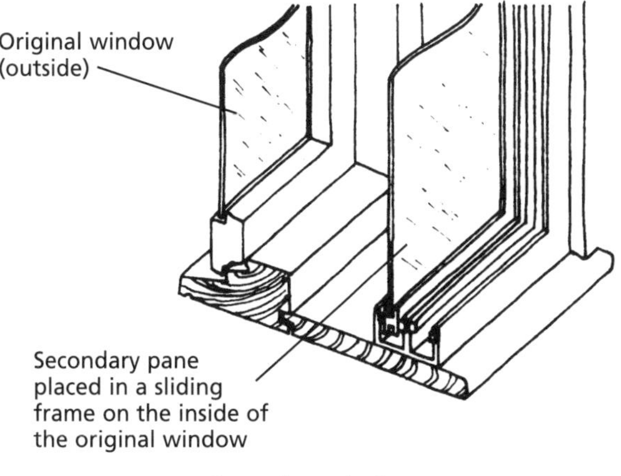

Secondary glazing

With these forms of secondary glazing, a second pane of glass is placed in a frame, and installed within the window recess itself, either on runners, so that the new pane can be pushed horizontally into place (sliding systems) or by hinges (hinged systems). Secondary panes like these can easily be opened for ventilation or cleaning, and also provide a good level of sound insulation, provided the space between the panes is at least 100 mm wide. Both hinged and sliding systems can be bought in kits and fitted by the householder, or made up to size and fitted by professional glazing firms.

Important points – secondary glazing

If secondary glazing is being applied to the windows of a room, ensure that at least one window in the room is either left uninsulated or can be easily opened to allow ventilation. This is particularly important if there are any fuel burning appliances in use.

Ensure that, in the case of an emergency, escape through a window can easily be achieved, even after the secondary glazing has been applied. Ensure also that everyone in the house knows how to remove, or break, the secondary glazing in such circumstances.

Contact details for organisations listed here are in Appendix 1.

REFERENCES

The Good Practice Guides (GPG) listed below are part of the 'Energy Efficiency Best Practice in Housing' (EEBPH) series and are available from **www.est.org.uk/bestpractice**

1 *Domestic Energy Efficiency Primer.* GPG 171. 2003.

2 Energy Efficiency Commitment 2002 – 2005. *Revised Technical Guidance Manual.* Issue 2 Ofgem. September 2002. **www.ofgem.gov.uk**

3 EST literature used by EEACs *It's Criminal to waste energy!* 2003.

4 *The effect of the Building Regulations (Part L 2002) on existing dwellings.* GIL 70. Housing Energy Efficiency Best Practice.

5 BS 5615. *'Specification for insulating jackets for domestic hot water storage cylinders'.*

6 BS 5803. Part 5 (1985). *Specification for the installation of man made mineral fibre and cellulose fibre insulation.* The Standard specifies the requirements when installing loft insulation into pitched roofed dwellings. (Part 1 covers mineral fibre quilt packed in rolls: Part 2 covers blown mineral fibre: Part 3 covers blown cellulose fibre.)

7 *Refurbishment site guidance for solid walled houses – roofs.* GPG 296. 2002.

8 *Cavity wall insulation in existing housing.* GPG 26. 2003.

9 *Refurbishment site guidance for solid walled houses – walls.* GPG 297. 2000.

10 *Energy efficient ventilation in housing. A guide to specifiers on the requirements and options for ventilation.* GPG 268. 1999.

11 BS 7386. 1997. *Specification for draughtstrips for the draught control of existing doors and windows in housing.*

12 *Refurbishment site guidance for solid walled houses – ground floors.* GPG 294. 2002.

13 *Windows for new and existing housing. A summary of Best Practice.* Energy Efficiency Best Practice in Housing. 2004.

FURTHER INFORMATION

British Fenestration Rating Council
www.bfrc.co.uk

Glass and Glazing Federation
www.ggf.org.uk

National Insulation Association
www.insulationassociation.org.uk

- Manufacturers' literature for a description of products.
- Case study reports from the Housing Energy Efficiency Best Practice Programme.
- For the benefits and savings of insulation methods in any particular dwelling type use energy auditing/energy rating software. (See Section 13.)

13

ENERGY RATING OF HOMES

Energy ratings provide a measure of energy efficiency of a dwelling. They are designed to provide a scale of energy efficiency which is easy to understand. They are used to:

- fulfil requirements of and demonstrate compliance with the Building Regulations [**1**]
- provide householders with a 'label' as an indication of how energy efficient their home is, and, at the most sophisticated level, to predict energy running costs of homes
- allow homes of different sizes to be compared with each other on an equal basis
- help landlords to assess the level of energy efficiency of their housing stock in order to prioritise improvements and set targets for higher energy ratings
- assess carbon dioxide emissions from homes and set targets for their reduction
- encourage the design of energy efficient homes
- provide the basis for the Energy Report in the proposed Home Information Pack (see 13.5).

13.1 WHAT IS AN ENERGY RATING?

An energy rating provides an indication of the energy efficiency of a dwelling. Data is collected about the dwelling and calculations are made about the annual energy running costs. The dwelling is provided with a 'label' or energy rating.

An energy rating has been described as being similar to the miles per gallon or 'mpg' of a car.

There are a number of energy labels which have developed since the early 1980s. They are all based on a model called BREDEM – The Building Research Establishment Domestic Energy Model. The most commonly used systems are:

- **The Standard Assessment Procedure (SAP).** This is the Government's recommended system for home energy ratings. The SAP calculation procedure is used for calculating both the SAP energy cost rating (SAP) and the Carbon Index (CI).
- **The National Home Energy Rating (NHER).** This is an energy rating scheme which provides the SAP rating and the Carbon Index as well as its own NHER rating.

13.2 SAP – THE STANDARD ASSESSMENT PROCEDURE

The Standard Assessment Procedure (SAP) was initially developed to compare different energy labels in the UK, and was published by the DOE (now DEFRA) and the BRE in 1993. All regulations, legislation and requirements involving the use of energy ratings use SAP.

SAP can be defined as follows:

SAP ENERGY COST RATING

'The SAP energy cost rating is based on energy costs for space and water heating under standard occupancy, heating pattern and location using UK three-year average fuel prices' [2].

The current SAP scale is rated from 1 to 120 – the higher the number the better the performance.

Official SAP logo
(SAP logo reproduced by permission of DEFRA)

The SAP calculations assume a standard occupancy and a standard heating pattern i.e. that a dwelling is heated in two periods for 9 hours in total on weekdays and 16 hours at weekends, that the living room is heated to 21°C and the rest of the dwelling to an average of 18°C.

SAP energy cost rating has gone through a range of amendments since it was introduced. In SAP 2001 the Carbon Index was introduced and the upper limit of the SAP rating raised from 100 to 120.

> As an indication of SAP ratings an average dwelling built to the 1990 Building Regulations would have a rating of approximately 60.

THE CARBON INDEX

The Carbon Index (CI) was introduced into the SAP calculation in 2001. It is a number between 0.0 and 10.0 based on the carbon dioxide (CO_2) emissions associated with space and water heating (under standard occupancy, standard heating pattern and at a standard location) [**2**]. The Carbon Index is expressed to the nearest single decimal place. The higher the number the better the performance.

Both the SAP rating and the CI are adjusted for floor area so that they are independent of dwelling size. They take into account a range of factors that contribute to energy efficiency:

- thermal insulation
- efficiency and control of the heating system
- ventilation characteristics of the dwelling
- solar gain characteristics of the dwelling
- fuel used for space and water heating.

SAP and CI calculations do not take into account the energy used by lighting, cooking and appliances or characteristics of the household occupying the dwelling, for example, household size and composition, the individual heating patterns and temperatures in the dwelling. Neither do the calculations take into account geographical location and hence climatic differences, so a given dwelling has the same rating in all parts of the UK.

THE BUILDING REGULATIONS

There are two ways in which SAP ratings are used in the Building Regulations:

- The Building Regulations [**1**] require SAP ratings to be notified to the local authority whenever a new dwelling is erected or formed by a conversion, although no minimum rating is required.
- The Carbon Index may be used to show compliance with Part L1 (England and Wales) and Part J (Scotland) if the Carbon Index method of compliance is used. The Approved Documents describe ways of demonstrating compliance with the energy efficiency requirements of the Building Regulations.

13.3 WHO PROVIDES SAP RATINGS?

SAP ratings can be calculated using a worksheet, accompanied by a series of tables, but they are far more commonly calculated by computer software which must be approved for SAP calculations by the Building Research Establishment (BRE).

A number of companies are authorised by the Government to issue a SAP rating and a CI on a certificate with an official SAP logo to indicate that the results are quality assured. These companies use computer software that has been approved by BRE as above and they also have in place quality assurance systems which ensure that the data being input is accurate e.g. staff training, monitoring systems etc. The authorised energy rating companies for SAP 2001 are listed at the end of this section [**3**]. See also The Federation of Authorised Energy Rating Organisations, FAERO.

SAP Certificate

26 Oakfield Street
Bristol BS22 1EJ

0012

Fred Smith

Surveyed: 11th Jun 2003

This MVM Home Energy Label confirms that the above dwelling has achieved the following SAP rating and STAR grading:

66

Good

Carbon Index: 4.7

Using the Government's Standard Assessment Procedure, this home is rated on the scale of 0 to 120 to be: 66

Issued by
Bill Brown
of
Greenville District Council

File: F:\s2mdata\demodata\support\example02.s4w

Issue Date: 30th July 2003

FS 71475

The calculation here was carried out in accordance with version 9.70 of the SAP worksheet, using version 2.7.3.79 of MVM's S2000Maxim software (incorporating SAPcalc 3.0)

SAPcalc 3.0 has been approved by the BRE on behalf of the DEFRA. Such approval, however, applies only to the software itself, so users are responsible for the accuracy of the data entered.

SAP certificate produced by MVM

There is also a list of other BRE approved software which can be used in connection with the Building Regulations and to provide SAP ratings and CI, but for which there is no quality assurance system and therefore no certificate with the SAP logo may be produced. (The output from this software is a printout of the SAP calculation that can be associated with the SAP worksheet.) The source for up to date approved software is provided at the end of this section [**4**].

13.4 THE NATIONAL HOME ENERGY RATING SCHEME (NHER)

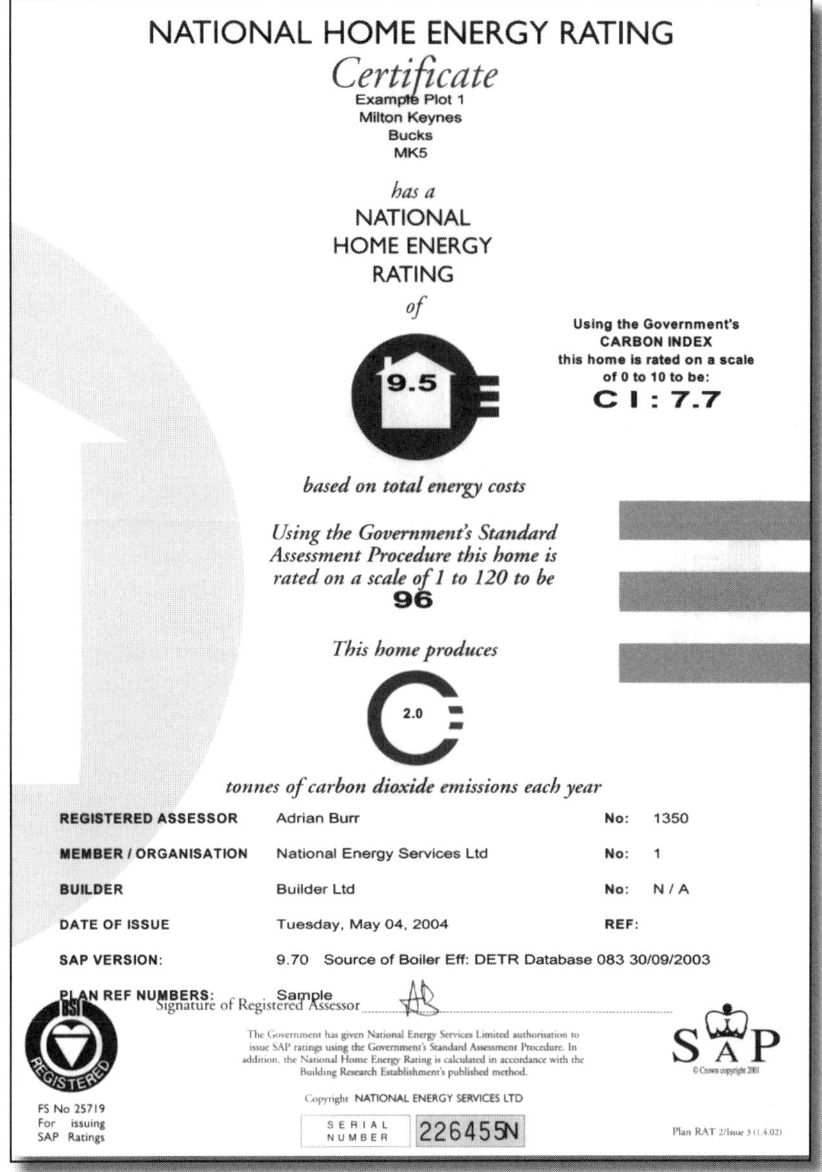

NATIONAL HOME ENERGY RATING

Certificate

Example Plot 1
Milton Keynes
Bucks
MK5

has a
NATIONAL
HOME ENERGY
RATING
of

9.5

Using the Government's
CARBON INDEX
this home is rated on a scale
of 0 to 10 to be:
CI : 7.7

based on total energy costs

Using the Government's Standard Assessment Procedure this home is rated on a scale of 1 to 120 to be
96

This home produces

2.0

tonnes of carbon dioxide emissions each year

REGISTERED ASSESSOR	Adrian Burr	No:	1350
MEMBER / ORGANISATION	National Energy Services Ltd	No:	1
BUILDER	Builder Ltd	No:	N / A
DATE OF ISSUE	Tuesday, May 04, 2004	REF:	
SAP VERSION:	9.70 Source of Boiler Eff: DETR Database 083 30/09/2003		
PLAN REF NUMBERS:	Sample		

Signature of Registered Assessor

BSI REGISTERED

FS No 25719
For issuing
SAP Ratings

The Government has given National Energy Services Limited authorisation to issue SAP ratings using the Government's Standard Assessment Procedure. In addition, the National Home Energy Rating is calculated in accordance with the Building Research Establishment's published method.

Copyright NATIONAL ENERGY SERVICES LTD

SERIAL NUMBER 226455N

SAP
© Crown copyright 2001

Plan RAT 2/Issue 3 (1.4.02)

The National Home Energy Rating Scheme (NHER) essentially differs from SAP ratings in that it takes into account the total annual fuel running costs for the dwelling (i.e. including cooking, lights and appliances).

In addition the NHER also takes into account the geographical location of the dwelling. NHERs are only calculated using computer software.

THE NHER IS DEFINED AS
'A number between 0 and 10 based on the total annual fuel running costs per square metre for the property, calculated using a standard occupancy and three-year average fuel prices' [5].

To give an indication of the scales of the rating, a dwelling built to 1990 Building Regulations would have an NHER of between 5 and 7 depending on where in the UK it was built.

A logo used for the National Home Energy Rating

The NHER scheme is a membership scheme, administered by National Energy Services Ltd. It operates as a professional institute by examining, registering and monitoring qualified assessors. NHER assessors and surveyors are required to pass appropriate NHER examinations, and the organisations for whom they work must be full members of NHER.

Whilst the NHER was the earliest energy rating based on BREDEM-12, there are now other software products which include an indication of total running costs based on BREDEM-12, for example MVM S2000Maxim total energy costs.

13.5 WHAT ENERGY RATING SOFTWARE IS USED FOR

The energy auditing process and the software available is used for a number of different purposes, few of which require the issue of energy rating certificates.

SAP is used as an indicator for energy efficiency for many purposes. It is often the increase in the SAP rating as a result of energy efficiency intervention which is of interest.

Some software programmes provide an accurate indication of running costs of a particular dwelling whereas others are less accurate and only suitable for reporting average energy ratings for a large number of dwellings.

Examples are shown below. This is not an exhaustive list. For full details of software and its applications, contact the organisations listed at the end of this section.

BUILDING REGULATIONS

SAP ratings and Carbon Index are issued in connection with the Building Regulations as described in 13.2.

DATA COLLECTION FOR HECA REPORTS AND BEST VALUE PERFORMANCE INDICATORS

The Home Energy Conservation Act (HECA) required housing authorities to report to Government on the rate of energy efficiency improvement in all domestic dwellings in their area. Therefore it has been necessary for authorities to collect data on the housing stock of all tenures within their boundaries.

Computer software is available which provides flexibility in the type of data which may be input to make up databases of the energy efficiency of the housing stock. The software can incorporate small amounts of data collected from a range of sources into the same database. For example the following types of information may be included:

- data collected during surveys of samples of the housing stock for house condition surveys
- information provided by scheme managers on energy efficiency measures or heating installed as part of grant schemes e.g. Warm Front
- data from other heating, insulation or relevant renovation programmes incorporating energy efficiency measures.

As part of their Best Value reporting, local authorities are also required to report on the average SAP and the annual improvement in that average, for their own housing stock. Energy rating software is used for this. The full set of data needed for a SAP calculation is unlikely to be available so reduced data set calculations can be carried out. There are default settings in the software to deal with this.

TARGETING INVESTMENT IN SOCIAL HOUSING

Social landlords may wish to target energy efficiency investment at housing with particularly low SAP ratings. Databases can be interrogated so that housing with the lowest SAP ratings are identified. Decisions can then be made on the most technically feasible and cost effective energy efficiency measures appropriate to the property. The software can also be used to determine the measures likely to improve the SAP rating the most.

ENERGY EFFICIENCY IN HOUSE CONDITION SURVEYS

The countries in the UK have national house condition surveys which include a section on energy efficiency. At a local level, house condition surveys provide local authorities with information on the energy efficiency of the housing stock, and can include sub groups of dwellings split for example by geographical area, tenure, age of dwelling, dwelling type, and by characteristics of the household.

This information provides the local authority with the basis for targeting local grants, loans or special schemes to groups of people or areas of housing which are identified as most energy inefficient.

EXAMPLE

A borough council conducted a Private Sector House Condition Survey in 2003. They discovered that the average SAP rating for the Borough was 46 compared to the national average (2001) of 51. Private rented and pre-1919 dwellings had the lowest SAP ratings, as did converted flats and detached houses. Households with particularly low SAP ratings had distinct characteristics such as single person households, special needs households, older people and those on low incomes.

The report looked in detail at ways in which the energy efficiency of dwellings could be improved in terms of increased SAP ratings and reduced running costs for occupants. The analysis included the impact of the energy improvement measures, the costs incurred if the improvements were carried out, and suggestions for targeting the improvements **[6]**.

ENERGY ADVICE REPORTS FOR HOUSEHOLDERS

Energy advice reports for individual households are produced by the collection of data on a questionnaire survey sheet, which may be completed by the customer or collected by a short home survey. (See Appendix 2 for an example of a home survey form.)

By entering this data into a computer, a report is generated detailing the appropriate energy efficiency measures for the dwelling, and advising the customer of the likely energy savings and priorities for each measure.

ENERGY EFFICIENT HOUSE DESIGN

Energy rating software can be used to compare the merits of different approaches to energy efficient house design, either for new build or refurbishment schemes. Energy efficient homes may be built to higher standards than those required by the existing Building Regulations.

THE HOME INFORMATION PACK

A number of mortgage lenders already produce indicative SAP ratings for existing dwellings for sale. The provision of energy reports will become formalised as a result of forthcoming European Union legislation.

The European Union Directive on Energy Performance in Buildings requires that all dwellings sold or let have an energy rating. The Housing Bill 2003 contains provisions for the introduction of Home Information Packs, which aim to simplify and speed up the home buying process.

Amongst other items, the Home Information Pack will contain a Home Condition Report. This in turn includes a standard Energy Performance Report which provides information on the current energy efficiency of the dwelling, improvements to the energy efficiency, and the potential energy rating if the improvements are undertaken [7].

A methodology for energy rating called 'Faster SAP' is being developed by FAERO members on behalf of the BRE for the energy report. Faster SAP will use a reduced data set, and deduce the data that cannot be collected on a survey. The full SAP will still be used to calculate the energy rating of new buildings.

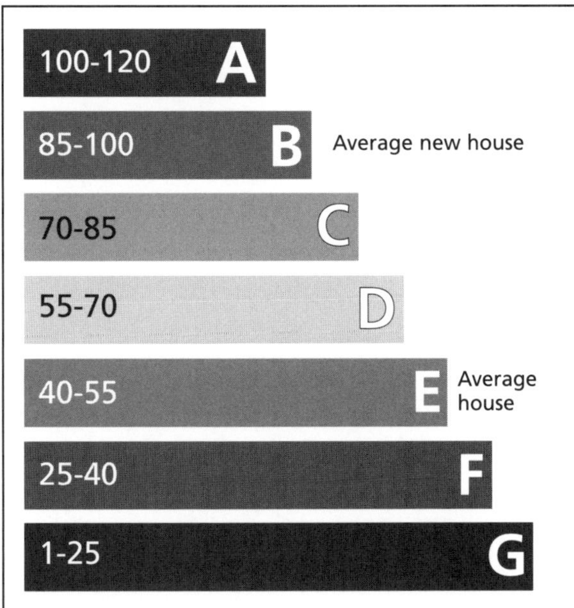

The energy rating is likely to be shown as a label in the Energy Performance Report

A consultation process has been undertaken by the EST on the format of the Energy Report. The chosen format will be on trial from 2004 [**7**], [**8**].

ASSESSMENT OF ENERGY RUNNING COSTS

Total household energy running costs depend on the following:

- the energy efficiency of the dwelling
- the size of the dwelling
- the geographical location (i.e. the altitude, exposure, latitude)
- the price of the fuel used
- occupancy (i.e. the number of occupants, hours of heating)
- the amount of fuel used for electrical appliances, lighting and cooking.

The SAP is an accurate indicator of energy efficiency of the dwelling, but energy efficiency is only one of the factors which affects the total running costs of the property. Assessments of energy use based on BREDEM-12 software allow the effect of all the factors above to be included in the running cost calculations.

(There is a worked example in Section 10.3 illustrating the difference in running costs of a dwelling when a householder wished to make a choice between oil and LPG as their main fuel.)

CALCULATING THE EXTENT OF FUEL POVERTY

A household is considered to be in fuel poverty if it cannot afford to keep warm at a reasonable cost. The definition used is that a fuel poor household is one which needs to spend more than 10% of its income on all fuel to heat the home to an adequate standard of warmth. An assessment of the extent of fuel poverty is carried out on a national scale as a part monitoring of the Government's Fuel Poverty Strategy [**9**].

In order to make an assessment of fuel poverty a calculation is made which compares the fuel cost of the household to the income of the household. Although currently under review to make the fuel poverty model more accurate, the fuel costs model is based on BREDEM-12 which includes estimates of the use of lighting, appliances and cooking as well as heating and hot water.

The energy rating companies have also developed software (in some cases using hand held calculators) based on BREDEM-12 to be used together with an assessment of household income to indicate whether the present occupants of a dwelling can afford to heat their home [**10**].

Contact details for organisations listed here are in Appendix 1.

REFERENCES

1 The Building Regulations (England and Wales Part L, Scotland Part J, and Northern Ireland Part F).

- Regulation 16 of the Building Regulations 2000 and in Regulation 12 of the Building (Approved Inspectors etc.) Regulations 2000 – in England and Wales.
- The Building (procedure) (Scotland) Regulations 1981, as amended – in Scotland.
- Building Regulations (Northern Ireland) 2000.

2 The Government's Standard Assessment Procedure for Energy Rating of Dwellings. 2001 edition: BRE.
www.bre.co.uk/sap2001

3 The following organisations are licensed by DEFRA to certify by means of a logo (the SAP logo) that the ratings have been issued by a body authorised by the Secretary of State:
Elmhurst Energy Systems,
MVM Consultants plc and
National Energy Services Ltd.
www.bre.co.uk/sap2001

4 List of BRE approved SAP software.
ww.bre.co.uk

5 NHER Plan Assessor Training Manual National Home Energy Rating Version 3.7, Issue1, Revision A.
www.nher.co.uk

6 *2003 Private Sector Stock Condition Survey.* Harrogate Borough Council.

7 Information provided by FAERO.
www.faero.org.uk

8 From EST website – link to partnership, link to what's new (April 2004).
www.est.org.uk

9 The UK Fuel Poverty Strategy. DEFRA. DTI.
www.defra.gov.uk
www.dti.gov.uk

10 NHER's Affordable Warmth Index and also MVM S2000 Fuel Poverty Indicator.

FURTHER INFORMATION

FAERO

The Federation of Authorised Energy Rating Organisations was set up to maintain high quality standards and consistency across the industry so that both professionals and the public could have confidence in ratings delivered by FAERO members.
www.faero.co.uk

Energy efficiency in new housing – a guide to achieving best practice. GPG 79. Energy Efficiency Best Practice in Housing. 2001.
www.est.org/bestpractice

14

APPLIANCES AND LIGHTING – OPERATION AND ENERGY EFFICIENCY

It is useful to understand how much electricity is consumed by lights and appliances so that high electricity bills can be explained, buying more efficient appliances becomes more straightforward, and ways to use appliances efficiently can be advised.

Although most energy in the home is used by heating and hot water systems, the proportion used by electrical appliances and lights will become more significant as improved insulation levels and efficient heating systems reduce the amount of energy needed for heating and hot water. In addition, electricity is a more polluting and more expensive fuel than gas and most other fuels used for heating and hot water. For example even though lights, cooking and appliances account for only 16% of energy use, they account for 32% of CO_2 emissions and 50% of fuel bills [**1**].

Domestic electricity consumption is increasing in the UK by around 1% per year [**2**]. As households acquire more variety of electrical appliances, and many are left on standby, there is considerable scope both for making sure that the most efficient appliances are bought, and that they are used efficiently.

This section looks at:

- how electricity is measured
- how to work out how much electricity appliances may use
- energy labels
- the operation and running costs of some large electrical appliances
- electricity consumption of appliances on 'standby'
- energy efficient lighting
- gas consumption of appliances other than heaters.

Note: a standard cost per unit (kWh) is used throughout this section. This is inclusive of VAT. Numbers of kWh are also given so that the reader may use another cost per kWh if it is more appropriate, if costs are out of date or regional variations are significant at the time of reading.

14.1 WORKING OUT RUNNING COSTS OF ELECTRICAL APPLIANCES

Working out the running costs of electrical appliances is useful if a consumer has a high electricity bill which they cannot explain. A useful method to analyse their electricity usage is to list the appliances they have, and look at how long they are switched on for. This may even involve keeping a diary. It is not uncommon for consumers to be unaware of the impact of using high wattage appliances or using low wattage appliances over long periods, some appliances are even left on permanently.

The amount of electricity used by appliances is measured in Units. A Unit is a kilowatt (1000 W or 1 kW) of electricity used for one hour (1 kWh). The wattage of an appliance is often marked on it, so it is possible to work out how much electricity the appliance uses, and therefore how much it costs to run. The higher the wattage, the more the appliance will cost per hour. For example, a 100 W light bulb will use one tenth of a unit in one hour, but a one bar electric fire rated at 1000 W (or 1 kW) will use 1 unit in one hour.

TABLE 14.1 TYPICAL WATTAGE OF SOME COMMON ELECTRICAL APPLIANCES [**3**]

Appliance	Typical rating in Watts
Cold Appliances	
Freezer	150
Refrigerator	100
Heating and Hot Water Appliances	
Immersion heater	3000
Instantaneous water heater	3000
Oil filled radiator	500 – 2500
Radiant heater/fire	1000 – 3000
Shower unit	6000 – 11000
Storage heater	2000 – 3000
Wet Appliances	
Dishwasher	3000
Tumble dryer	2500
Washing machine	2500
Cooking Appliances	
Cooker hood	130
Deep fat fryer	2000
Electric hob 4 rings	2500
Grill (alone)	2500
Kettle	1800 – 2500
Microwave oven	800
Toaster	1050 –1360
Breadmaker	500
Lighting Appliances	
Light (common incandescent)	100
Light (compact fluorescent, equivalent light to above)	20
Home Entertainment	
Portable radio/CD/cassette player	18
Compact disc player	15
DVD player	15
TV widescreen	70
TV widescreen standby	5
Video cassette recorder	35
Playstation	50
Miscellaneous Appliances	
Blanket (under)	60 – 120
Blanket (over)	150 – 350
Dehumidifier	200
Fan extractor	75
Food processor	200 – 700
Hair dryer	400 – 1200
Iron	1200
Drill	250 – 500
Grass mower	1300
Vacuum cleaner	900

TABLE 14.2 AMOUNT OF ELECTRICITY USED BY A VARIETY OF APPLIANCES (1 UNIT = 1 KWH) [**4**]

Appliance	
Cold Appliances	
Freezer (upright or chest)	About 1 to 1.5 units a day
Fridge/freezer	About 1.5 units a day
Refrigerator (larder)	Less than 1 unit a day
Heating and Hot Water Appliances	
Convector heater (2 kW)	half hour's warmth – 1 unit
Fan heater (2 kW)	half hour's warmth – 1 unit
Infra-red heater (1 kW)	1 hour's warmth – 1 unit
Oil-filled radiator (500 W)	2 hours' warmth – 1 unit
Panel heater (1.5 kW)	40 minutes' warmth – 1 unit
Electric heater (3 kW)	20 minutes' warmth – 1 unit
(Note that a 2 kW heater provides twice as much heat as a 1 kW heater)	
Wet Appliances	
Dishwasher	One full load – about 1.5 units
Tumble dryer	Full load of cottons – about 3.5 units Full load of synthetics – about 2 units
Washing machine	Load of synthetics at 40°C – less than 1 unit Load of cottons at 60°C – about 1 unit
Cooking Appliances	
Cooker and hob	Average about 1.5 units a day
Kettle	12 pints of boiling water – 1 unit
Microwave (850W)	20 minutes on Full power – less than 0.5 unit
Toaster	60 slices of toast – about 1 unit
Miscellaneous Appliances	
Single underblanket	1.5 hours each night for 1 week ` – less than 1 unit
Extractor fan	24 hours' use – 1 to 2 units
Hair dryer (500 W)	12 ten minute sessions – 1 unit
Iron	1 hour's use – 0.5 to 1 unit
Shower (7 kW)	5 minute shower 7 days a week – 4 units
For more information on efficient use and running costs of these appliances see Section 14.3 below and Table 14.5	

It is a useful exercise to advise householders to look around their homes room by room and note down a list of electrical appliances in use in each room, and to look at the wattages. Many small appliances have the rating in Watts written on them. For large appliances consult manuals.

To work out the running costs of electrical appliances multiply the rating by the amount of time it is on to give the number of kWh. Then multiply the cost per kWh (look at a recent electricity bill or tariff leaflet for the appropriate figure).

Wattage ÷ 1000 x time in minutes ÷ 60 = kWh
kWh x cost in pence = Cost

e.g. A 900 W vacuum cleaner used for 15 mins
900 ÷ 1000 x 15 ÷ 60 = 0.225 kWh
Cost = 0.225 x 6.6p = 1.5p

Appliances with heating elements incorporated in them tend to be the most expensive to use, followed by appliances with motors. Some appliances have both, for example washing machines and dishwashers.

We accept that this is a fairly crude way to measure the electricity usage as many appliances have thermostats so that when the operating temperature is reached the appliance is switched off. It is more difficult to estimate the running costs of these appliances. For those appliances which have energy labels (see 14.2 for details of labels) running costs are shown for appliances under test conditions.

The tables on page **14**–2 show the electricity consumption of appliances in two different ways. Table 14.1 shows wattage of a number of common appliances. Table 14.2 shows what use you could get out of a variety of appliances for a given number of units. Where appropriate this takes into account thermostatic control.

14.2 ENERGY LABELS

The energy efficiency of electrical appliances varies from model to model, which influences running costs and CO_2 emissions.

It may be difficult to tell how energy efficient an appliance is without an energy label. Compare the technical information on the manufacturer's literature for details of wattages or other running costs.

The European Union (EU) Energy Label must be displayed by law on all new household appliances in the following categories which are displayed for sale, hire or hire purchase (including catalogues and Internet advertising).

- refrigerators, freezers and fridge freezer combinations (A+ and A++ labels are being introduced from July 2004)
- washing machines
- electric tumble dryers
- dishwashers
- light bulbs (packaging)
- electric ovens
- other labels are planned

The labels rate appliances from A (green colour – most efficient) to G (red colour – least efficient). They also provide other information, for example water consumption, noise and the wash and spin performance of washing machines.

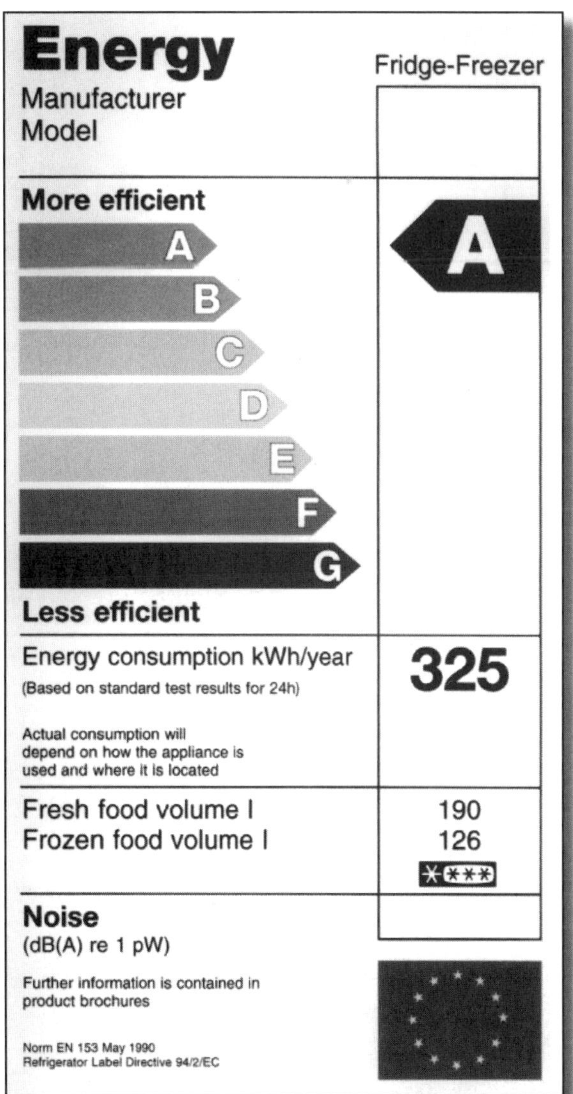

Example of an EU Energy Label for a fridge freezer

When buying appliances look at similar models, for example when buying fridge freezers, compare like with like, i.e. similar volume of freezer and fresh food, and look at the comparative energy consumption.

On this example the fridge freezer under test conditions consumes 325 kWh per year. Multiply this by your cost per kWh to work out annual running costs.

If the cost per unit is 6.6p the annual running costs are 325 x 6.6 = £21.25

The example of the washing machine shows the energy consumption per cycle. In this example it uses 1.05 kWh per 60°C wash. This example also has A rated spin performance which means that tumble drying clothes would be quicker than those with poorer spin efficiency.

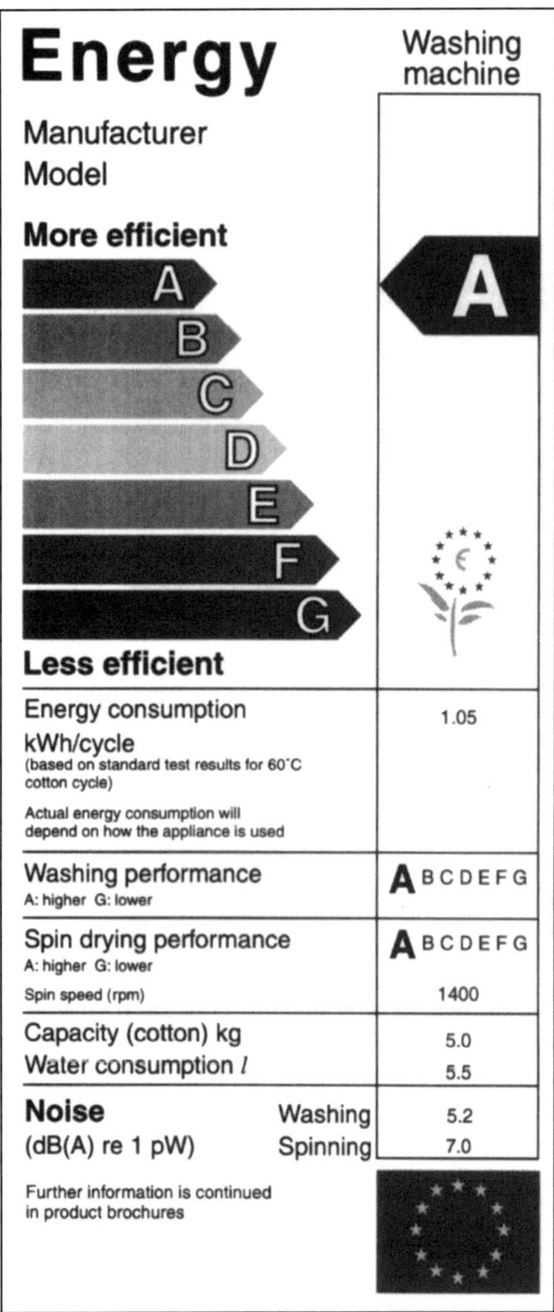

Example of an EU Energy Label for a washing machine

ENERGY EFFICIENCY RECOMMENDED LOGO

The Energy Efficiency Recommended logo helps customers to identify and buy energy efficient products.

The logo makes the most efficient products instantly recognisable and complements the EU Energy Label, making it even easier to buy energy efficient products.

Energy Efficiency Recommended logo

Only products that meet or exceed the energy efficiency criteria set by the Energy Saving Trust and backed by Government can use the Energy Efficiency Recommended logo.

The logo appears on a wide (and continually growing) range of products including energy saving light bulbs and light fittings, refrigeration, laundry and dishwashing appliances, gas boilers and heating controls. For an up to date list of Energy Efficiency Recommended products and the criteria they have to meet see [**5**].

14.3 OPERATION OF SOME MAJOR ELECTRICAL APPLIANCES [6]

FRIDGES AND FREEZERS

How do fridges and freezers work?

Most fridges and freezers maintain a cold environment inside the appliance by the evaporation of a refrigerant (a special chemical which circulates in a piped heat exchanger). The refrigerant removes heat from inside the appliance and can maintain cold temperatures lower than –18°C in the case of freezers. The heat removed is then given out from a heat exchanger at the back of the appliance. This usually looks like a black serpentine of finned piping. A thermostat recognises the temperature inside the appliance and switches the compressor (motor) on and off. The refrigerant is recirculated by the compressor – this is the 'humming' noise heard when the thermostat brings the compressor on.

Refrigerants used in cold appliances have been changed in recent years so that the chemicals have minimum impact on the environment. However, old appliances will invariably use the older type of refrigerants (known as CFCs) and must be disposed of properly to ensure the chemicals do not escape. They are usually taken away by the local authority or special contractor.

Efficient fridge freezers may have:

- More insulation (thicker walls)
- Vacuum sealed insulation (better insulation)
- Efficient compressors (better operation).

How to use fridges and freezers more efficiently

- Defrost freezers regularly.
- Keep fridges and freezers away from heat sources such as cookers or boilers.
- Keep out of rooms where temperatures get very high e.g. conservatories.
- Ensure a free flow of air over the condenser (the heat exchanger at the back). This is particularly important if the appliance is built-in – there should be a 'grille' in a work surface above the appliance.
- Try to keep fridges and freezers at least two thirds full.
- Don't put hot food straight into the fridge.
- Keep the door closed whenever possible.
- Don't set temperature settings too low.

Example of small upright freezer (this is an A rated freezer using 208 kWh/year)

TUMBLE DRYERS

How do tumble dryers work?

An electric, or less commonly gas, heater heats the air that is drawn through the clothes as they tumble. The hot air then heats up the clothes and the water in them.

Vented dryer:

The water from the clothes is absorbed as water vapour in the surrounding hot air in the drum. The hot, wet air is then discharged from the dryer to the outside of the house through an exhaust vent. (It is important that tumble dryers are not vented into the house or there may be serious condensation problems.)

Condensing dryer:

The wet exhaust air is cooled by air drawn into the machine from the house which makes the water condense out like dew. This may be plumbed in to the waste water disposal or, more commonly, fills a container which regularly needs emptying. The drier exhaust air is then reheated and fed back into the dryer. The air used for cooling is returned into the home hotter than it went in.

More efficient dryers tend to:

- Have a sensor to optimise drying (this can save 5 – 10% of energy consumption)
- Use longer cycles at lower temperatures
- Ensure that the air and clothes mix well in the drum, reverse tumble helps
- Recover some of the heat that is being vented

Drying clothes efficiently

- Dry clothes outside in warm weather. Not using the tumble dryer makes a 100% saving.
- Pick a washing machine with good spin efficiency, and spin clothes at as high a speed as possible to remove maximum moisture. Spinning at 1000 rpm, rather than 800 rpm, saves 46 kWh per year and spinning at 1400 rpm, rather than 800 rpm, saves 87 kWh per year.
- Use a gas tumble dryer – the fuel costs and carbon emissions are lower. Typical running costs are likely to be less than half that of an equivalent electric dryer.
- Using Economy 7 (for an electric dryer) would be cheaper but would not use less energy. A quieter running machine with a timer would be most suitable.
- Switch the tumble dryer off after use.
- Keep the tumble dryer fluff-free, especially the condenser in condensing dryers.
- Use a dryer which has the best energy rating (the lowest kWh/cycle on the Energy Label) and a sensor.

WASHING MACHINES

How do washing machines work?

- A fixed tub contains the water. A drum holds the clothes and revolves within the tub.
- Automatic taps let the water in and a pump pumps out water. Sensors in the machine decide when enough water has been added.
- A combination of detergent, wash temperature, wash time, water level and agitation is used to clean the clothes. Sensors in the machine ensure the water is at the correct temperature.
- A wash cycle can consist of a pre-wash, main wash, up to 4 rinses and a final spin dry.

If the washing machine is 'cold fill' the water for the washes and rinses is taken from the cold supply only. All of the heating is done by electricity in the machine. If the washing machine is connected to both the hot and cold water supply in the house, some hot water is used to fill up for some washes, but some heating by electricity will still take place.

More efficient washing machines tend to:

- Minimise the water needed to be heated to do a standard wash.
- Match water use to the load size by using sensors to check how much water is absorbed by the clothes. Less water means less heating. This can save 10% of energy and water consumption.
- Have fuzzy logic to help optimise machine performance for each individual load and phase of the wash.
- Have larger tubs and drums – only efficient if larger loads are washed.

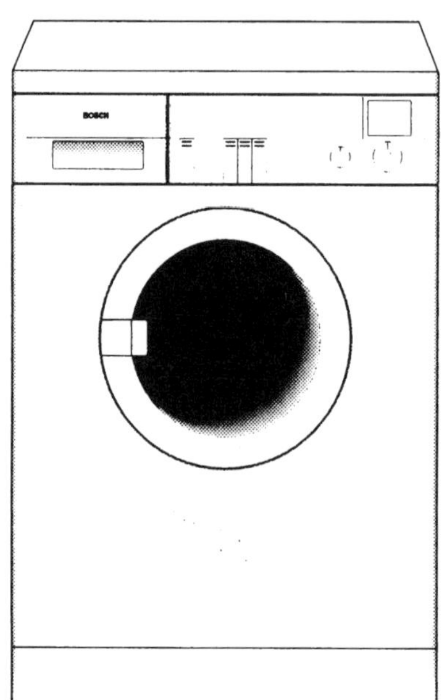

Example of washing machine

How to use washing machines efficiently

- Use the lowest possible temperatures for washes.
- Fill the machine to its rated capacity. As a guide, a 5 kg load is equivalent to about 30 shirts.
- Spin the clothes at as high a speed as possible to remove as much moisture as possible if clothes are to be dried in a tumble dryer.
- Using Economy 7 would be cheaper but would not use less energy. A quieter running machine with a timer would be most suitable.
- Use a washing machine with an 'A' energy rating. Some 'A' rated machines are better than others – check the label.
- Real life electricity use per cycle maybe 33% less than stated on the Energy Label if most washes are done at 40°C. Modern machines may also use less because they can sense how much water and energy is needed for part load washes.
- Switch off on the front of the machine after use.

DISHWASHERS

How do dishwashers work?

- The dishes are held in baskets and normally have arms spraying water from above, below, or both above and below.
- Automatic taps let the water in. Used water is pumped out of the machine. A filter stops large pieces of food blocking up the spray arms or pump.
- A combination of detergent, wash temperature, wash time, and water pressure is used to clean the dishes. Washes can be at temperatures as high as 65°C, but most modern machines used with modern detergents give good wash performance at 55°C. Sensors in the machine ensure that water reaches the correct temperature.
- A wash cycle can consist of a pre-wash, main wash, up to 3 rinses and a final drying period. After each main step the water is usually pumped away before the next step.
- Most dishwashers in the UK only use cold fill (taking from the cold supply). All of the heating is done by electricity in the machine.

More efficient dishwashers tend to:

- Give good washes at 55°C or even 50°C rather than the standard 65°C.
- Minimise the water needed to be heated to do a standard wash.
- Recycle the heat from each stage of the process to heat up the water for the next stage.
- Add no extra heat in the drying stage – just use the heat from the last rinse and, sometimes, a small fan.

How to use dishwashers efficiently

- Use a dishwasher with an 'A' energy rating. Some 'A' rated machines are better than others – check the label.
- Use the lowest possible temperatures for washes. Fill the machine up as much as possible.
- Using Economy 7 would be cheaper but not use less energy. A quieter running machine with a delay timer would be most suitable.
- Switch the dishwasher off on the front panel.
- Real life electricity use per cycle may be 30% more than stated on the Energy Label if most washes are done at 65°C.

OVENS

How do ovens work?

Conventional Electric Oven – switches an electric heater on and off to ensure that the oven stays at the correct temperature. The heating elements can be at the top and bottom of the oven, or on either side.

Fan Electric Oven – the air in the oven is heated by blowing it across an electric heating element outside the main oven compartment. This helps to distribute the heat evenly around the oven.

Multi-Function Oven – has the heating elements of both a conventional and fan oven which are used in a combination best suited to the food being cooked.

Halogen Light Oven – these are relatively new and use high-wattage halogen lamps. Cooking times and energy use are reported to be about 40% less than a conventional electric oven [**6**]. These are currently only available as built-in or to stand on a work surface (like a microwave).

Gas Oven – uses gas flames instead of an electric heater and costs 70% less per year to run than electric ovens.

Self-Cleaning (Pyrolytic) Ovens – these work by taking the oven to a very high temperature during the cleaning cycle and 'burning' off burnt on food. They tend to be better insulated to ensure the outside of the oven is at a safe temperature during the high temperature clean. The energy used for cleaning may cancel out the operating savings due to the good insulation.

More efficient ovens tend to:

- Be fuelled by natural gas.
- Be better insulated.
- Have better door sealing.
- Have no clock and timer or one that doesn't use much energy.
- If electric, be a fan oven because it takes less time to heat up.

How to use ovens efficiently

- Cook several dishes at once – 85% of the energy put into the oven is used to heat up the oven.
- If the oven is self-cleaning, start the self-cleaning cycle just after the oven has been used.
- Use half width option for grilling wherever possible.
- Turn off ovens before cooking is finished to utilise the residual heat.

HOBS

How do hobs work?

Electric Coil Element – passes electric current through a coil which produces heat, range from 700 W – 1.2 kW.

Solid Disc – similar to the coil element but using a solid disc.

Ceramic – a coil element, but under a ceramic top.

Halogen – essentially a very powerful type of light bulb mounted under a ceramic top.

Induction – works by heating up metal pans directly using focused electro-magnetism – 50% cheaper than solid disc.

Gas – gas flame provides heat. Costs 70% less than an electric coil element to run.

More efficient hobs tend to:

- Be fuelled by natural gas.
- Use electric induction.

How to use hobs efficiently

- Use lids on pans – 25% saving.
- Use a pressure cooker instead of two or more pans – 20% saving over lidded pans.
- Use a steamer when possible instead of extra pans.
- Match the ring size to the saucepan being used.
- Use electric steamers – these can save about 30% of the energy of electric rings.
- Use a microwave instead of an electric hob, whenever practicable.

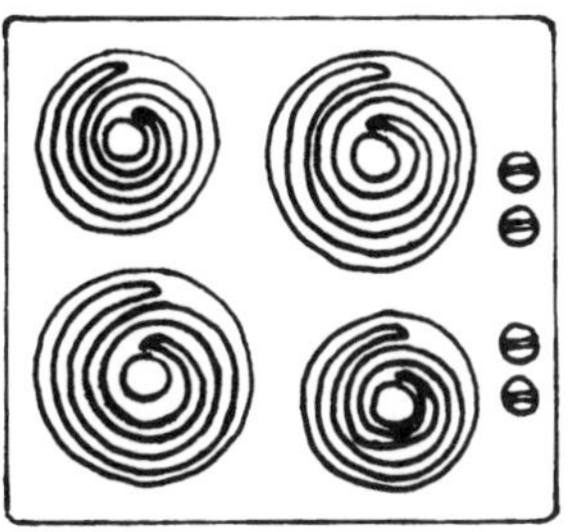

Electric coil element

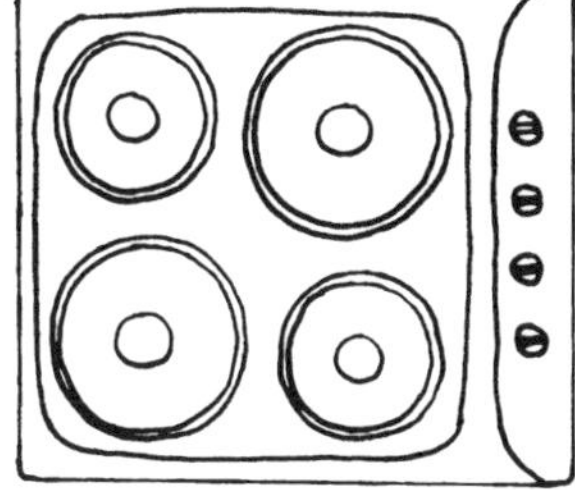

Solid disc

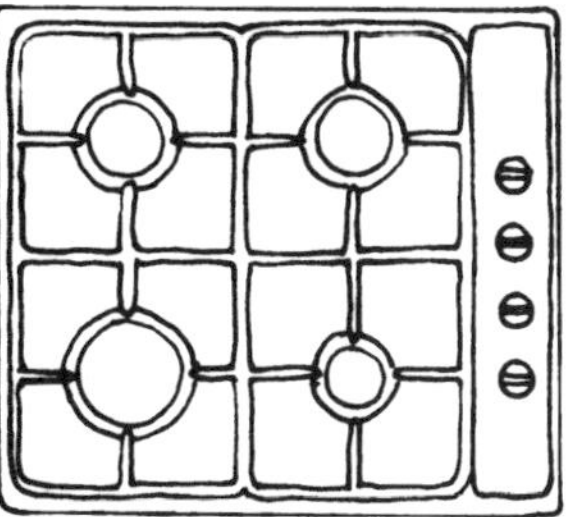

Gas hob

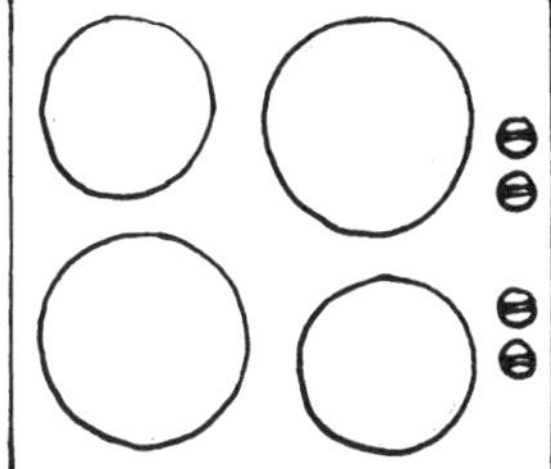

Ceramic hob (flat and black)

Examples of hobs: Halogen and induction hobs are also flat and usually black.

14.4 STANDBY

WHAT IS STANDBY?

- Most appliances consume power when connected to the mains even when they are switched off. Power packs that are supplied with products ranging from mobile phones, games machines, printers and baby monitors also use energy when connected to the mains, even when not connected to anything. Feel one when it is plugged in and it will be warm.
- Some components in appliances are always 'live' and use electricity, for example clocks and timers (e.g. on video recorders or ovens) cost a surprising amount to run every year. 80% of the energy used to run a video recorder is consumed when the video recorder is not in use.
- Power consumption can be anything from 0 to 20 watts (W). Most homes will have at least 10 items that are constantly using energy.

Below is a table of typical standby wattages, shown on permanently. In future, standby wattages should be lower.

Table 14.4 TYPICAL STANDBY WATTAGES [**7**]

Typical Standby Wattages and Consumption			
	W	**kWh per year (i.e. x 8760 hours)**	**£ per year (at 6.6p per kWh)**
Microwave	7	61.32	4.05
Cooker	5	43.8	2.89
TV	5	43.8	2.89
VCR	5	43.8	2.89
Mobile phone charger	6	52.56	3.47
Cordless phone	8	70.08	4.63
Answer machine	8	70.08	4.63
Stereo	10	87.6	5.78
Digital decoder	15	131.4	8.67
Washing machine	2	17.52	1.16
PC	10	87.6	5.78
Printer	15	131.4	8.67
PC speakers	5	43.8	2.89

Note: The typical cost for any household depends on the number and type of appliances left on standby.

Lower standby consumption is possible if:

- Appliances have an off switch which cuts off the power as it enters the appliance.
- Features such as clocks are omitted.
- Appliances and power packs are disconnected from the mains when not in use.
- PCs are turned off once they have been shut down. The screensaver is designed to save the screen. It does not save much energy. If you are not using the printer for a while, switch it off.
- If appliances with low standby power are purchased. This can be difficult to find out, but there are websites that can help [**8**].
- If TVs and videos are turned off at the mains rather than using the 'off' button on the remote control. Look for a video player with a battery back-up so that you don't need to set the clock every time!
- If washing machines, tumble dryers and dishwashers are turned off at the front panel after use.
- If stereos are turned off at the mains. It is likely that the annual standby consumption of your stereo will be more than actually used when listening to music or the radio.
- If IRDs (Integrated Receiver Decoders e.g. satellite or cable TV receivers) are turned off at the mains. These are amongst the heaviest consumers of power in the standby mode (NB please check the contract with the service provider as it may require the receiver to be kept on for a set period).

Energy labels for Standby

Energy labels do not yet cover standby consumption of appliances or power packs. However, some manufacturers have voluntarily agreed with the European Commission to reduce the standby consumption of TVs, VCRs and power supplies. There is often no way to identify these items but manufacturers are starting to publish standby consumption in the technical specifications of the products.

ENERGY STAR

ENERGY STAR is an international initiative for energy efficient electronic office equipment, created by the US Environment Protection Agency (EPA) in 1992. It has now been adopted by several countries including the EU for some products. If a computer, printer or monitor has the ENERGY STAR standard it can automatically switch itself into power saving mode after a certain amount of idle time. When a key is pressed or mouse moved it 'wakes up'. Not all PCs that are ENERGY STAR compliant have been set to save energy. Check from the Control Panel, look at Display (or Appearance and Themes), select the Screen Saver tab (may be more than one link), then click Settings (or Power) button next to the ENERGY STAR logo.

Table 14.5 SUMMARY OF ENERGY CONSUMPTION AND RUNNING COSTS OF MAJOR APPLIANCES AND 'STANDBY' FOR AVERAGE USE [**9**].(Information is based on an average age of appliance and average usage. kWh per use are provided so that higher or lower usage can be calculated – as can changes in electricity prices.)

Washing Machines	
Running cost	**Approx. £14 per year.** If used on various programmes at an average of 0.77 kWh per cycle. Cost @ 6.6p/kWh = 5.1p/cycle. At 274 uses/yr [**9**] x 0.77 kWh = 212 kWh/yr.
Economy 7	Save around £9/yr (@ 2.4p/kWh).
Information on Energy Labels	Tested on full cotton load washed at 60°C with cold fill only. Example: energy use 1.2kWh/cycle Water Example: 50 litres/fill @ 0.12p/litre = 6p/cycle = £16/yr based on 274 uses/yr.
Dishwashers	
Running cost	**Approx. £22 per year.** If used on various programmes at an average of 1.33 kWh/cycle. Cost @ 6.6p/kWh = 8.8p/cycle. At 250 uses/yr [**9**] x 1.33 kWh = 333 kWh/yr.
Economy 7	Save around £14/yr (@2.4p/kWh).
Information on Energy Labels	Tested on full load. Example: energy 1.5 kWh/cycle. Water Example: 20 litres/wash @ 0.12p/litre = 2.4p/wash = £6/yr based on 250 uses/yr.
Tumble Dryers	
Running cost	**Approx. £23 per year.** Consumption varies depending on cotton/synthetics and spin performance of washing machine. On average uses 2.36 kWh/cycle. Cost @ 6.6p/kWh = 15.6p/cycle. At 148 uses/yr [**9**] x 2.36 kWh = 350 kWh/yr.
Washing machine spin savings	Compared to 800 rpm, 1200 rpm saves £5/yr and 1400 rpm saves £8.50/yr.
Gas fired dryer	Save around £20/yr.
Economy 7	Save around £15/yr (@2.4p/kWh).
Information on Energy Labels	Tested on full cotton load which has been spun at 800 rpm. Example: as above.
Hobs	
Running cost	**Approx. £18 per year.** Each use at 0.72 kWh. Cost @ 6.6p/kWh = 4.8p/use. At 369 uses/yr [**9**] x 0.72 kWh = 266 kWh/yr.
Gas	60 – 70% saving to normal electric hobs.
Induction hob	50% saving to normal electric hob = £10 saving/yr.
Ovens	
Running cost	**Approx. £20 per year.** Each use at 1.4kWh. Cost @ 6.6p/kWh = 9.24p/use. At 223 uses/yr [9] = 312kWh/yr.
Standby – various appliances	
Annual cost in average home	**Approx. £29 per year.** 10 appliances at 5 W [**6**] = 50 W. Cost@ 6.6p/kWh = 0.33p/hour. All on for 24 hrs/day for 365 days = 438 kWh/yr. (Depends on wattage – see Table 14.4.)

Table 14.6 SAVINGS IF REPLACING AN APPLIANCE BOUGHT IN 1990 WITH AN A RATED APPLIANCE (AT 6.6P/KWH) [**10**]

	Cost / yr (1990)	Cost / yr (A rated)	Saving /yr
Fridge freezer	£52	£17	**£35**
Chest freezer	£37	£10	**£27**
Larder fridge	£25.50	£ 8.50	**£17**
Washing machine	£15.50	£11	**£ 4.50**
Dishwasher	£27.50	£15	**£12.50**

14.5 LIGHTING

Lighting consumes a significant amount of electricity – In 1998 the average household had 22 light bulbs in use and this number was set to rise [**11**]. Most of these were traditional light bulbs (GLS incandescent bulbs) which consumed 84% of the energy used for lighting in 1998. The 60 W bulb was the most common.

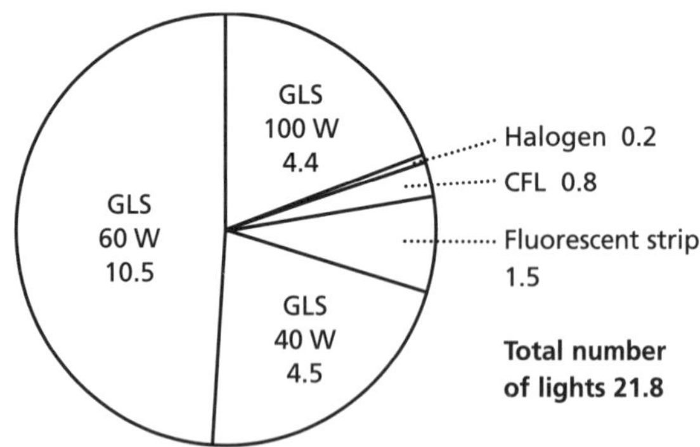

Average number of lights per 1998 household

There are different types of lights available on the market which are suitable for different purposes, and provide varying types of light. A householder's choice of lights will probably be determined as much by fashion and design as by energy efficiency, and any household will probably have a mixture.

There has been a large amount promotional work in recent years to encourage consumers to use more CFLs. (Compact fluorescent lights or low energy light bulbs). This is largely driven by the energy suppliers' requirements to promote energy efficiency to reduce CO_2 emissions. CFLs are frequently given away free, or offered at discount prices.

Light sources can be classified into five general categories, as summarised in **Table 14.7**.

INCANDESCENT LIGHTS

Traditional (GLS incandescent) light bulbs are the most commonly used light source in homes. (GLS stands for General Lighting Service.) People are familiar with them, the bulbs are cheap and easy to use, have good colour rendering properties and can be dimmed. However, they are the least efficient light source and have a short life.

Halogen bulbs are an improvement on GLS bulbs – the technology is essentially the same but with the filament enclosed in halogen gases. This extends the life of the filament and improves both efficacy and light output. Halogen infrared-reflecting (HIR) bulbs have an even higher efficacy. Screw and bayonet based halogens are available, but the majority are pin-based and so require specially designed fixtures.

Low-voltage halogens may vary between 15 – 65 W but they may operate at 12 V or 24 V and therefore require a transformer, which uses additional power – around 10 to 20% of the bulb wattage. The use of

Table 14.7 BASIC PROPERTIES OF THE KEY DOMESTIC LIGHT SOURCES [**12**]

Light source (illustrations not to scale)	Bulb wattage (W)	Efficacy* (lumen / W)	Average life (h)
Incandescent			
GLS (traditional light bulbs)	15 – 150	6 – 18	750 – 1500
Halogen small directional lights – some need transformer	15 – 65	8 – 20	2000 – 4000
Halogen uplighters ~/floodlights	75 – 500	13 – 29	2000
Fluorescent			
Fluorescent strips	4 – 58	65 – 100	10000 – 20000
Compact fluorescent light (CFL)	5 – 36	42 – 82	10000 – 15000

*Efficacy – a measure of the light provided (measured in lumens, lm) per unit of input power (Watts). The higher this is, the more efficient the light source.

reflectors in these bulbs produces a focused beam of light in one direction. This type of halogen is often used for accent lighting and desk lamps and has become popular as recessed lighting in ceilings.

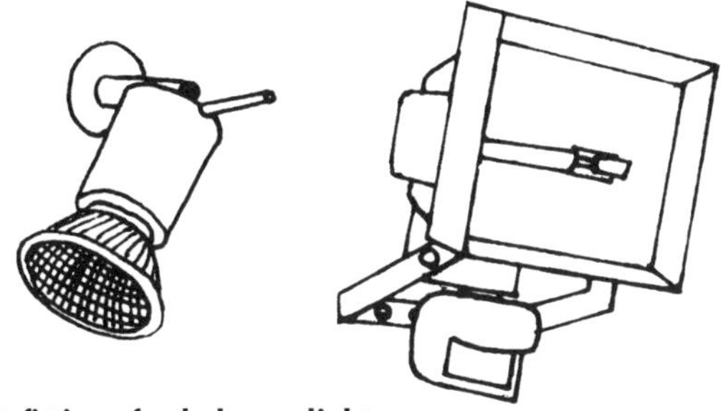

Light fittings for halogen lights

High-voltage halogens are non-directional light sources commonly used in uplighters, typically using 300 – 500 W halogen bulbs, providing a bright, indirect and diffuse light. These are also fitted in outdoor floodlights and security lights.

FLUORESCENT LIGHTS

The two main classes of fluorescent light sources used in homes are strip lights and CFLs (compact fluorescent lights). These are both based on the same technology (a CFL is a small folded fluorescent tube) which is different and more complex than incandescent lights and is also more efficient.

Energy savings from fluorescent lights

Fluorescent lights use less electricity than other forms of lighting. Fluorescent strips are very efficient but have diminished in popularity. The CFL is promoted as the principal low energy light in domestic situations. The CFL lasts for 12000 to 15000 hours compared to about 1000 hours for an incandescent light, but more importantly it only uses between one fifth and one quarter of the amount of electricity for the same amount of light.

Table 14.8 COMPARISON OF THE COSTS OF USING LOW ENERGY LIGHT BULBS (CFLS) AND TRADITIONAL INCANDESCENT LIGHT BULBS OVER 12000 HOURS (THE LIFE OF A LOW ENERGY BULB)

	Compact fluorescent 20W	Traditional incandescent GLS 100W
Electricity consumption during 12000 hours	240 kWh	1200 kWh
Running cost at 6.6p/kWh	£15.84	£79.20
Saving per bulb = 960 kWh (@6.6p per kWh) = £63.36 (over 12000 hours) This is often quoted as an annual figure of £7–10 per year		
Capital costs are not included. Low energy lights may be free, or on special offer. Full price may be up to £10, but the cost should be compared to buying 12 incandescent bulbs at £0.50 each (approximately £6).		

The higher the wattage of the light replaced the more electricity will be saved per light.

GLS bulb	CFL equivalent	Saved energy
40 W	8 – 11 W	29 – 32 W
60 W	15 – 18 W	42 – 45 W
100 W	20 – 25 W	75 – 80 W

Savings figures usually compare a four or five to one ratio, i.e. replacing a 100 W GLS bulb with a 20 W CFL bulb. However, because of the way light is radiated it may be necessary to choose the next wattage up to achieve the same brightness, i.e. replacing a 60 W GLS bulb with a 20 W CFL bulb.

Other aspects of CFLs

CFLs are produced in a variety of shapes and sizes to fit screw or bayonet light fittings. It is not always easy to find light fittings to accommodate the bulkier and usually longer shape of the CFL – it may be necessary to shop around.

Fluorescent light sources need a ballast to work. The type of ballast used (magnetic, electronic or a mixture), determines the light's efficacy and other aspects of the way the lights work. Higher wattage CFLs and those operating on electronic ballasts, rather than magnetic, tend to be the most efficient. Flicker, hum and long 'light up' times are also associated with magnetic ballasts. Electronic ballasts are now more common and suffer from fewer drawbacks, being silent, lighter-weight and more efficient.

Most consumers are not aware of the difference between the two ballast types and may assume that any problems experienced with magnetic ballasts are true for all CFLs. Those people who bought CFLs when they first appeared on the market may not realise that the technology has now vastly improved.

In addition tests on high quality electronic ballast CFLs show that their operating life is not affected by turning the lights on and off frequently (tests were based on a cycle of three minutes on and five minutes off for up to 20000 ignitions) [**12**].

CASE STUDY

A householder replaced two 50 W fluorescent strips in the kitchen with 15 50 W halogen lights. In one winter's week the lighting was on for 56 hours (2 hours in the morning and 6 hours in the evening).

Energy used and cost

Old lights:
100 W x 56 hrs = 5.6 kWh @ 6.6p = 37p per week
New lights:
750 W x 56 hrs = 42 kWh @ 6.6p = £2.77 per week

The new lights cost more than 7 times the old to run.

14.6 RUNNING COSTS OF GAS APPLIANCES [13]

Apart from heating and hot water appliances, the two main gas appliances in the home are cookers and tumble dryers (gas fridges are now very uncommon). Generally speaking the cost of gas is approximately one third that of electricity (unless Economy 7 or similar tariff is used). The approximate energy usage and running costs are:

Gas Cooker	Fuel used in kW	Cost per hour at 1.4p/kWh
Grill on full	4.4	6.0p
One burner on full	3.2	4.5p
One burner on low	0.25	0.35p
Oven at Mark 7	1.5	2.1p
Oven at Mark 2	0.8	1.1p
Gas tumble dryer	To dry a 10 lb load of towelling costs 6.0p Normal Dryer, 6.5p High Speed Dryer	

Contact details for organisations listed here are in Appendix 1.

REFERENCES

1 *Domestic heating and hot water – choice of fuel and system type. 2002.* GPG 301. Energy Efficiency Best Practice Programme.

2 *Lower Carbon Futures* (Executive Summary). Environmental Change Institute – (ECI) University of Oxford. March 2000.

3 *Home Electric Information.* Electricity Council 1987. Updated in 2003 by examination of typical appliances available in retailers', and manufacturers' technical specifications on product literature.

4 *Electricity and You – A Guide to Running Costs.* Electricity Association leaflet. Figures amended in line with more recent data (Table 14.5).

5 For details of the Energy Efficiency Recommended logo.
www.saveenergy.co.uk

6 Information from EST and Energy Efficiency Partnership for Homes Appliances Group.

7 EST information. These wattages were typical in 2003. Conservative estimates indicate wattages at approximately half of these, and standby wattages are due to fall in the future.

8 For information on appliances with low standby power.
www.mtprog.com and **www.ukepic.com**

9 *Lower Carbon Futures:* Table 2.7 Usage patterns of selected lighting, appliances and water heating and Table 2.8 Power demand of average new appliances in 1990/98/2020.

10 Energy Efficiency Commitment 2002 – 2005. Technical Guidance Manual Issue 2. Ofgem Sept 2002.

11 *Domestic Lighting in the UK A Sector Review Paper on Projected Energy Consumption for DEFRA.* (Information provided by ECI University of Oxford) January 2001.

12 *DELight* Energy and Environment Programme, Environmental Change Unit. University of Oxford. 1998.

13 Updated from second edition of Heating Advice Handbook. Energy Inform 1993. Original information supplied by British Gas.

FURTHER INFORMATION

Which? Magazine Jan 2004 p26 *'Sound light' cut your electricity bill and help save the planet by switching to low-energy light bulbs.*

Low energy domestic lighting. GIL 20. Housing Energy Efficiency Best Practice Programme. 2002.

15

RENEWABLE ENERGY

There is increasing consumer interest in renewable energy and the contribution it can make to sustainable lifestyles. Renewable energy uses natural energy flows – the sun, wind, falling water, waves and tides. It does not run out and it does not rely on burning fossil fuels such as coal, oil or gas, which are finite resources. When fossil fuels are burned they release harmful greenhouse gases like carbon dioxide (CO_2) and methane, which contribute to climate change. Renewable energy therefore has an important role to play in helping tackle climate change.

Some renewable technologies can be used directly in the home, especially if they are planned into house design. Others are used for the production of electricity, the generation of heat, and energy for transport. The technologies most applicable to homes will depend on a number of factors: location, the orientation of the building and local resources.

This section briefly covers:

- different types of solar energy
- wind power
- ground source heat pumps
- biofuels
- hydroelectricity.

15.1 RENEWABLE ENERGY POLICY

The Government has taken action to encourage greater use of renewables by requiring more electricity to be generated from renewable sources and by providing grant aid and increased research and development for a range of renewable technologies – some of which are applicable to homes.

In April 2002 the Renewables Obligation called on all licensed electricity suppliers in England and Wales to supply a specified and growing proportion of their electricity sales from a choice of renewable sources (Renewables Obligation Scotland in Scotland). The aim is that by 2010, 10% of the UK's electricity should be supplied by renewable sources. The targets rise from 3% of electricity sales in 2003 to 10.4% of sales in 2011 [**1**].

As well as helping the UK to meet its targets for the reduction of CO_2 and other greenhouse gas emissions, the UK policy also aims to help provide diverse, secure and sustainable energy supplies, and to stimulate the development of new technologies and help the UK renewables industries.

15.2 SOLAR ENERGY

Solar energy is the most appropriate source of renewable energy of direct relevance to domestic use. There are three different uses of the sun's energy:

- passive solar design
- solar water heating
- photovoltaics or Solar PV.

PASSIVE SOLAR DESIGN

Passive solar means to use the design of a building to maximise the benefit of the sunshine (solar gain) falling on it, particularly through features which allow solar energy to contribute to the space heating. Passive solar design is mainly aimed at new buildings (although refurbishment can also incorporate passive solar features). In a new dwelling it can significantly reduce the need for heating and lighting, and may add nothing to the cost of the building.

Studies on houses in Milton Keynes have shown that low cost passive solar design features and draught-proofing and insulation measures reduced heating bills by 40%. Savings paid back the costs in two years [**2**].

To maximise the amount of sunshine falling on a dwelling, it should face south – the windows and glazed areas should be concentrated on the south facing (or within 30° to the south east or south west) side of the building with only small areas on the north facing side, which gets little or no sunshine. Larger frequently used rooms (with larger windows) should be designed on the south facing side, with less frequently used rooms (with smaller windows) designed on the north side. The dwellings should not be overshadowed by trees and other buildings, though care should be taken to provide some shading for the most intense sunshine of the summer months. Unfortunately these considerations are not likely to be of high priority to developers whose site layout of new dwellings is more likely to be about numbers of dwellings on a plot of land rather than their orientation.

The dwellings should contain material which has a high thermal mass, e.g. stone, concrete or brick. This sort of material absorbs heat and so reduces temperature peaks during the day and means that the stored heat warms the dwelling at night. The dwelling should be well insulated and an efficient heating system installed. It is important that the heating controls allow rooms already warmed by the sun to get less heat from the heating system, e.g. by installing thermostatic radiator valves. Otherwise the rooms with high solar gain may simply be overheated, wasteful and uncomfortable.

Passive solar measures can be applied to existing buildings, for example by adding conservatories, or atria (an atrium is a space or courtyard in the middle of a building – in this case it would be glazed over). Where passive solar measures are incorporated, it is best to use energy conservation measures as well. Fitting conservatories, atria or greenhouses on existing dwellings can be expensive and cannot be justified on the grounds of energy efficiency alone, but a well-designed conservatory can provide an extra unheated living space which also provides significant warmth from the sun. It acts as extra insulation for the dwelling as the ventilation air is pre-warmed and the wall between the dwelling and the conservatory is warmed up.

South elevation: larger windows in the lounge, dining room and two main bedrooms.

Example of passive solar design – these houses are arranged on an estate so that most of them are orientated within 30° of south (courtesy of Lovell Homes)

Sunshine on the sunspace or conservatory warms the walls and pre-warms the ventilation air into the dwelling

House with 'sunspace' or conservatory

However, the positive energy gains of a conservatory are lost if the space is heated like the rest of the building. It is also important that the conservatory is not permanently open to the rest of the building.

SOLAR WATER HEATING

Solar hot water collectors on the roof of a house

Solar water heating uses the sun's energy to provide a portion of the energy needed for domestic hot water. In the UK solar water heating systems are normally designed to provide about half the hot water requirements over a 12 month period. Usually this is done by the use of solar collectors on the roofs of dwellings. There were about 42000 active solar heating systems in use in the UK in 1994, but by 2001 this would have been significantly higher, if not double [**3**].

There are a number of different designs and systems which can be used for solar water heating. They are basically panels or 'collectors' containing a fluid which circulates from the collectors where the fluid is heated by the sun, through pipes to a heat exchanger or coil within the hot water storage cylinder. The cylinder can be placed above the collectors as in a 'thermosyphon' layout – (hot water rises into the cylinder so no pump is needed) or, more commonly in the UK, the cylinder is below the collectors in a pumped system. The collectors are black to absorb the maximum amount of solar radiation.

The following types of solar collector are used in the UK:

- evacuated tube collectors – metal collectors within a tube. The outer chamber contains a vacuum which cuts down the heat loss from the collectors.
- flat plate collectors with or without selective surface – these are 'flat plate' collectors often coated in black paint and single or double glazed to cut down heat loss.

The size of a solar water collector will vary according to its design and the hot water needs of the house concerned. Typically it could be anywhere between 2 m^2 and 7 m^2. For an average house 4 m^2 of collector area is usually enough. In addition to the collector a hot water cylinder and some simple plumbing will be required.

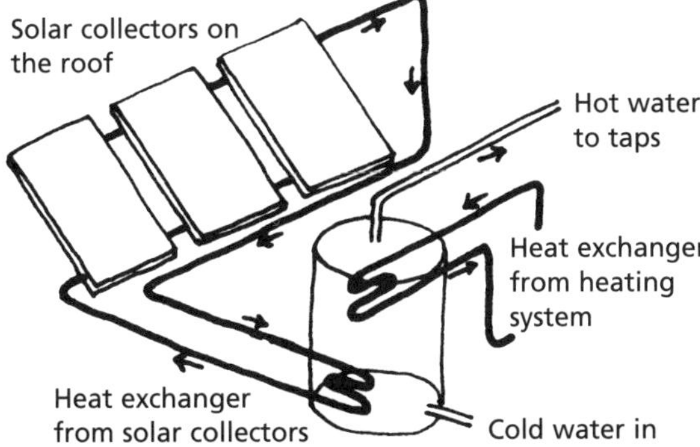

The hot water from the collector circulates inside the hot water cylinder

A well-designed system should provide about 50% (1500 kWh to 2000 kWh per year) of a household's hot water needs. In the summer the panels may provide all the hot water needs. In winter energy is captured even on overcast days. On a sunny winter's day the water temperature may be raised up to 45 – 50°C, which would then be heated to 60°C by the other source of fuel e.g. a gas central heating system.

Costs

Typical costs range from less than £2500 to over £4000 for professionally installed systems. Domestic hot water in a typical household costs between £50 to £200 a year to heat. Therefore the simple payback period (i.e. the amount of time the capital cost of the system is paid back by savings in energy costs) varies according to circumstance and can be quite long [**4**]. However, average active solar heating systems provide 20 years or more reliable service. Grants are available through the Clear Skies Programme for SCHRI in Scotland. (See Section 7) [**16**].

Payback times will be shorter if:

- there is higher hot water use than average, particularly during the summer months
- water is currently heated using a high cost fuel such as peak rate electricity or LPG
- solar hot water heating is incorporated into a new building, reducing installation costs
- there is a bulk order for a number of houses
- solar hot water heating is installed on a DIY basis (although grants are not available for DIY construction).

There are DIY solar hot water heating kits available. The Centre for Alternative Technology (CAT) produces a system, the National Energy Foundation (NEF) also provides a list of contacts for DIY systems. See end of this section for contacts.

SOLAR PHOTOVOLTAICS (SOLAR PV)

Solar photovoltaic cells convert light energy into electrical energy. The technology was first used in space, most notably in satellites with large arrays, and is common for small products such as calculators. Solar PV cells can also be seen in the UK powering road signs, parking meters, etc. They are also being used in developing countries, especially in remote areas where small kits can run small appliances, radios, and lights.

Solar PV technology is still expensive but installation of schemes is increasing due to the Government's targets to increase the use of renewable energy, and the availability of grants for Solar PV projects (see Section 7).

How does Solar PV work?

There are three main types of Solar PV cells:

- **monocrystalline:** high quality and most expensive, made from thin slices of silicon wafer. The most efficient of the PV technologies in good light conditions.
- **polycrystalline:** slightly cheaper – made from off cuts of silicon wafer – not quite such good performance but efficient in good light conditions. Less energy used for its manufacture.
- **thick film:** efficient in poor light conditions. Low energy used in manufacture so the most environmentally friendly form of PV.
- **thin film silicon:** this is usually deposited on a glass or metal base so it is sturdy. Efficient in low light conditions but performance may fade with time.

Examples of Solar PV panels

Monocrystalline PV

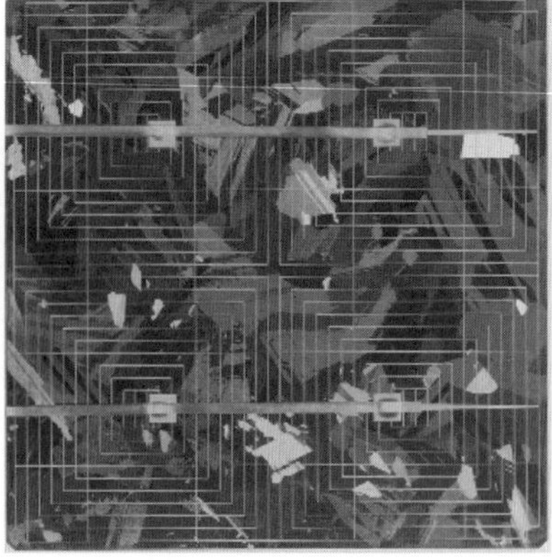

Polycrystalline PV

Thin film PV

When the silicon is exposed to light, electrical charges are generated and conducted away by metal contacts. Usually an array of solar cells is connected together as each one of them only generates a small amount of electricity. The array of cells is usually placed on the roof in a domestic situation. They should face due south in order to capture as much sunlight as possible, although they could be placed within 45° of south. Shade on the array can cause a considerable reduction in output of electricity even if only one cell is shaded, so should be avoided if possible.

The cells can be used in newly built or existing dwellings and are often put on roofs because a tilted array receives more light than a vertical one. Cells can be put together in a variety of shapes and sizes including roof tiles and cladding material, so they can be incorporated into the structure of the building, including on conservatory roofs, sun shades, etc.

In a typical domestic system the array of photovoltaic cells would cover an area of 5 – 10 m^2 (crystalline) or 15 – 25 m^2 (thin film – a larger area is needed because thin film is less efficient).

How much electricity do PV cells generate?

In a domestic system of 2 kWp, a system could produce 1500 kWh in a year. This could reduce a domestic electricity bill by 30 – 50% [**5**]. (kWp is the peak kilowatt rating for the solar panels – the maximum output of the array under full sun conditions, usually about 1 kW / m^2. This will vary throughout the year and throughout the day and in the UK PV produces approx 750 kWh per kWp per year.

The electricity output from the cells is direct current (DC), whereas domestic electricity is alternating current (AC), so an inverter is needed to turn the current from DC to AC. The electricity generated is used directly in the home. Any which is unused can be connected to the electricity grid or stored in batteries (though storing in batteries is rare). Connection to the electricity grid needs permission from the local Distribution Network Operator (DNO) but does avoid the need for storage in batteries. The electricity fed into the network must be metered because the energy supplier (in this case the householder) 'exports' the electricity into the grid when it is sunny and 'imports' it when their demand is high or the sun isn't shining. The supplier (householder) is paid for the electricity, although often at a lower rate than they themselves pay for electricity. It may be necessary to shop around for a different electricity supplier for the best price for PV generated electricity, preferably one who buys the electricity at the same price that they sell it.

Solar PV must be fitted by approved installers as there are safety issues about the electrical connections.

Costs

Installation costs for systems in 2003 were £9000 - £10000 for a 1.5 kWp system. Costs have fallen in recent years and are expected to continue to fall as the technology becomes more popular. The Department of Trade and Industry (DTI) has been funding PV projects since 1999 [**6**]. (See Section 7 for more information on grants.)

A large array of Solar PV cells – These 20 x 120 W panels are on the roof of a primary school and form a hybrid system with a 6 kW wind turbine

15.3 WIND POWER

The UK has the largest potential wind energy resource in Europe. Wind energy ranges from small battery charging applications producing electricity where the location is remote from the electricity distribution network, to large wind farms producing electricity for the national grid. We currently get less than 1% of electricity from wind. There is the potential for wind to provide 10% or more of our power requirements. The Government announced in July 2003 a major new programme for the development of up to 6 gigawatts (GW) of offshore wind farms in 3 different areas around the coast.

Wind power is not commonly used for domestic applications except in remote locations or where electricity is needed for other uses, e.g. farms or light industry. However, the technology is constantly developing.

HOW DOES A WIND TURBINE WORK?

The blades of a wind turbine generator may be up to 150 metres in diameter. When the wind blows, the blades and hub turn a shaft which rotates inside the generator which produces electricity. The amount of power generated depends on the size of the blades and the speed of the wind. The electricity is carried away by cables running underground to the electricity grid, or is sometimes used to power a stand-alone application. Overall wind energy projects are simple, clean and cheap to maintain. The land can still be part of the agricultural system.

Wind turbines

One 600 kW wind turbine (that is the size of one turbine currently typical in a wind farm – though the newest wind farms have turbines producing twice this power) would produce enough electricity for the annual needs of 375 households [**7**].

SMALL SCALE WIND TURBINES

Although large wind turbines generate electricity competitively with other sources of generation, domestic sized turbines would not be financially viable compared to electricity bought from the grid. Wind turbines need to be large in relation to the power they produce. To power a modern home on a windy site the blades would need to span 5 metres from tip to tip. A 2-metre blade could generate up to 500 kWh of electricity per year – which is only about a ninth of the average domestic electricity consumption of 4500 kWh per year [**8**].

Small scale wind turbine (20 kW) provides electricity for a dairy farm

Small scale wind turbines can, however, benefit communities or farms. Very small wind turbines (less than 1 kW) are being developed for individual properties.

Costs

For more than one household, a 6 kW system could provide 12000 kWh to 15000 kWh of electricity per year. Systems can cost between £5000 and £25000 including the turbine, mast, inverters, storage and installation, depending on the size and type of system installed [**9**].

Small stand-alone systems are available for charging batteries to run small electrical applications, such as for small pumps, electric fences, caravans and boats etc. Their output is about 0.5 – 1 kWh per day and may only cost a few hundred pounds to install. There is information on small DIY wind turbines, although the author points out that building turbines is not a simple matter [**10**].

Electricity generating wind turbines should not be confused with windmills used directly as pumps. These have more blades and work more slowly and powerfully to pump water along drainage ditches, e.g. in the Norfolk Broads.

15.4 GROUND SOURCE HEAT PUMPS

The earth contains heat in two ways, first as geothermal energy which results from geological processes creating heat within the earth. One example of how this is used is geothermal aquifiers which occur in specific geographical locations, not many of which are in the UK. In these, groundwater collects in porous rock and boreholes are drilled to extract the warm water.

The second way in which the earth contains heat is when the sun shines on the ground and the heat is absorbed and stored in the earth's surface. This source of heat is most commonly used in the UK by the use of ground source heat pumps.

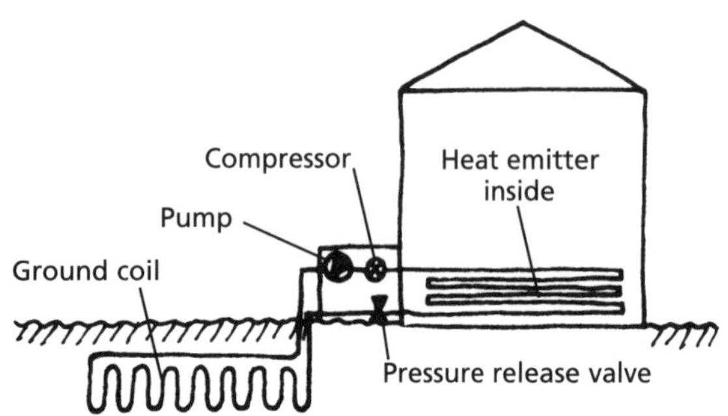

Typical schematic layout of ground source heat pump

Ground source heat pumps rely on the heat available in the ground close to the building to be heated. In the UK the ground is about 12°C. Loops of pipes are laid in the ground, either vertically in a bore hole or horizontally in trenches, often with loops of piping. The heat is extracted from the ground in a similar way to which the heat is extracted from a refrigerator. (Notice that the finned coil at the back of a fridge becomes warm – this is a similar process.) By the compression and evaporation of a special fluid, heat can be moved from one place to another. The heat exchanger provides heat which is distributed around the building as in a conventional heating system. However, because the maximum heat output temperature is usually around 55°C, special low surface temperature radiators would need to be used or wet under floor heating. The temperature of hot water would need to be boosted to 60°C.

Because the system needs electricity to run the compressor and the pump, the comparison between energy used and energy produced is described as the Coefficient of Performance (CoP). The higher the CoP the better. An efficient heat pump should extract 2.5 – 3.5 kWh of heat from the ground for every 1 kWh used. This is why ground source heat pumps are regarded as a type of renewable energy.

Because the heat pump requires electricity to run, for it to be a fully renewable technology this electricity should be generated by a renewable source too. (The easiest way to do this is to buy a green electricity tariff.) Although widely used in other Northern European countries, there are limited examples of heat pump uses in the UK [**11**].

Costs

Installation costs range between £6500 and £9500. Based on a CoP of 3 – 4 a ground source heat pump can be a cheaper form of heating than oil, LPG or electric storage heaters, but more expensive than gas [**12**].

15.5 BIOFUELS

Biofuels are fuels either used directly (e.g. wood or wood products), or produced by the breakdown of organic products to produce gas. They include agricultural and forestry by-products, energy crops, landfill gas and biodegradable waste.

BIOMASS

Biomass is the term commonly used for organic material such as wood grown specifically for fuel or waste wood or other vegetation used to burn in power stations to generate electricity, and also to provide heat. Although biomass does release CO_2 when it is burnt it is considered to be a 'carbon neutral' because the crops that are grown reabsorb this CO_2. Energy crops are, for example, willow or miscanthus – a type of large grass, grown and coppiced (cut down) which will continue to regrow.

SMALL SCALE BIOMASS

Biomass may also be used as a term to describe the burning of wood, wood pellets or wood chips directly in the domestic situation. There are many domestic scale log, wood-chip and wood pellet burning central heating boilers available [**13**].

Wood burning stoves are not uncommon in rural areas where there may be no gas but easy access to logs. They may be stand-alone stoves or they may have a back boiler supplying domestic hot water. Ranges, used for cooking as well, may run central heating and hot water systems.

Wood pellets and wood chip can both be used in automatically fed boilers so they do not have the inconvenience of needing to be manually fed. Wood pellets are a compacted form of wood, which have a low moisture content and a high energy density. In other European countries the use of wood pellets is expanding and the technology is sophisticated. Wood pellets are currently more expensive than logs and wood chip.

The capital cost of wood chip and pellet boiler installation is significantly greater than conventional systems because of the more complicated feeding mechanisms and the smaller market for the boilers.

Biomass pellets

There are grants for some types of biomass heating systems. See reference [**16**] for information on Clear Skies grants (or SCHRI in Scotland).

BIOGAS

Landfill gas is mostly a mixture of CO_2 and methane formed by the breakdown of waste in landfill sites. The anaerobic digestion of animal waste and other compostable wastes on farms also produces biogas. This can be used directly to produce heat or to generate electricity. It may also be used for both by being connected to a Combined Heat and Power plant (CHP).

15.6 HYDROELECTRICITY

Hydroelectricity uses the power of water to generate electricity. Typically this occurs at hydroelectric power stations located at dams or in mountainous regions. The technology is proven and the power stations can work for over 50 years.

On a smaller scale, water has been used for centuries to produce power for a range of uses. 'Micro hydro' is now being considered seriously again. Electricity can be generated by a 'head' of water falling 2 – 3 metres. The falling water turns a turbine which generates electricity.

A site for micro hydroelectricity needs the following features:

- enough water flow, e.g. drop or head of 2 metres
- a control of the flow of water
- a pipe to take the water to the turbine
- the powerhouse including the turbine and generator
- an outflow for the water to flow away
- cables to carry electricity to where it will be used, or the grid.

In some cases there may also be a dam to store water or create a sufficient head. Specialised advice should be sought to design and build a micro hydro system.

Costs

For dwellings with no mains electricity supply, a good hydro system can generate a reliable electricity supply, but can be expensive to build and depend on the site. For example in 2003 a scheme with a medium head of water would cost around £20,000 – £25,000 for a domestic 5kW scheme [**14**]. Larger schemes as community projects may work out more cost effective as long as there are enough water resources.

Small systems would be most suitable to charge batteries, e.g. as a back up to a diesel generator [**15**] though they can also be grid connected in the same way as solar PV (see Section 15.2).

15.7 GREEN ELECTRICITY

Not all households will be able to make use of renewable energy directly, but they can potentially still make a contribution to renewable energy by buying 'green electricity'.

WHAT IS GREEN ELECTRICITY?

Green electricity is produced from renewable energy sources. There are two types of green electricity.

- **Energy tariff** There is a direct relationship between the amount of energy bought by the customer and the supplier's use of electricity from renewable sources, i.e. the supply will match all (or a specific percentage) of the customer's energy supply bought from renewable sources.
- **Fund tariff** The supplier makes a financial contribution on the customer's behalf to bring about environmental benefit. The contribution may be a fixed payment or related to energy consumption.

Some suppliers offer a mixture of energy tariffs and fund tariffs.

HOW TO IDENTIFY A TRUE 'GREEN TARIFF'

There has in the past been confusion about the term green electricity and it is not as straightforward as it may at first seem. Ofgem has produced guidelines on green tariffs [**17**] and Friends of the Earth have produced a green electricity league table to help consumers work out exactly what is contained in each tariff [**18**].

One of the main issues is whether the green electricity being bought in the tariff (often at a premium price) is simply the green electricity the energy suppliers now have an obligation to buy under the Renewables Obligation. Someone being sold this 'obligated' green electricity in the tariff is contributing no more to renewable energy than someone not buying it – as the suppliers have to buy it under the obligation anyway.

Contact details for organisations listed here are in Appendix 1.

REFERENCES

For website references it is usually necessary to look for the link to renewables.

1 Department of Trade and Industry. **www.dti.gov.uk**

2 *Overview of renewable technologies. Passive Solar overview.* NEF renewables. **www.greenenergy.org.uk**

3 *Promoting Solar Energy.* Briefing note. **www.practicalhelp.org.uk**

4 *Solar water heating* NEF. renewables. **www.greenenergy.org.uk**

5 *Promoting Photovoltaics.* Briefing note. **www.practicalhelp.org.uk**

6 DTI *PV field trial information.* **www.solarpvgrants.co.uk**

7 *Wind energy. Frequently asked questions.* British Wind Energy Association. **www.bwea.com**

8 *Build your own wind turbine.* British Wind Energy Association. **www.bwea.com**

9 *Small-scale wind energy.* EST Fact sheet 6. Renewable Energy Technologies. **www.est.co.uk**

10 *Build your own wind turbine Wind energy in agriculture.* Hugh Piggott. Available from Centre for Alternative Technology (CAT) in Wind Energy books section.

11 *Sustainable Energy Technology Route Maps: Biofuels, Geothermal Energy,* DTI. **www.dti.gov.uk**

12 *Ground source heat pumps.* EST Fact sheet 5 Renewable Energy Technologies. **www.est.co.uk**

13 National Energy Foundation; Information on wood as a fuel and a list of suppliers of stoves, boilers and database of wood fuel suppliers. **www.greenenergy.org.uk**

14 *Small scale hydroelectricity.* EST Fact sheet 7. Renewable Energy Technologies.

15 *Small scale hydropower* NEF. renewables. **www.greenenergy.org.uk**

16 Clear Skies programme. **www.clear-skies.org**

17 *Guidelines on Green Supply Offerings.* Ofgem. April 2002.

18 *Friends of the Earth League Table of UK Green Electricity Tariffs.* **www.foe.co.uk**

FURTHER INFORMATION

The EST has produced a series of Fact sheets on Renewable Energy. They are:

Renewable energy – an introduction
Green electricity tariffs
Solar water heating
Solar photovoltaics
Ground source heat pumps
Small scale wind energy
Small scale hydroelectricity
Biomass – small scale

The following publications are available from Energy Efficiency Best Practice in Housing (EEBPH) at **www.est.org/bestpractice**:

Renewable energy in housing – case studies. CE28. 2003

Renewable energy sources for dwellings in urban environments. CE69. 2004

Renewable energy sources for dwellings in rural environments. CE70. 2004

Building a sustainable future – homes for an autonomous community. GIR53 2003

Heat pumps in the UK – a monitoring report. GIR72. 2000

Domestic ground source heat pumps. GPG339. 2003

Solar hot water systems in new housing – a monitoring report. GIR88. 2001

BedZED – Beddington Zero Energy Development, Sutton. GIR89.

Passive solar design – the Farrans study. GIL25.

USEFUL CONTACTS

For further information on renewables, local advice services, projects, case studies and training courses.

Energy Saving Trust (EST):
www.est.co.uk
Centre for Alternative Technology:
www.cat.org.uk
National Energy Foundation:
www.greenenergy.org.uk
Centre for Sustainable Energy:
www.cse.org.uk

16

CONDENSATION AND DAMPNESS

A section on condensation is included in this Handbook because condensation is a problem which, in many cases, can be solved by the same solutions which make dwellings more affordable to heat and more energy efficient.

Condensation is a form of dampness caused in the home by warm moist air hitting a cold surface. The resulting dampness may be severe and may be accompanied by mould growth. Condensation is complex in nature as it is the result of a number of inter-related conditions. It is not within the scope of this Handbook to provide a detailed technical analysis. Most of the information in this section is based on the work of the Building Research Establishment [**1**], [**2**]. This section covers:

- a description of the causes of dampness in homes so that condensation can be identified
- an explanation of the conditions which interact to cause condensation
- ways to reduce the risk of condensation
- procedures for diagnosing and remedying condensation
- equipment to help reduce condensation and mould
- the legal position for tenants whose homes suffer from condensation.

16.1 THE CAUSES OF DAMPNESS

It is often difficult to identify the cause of dampness. When faced with a dampness problem, it is necessary to consider all the causes as there may be more than one. It is important to note that the damp structure of a building can take a long time to dry out (depending on the weather, heating and other factors – but up to a year is not uncommon) even after the cause has been removed. Damp areas usually appear as stains or patches of mould. Table 16.1 helps to identify the cause.

RISING DAMP

This is dampness rising up into the building fabric from the ground. It happens because the masonry is porous and water may be soaked up into the wall by 'capillary action'. (This is the same physical process as that which draws ink into blotting paper.) It will not generally rise more than one metre up walls, and will leave a characteristic 'tide mark' on wall-paper or painted surfaces.

Rising damp can be prevented by a 'damp-proof course'. This is a barrier created by the physical insertion of either slates or a layer of plastic or bitumen into the wall, or by drilling holes in the base of the wall and injecting a solution of water repellent.

Rising damp usually occurs as a result of one of the following:

- there is no damp-proof course
- the damp-proof course has failed
- the damp-proof course has been bypassed or 'bridged' in some way.

It is possible for a damp-proof course to have failed and to have been bridged.

Where there is a damp-proof course, bridging is a common cause of rising damp. Look for this first.

If bridging of the damp-proof course is discovered, it should be eliminated. For example, any earth piled up against an external wall should be removed. If internal plaster or external render are forming the bridge these should be cut back to just above the damp-proof course.

A failed damp-proof course must be repaired or replaced. If there is no damp-proof course at all (such as in the case of an old solid walled building) one can be installed. New injected damp-proof courses must be installed properly to be effective.

Table 16.1 RECOGNISING THE CAUSE OF DAMPNESS

Cause	Position	Appearance	Timing and permanence
Rising damp	Lower part of walls on ground floor, or on higher floors adjacent to pools of standing water on walkways.	Usually a horizontal tidemark with a well defined edge usually about 600–900 mm (2–3 ft) above ground level on external walls. Often white salts deposited.	Often looks the same for long periods (months or years).
Rain penetration through faults in building fabric. Faulty rainwater disposal	Localised patches usually on outside walls – no particular position. Damp may move horizontally as well as vertically and therefore appear at some distance from cause of problem.	Patches with well defined edges.	Tends to increase in wet weather, especially after driving rain. May fade away completely in long dry spell.
Plumbing defects	Localised patches – no particular pattern or position.	Patches with well defined edges.	May stay the same or progressively increase with time. Not much affected by weather conditions unless caused by burst pipes.
Condensation dampness	Tends to occur: • in rooms where a lot of moisture is generated • on cold surfaces • in poorly ventilated spaces • on 'cold bridges'	Patches without the definite edges characteristic of other types of dampness. Often associated with black mould.	Tends to increase in cold weather.

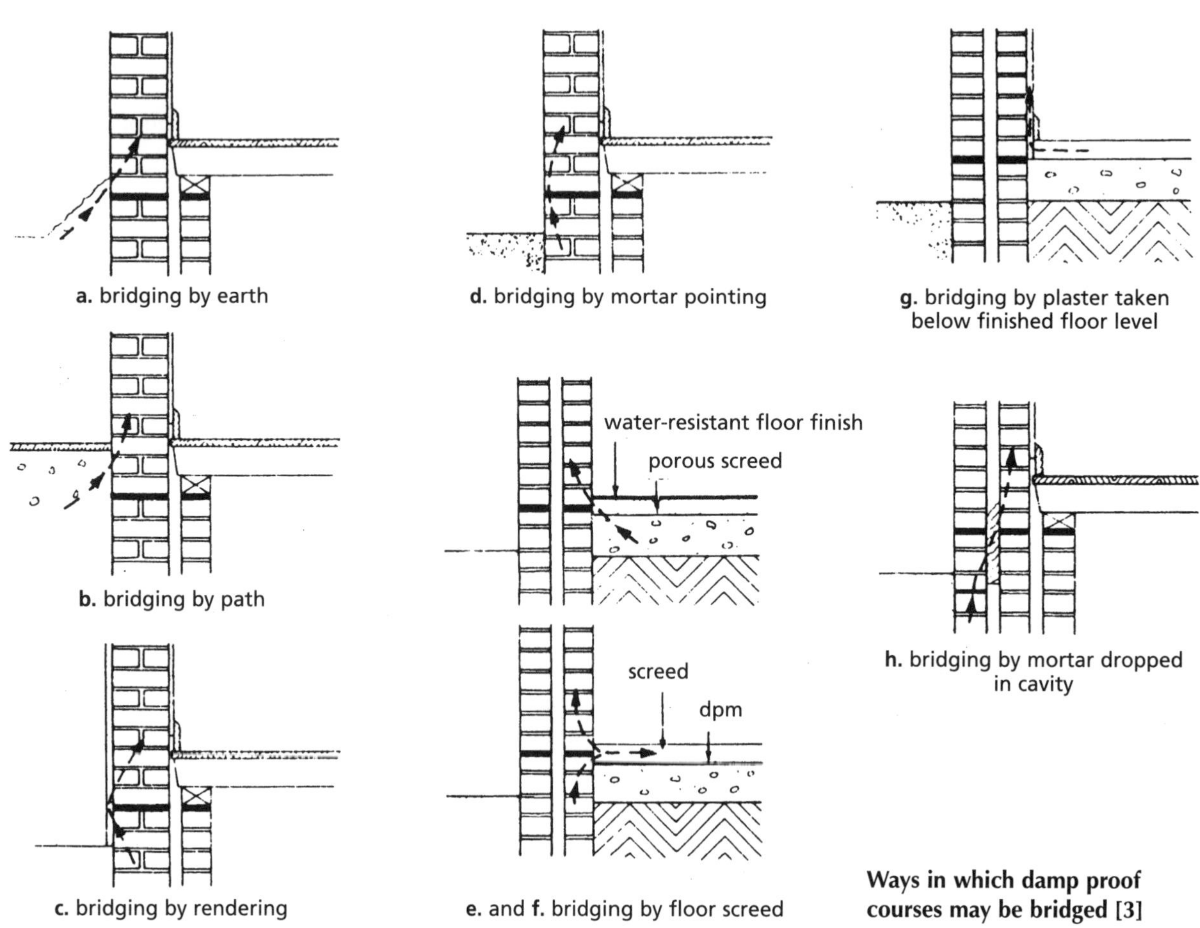

a. bridging by earth

b. bridging by path

c. bridging by rendering

d. bridging by mortar pointing

e. and **f.** bridging by floor screed

g. bridging by plaster taken below finished floor level

h. bridging by mortar dropped in cavity

Ways in which damp proof courses may be bridged [3]

RAIN PENETRATION

Building materials, such as brickwork, stonework or concrete are not perfectly 'waterproof', and will allow water penetration to a certain extent. In addition to this, rain may get in through cracks or unsealed joints.

Typical examples of building fabric in bad condition are cracked rendering, or brickwork in need of re-pointing. Except in cases where the building fabric is actually inadequate in design, rain penetration can be avoided by repair and maintenance.

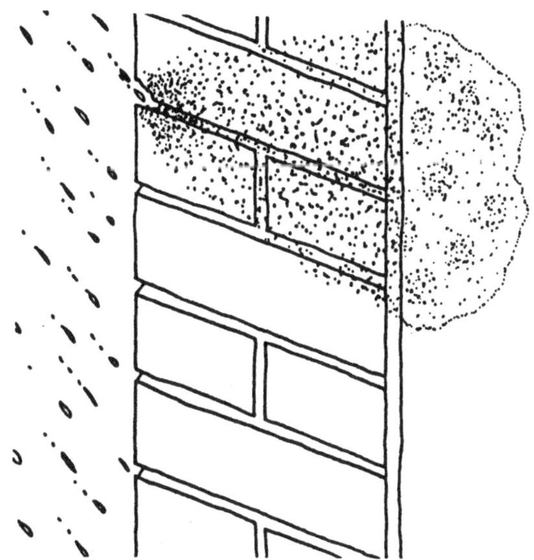

Water penetration as a result of faulty pointing

FAULTY RAINWATER DISPOSAL

Common causes are blocked, broken or disconnected downpipes and gutters, causing water to pour down wall surfaces. Guttering is sometimes placed either too close to or touching the wall, and this can cause water to spill onto the wall. If the guttering is fixed with too little slope, the same thing can happen.

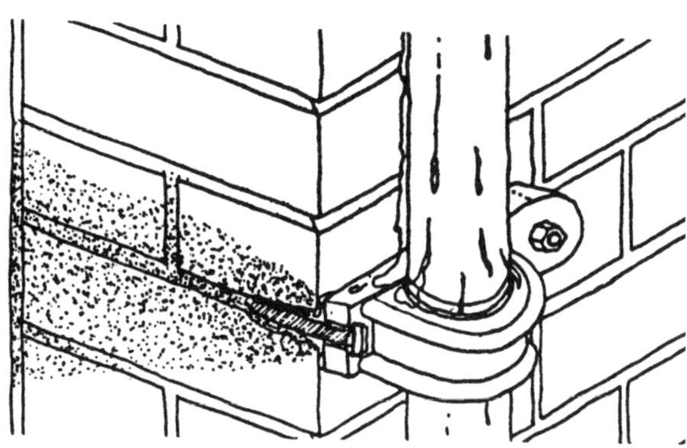

Water penetration as a result of faulty rainwater disposal

PLUMBING DEFECTS

These need no explanation, except to say that dampness may be caused either by a serious leak or by quite a small one over a period of time. The former may be dramatic, for example, a burst pipe following a freeze/thaw. The latter may be a leaking pipe or joint or even an unsealed gap between a bath or basin and the wall. A common plumbing defect is a dripping overflow pipe which gradually saturates the wall below it. Regular maintenance and prompt repair of plumbing defects should prevent problems of this kind.

CONDENSATION DAMPNESS

Air contains moisture which is held as water vapour. The amount of moisture the air can hold is determined by temperature. The higher the temperature, the more moisture can be held. Condensation occurs when this moist air hits a cold surface. The moisture 'condenses' forming water droplets.

Some condensation on the glass surface of single glazed windows may be unavoidable in cold weather, and can be wiped off. Condensation becomes a problem when it is bad enough to cause damp areas on internal wall surfaces, furniture or fittings, to rot or rust window frames, or to necessitate frequent wiping to prevent damage to decorations. A problem associated with severe condensation dampness is the growth of black or green mould. This is a health hazard [**4**].

The most familiar type of condensation is surface condensation as described, which occurs on visible surfaces. However, condensation can also form within the structure of a building, where it cannot be seen. This is known as 'interstitial condensation' and will eventually damage the fabric of the building.

Where condensation is formed

Condensation is most likely to occur:

- in rooms where lots of moisture is produced such as bathrooms and kitchens
- on cold surfaces, such as single glazed windows or metal window frames
- on walls in unheated rooms, particularly at the corner of two external walls
- on 'cold spots' caused by cold bridging
- in poorly ventilated spaces, such as inside cupboards or wardrobes or behind furniture placed against outside walls.

It is important to realise that condensation can occur in rooms a long distance away from the source of the moisture production. Warm moist air will move to colder areas and condense on cold surfaces. For example, a common problem in homes that are not centrally heated is that moisture-laden air moves to unheated rooms (often bedrooms) and causes condensation.

16.2 MOULD GROWTH

Mould growth is one of the most serious consequences of dampness. It is a health hazard and damages possessions. It also smells, looks unpleasant, and can cause a great deal of distress.

Typical mould growth caused by condensation

Mould is a type of fungus and is propagated by spores. Spores can cause respiratory allergies such as asthma to sensitive people. Air almost always contains spores, in varying concentrations. In homes unaffected by mould growth this does not usually exceed five hundred spores per cubic metre, but in homes with mould growth problems there may be more than ten times this concentration.

Moisture is necessary for the germination of spores. A term often used in relation to condensation and mould growth is 'relative humidity'. Relative humidity is the amount of water vapour in the air as a proportion of the maximum amount that the air can hold at a particular temperature.

If the relative humidity is 100%, the air is holding as much water vapour as it can at that temperature. The BRE has found that if the humidity in a room is over 70% for long periods, moulds will spread [**4**]. However, this depends also on the temperature and humidity at the surfaces themselves. The nature of the surface is significant – especially the extent to which it can absorb and retain water.

16.3 UNDERSTANDING CONDENSATION

A great deal of misunderstanding has arisen in the past, particularly between landlords and tenants, over the cause of condensation dampness. The reaction to condensation has frequently been to provide excessive ventilation. 'Open the windows and turn up the heating' was not an unfamiliar order from the landlord to the tenant. No one on a tight budget for fuel is likely to heed such advice.

Condensation is nearly always the result of a combination of conditions which lead to an air moisture content too high in relation to temperature, or temperature too low in relation to air moisture content. In real terms this situation can happen if a building lacks an adequate and affordable heating system, it has inadequate thermal insulation causing cold walls and other cold spots, and/or it lacks appropriate ventilation.

The householder is in control of the amount of moisture produced in the building, and, to some degree, its removal, so there are some things which she/he can do to help alleviate the problem. There may be situations where condensation is caused by excessive moisture generated by the householder, but these are unusual. Poor design of buildings and their services as described above are commonly the underlying causes of condensation.

16.4 REDUCING THE RISK OF CONDENSATION

The risk of condensation can be reduced by:

- increasing the temperature of the air and of internal surfaces (by providing adequate heating and insulation)
- reducing the moisture content of the air (either by producing less moisture or removing moisture by ventilation in the right places).

The four main factors to consider in the control of condensation are therefore:

- adequate heating
- adequate insulation
- reducing moisture production
- appropriate ventilation.

To successfully remedy condensation a comprehensive approach should be taken, and these four conditions should not be treated in isolation from each other. In practice more than one often requires attention. What follows should help to clarify some of the causes and remedies for condensation. Most of the information is based on the work of the BRE, see references [**1**] and [**2**].

ADEQUATE AND AFFORDABLE HEATING

A reasonable level of heating will help to reduce the risk of condensation. Heating means that the air will be able to hold more moisture, and the internal surfaces of the building will be kept warm. Around 14°C is the temperature at which the risk of condensation is reduced for most structures in existing dwellings.

In practice, the following points are important with regard to condensation risk:

- The running costs of heating systems should be affordable, or they are not likely to be used.
- Heating the whole building at a low level is better than heating one room and leaving the others completely unheated. Modern controls on heating systems, for example thermostatic radiator valves on wet systems, allow for individual room control.
- Constant heating is less likely to cause condensation than intermittent heating.
- Moisture producing heaters should be avoided, for example bottled gas and paraffin, which generate water vapour as the fuel burns.
- Warm air systems should not circulate air from the moisture producing areas such as kitchen and bathroom to other rooms.
- In two storey dwellings with unheated bedrooms, the heat rising from downstairs may be enough to reduce the risk of condensation but this is not the case in unheated bedrooms in flats or bungalows.

ADEQUATE INSULATION

Insulation in dwellings helps reduce the risk of condensation in two ways. It raises the air temperature so the air can hold more moisture. It also raises the temperature of internal surfaces so that condensation is less likely to occur.

The Building Regulations lay down standards for insulation in new dwellings (and extensions to existing dwellings) which should ensure that roofs, walls and floors are insulated. Care needs to be taken to ensure that 'cold spots' or 'cold bridges' are not built into the structure, and guidance is provided by the BRE on this matter.

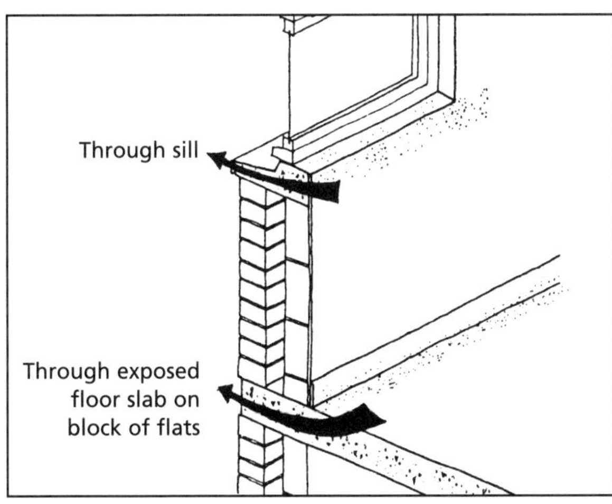

Examples of 'cold bridging'

Dwellings built before the existence of current insulation standards may suffer from high heat loss and it may be difficult to maintain adequate temperatures inside the dwelling, particularly if the heating system is expensive to run.

Roof insulation and wall insulation are commonly used to reduce heat loss from large areas of dwellings. It is also necessary to insulate parts of buildings which may, due to design faults, contain 'cold bridges'.

REDUCING MOISTURE

Water is produced by ordinary household activities and by human beings. The more people there are in a dwelling, the higher the moisture content is likely to be. Overcrowding is not, however, generally a matter of choice. Some household activities produce more moisture than others and there may be scope for reduction in moisture production.

Table 16.2 RANGE OF TYPICAL MOISTURE EMISSION RATES IN A FOUR-PERSON HOUSEHOLD [**4**]

Source	Moisture emission per 24 hours (litres)
4 persons asleep for 8 hours	1 – 2
2 persons active for 16 hours	1.5 – 3
Cooking	2 – 4
Bathing, dish washing etc.	0.5 – 1
Normal daily total	5 – 10
Additional sources of moisture	
Washing clothes	0.5 – 1
Drying clothes (e.g. unvented tumble dryers)	3 – 7.5
Paraffin or bottled gas heater during evening	1 – 2
Maximum daily total	10 – 20

Washing clothes – There is often no alternative to washing and drying clothes in the home because of launderette costs and lack of alternative facilities. In this case, general tips are:

- dry clothes outside if possible
- vent tumble dryers to the outside or use a condensing tumble dryer
- do not soak clothes any more than necessary
- keep the lid on top-loading washing machines as much as possible
- open the window and close the internal door in a room where washing and drying is going on.

Unflued heating appliances – Some gas or oil appliances do not have a chimney or flue (a passage for the removal of gases produced by burning the fuel). Burning gas or oil produces water vapour and, if no flue is used, this water vapour is released into the room. Examples of this are bottled gas fires and paraffin stoves. There may not be an alternative source of heat but, if there is, then the use of such appliances should be minimised, as they can contribute to condensation. It should be noted that gas cookers are also unflued, and should not be used for heating.

Boiling – Avoid boiling things for any longer than necessary, and keep a lid on as much as possible. Simmering is preferable to a fast boil.

APPROPRIATE VENTILATION

The moisture content of air inside a dwelling is normally greater than the moisture content of the air outside. Ventilation to the exterior therefore reduces moisture levels in the building.

Because condensation is a result of the relationship between the moisture in the air and temperature, it is important to achieve sufficient ventilation in the right places. This does not simply mean increasing ventilation. The BRE advise that approximately 0.5 to 1.5 Air Change per hour ('ach') will help prevent condensation, but an increase in ventilation over 1.5 'ach' may reduce room temperatures to such an extent that the risk of condensation is increased. The following are important considerations for reducing the risk of condensation:

- Air from the dwelling should be extracted as near to the source of moisture as possible so as to minimise the movement of wet air to the drier areas of the home. In practice this means using extractor fans or opening windows in kitchens and bathrooms when moisture is being produced. (The Building Regulations require the fitting of extractor fans to kitchens and bathrooms in new homes.)
- Opening windows in kitchens and bathrooms should be small enough so as not to discourage their being opened in winter.
- Extractor fans and extractor cooker hoods have an advantage over windows where there is no wind. Humidistat controlled extractor fans are particularly useful as they automatically react to relative humidity levels in the dwelling.
- The moisture producing areas in the dwelling should be isolated from the drier areas by keeping internal bathroom and kitchen doors closed.
- Background ventilation should be maintained in all other rooms in the dwelling.

16.5 PROCEDURES FOR DIAGNOSING AND REMEDYING CONDENSATION PROBLEMS

Condensation is a complex subject. In addition to levels of heating, insulation, ventilation and moisture production there are other factors which may contribute to any one condensation problem. The weather conditions, the orientation of the dwelling and the absorbency of the building structure all play some part.

A great deal of work has been done by the BRE along with other organisations and local authorities in recent years on tackling the problems of condensation in dwellings. The BRE state in the publication 'Tackling condensation' [**1**] that 'a comprehensive understanding of the nature of condensation more than any other factor will enable readers to deal with most of the problems in the domestic situation'.

Experience has shown that unless a whole housing estate or house type is beset by a known problem it is generally necessary to make a diagnostic visit to a dwelling. The BRE recommend that a site investigator has a working knowledge of BS 5250 [**5**]. The following points provide a general procedure for investigating and remedying condensation.

1. **Diagnose the source of dampness:**
   ensure that the problem is condensation, not due to another source of dampness.
2. **Look at the factors:**
   the heating and insulation levels in the building and any design features causing cold bridging; the occupants and their life styles; ventilation; moisture production, weather and external environment.
3. **Identify the cause of condensation:**
   given the factors above to consider, is the dwelling too cold, too wet or is there poor ventilation?
4. **Selecting and applying the remedy:**
   depending on the cause, the remedy may be a combination of increasing heating, increasing insulation, reducing unwanted ventilation, increasing controllable ventilation and reducing moisture production. The use of fungicidal washes and paints to affected areas and the provision of advice to residents are also features of the remedial package.
5. **Following up:**
   follow up interviews provide feedback on the effectiveness of the remedies.

16.6 EQUIPMENT TO HELP REDUCE CONDENSATION AND MOULD GROWTH

Positive input ventilation systems

Positive input ventilation is the usual name for systems which supply fresh air via a fan into a dwelling from the roof space (or inlet pipes in a dwelling without a roof space). The system was developed in the 1970s to deal with condensation. Typically the air is drawn through the loft and warmed up by solar gain and warmth from the house. The air is passed through a diffuser into the dwelling where it provides a continuous unobtrusive supply of air, pushing out moisture laden stale air through gaps in the dwelling structure.

Tests by the BRE in 1998 on 12 dwellings which suffered from condensation and mould [**5**] concluded that almost all the tenants felt that the conditions in their homes had improved. Test results showed that the risk of condensation was reduced in all rooms, although the effect was less in the rooms furthest away from the air input of the equipment. One drawback with the systems identified by the BRE was that the loft space will be cooler with the system operating so unlagged pipes would be more likely to freeze in very cold weather.

Dehumidifiers

Dehumidifiers are electrically operated machines that both dry and warm the air. Warm moist air is drawn into the dehumidifier. It passes over a cold coil so that moisture condenses and collects in a container which must be emptied. The dehumidifier stops operating automatically when the container is full.

A feature of all dehumidifiers is that the amount of water they extract is dependent on the temperature and humidity of the air. They are much more effective in warmer homes, where condensation is a result of a great deal of water vapour, than in the more typically condensation prone homes where condensation is a result of low room temperatures.

Fungicides

There are a large number of fungicidal washes and paints available for killing mould fungi on walls. These may also help to prevent future growth. Some are more effective than others, but there is little point in using them if the underlying cause of mould growth is not removed. However, if the cause of condensation has been dealt with, it is important to clean and treat the affected surfaces with an approved fungicide.

16.7 LEGAL POSITION OF TENANTS

Many of the remedies for condensation, for example the provision of affordable heating and improvements in insulation and ventilation, are outside the control of tenants. If a tenant lives in a dwelling which suffers from condensation and the landlord does not arrange for necessary work to be done, a tenant can resort to the law. It is beyond the scope of this Handbook to deal with detailed legal issues. The intention is to indicate the most likely course of action and refer the reader to relevant sources of advice and information [**7**], [**8**].

Although the law varies from England and Wales to Scotland, it is normally most effective for tenants to take landlords to court using the Environmental Protection Act 1990. The Act gives remedies to any person 'aggrieved' by a 'statutory nuisance', which in this case is 'a premises in such a state as to be prejudicial to health'. Severe condensation and associated mould growth will certainly be a health hazard (see Section 3) although the tenant will need to show that it is the condition of the building and services and not their use of it that is at fault. In order to win a case at the Magistrates Court (or Sheriffs Court in Scotland) it is necessary to prove three main things:

- the conditions are sufficiently bad as to be prejudicial to health
- condensation dampness is due to the structure of the home and the provision of services (e.g. provision of heating, and ventilation)
- the correct legal procedure has been followed.

It is important to get good legal advice. Cases need to be carefully prepared with the support of solicitors and building surveyors. The Health and Housing Group is a group of independent environmental health consultants active in all parts of England and Wales, and the Law Centres Federation can provide contacts for the nearest law centre – see Contacts. For further details of taking a case forward, see references [**7**] and [**8**].

Contact details for organisations listed here are in Appendix 1.

REFERENCES

1 *Tackling Condensation: A guide to the causes of and remedies for surface condensation and mould in traditional housing.* J Garratt and F Nowak, Building Research Establishment, 1991.

2 *BRE. Remedies for condensation and mould in traditional housing,* Building Research Establishment. 60 minute presentation accompanied by summary leaflets and background publications.

3 *Rising damp in walls – diagnosis and treatment.* BRE Digest 245. (Reproduced by permission of the controller, HMSO. Crown copyright.)

4 *Surface condensation and mould growth in traditionally built dwellings,* BRE Digest 297. (Table 16.2 reproduced with the permission of the controller, HMSO. Crown copyright.)

5 BS 5250: 1989 *Code of Practice: the control of condensation in dwellings,* London BSI, 1989.

6 *Monitoring and Evaluation of Domestic Supply Ventilation Systems,* foe, The Scottish Office Construction and Building Control Group, BRE Scottish Laboratory, 1998 (Executive Summary only).

7 *Action on Damp Homes,* tris (tenants' resource and information service), 1995

8 *Fuel Rights Handbook.* 12th edition. Catherine Bartholomew. Child Poverty Action Group. 2002.

FURTHER INFORMATION

BRE Digests
370 *Control of lichens, mould and similar growths*
380 *Damp proof courses*
180 *Condensation in roofs*

BRE Good Repair Guides
30 *Remedying condensation in domestic pitched tiled roofs*
5 *Diagnosing the cause of dampness*

www.bre.co.uk
for publications – **www.brebookshop.com**

CONTACTS

Law Centres Federation
Heath and Housing Group

17 VENTILATION

This section on ventilation is primarily written to cover safety, good air quality, and the consideration of energy efficient ventilation methods.

Some types of heating systems and fires require fixed ventilation and it is important to recognise this when advice is given in the home – in particular so that householders do not block up essential air vents. In addition, levels of ventilation can influence condensation and contribute to poor air quality and the build up of moulds and other allergens which can cause respiratory disorders. It is necessary for householders to understand the importance of ventilation and how to use the system they have effectively.

Ventilation is not simple to measure. There are regulations relating to ventilation requirements in housing which use a variety of definitions. The material in this section is not intended as a technical guide but to raise awareness of advisors to situations where inadequate ventilation could cause problems. For heating systems, insulation or ventilation installation, relevant Building Regulations or industry guidelines should be consulted. Ventilation heat loss is described in Section 11.

This section covers:

- air supply requirements for fuel burning appliances
- the dangers of carbon monoxide poisoning
- ventilation to help prevent condensation
- the ways ventilation is provided in a dwelling
- energy efficient ventilation methods.

17.1 HOW MUCH VENTILATION?

Ventilation is necessary in order to:

- provide air for combustion for some appliances
- remove the products of combustion from appliances which don't have flues
- ensure the proper operation of 'open' flues
- remove moisture laden air to help prevent condensation and the build up of allergens
- provide fresh air for the occupants to breathe
- remove odours.

For these reasons it is important that ventilation rates do not drop below certain minimum levels. At the same time though, it is desirable to avoid unnecessary ventilation which would cause heat loss from the dwelling.

The rate at which air leaves a building and is replaced by air entering a building is normally expressed in terms of 'air changes per hour' (written 'ach'). An air change rate of 1 'ach' is equivalent to removing the whole volume of air out of the building and replacing it with fresh air once every hour. This can be applied to a room, a flat or maisonette within a building, or a whole building. The measurement of 'air changes per hour' requires specialised equipment.

With the exception of the specific air supply requirements for fuel burning appliances (considered separately in 17.4) the most significant reason for ventilation is to remove moisture to avoid condensation problems. It follows that if the ventilation is adequate to control moisture levels, (between 0.5 and 1.0 'ach') then other pollutants will also be controlled [**1**].

Ventilation rates in any one dwelling will be determined by uncontrolled draughts from cracks, holes and gaps around windows, doors and in the building fabric, as well as deliberate and controlled ventilation. To a certain extent this depends on the age, type of construction and condition of the building. In general, the problem in older housing is too much ventilation. More recent housing tends to have lower background ventilation rates as it has fewer permanent openings, such as air bricks or chimneys. The average level of uncontrolled ventilation in UK housing is around 0.7 'ach', so there would appear to be about the right level of ventilation present. However, it is unlikely to be in the places and at the times it is needed. In windy conditions the dwelling will become draughtier.

The objective of a good ventilation strategy is to provide the balance between good air quality and energy efficiency. 'Build tight – ventilate right' is quoted by the BRE, meaning making the building as airtight as practicable and then providing a controllable ventilation system [**1**].

In new dwellings the Building Regulations Part F set down requirements for ventilation. The Approved Document F recommends ways of achieving Part F of the Regulations [**2**]. There are a number of ways to comply with these. Separately there are minimum levels of ventilation required when fuel-burning appliances are present in a dwelling. The Building Regulations Part J [**3**] and British Standards Codes of Practice [**4**], [**5**], [**6**] require the fitting of flues and the provision of adequate air supply to the appliances.

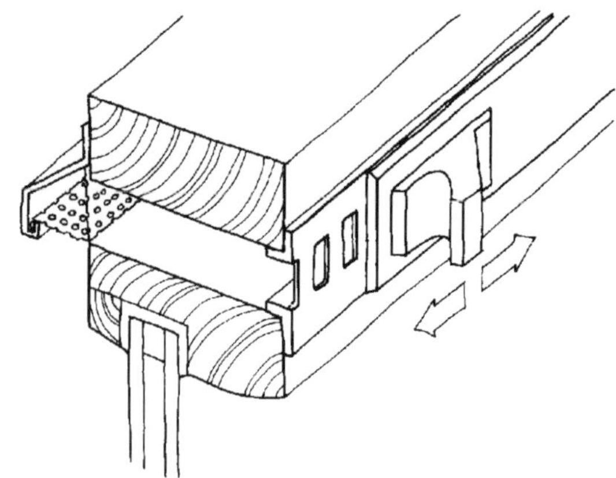

Trickle vent

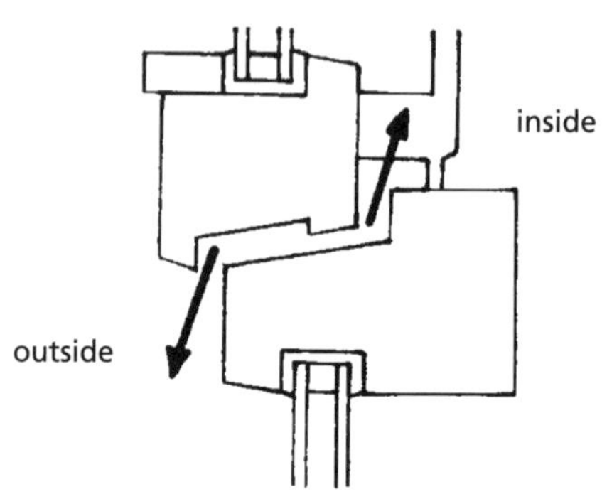

Window with adjustable locking positions

17.2 DIFFERENT TYPES OF VENTILATION

Different levels of ventilation are needed depending on what sort of activities are going on in the dwelling. The main types of ventilation are:

- rapid ventilation – e.g. an opening window
- background ventilation – e.g. trickle ventilators
- extract ventilation – either mechanical extract fans, passive stack ventilation or an open flued heating appliance e.g. with a chimney.

Ventilation problems often arise for householders as a result of the position (and to some extent the timing) of the ventilation. The source of uncomfortable draughts will often be blocked by the householder. This does not matter if the ventilation was excessive, but it is important that householders understand when essential ventilation must be maintained, and when it is important to avoid condensation.

For example, gaps around doors and windows or an air brick placed in a wall at ankle or table height (or bed height in a bedroom) can cause draughts and great discomfort. It is possible to replace uncomfortable draughts with controlled ventilation as long as it is adequate. This can be done for example by placing trickle ventilators in the frames of windows, or by re-positioning air vents.

Higher levels of ventilation are needed in kitchens and bathrooms (see Section 16) than in other rooms in the dwelling but only during or a while after moisture-producing activities such as cooking and bathing. The additional ventilation necessary in these rooms can therefore be flexible (adjustable or humidity controlled), to avoid unnecessary discomfort and heat loss at other times.

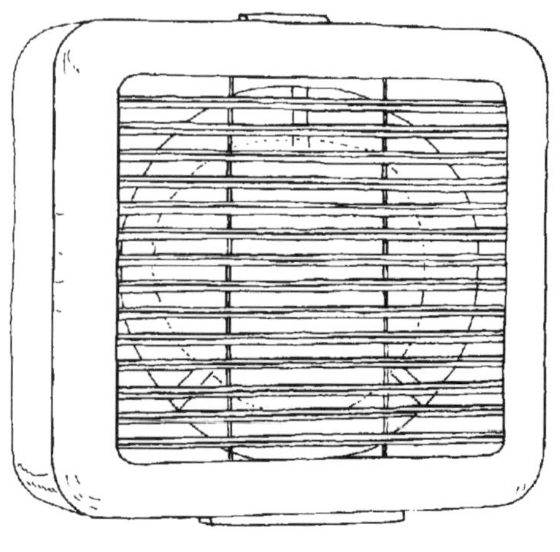

Extract fan

17.3 VENTILATION REQUIREMENTS FOR THE BUILDING REGULATIONS

Table 17.1 is reproduced from The Building Regulations (England and Wales) Approved Document F1 [**2**] and includes Building Standards (Scotland) Regulations 1990 including up to date amendments Part K. These requirements relate to new buildings.

Table 17.1 VENTILATION OF ROOMS CONTAINING OPENABLE WINDOWS (i.e. LOCATED ON AN EXTERNAL WALL)

Room	Rapid ventilation (e.g. opening windows)	Background ventilation (e.g. trickle vents)*	Extract ventilation fan rates or passive stack (PSV)
Habitable room	1/20th of floor area 1/30th (Scotland)	80 cm^2	-
Kitchen	opening window (no minimum size)	40 cm^2	30 litres/second (cooker hood) adjacent to a hob or 60 litres/second (extract fan) elsewhere or PSV
Utility room	opening window (no minimum size)	40 cm^2	30 litres/second or PSV
Bathroom (with or without wc)	opening window (no minimum size)	40 cm^2	15 litres/second or PSV
Sanitary accommodation (separate from bathroom)	1/20th of floor area	40 cm^2	6 litres/second (3 'ach' in Scotland)

Note: *Alternative approach is overall provision of background ventilation of 60 cm^2 per room with a minimum level of 40 cm^2 in each room.

17.4 VENTILATION REQUIREMENTS FOR FUEL BURNING APPLIANCES

Ventilation is needed for fuel burning appliances in order to provide oxygen for them to burn properly and to remove the products of combustion. If an appliance does not have enough oxygen to burn it will not work properly so carbon monoxide gas may be produced.

WHAT IS CARBON MONOXIDE (CO)?

Carbon monoxide (CO) is a highly poisonous gas that can be produced by burning any fossil fuel such as coal, wood or gas without enough oxygen. CO is particularly dangerous because it is colourless, odourless and tasteless, so you won't know when it is present. It can kill or cause permanent damage within a matter of hours. People are particularly vulnerable when asleep. The elderly and the young are particularly vulnerable. Around 50 people die each year as a result of CO poisoning and many more are seriously injured [**7**].

The symptoms of CO poisoning include tiredness, drowsiness, headache, dizziness, chest pains and nausea. Because these are symptoms of other illnesses, they often go ignored. CO poisoning is mostly caused by inadequate ventilation or a lack of correct maintenance of appliances, flues and chimneys. It is very important then to take action to avoid the presence of CO by the correct installation and maintenance of appliances and flues, and to look out for the danger signs.

A CO detector will warn of the presence of CO and can be used as a second line of defence although they should not be relied upon totally. Look out for the other danger signs. Models with an audible warning signal are recommended approved to BS7860 [**7**].

Danger signs that CO may be produced include:

- gas flames which normally burn blue, burning orange or yellow instead
- signs of staining, discolouration on or around gas fires, boilers or water heaters
- fumes or smoke in the house
- slower than usual burning of solid fuel fires.

There are regulations about who should install and maintain gas appliances, and how frequently they should be checked.

FLUES AND VENTILATION REQUIREMENTS

Fuel burning appliances can be divided into three categories with regard to flueing and ventilation requirements (full descriptions of flues are found in Section 8):

Flueless: these have no flue at all. The air for combustion is taken directly from the room and gases produced by combustion are released into the room. Extra ventilation is needed to provide combustion air and remove these gases. Examples are flueless gas fires or gas cookers.

Open-flued: these take their air for combustion from the room, but have a chimney or a flue taking the gases produced by combustion directly to the outside. Extra ventilation is needed, to replace air drawn up the chimney or flue and to ensure that the flue can work properly. An example is a gas fire with a back boiler fitted on a chimney breast. (See Section 8.)

Room sealed (often balanced flue): these take their combustion air from outside and are vented directly to the outside. No extra ventilation is needed. Examples include most modern gas wall-mounted boilers. (See Section 8.)

Tables 17.2 and 17.3 provide details of the air supply requirements for fuel-burning appliances. The tables are derived from Building Research Establishment Digest 306 [**8**] (reproduced by permission of the Controller, HMSO, Crown Copyright). They have been revised and updated by further material from the current Building Regulations and British Standards.

Table 17.2 AIR SUPPLY REQUIREMENTS FOR FLUELESS DOMESTIC GAS APPLIANCES OTHER THAN HEATERS [**3**]

Type of appliance	Room volume m^3	Requirements for permanent opening to the outside air (Openable window or equivalent is also required)
Gas oven, hotplate, grill or any combination thereof# [3] [4]	Less than 5	Permanent opening of 100 cm^2
	5 to 10	Permanent opening of 50 cm^2 *
	Greater than 10	No permanent opening required
Instantaneous water heater (max input of 11 kW)# [4]	Less than 5	Installation not permitted
	5 to 10	Permanent opening of 100 cm^2
	10 to 20	Permanent opening of 50 cm^2
	Greater than 20	No permanent opening required

The appliance, unless a single burner hotplate/boiling ring, is not to be installed in a bed sitting room of less than 20 m^3 volume.

*If the room or internal space containing these appliances has a door which opens directly to outside, no permanent opening is required.

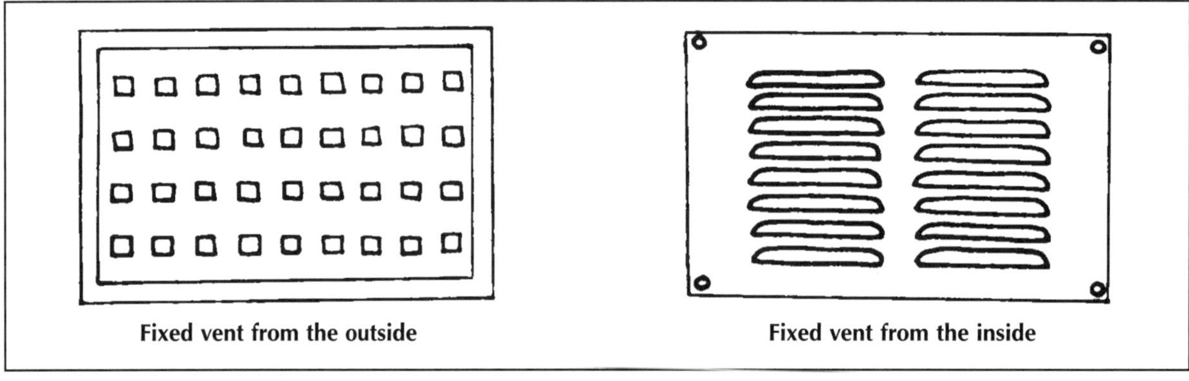

Fixed vent from the outside
Fixed vent from the inside

Table 17.3 AIR SUPPLY REQUIREMENTS FOR FUEL-BURNING HEATING APPLIANCES
Requirements for permanent opening to the outside air in the room or space containing appliance as specified in Building Regulations [**3**] or British Standards [**4**], [**5**], [**6**].

Type of appliance	Requirements for permanent openings
Room sealed heating appliance in a room or space (e.g. wall hung boiler)	None – air supply provided directly from outside. Boilers in compartments need extra ventilation for cooling[a].
Open flued gas appliance (e.g. floor mounted boiler, back boiler) [**3**] see example 1	Permanent opening required – an area of 5 cm^2 for every kW of input rating over 7 kW (net). Boilers in compartments need extra ventilation for cooling[a].
Room gas fire, open-flued [**4**], [**6**]	
a) Gas fire	Not normally required up to 7 kW input (net).
b) Inset live fuel effect gas fire	Not normally required up to 7 kW input (net).
c) Decorative fuel effect gas fire	Purpose provided ventilation of at least 100 cm^2 normally required up to 20 kW input[b].
Flueless gas space heater located in either [**3**]	Permanent ventilation required:
a) a room (max input 45 W/m^3) or	100 cm^2 plus 55 cm^2 for every kW (net) by which the appliance rated input exceeds 2.7 kW (net).
b) an internal space (a hall or passageway) (max input 90 W/m^3) see example 2	100 cm^2 plus 27.5 cm^2 for every kW (net) by which the appliance rated input exceeds 5.4 kW (net).
Open solid-fuel fire [**3**], (**5**]	An air entry opening or openings with a total free area of at least 50% of the throat opening area.
Other solid fuel flued appliance including stove, cooker or boiler [**3**], (**5**]	An air entry opening or openings with a total free area of at least 5.5 cm^2 per kW of rated output above 5 kW. Where a flue draught stabiliser is used the total free area should be 3 cm^2 per kW for the first 5 kW of output and 8.5 cm^2 for every kW by which the appliance exceeds 5 kW.
Oil burning flued appliance in a room or space [**3**]	Permanent opening of at least 5.5 cm^2 per kW of appliance rated output above 5 kW. In Northern Ireland the definition is 5.5 cm^2 plus 5.5 cm^2 for each kW of appliance output above 6kW. Boilers in compartments need extra ventilation for cooling[a].

[a] Some boilers need to be cooled to protect the controls from overheating.
The air for cooling may be drawn from a larger indoor space – it does not need to be drawn from outside. See reference [**3**].

[b] May not be necessary if fire input is less than 7 kW. See reference [**3**].

EXAMPLES:

1 A gas fired back boiler is rated at 14 kW input. The vent should be (14 – 7) x 5 cm^2 = 35 cm^2.

2 A hallway contains a flueless gas heater rated at 7 kW input. The vent should be 100 cm^2 plus (7 – 5.4) x 27.5 = 144 cm^2.

INTERACTION OF EXTRACT VENTILATION AND OPEN FLUED APPLIANCES

Mechanical extract ventilation can cause the 'spillage' of flue gases from open flued appliances whether or not the fans and appliances are in the same room (that is, they draw the gases back into the room). This is dangerous. The appliance needs to be able to operate safely whether or not the fan is running. The Building Regulations Approved Document J [**3**] states that for gas appliances, where the appliance and fan are in the kitchen, the maximum extract rate of the fan should be reduced (20 litres/second) and where they are in different rooms a spillage test is carried out. For oil-fired appliances, advice should be obtained from OFTEC [**9**], and for solid fuel appliances mechanical extract fans should not be provided in the same room.

17.5 VENTILATION AND CONDENSATION

This subject has largely been covered in Section 16, but there are recommendations for ventilation to avoid condensation.

An ideal rate of ventilation between 0.5 and 1.0 air changes per hour (ach) is recommended because:

- With less than 0.5 ach, the relative humidity rises sharply regardless of heat input or insulation level, so increasing the risk of condensation problems.
- Much more than 1.0 ach does not help to reduce the relative humidity and the home gets much colder for a given amount of heating. At high ventilation rates, condensation may even get worse because of lower temperatures [**10**].

It should be noted that roof and loft spaces must also be adequately ventilated, as must space under suspended timber floors. This is especially important with well insulated lofts, as the loft space will be colder, so more likely to suffer from condensation (see Section 12).

Moisture should be removed at as close to source as possible so higher ventilation levels are required in kitchens and bathrooms following moisture generation. Small windows should be opened or extract fans used.

17.6 ENERGY EFFICIENT VENTILATION METHODS

The Good Practice Guide 268: Energy efficient ventilation in housing [**1**] reviews ventilation methods with their advantages and disadvantages. A short summary is provided here.

PASSIVE STACK VENTILATION (PSV)

Passive stack ventilation was introduced into the Building Regulations in 1995 as an alternative to mechanical extract fans in kitchens, bathrooms and utility rooms. Commonly installed in Europe, the system works in a similar way to the chimney of an open fire. Warm moist air rises up vertical ducts out of the dwelling as it is lighter. The effect of the wind also draws the air up. The energy efficiency of the systems is comparable with mechanical extract fans [**11**]. It is difficult to fit passive stack ventilation systems in anything except new or refurbished dwellings. The advantages are the continuous background ventilation which is silent with no running costs, which is capable of keeping humidity to a level which avoids condensation.

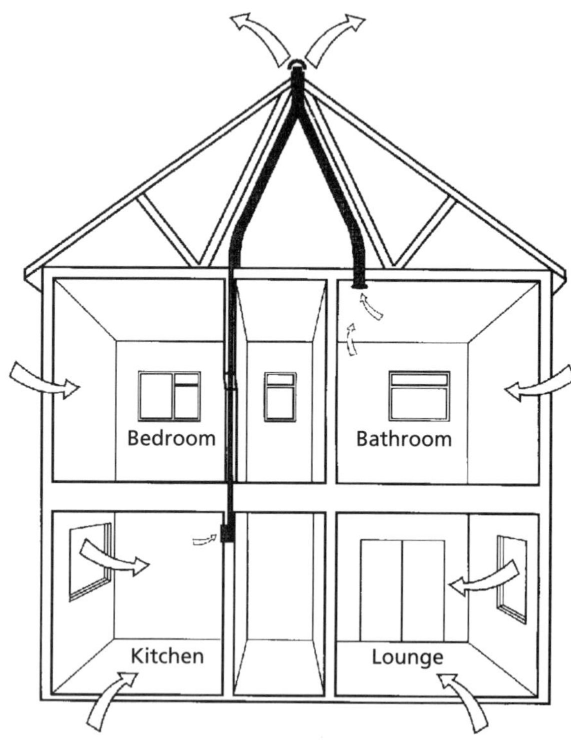

Passive stack ventilation

HEAT RECOVERY ROOM VENTILATOR

Local extract fans in the kitchen and bathroom incorporate a heat exchanger which recovers approximately 60% of the heat from the outgoing

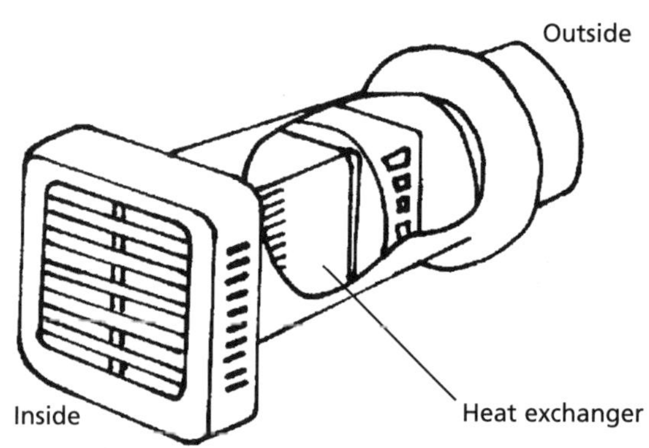

Heat recovery room ventilator

air [**1**]. This pre-warms incoming fresh air. They run at a 'trickle' rate and are boosted up to high rate by either manual or humidistat control. As with all extractor fans these may be switched off by occupants who find them noisy, so the quiet trickle rate is an advantage.

POSITIVE PRESSURE VENTILATION

In this system air, usually from the loft space, is drawn by a fan down into the dwelling which creates a positive pressure within the house so pushing stale air out through gaps in the building. As the air is drawn from the loft space in houses it is pre-warmed by otherwise wasted heat in the loft space. (See also Section 16.) This system is simple in operation, but may be perceived to be noisy so may be switched off by occupants.

WHOLE HOUSE MECHANICAL VENTILATION WITH HEAT RECOVERY

This system is appropriate to new buildings or to major refurbishment. The system both extracts stale air mainly from the 'wet' areas of the dwelling and provides pre-heating for fresh air throughout the house which is distributed through ducting. It is important that the house is otherwise airtight for the system to work properly. The system can provide continuous pre-warmed fresh air and so contributes to energy efficiency and good air quality, although the energy used by the continually running fans largely offsets savings by heat recovery. The initial costs of whole house ventilation are high.

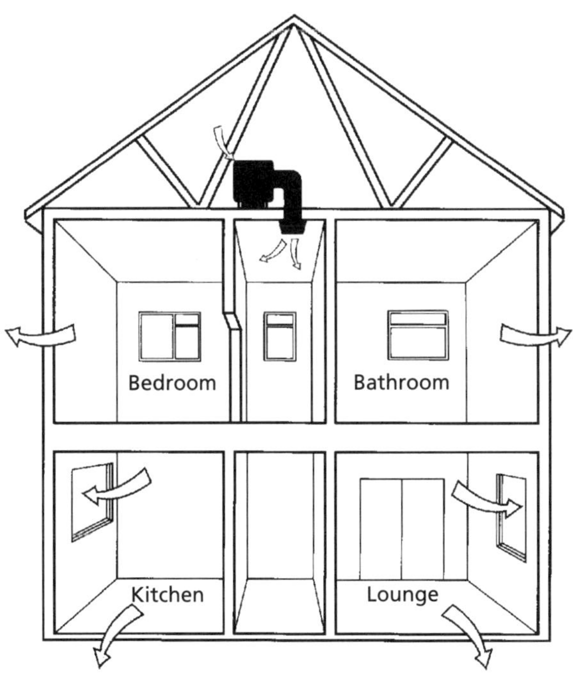

Positive pressure ventilation

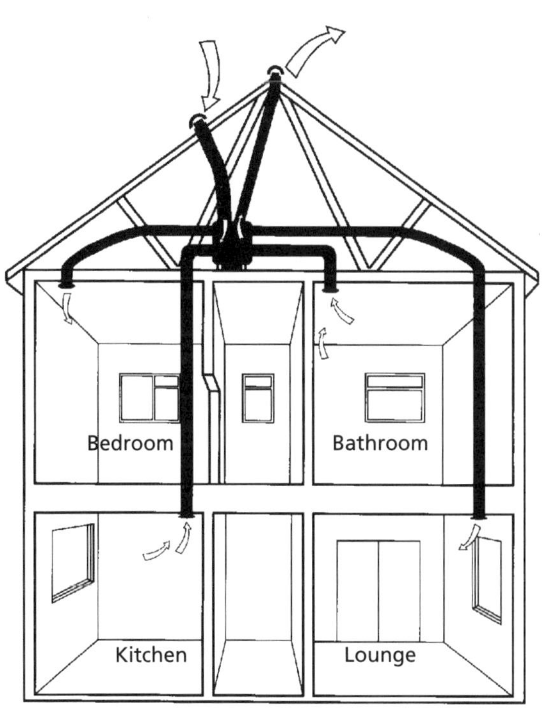

Whole house mechanical ventilation

See page **17–8** for references.

Contact details for organisations listed here sare in Appendix 1.

REFERENCES

1 *Energy efficient ventilation in housing. A guide to specifiers on the requirements and options for ventilation.* Energy Efficiency Best Practice. GPG 268. Housing 1999.
www.est.org.uk/bestpractice

2 *The Building Regulations Approved Document F – Ventilation*: 1995 Edition, amended 2000. The Stationery Office.
www.odpm.gov.uk/buildingregulations

3 *The Building Regulations Approved Document J – Combustion appliances and fuel storage systems*: 2002 edition. The Stationery Office.
www.odpm.gov.uk/buildingregulations

4 BS 5440: Part 2: 2000. British Standards Institution. *Installation of flues and ventilation for gas appliances of rated input not exceeding 60kW (1st, 2nd and 3rd family gases).* Specification for installation and maintenance of ventilation for gas appliances.

5 BS 8303: Part 1: 1994. British Standards Institution. *Code of practice for installation of domestic heating and cooking appliances burning solid mineral fuels.*

6 BS 5871: Part 3: 2001. British Standards Institution. *Specification for installation of gas fires, convector heaters, fire/back boilers and decorative fuel effect gas appliances.*

7 British Gas leaflet: *'Setting the Standards – Our pledge to you'*. 2002.

8 BRE Digest 306, *Domestic draughtproofing ventilation considerations.* BRE. Feb, 1986.

9 *The Gas Safety (Installation and Use) Regulations 1998*: Statutory Instruments 1998 No. 2451.

10 OFTEC Oil Firing Technical Association for the Petroleum Industry.
www.oftec.org

11 *Tackling Condensation: a guide to the causes of and remedies for surface condensation and mould in traditional housing.* J Garratt and F Novak. BRE Report. 1991.

12 BRE Good Repair Guide 21. *Improving ventilation in housing.* 1998.

Appendix 1

USEFUL ADDRESSES

Organisations listed here are in alphabetical order to avoid multiple entries. (The exception is the list of gas and electricity suppliers which are listed under F for Fuel Suppliers.) The majority of these organisations have been referred to at the end of each relevant section of the Handbook.

A

Age Concern England
Astral House
1268 London Road
London
SW16 4ER

0800 009966
www.ace.org.uk

Approved Coal Merchants
See Solid Fuel Association

Association for the Conservation of Energy (ACE)
Westgate House
Prebend St
London
N1 8PT

020 7359 8000
www.ukace.org

Association of Plumbing and Heating Contractors (APHC)
14 Ensign House
Ensign Business Centre
Westwood Way
Coventry
CV4 8JA

02476 470626
www.aphc.co.uk

B

British Board of Agrement (BBA)
PO Box 195
Bucknalls Lane
Garston
Watford
Herts
WD25 9BA

01923 665 300

British Photovoltaic Association
National Energy Centre
Davy Avenue
Knowlhill
Milton Keynes
MK5 8NG

01908 442291
www.pv-uk.org.uk

British Standards Institution
Head Office
389 Chiswick High Road
London
W4 4AL

0208 996 9000
www.bsi.org.uk

British Wind Energy Association
Renewable Energy House
1 Aztec Row
Berners Road
London
N1 0PW

020 7689 1960
www.bwea.com

Building Research Establishment (BRE)
Garston
Watford
WD25 9XX

01923 664258
www.bre.co.uk

C

Cavity Insulation Guarantee Agency (CIGA)
CIGA House
3 Vimy Court
Leighton Buzzard
Beds
LU7 1FG

01525 853 300
www.ciga.co.uk

Cavity Foam Bureau
PO Box 79
Oldbury
Warley
West Midlands
B69 4PW

0121 544 4949

Centre for Alternative Technology (CAT)
Machynlleth
Powys
SY20 9AZ

01654 705950
www.cat.org.uk

Centre for Sustainable Energy (CSE)
The CREATE Centre
Smeaton Road
Bristol
BS1 6XN

0117 929 9950
www.cse.org.uk

Chartered Institution of Building Services Engineers (CIBSE)
222 Balham High Road
Balham
London
SW12 9BS

020 8675 5211
www.cibse.org

Child Poverty Action Group (CPAG)
94 White Lion Street
London
N1 9PF

020 7837 7979
www.cpag.org.uk

Clear Skies
BRE Ltd
Building 17
Garston
Watford
WD25 9XX

08702 430 930
www.clear-skies.org

Combined Heat and Power Association (CHPA)
Grosvenor Gardens House
35/37 Grosvenor Gardens
London
SW1W OBS

020 7828 4077
www.chpa.co.uk

Community Legal Services (CLS) Legal Help Scheme

0845 608 1122
www.justask.org.uk

Consumers' Association
2 Marylebone Road
London
NW1 4DF

020 7770 7000
www.which.net

Council for Registered Gas Installers (CORGI)
1 Elmwood
Chineham Business Park
Crockford Lane
Basingstoke
Hants
RG24 8WG

01256 372 200
www.corgi-group.com

CPAG in Scotland
Unit 09 Ladywell
94 Duke Street
Glasgow
G4 0UW

0141 552 3303
www.cpagscotland.org.uk

CREATE (Centre for Research Education and Training in Energy)
Kenley House
25 Bridgeman Terrace
Wigan
WN1 1TD

01942 322271
www.create.org.uk

D

Department for Environment, Food & Rural Affairs (DEFRA)
Nobel House
17 Smith Square
London
SW1P 3JR

08459 33 55 77
www.defra.gov.uk

Department of Trade and Industry (DTI)
1 Victoria Street
London
SW1H 0ET

020 7215 5000
www.dti.gov.uk

Domestic Heating Controls Group
TACMA
Westminster Tower
3 Albert Embankment
London
SE1 7SL

020 7793 3008
www.heatingcontrols.org.uk

E

Eaga Charitable Trust
23 Macadam Gardens
Penrith
Cumbria
CA11 9HS

01768 210220
www.eaga.co.uk

Eaga Partnership Ltd
Eaga House
Archbold Terrace
Jesmond
Newcastle upon Tyne
NE2 1DB

0191 247 3800
www.eaga.co.uk
(for grant information in England, Wales, Scotland and Northern Ireland see Section 7)

Elmhurst Energy Systems Ltd
Elmhurst Farm
Bow Lane
Withybrook
Nr Coventry
CV7 9LQ

01788 833386
www.elmhurstenergy.co.uk

Energy Action Scotland
Suite 4a
Ingram House
227 Ingram St
Glasgow
G1 1DA

0141 226 3064
www.eas.org.uk

Energy Advice Providers' Group
See Energy Efficiency Partnership for Homes

Energy Efficiency Advice Centres (EEACs)
There are 52 EEACs around the UK. Call the freephone number to link to the EEAC covering your area.

0800 512 012

Energy Efficiency Best Practice in Housing
See Energy Saving Trust
www.est.org.uk/bestpractice

Energy Efficiency Partnership for Homes
See Energy Saving Trust
www.est.org.uk/partnership

Energy Inform Ltd
5 Hawkyard
Greenfield
Oldham
OL3 7NP

01457 873610
www.energyinform.co.uk

Energy Saving Trust (EST)
21 Dartmouth Street
London
SW1H 9BP

020 7222 0101
www.est.org.uk

energywatch
Head Office, 4th Floor
Artillery House
Artillery Row
London
SW1P 1RT

08459 06 07 08
www.energywatch.org.uk

Environmental Change Institute University of Oxford
5 South Parks Road
Oxford
OX1 3UB

01865 281180
www.eci.oc.ac.uk

F

Federation of Authorised Energy Rating Organisations (FAERO)
See NHER
www.faero.co.uk

FIAC (Federation of Independent Advice Centres)
4 Dean's Court
St Pauls Churchyard
London
EC4V 5AA

020 74891800
www.yourrights.org.uk

Friends of the Earth
26-28 Underwood Street
London
N1 7JQ

020 7490 1555
www.foe.co.uk

FUEL SUPPLIERS
Domestic suppliers of gas and electricity. (Some suppliers are listed under group headings showing which have merged or are working together.)

Atlantic Electric and Gas
Southgate House
Southgate Street
Gloucester
GL1 1UB

Customer Services:
0870 013 2080
Energy Efficiency:
0845 330 0648
www.atlanticeg.com

British Gas Trading
National Sales Office
Helmont House
Churchill Way
Cardiff
CF1 4NB

Customer Services:
0845 6070200
Energy Efficiency:
0845 602 0155
www.house.co.uk
(England & Wales)

British Gas Trading (trading as Scottish Gas)
4 Marine Drive
Edinburgh
EH5 1YB

Customer Services:
0845 6070300
(Scotland)

EDF Energy
Energy Efficiency:
0800 096 9966
www.edfenergy.com

London Energy
40 Grosvenor Place
Victoria
London
SW1X 7EN

Customer Services:
0800 096 5010
www.london-energy.com

Seeboard Energy
Freepost 3815
Hove
BN3 5AW

Customer Services:
0800 096 9696
www.seeboard-energy.com

SWEB Energy
Osprey Road
Exeter
EX2 7HZ

Customer Services:
0800 365 000
www.sweb-energy.com

Virgin Home Energy
Freepost LON14908
Exeter
EX2 7BF

Customer Services:
0800 028 8269
www.virginhome.co.uk

npower
Tyne House
Birchwood Drive
Peterlee
County Durham
SR8 2YA

Customer Services:
0800 389 2388
Energy Efficiency:
0800 022 220
www.npower.com

Powergen
Raw Dykes Road
Leicester
LE2 7JY

Customer Services:
0800 363 363
Energy Efficiency:
0800 195 0101
www.powergen.co.uk
Amerada acquired by Powergen
TXU Energi acquired by Powergen

Scottish & Southern Energy
PO Box 6009
Basingstoke
RG21 8ZD

Energy Efficiency
0845 777 6633
www.scottish-southern.co.uk

Scottish Hydro Electric
Customer Services:
0845 300 2141 (electricity)
Customer Services:
0845 755 2233 (gas)
www.hydro.co.uk

Southern Electric
Customer Services:
0845 744 4555 (electricity)
Customer Services;
0845 758 5401 (gas)
www.southern-electric.co.uk

SWALEC
Customer Services:
0800 052 5252 (electricity)
Customer Services:
0800 052 0567 (gas)
www.swalec.co.uk

Scottish Power
Cathcart House
Spean Street
Glasgow
G44 4GG

Customer Services:
0800 400 200
Energy Efficiency:
0800 332233
www.scottishpower.co.uk

Manweb owned by ScottishPower

G

The Glass and Glazing Federation (GGF)
44-48 Borough High St
London
SE1 1XB

020 7403 7177
www.ggf.org.uk

H

Health and Housing Group
120 Wilton Road
London
SW1V 1JZ

0207 233 7780

Heating & Hotwater Information Council
36 Holly Walk
Leamington Spa
Warwickshire
CV32 4LY

0845 600 2200
www.centralheating.co.uk

Heating and Ventilating Contractors' Association (HVCA)
ESCA House
34 Palace Court
London
W2 4JG

020 7313 4900
www.hvca.org.uk

HMSO (The Stationery Office)
PO Box 276
London
SW8 5DT

0870 600 5522
www.hmso.gov.uk

I

Institute of Domestic Heating and Environmental Engineers (IDHE)
Dorchester House
Wimblestraw Rd
Berinsfield
Wallingford
Oxon
OX10 7LZ

01865 343 096
www.idhe.org.uk

Institute of Plumbing (IoP)
64 Station Lane
Hornchurch
Essex
RM12 6NB

01708 472 791

L

Law Centres Federation
Duchess House
18-19 Warren Street
London
W1T 5LR

020 7387 8570
www.lawcentres.org.uk

The LP Gas Association
Pavilion 16
Headlands Business Park
Salisbury Rd
Ringwood
Hampshire
BH24 3PB

01425 461612
www.lpga.co.uk

M

Market Transformation Programme
Future Energy Solutions
Harwell
Didcot
Oxfordshire
OX11 0QL

0845 600 8951
www.mtprog.com

MVM Consultants plc
MVM House
2 Oakfield Road
Clifton
Bristol
BS8 2AL

0117 974 4477
www.mvm.co.uk

N

National Assembly for Wales
Cardiff Bay
Cardiff
CF99 1NA

02920 825111
www.wales.gov.uk

National Association of Citizens' Advice Bureaux (NACAB)
Myddelton House
115-123 Pentonville Rd
London N1 9LZ

www.nacab.org.uk

National Audit Office (NAO)
157-197 Buckingham Palace Rd
London
SW1W 9SP

0207 798 7000
www.nao.org.uk

National Debtline
The Arch
48-52 Floodgate Street
Birmingham
B5 5SL

0808 808 4000
www.nationaldebtline.co.uk

National Energy Services (NES Ltd)
The National Energy Centre
Davy Avenue
Milton Keynes
MK5 8NA

01908 672787
www.nesltd.co.uk

National Heart Forum
Tavistock House South
Tavistock Sq
London
WC1H 9LG

020 7383 7638
www.heartforum.org.uk

National Insulation Association
PO Box 12
Haslemere
Surrey
GU27 3AH

01428 654 011
www.insulationassociation.org.uk

NEA (National Energy Action)
St Andrew's House
90-92 Pilgrim Street
Newcastle upon Tyne
NE1 6SG

0191 261 5677
www.nea.org.uk

NEA Northern Ireland
64-66 Upper Church Lane
Belfast
BT1 4QL

02890 239909
www.nea.org.uk

NEA Wales
See NEA

NEF Renewables
The National Energy Foundation
Davy Avenue
Knowlhill
Milton Keynes
MK5 8NG

01908 665555
www.greenenergy.org.uk

NHER (National Home Energy Rating)
The National Energy Centre
Davy Avenue
Milton Keynes
MK5 8NA

01908 672787
www.nher.co.uk

O

Ofgem (The Office of Gas and Electricity Markets)
9 Millbank
London
SW1P 3GE

020 7901 7000
www.ofgem.gov.uk

OFTEC (Oil Firing Technical Association)
Foxwood House
Dobbs Lane
Kesgrave
Ipswich
IP5 2QQ

0845 65 85 080
www.oftec.org

P

Photovoltaics (PV)
See British Photovoltaic Association

Powergen
(Warm Front Grants only. See also Fuel Suppliers)

0800 952 1555
www.powergen-warmfront.co.uk

R

Renewable Energy Enquiries Bureau
Future Energy Solutions
Harwell
Didcot
Oxfordshire
OX11 0QJ

0870 190 6349
www.dti.gov.uk/renewables

S

SALKENT
202 Tonbridge road
Wateringbury
Kent
ME18 5NU

01622 817095
www.salkent.co.uk

Scottish Community and Householder Renewables Initiative (SCHRI)

0800 138 8858
www.est.co.uk

link to Scotland, link to Scottish Community and Householder Renewables Initiative

Scottish Executive

0131 556 8400
www.scotland.gov.uk

Scottish and Northern Ireland Plumbing Employers' Federation (SNIPEF)
2 Walker St
Edinburgh
EH3 7LB

0131 225 2255
www.snipef.org.uk

Solar Trade Association
The National Energy Centre
Davy Avenue
Knowlhill
Milton Keynes
MK5 8NG

01908 442290
www.solartradeassociation.org.uk

Solid Fuel Association
7 Swanwick Court
Alfreton
Derbyshire
DE55 7AS

0845 601 4406
www.solidfuel.co.uk

T

TACMA
See Domestic Heating Controls Group

U

UK Environmental Product Information Consortium (UKEPIC)
See Market Transformation Programme

www.ukepic.com

Utilities
See Fuel Suppliers

W

Which? Magazine
See Consumers' Association

Appendix 2

HOME SURVEY QUESTIONNAIRE

This questionnaire is based loosely on the Home Energy Check used by the national network of Energy Efficiency Advice Centres (EEAC). It may be used as a guide and modified for your own purposes.
It must NOT be filled in and sent to an EEAC.

Customer Details

Title: Mr ☐ Mrs ☐ Miss ☐

Other ______

First Name/Initial: ______

Surname: ______

Address: ______

______

______

Postcode: ☐☐☐☐ ☐☐☐☐

Contact tel. no: ______

In what year was your house built? (Tick one)

Before 1900	☐	1965 – 1974	☐
1900 – 1918	☐	1975 – 1980	☐
1919 – 1929	☐	1981 – 1990	☐
1930 – 1944	☐	1991 – 1995	☐
1945 – 1949	☐	1996 or later	☐
1950 – 1964	☐		

Property type? (Tick one)

Detached	☐	Semi-detached	☐
End terrace	☐	Mid terrace	☐
Top floor flat	☐	Middle flat	☐
Ground floor flat	☐		

Do you own your home or do you rent?

Own/buying on mortgage ☐

Rent from Council ☐

Rent from Housing Association ☐

Rent privately ☐

Tied/other ☐

Property Details

Does your home have a loft?

Yes ☐ No ☐

If yes, is there a heated room that's in regular use within the loft?

Yes ☐ No ☐

Insulation Details

How much loft insulation do you have?
(If this is going to be difficult, please take an educated guess)

None ☐ 1″ ☐ 2″ ☐ 3″ ☐

4-5″ ☐ 6″ ☐ 8″ ☐

I have some but don't know how much ☐

Don't know ☐

What type of outside walls do you have?

Solid brick	☐	Mixed (solid/cavity)	☐
Solid concrete	☐	Timber frame	☐
Solid stone	☐	Don't know	☐
Cavity – insulated	☐		
Cavity – uninsulated	☐		

Which type of windows do you have?

All single glazed ☐

Some double or secondary glazed ☐

Most double or secondary glazed ☐

All double or secondary glazed ☐

Is there any draughtproofing on windows and external doors? (Assume double glazed windows and doors to be draughtproofed)

None ☐ Some ☐ Most ☐ All ☐

Heating and Hot Water

What is your main heating system?

Boiler/radiators ☐

Warm air ☐

Storage heaters ☐

Room heaters/fires ☐

Other ☐

What is your main heating fuel?

Mains gas ☐ Solid fuel ☐

LPG (bulk) ☐ Electricity ☐

Bottled gas ☐ Oil ☐

What heating controls do you have? (Please tick all that apply)

Timer/programmer ☐

Room thermostat ☐

Thermostatic radiator valves ☐

Storage heater dials ☐

None ☐

If you have a bolier, how old is it?

Under 5 years ☐

5–10 years ☐

11–15 years ☐

over 15years ☐

How is your hot water usually provided?

Gas instantaneous/Combi ☐

From heating system ☐

Electric instantaneous ☐

Gas, oil or coal range ☐

Electric immersion (on peak) ☐

Back boiler ☐

Electric immersion (off peak) ☐

Dual electric immersion ☐

Other ☐

How would you describe your hot water tank insulation?

Solid foam insulation ☐

Jacket ☐

No insulation ☐

No tank ☐

Lights and Appliances

How many of your lights have low energy bulbs fitted?

None ☐

One ☐

Some ☐

Most ☐

Don't know ☐

All ☐

Which of the following household appliances do you have? If possible, could you also tell us how old the appliance is?

	Please tick	Age in years 0–5	6–10	11+
Fridge/Freezer	☐	☐	☐	☐
Fridge	☐	☐	☐	☐
Freezer	☐	☐	☐	☐

Household Details

The following questions will be used to help us evaluate whether or not you may be eligible for a grant.

Is a member of your household over 60?

Yes ☐ No ☐

Is a member of your household in receipt of benefits?

Yes ☐ No ☐

Appendix 3

HOW TO WORK OUT APPROXIMATE WEEKLY FUEL COSTS FROM METER READINGS

Electricity and gas tariffs can be complicated, making it difficult to work out running costs from meter readings in a simple way. The charts here cut out some of the steps needed for accurate bill calculations, but should still provide an adequate guide to likely fuel costs. These are examples so up to date local costs should be used. Here we provide blank templates which can be copied to produce weekly monitoring sheets.

These meter readings should remind you how to read various meters.

Electricity digital meter – this meter reads 29897

Gas meter reading cubic feet – this meter reads 1668.

Electricity dial meter – this meter reads 10851

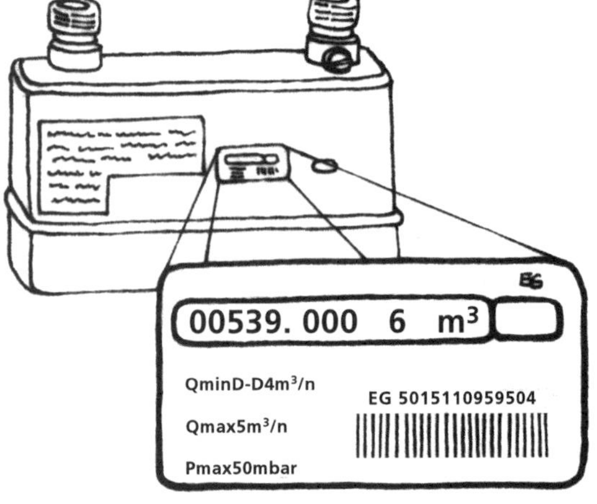

Gas meter reading cubic metres – this meter reads 00539.

Electricity Economy 7 meter – this meter reads low 97666, normal 45338

FUEL MONITORING CHART – ELECTRICITY

(See Section 5 for identification of meters and accurate calculations)

- Read the meter and record the reading.
- Read the meter a week later and record the reading.
- Subtract the first reading from the second to give the umber of units (kWh) used.
- Multiply the answer by the cost of a kWh of electricity. IMPORTANT – USE YOUR KNOWN COST
- Add in a figure (we have used 15p per day) to represent the weekly standing charge (or equivalent) and VAT to provide the weekly cost.

Fuel Monitoring Chart – Electricity – Example

Wk No	**METER READING**	**UNITS in kWh** Subtract previous week from current week's reading	**COST** (6.6p per unit)	**Other costs to add in** (Either add the weekly standing charge, or a similar amount if there is a split tariff instead of a standing charge. VAT also needs to be added. These costs are not likely to be more than 15p per day.)	**Approx Weekly Cost**
1	21602				
2	21802	200	£13.20	Add 7x15p = £1.05	£14.25
3	22014	212	£13.99	Add 7x15p = £1.05	£15.04

Fuel Monitoring Chart – Electricity

Wk No	**METER READING**	**UNITS in kWh** Subtract previous week from current week's reading	**COST** (6.6p per unit)	**Other costs to add in** (Either add the weekly standing charge, or a similar amount if there is a split tariff instead of a standing charge. VAT also needs to be added. These costs are not likely to be more than 15p per day.)	**Approx Weekly Cost**
1					
2					
3					
4					
5					
6					
7					
8					
9					
10					
11					
12					
13					
QUARTERLY TOTALS					

FUEL MONITORING CHART – GAS (WITH A METER READING IN CUBIC FEET)

(See Section 5 on identification of meters and accurate calculations)

- Read the meter and record the reading.
- Read the meter a week later.
- Take the first reading from the second reading to give the number of units (or hundreds of cubic feet) used.
- Multiply the answer by 31 to give kWh.
- Multiply that answer by the cost of a kWh of gas. IMPORTANT – USE YOUR KNOWN COST.
- Add in a figure (we have used 15p per day) to represent the weekly standing charge (or equivalent) and VAT to provide the weekly cost.

Fuel Monitoring Chart – Gas (with a meter reading cubic feet) – Example

Wk No	**METER READING**	**100s of cubic feet** Subtract previous week from current week's reading	**UNITS in kWh** (100s cu ft x 31)	**COST** (1.5p per unit)	**Other costs to add in** (Either add the weekly standing charge, or a similar amount if there is a split tariff instead of a standing charge. VAT also needs to be added. These costs are not likely to be more than 15p per day.)	**Approx Weekly Cost**
1	3211					
2	3229	18	558	£8.37	Add 7x15p = £1.05	£9.42
3	3252	23	713	£10.69	Add 7x15p = £1.05	£11.74

Fuel Monitoring Chart – Gas (with a meter reading cubic feet)

Wk No	**METER READING**	**100s of cubic feet** Subtract previous week from current week's reading	**UNITS in kWh** (100s cu ft x 31)	**COST** (1.5p per unit)	**Other costs to add in** (Either add the weekly standing charge, or a similar amount if there is a split tariff instead of a standing charge. VAT also needs to be added. These costs are not likely to be more than 15p per day.)	**Approx Weekly Cost**
1						
2						
3						
4						
5						
6						
7						
8						
9						
10						
11						
13						
QUARTERLY TOTALS						

FUEL MONITORING CHART – GAS (WITH A METER READING IN CUBIC METRES)

(See Section 5 for identification of meters and accurate calculations)

- Read the meter and record the reading.
- Read the meter a week later.
- Take the first reading from the second reading to give the number of cubic metres used.
- Multiply the answer by 11 to give kWh.
- Multiply that answer by the cost of a kWh of gas. IMPORTANT – USE YOUR KNOWN COST.
- Add in a figure (we have used 15p per day) to represent the weekly standing charge (or equivalent) and VAT to provide the weekly cost.

Fuel Monitoring Chart – Gas (with a meter reading cubic metres) – Example

Wk No	**METER READING**	**Cubic metres** Subtract previous week from current week's reading	**UNITS in kWh** (cubic metres x 11)	**COST** (1.5p per unit)	**Other costs to add in** (Either add the weekly standing charge, or a similar amount if there is a split tariff instead of a standing charge. VAT also needs to be added. These costs are not likely to be more than 15p per day.)	**Approx Weekly Cost**
1	02412					
2	02472	60	660	£9.90	Add 7x15p = £1.05	£10.95
3	02545	73	803	£12.05	Add 7x15p = £1.05	£13.10

Fuel Monitoring Chart – Gas (with a meter reading cubic metres)

Wk No	**METER READING**	**Cubic metres** Subtract previous week from current week's reading	**UNITS in kWh** (cubic metres x 11)	**COST** (1.5p per unit)	**Other costs to add in** (Either add the weekly standing charge, or a similar amount if there is a split tariff instead of a standing charge. VAT also needs to be added. These costs are not likely to be more than 15p per day.)	**Approx Weekly Cost**
1						
2						
3						
4						
5						
6						
7						
8						
9						
10						
11						
13						
QUARTERLY TOTALS						

Appendix 4

UNITS OF TEMPERATURE, ENERGY AND CO_2

UNITS

The use of several different units for the same thing can cause a great deal of confusion. Everyday examples are our use of metres or feet and inches in the measurement of length, and of degrees Fahrenheit or degrees Celsius (also called Centigrade) or Kelvin for the measurement of temperature.

HEAT

Heat is a form of energy. It flows from a hotter to a colder object, but is often invisible. It is not the same thing as temperature, which is something we can actually sense – as relative coldness or hotness.

TEMPERATURE

Temperature can be visualised as the degree of movement or 'excitement' of the atoms in a material. If an object comes into contact with a colder object then this energy will be transferred as heat flow from the warmer to the colder material, until the temperatures are the same, at which point the flow of heat will stop. The bigger the difference in temperature, the faster the heat flows.

In some books K is used instead of °C. It refers to degrees Kelvin, a scale starting at absolute zero (-273°C). The size of the 'degree steps' is identical in the two scales, so for differences in temperature, either can be used (for example in U-values).

Temperatures are usually stated in Centigrade °C but some people may be more familiar with Fahrenheit °F so it is useful to be able to convert from one scale to another. Here is the formula, a conversion chart, and some common temperatures often found in domestic situations.

Temperature

Units used	**Written**
Degrees Fahrenheit	°F
Degrees Centigrade	°C

Rule for conversion:

°C to °F

°C x 1.8 + 32 = °F

°F to °C

°F – 32 ÷ 1.8 = °C

Quick conversion chart

°C	**°F**
-10	14
-5	23
0	32
5	41
10	50
15	59
16	61
18	64
20	68
21	70
22	72
25	77
30	86
60	140
100	212

EVERYDAY EXAMPLES OF TEMPERATURES

- Body temperature should be 37°C (98.6°F).
- Most people are comfortable with living room temperatures of around 19° to 21°C (66° to 70°F).
- Bath water is comfortable at 40°C (104°F) to most people.
- 'Hand hot' water, for washing up, is usually 40°C (104°F) but can reach as high as 50°C (122°F).
- At normal pressures, water boils at 100°C (212°F) and freezes at 0°C (32°F).

ENERGY

Units used	**Written**
Kilowatt hours	kWh
Joules	J
Kilojoules = 1,000 Joules	kJ
Megajoules = 1,000,000 Joules	MJ
Gigajoules = 1,000,000,000 Joules	GJ

1 Joule/second = 1 watt

POWER

Units used	**Written**
Watts	W
Kilowatts	kW

CARBON DIOXIDE – CO_2

Carbon dioxide emissions vary from one fuel to another. This list illustrates that some fuels are more polluting than others.

Carbon dioxide emission factors for delivered energy (SAP 2001- See Section 13 for information on SAP)

	kgCO_2 per GJ
Gas (mains)	54
Bulk LPG	69
Bottled gas (propane)	69
Heating oil	79
House coal	81
Anthracite	88
Smokeless solid fuel	109
Electricity	115
Wood	7
Household waste	12
Biomass	7
Biogas (landfill)	7
Waste heat from power stations	5

Appendix 5

BASIC AND BEST PRACTICE SPECIFICATIONS FOR CENTRAL HEATING SYSTEMS (YEAR 2002)

These specifications are taken from: *Central Heating System Specification (CHeSS)* 2002. GIL 59. Energy Efficiency Best Practice in Housing.
www.est.org.uk/bestpractice

See the reference for full details.

Basic Central Heating Specification (Year 2002) Combi or CPSU boiler
(For Basic Central Heating Specification for a regular boiler see page **8**–7)

Reference	CHeSS – HC3 (2002)
Description	Domestic wet central heating system with combi or CPSU boiler.
Boiler	A combi or CPSU boiler which has a SEDBUK efficiency of at least: 78% (natural gas) 80% (LPG) 82% (oil)
Hot water store	None, unless included within boiler.
Controls (See Section 9)	Timeswitch. Room thermostat. Boiler interlock. TRVs on all radiators, except in rooms with a room thermostat. Automatic bypass valve.
Installation	The design and installation of the system must be in accordance with relevant specifications and regulations.

Recommended Best Practice Central Heating Specification. Regular boiler (Year 2002)

Reference	CHeSS – HR4 (2002)
Description	Domestic wet central heating system with regular boiler and separate hot water store.
Boiler	A regular boiler (not a combi) which has a SEDBUK efficiency of at least: 86% (natural gas) 88% (LPG) 89% (oil) These levels of efficiency can only be achieved by condensing boilers.
Hot water store	EITHER High-performance hot water cylinder, OR High-performance thermal (primary) storage system.
Controls (See Section 9)	Programmable room thermostat, with additional timing capability for hot water. Cylinder thermostat. Boiler interlock. TRVs on all radiators, except in rooms with a room thermostat. Automatic bypass valve.
Installation	The design and installation of the system must be in accordance with relevant specifications and regulations.

Recommended Best Practice Central Heating Specification. Combi or CPSU boiler. (Year 2002)	
Reference	CHeSS – HC4 (2002)
Description	Domestic wet central heating system with combi or CPSU boiler.
Boiler	A combi or CPSU boiler which has a SEDBUK efficiency of at least: 86% (natural gas) 88% (LPG) 86% (oil) These levels of efficiency can only be achieved by condensing boilers.
Hot water store	None, unless included within boiler.
Controls (See Section 9)	Programmable room thermostat. Boiler interlock. TRVs on all radiators, except in rooms with a room thermostat. Automatic bypass valve.
Installation	The design and installation of the system must be in accordance with relevant specifications and regulations.

GLOSSARY

ANTHRACITE
A naturally occurring smokeless fuel which is slow burning and particularly suited to room heaters, boilers and cookers.

BALANCED FLUE
A duct which links the boiler with the outside atmosphere and where the inlet (for air coming in) and the outlet (for waste products of burning going out) have the same, or balanced, pressure. An appliance using this type of flue is completely sealed off from the room.

BOTTLED GAS
Liquid Petroleum Gas supplied in a bottle or cylinder. See LIQUID PETROLEUM GAS.

BUDGET METER
A form of prepayment meter operated by an electronic key or tokens. This may also be called token meter, Smart Card meter or prepayment meter.

BUDGET PAYMENT SCHEME
A method of paying for fuel whereby the consumer makes regular payments at fixed intervals.

BUTANE GAS
A particular type of liquid petroleum gas. See LIQUID PETROLEUM GAS.

CALIBRATION (of prepayment meters)
The way in which a meter is set, that is how much fuel you can get from it for the money you put in. For example, a meter can be calibrated so that the consumer pays in advance for fuel, and pays off any previously incurred debt.

CALOR GAS
This is a trade name. See LIQUID PETROLEUM GAS.

CALORIFIC VALUE
The quantity of heat produced per unit of fuel burned. It is used as a way of measuring the quality of a fuel in terms of the amount of heat it can provide.

CARBON DIOXIDE
Carbon dioxide (CO_2) is a gas produced when fossil fuels are burned and is one of the 'greenhouse gases'. UK energy policy aims to cut carbon dioxide emissions.

CENTRAL HEATING
A heating system which provides heat to the whole home from a central source, such as a boiler.

COMBI
A combi is a combination boiler which provides heating and hot water without the need for a hot water storage cylinder.

COMBINED HEAT AND POWER
A type of power station which uses the waste heat from the generation of electricity (normally dumped into the atmosphere, rivers or the sea) to provide heating and hot water.

CONDENSATION
A change of state from gaseous to liquid (e.g. from water vapour to water).

CONVECTED HEAT
Heat which is transported by the movement of a heated substance, such as air or water. Warm air (or water) rises and cool air (or water) falls.

CREDIT METER
A meter which records fuel consumption so that the customer is charged each quarter for fuel already used.

DAMPER
A movable plate to regulate the draught in a fire/stove or other solid fuel burning appliance.

DEHUMIDIFIER
A machine which dries and heats air. It works along the same lines as a refrigerator by creating a very cold surface for moisture in the air to condense on (in preference to condensing on the fabric of the building).

DISTRICT/GROUP COMMUNITY/HEATING
A large heating system where one central boiler serves a group of dwellings. Large-scale district heating systems can serve whole towns.

DRY LINING
Insulation of a wall, usually a solid wall, from the inside by lining the room with plasterboard and insulation.

FLOATING FLOOR
A floor of discontinuous construction, for sound or thermal insulation. The surface of the floor is separated from the loadbearing part of the building structure, whether that is concrete or wooden. A layer of insulation is laid on the rough floor, battens laid on it without nailing, and the floorboards nailed to the battens.

FLUE
A duct through which the waste products of burning fuel can escape to the outside atmosphere.

FUEL DIRECT
A system where the Benefits Agency deducts money at source from a person's Income Support and pays direct to the fuel company money to cover payments towards arrears (a fixed weekly amount) and current consumption (a weekly amount based on average consumption for the previous year divided by 52).

FUEL POVERTY
The condition which households are in when they cannot afford to heat their homes to an adequate standard. The definition of a household in fuel poverty is one which needs to spend 10% of their income on all fuel, in order to heat their home to an adequate standard.

GLOBAL WARMING
The effect which occurs when the radiant heat from the sun passes through the atmosphere and is trapped by greenhouse gases. This increases the temperature of the earth's surface.

GREENHOUSE GASES
See GLOBAL WARMING.

GROUP HEATING
See DISTRICT/GROUP HEATING.

HEAT EXCHANGER
Anything that transfers heat between two materials without those materials coming into contact. A common example of the use of a heat exchanger in a domestic heating system is in the hot water cylinder. Here, very hot water from the boiler passes through a coil of pipe inside the cylinder and transfers heat into the water stored in the cylinder. The water in the boiler circuit never mixes with the water in the cylinder, which is the water that comes out of the taps.

HYPOTHERMIA
An abnormally low deep inner body temperature, defined by the Royal College of Physicians and the British Medical Association as a core temperature of 35°C (95°F) or below.

IMMERSION HEATER
An electric heater element inside a hot water storage tank which heats up the water stored around it. The heater takes time to heat up the water rather than producing hot water instantly.

INDIVIDUAL HEATER
An individually controlled heater which is not part of a central heating system.

INSTANTANEOUS HEATER
A type of water heater which produces hot water instantly when the tap is turned on rather than storing hot water.

INSULATION
Material which is a very poor conductor of heat, used to minimise the rate at which heat is lost from inside a warm building to a cold environment outside.

JOULE (J)
A very small unit of energy. It takes 4200J to raise the temperature of one kilogram of water by one degree Centigrade. Because these units are so small it is more usual to use a unit of millions of joules. This is known as a megajoule (MJ) and is equal to 1,000,000 joules.

KEY METER
See BUDGET METER.

KILOWATT (kW)
A rate of flow of energy equal to one thousand watts. This power rating is applied to heating appliances to define the rate at which they are able to give out heat or power. See WATT.

KILOWATT HOUR (kWh)
A unit for measuring energy. An appliance with a power rating of one kilowatt, running for exactly one hour will use one kilowatt hour of energy. The electricity and gas suppliers use this unit to measure the amounts of fuel they supply. 1 kilowatt hour equals 1000 watt hours.

LIQUID PETROLEUM GAS (LPG)
This is gas made liquid under extreme pressure. Two types are commonly used for heating, these being butane and propane. Butane is usually supplied in cylinders (or 'bottles') and is the type used in free standing room heaters. Propane is more likely to be delivered in bulk to a storage tank outside a property and is used to run a more conventional boiler.

MEGAJOULE (MJ)
See JOULE.

MOULD
A type of fungus propagated by spores which grows on some surfaces where dampness is present.

MULTIPOINT (gas water heater)
A type of instantaneous water heater which provides hot water to a number of outlets (such as sinks, baths and basins) rather than just one.

NATURAL GAS
This is the type of gas which is provided via the gas main in the UK. It is naturally occurring, rather than manufactured, and is essentially methane.

OFF PEAK ELECTRICITY
Electricity charged at a lower rate per kWh, usually during night time hours.

ON PEAK ELECTRICITY
The higher rate per kWh for domestic electricity, usually during the day.

PREPAYMENT METER
A meter which records consumption of fuel and where the customer pays in advance. The main types of prepayment meters use tokens, keys or cards.

PRESERVED TARIFF
A special tariff applicable to some types of heating system (e.g. old storage heaters or under floor electric heating). Names of preserved tariffs and hours of operation vary regionally.

PROGRAMMER
A device which controls the time at which heating and hot water systems are turned on and off. Some can operate heating and hot water programmes independently of each other.

PROPANE GAS
A particular type of LIQUID PETROLEUM GAS.

RADIANT HEAT
Heat which travels in straight lines directly from the heat source, warming up any objects in its path, without appreciably heating up the air it passes through.

RELATIVE HUMIDITY
The amount of water vapour in the air as a proportion of the maximum amount of water vapour the air can hold at a given temperature.

ROOM THERMOSTAT
A device which controls the overall space temperature of a dwelling by responding to air temperature where it is sited and regulating the source of heat.

SOLAR ENERGY
The energy from the sun is used in different ways in domestic buildings. These are passive solar heating, solar hot water heating and solar photovoltaics.

SOLID FUEL
Solid fuel includes: coal and fuels made from coal.

SOLID WALL
An external wall without a cavity, usually brick or stone (plus internal plaster and sometimes external render).

STANDING CHARGE
A charge levied by some electricity and gas suppliers in return for providing a fuel supply, whether or not any fuel is actually used.

SUSPENDED FLOOR
Any floor which is suspended at its ends, not in the middle.

TARIFF
The rate at which electricity or gas is charged.

THERMOSTAT
A device which maintains a system at a constant temperature.

TIMER/TIMECLOCK
A device which controls the times at which the heating and/or hot water are turned on or off.

UNIT (electricity)
A measure of electricity. One unit is equal to one kilowatt hour of electricity, or one kilowatt used for one hour.

U-VALUE
A measure of the rate at which heat passes through building fabric, measured in watts per square metre per degree Celsius (Centigrade). The higher the U-value the greater the rate of heat loss.

WATT (W)
A watt is the SI unit of power. This is the rate of flow of energy, equivalent to one joule per second.

WET CENTRAL HEATING
A central heating system which uses hot water to distribute heat through the home in pipes and radiators (or sometimes under the floor).

INDEX

Numbers in the index refer to page numbers, not section numbers.

A

Action flow charts, **2**–3
Advice, energy, **1**
  Code of Practice, **1**–3
  definition, **1**–1
  delivery, **1**–2
  effectiveness, **1**–2
  reports, **13**–5
Air
  changes per hour (ach), **16**–6, **17**–1, **17**–6
  supply requirements for fuel burning appliances, **17**–5
Anthracite, **8**–8
Appliances, **14**
  calculating running costs, **14**–1
  energy labels, **14**–3
  energy use, **14**–2
  energy efficient, **14**–4
  heating, **8**–15
  operation of, **14**–4
  running costs
    – electricity, **14**–9
    – gas, **14**–12
Arrears for fuel
  definition of, **6**–4
  ways to pay off, **6**–5

B

Balanced flues
  ventilation for, **17**–4
Benefit take up, **7**–4
Bills
  estimated, **5**–12
  information on, **5**–8, **5**–13
  ways to pay, **6**–1
Biofuels, **15**–6
Biogas, **15**–7
Biomass, **15**–6
Boiler(s)
  back, **8**–5
  combination, **8**–5, **8**–18, **9**–4
  condensing, **8**–6
  CPSU, **8**–5, **9**–4
  efficiency, **8**–6, **10**–3
  electric, **8**–8
  energy management systems, **9**–7
  fuels, **8**–2
  gas, **8**–5
  interlock, **9**–5
  LPG, **8**–5
  oil, **8**–5
  solid fuel, **8**–8
  thermostat, **9**–2
Bottled gas heaters, **8**–17
BREDEM, **13**
British Standards
  BS 5250, **16**–8
  BS 5440, **17**–8
  BS 5615, **12**–2
  BS 5803, **12**–4
  BS 5871, **17**–8
  BS 7386, **12**–8
  BS 8303, **17**–8
Budget meter(s), see Prepayment meters
Budget scheme(s), **6**–2
Building Regulations – compliance with
  heating, **8**–20
  heat loss, **11**–1
  insulation, **12**–2
  SAP ratings, **13**–1
  ventilation, **17**–3

C

Calorific value, **5**–9
Calor gas fire(s), see Bottled gas heaters
Carbon dioxide emissions, **15**–1, **A**–12
Carbon Index, **11**–7, **13**–2
Carbon monoxide, **17**–3
Card meter, see Prepayment meters
Cavity wall insulation, **12**–6
Central heating
  appropriateness for the user, **8**–4
  boilers, **8**–5
  controls, **9**–1
  cost to run, **10**–2
  electric, **8**–8, **8**–12
  gas **8**–4, **8**–11
  LPG, **8**–4
  oil, **8**–5
  Programme (Scotland), **7**–2
  solid fuel, **8**–8
  wet systems, **8**–4
Charitable funds, **7**–4
CHeSS, **8**–7, **9**–4, **A**–13
Circulation of hot water in a wet system, **8**–9
Clear Skies, **7**–4
Coal – see Solid fuel
Codes of Practice

Numbers in the index refer to page numbers, not section numbers.

from gas and electricity suppliers, **6**–3
The Domestic Energy Efficiency Advice Code of Practice, **1**–3
Cold
bridging, **11**–5, **16**–3
health risk, **3**–2
weather payments, **7**–4
Combi (Combination) boilers, **8**–5, **8**–18, **9**–4
Combined
Heat and Power (CHP) Scheme, **8**–14
Primary Storage Unit (CPSU), **8**–5
Community heating, **8**–14
Compact Fluorescent Lights (CFLs), **14**–11
Comparative
cost of heating, **10**–2
efficiencies of heating, **10**–2
running costs, **10**–2
Compression seals (draughtproofing), **12**–8
Condensation, **16**
diagnosing, **16**–2, **16**–6
dehumidifiers, **16**–7
fungicides, **16**–7
legal position of tenants, **16**–8
mould growth, **16**–4
reducing, **16**–4, **16**–6
roofs, **12**–5
understanding, **16**–4
ventilation, **16**–6, **17**–6
Condensing boilers, **8**–6
running costs, **10**–3
specification (CheSS), **A**–13
Consumer Advice Organisations
energywatch, **4**–4
Ofgem, **4**–4
Controls, **9**
electric heating, **9**–10
hot water, **9**–11
how to use, **9**
solid fuel system, **9**–9
specification for efficiency, **9**–4
wet system, **9**–2
Controlling temperature
dwelling, **9**–2
hot water, **9**–3
Convector heaters, **8**–15
Convectors, **8**–11
Cost (running)
appliances, **14**–9
central heating and hot water, **10**–3
heating one room, **10**–4
Costs and payback of insulation, **12**–3
Credit meters
electricity, **5**–1
gas, **5**–3
payment for fuel, **6**–1
Cylinder(s)
controls, **9**–3, **9**–11
indirect, **8**–17
insulation, **12**–2

D

Damper(s), **9**–9
Damp-proof course, **16**–1
Dampness
causes of, **16**–1
condensation, **16**
faulty rainwater disposal, **16**–3
plumbing defects, **16**–3
rain penetration, **16**–3
rising damp, **16**–1
Decorative effect gas fire, **8**–16
cost to run, **10**–4
Debt, **6**
fuel, **6**–4
multiple, **6**–7
Dehumidifiers, **16**–7
Delivery methods for advice, **1**–2
Digital timer/programmer, **9**–6
Direct Debit, **6**–1
Disconnection of fuel supply, **6**–6
Code of Practice, **6**–6
preventing, **6**–6
Dishwashers, **14**–6
District Heating System(s), **8**–14
Domestic appliances, see Appliances
Doors, draughtproofing, **12**–9
Double glazing, **12**–11
cost and payback time, **12**–3
Draughtproofing, **12**–8
compression seals, **12**–8
doors, **12**–9
gap filling seals, **12**–9
low friction seals, **12**–8
sash windows, **12**–9
suspended timber floor, **12**–9
ventilation, **12**–8
wooden hinged windows, **12**–9
wiper seals, **12**–8
Dry lining, **12**–7
Ducts, **8**–11

E

Economy 7, **5**–7
meters, **5**–2
electric boilers, **8**–8
storage heaters, **8**–12
water heating, **8**–18, **9**–11
Efficiency
of appliances and lighting, **14**
of boilers, **8**–6
of gas fires, **8**–16
of systems, **10**–3

Numbers in the index refer to page numbers, not section numbers.

Electric
- appliances, **14**
- blankets, **14**–2
- boilers, **8**–8
- fires, and other heaters, **8**–15
- storage heaters, **8**–12
- under floor heating, **8**–13

Electricity
- bills, **5**–8
- dial meters, **5**–2
- digital meters, **5**–1
- disconnection, **6**–6
- heating, **8**–3
- hot water systems, **8**–18
- prepayment meters, **5**–3
- suppliers, **4**
- tariffs, **5**–6

Elemental method, **11**–7

Energy
- advice
  - – Code of Practice, **1**–3
  - – definition, **1**–1
  - – delivery, **1**–2
  - – effective, **1**–2
  - – reports, **13**–5
  - – auditing software, **10**–5
- efficient appliances and lights, **14**–3
- Efficiency Advice Centres, **A**–2
- Efficiency Commitment (EEC), **7**–3
- Efficiency Recommended label, **14**–4
- labels, **14**–3
- Retail Association, **4**–5
- rating, **13**
- Saving Trust, **14**–4
- units of, conversion table, **A**–12

energywatch, **4**–4

Enforcement matters
- Ofgem, **4**–4

Estimated bills, **5**–12

Excess winter deaths, **3**–1

Exposure, **11**–5

External wall insulation, **12**–8

Extract fans
- energy use, **14**–2
- fuel burning appliances, **17**–3
- ventilation, **17**–2

F

Fabric heat loss, **11**–1

Fan heaters, **8**–15

Flat roof insulation, **12**–5

Floor(s)
- exposed, **11**–3
- heat loss, **11**–2
- insulation, **12**–10
- tile warming, **8**–13

Flue(s), **8**–8, **17**–4

Fluorescent lights, **14**–11

Friction seals, draughtproofing, **12**–8

Fridges and freezers, **14**–4

Fuel
- bills, **5**–7
- choice of, **8**–2
- consumption, monitoring, **10**–6
- debt, **6**–4
- Direct, **6**–5
- payment methods, **6**
- poverty, **7**–1
- price comparison, **4**–2
- Rights Handbook, **6**–1
- running costs, heating, **10**–2
- stamps, **6**–2
- suppliers, **4**, **A**–3
  - choice of, **4**–1
  - changing, **4**–2
  - services, **4**–3

Fungicides, **16**–7

G

Gas
- appliances, **14**
- bills, **5**–7
- central heating, **8**–2
- cost of heating one room, **10**–4
- costs of central heating, **10**–3
- digital meter, **5**–3
- fires and heaters, **8**–15, **10**–5
- prepayment/quantum meter, **5**–4
- tariffs, **5**–6

Glazing
- double, **12**–11
- heat loss, **11**–2
- secondary, **12**–11

GLS lightbulbs, **14**–10

Government grants, **7**–1

Grants, **7**
- energy efficiency, **7**–1
- heating, **7**–2
- Information Database (GID) **7**–5
- renewable energy, **7**–4

Gravity heating system, **8**–9

Green,
- electricity, **15**–7
- tariff, **15**–7

Ground source heat pumps, **15**–6

Group Heating, see Community Heating

H

Halogen lights, **14**–10

Hardship
- funds, **7**–4

Numbers in the index refer to page numbers, not section numbers.

related grant schemes, **7**–3
Health risks, **3**
from the cold, **3**–2
from damp homes, **3**–3
Heating, **8**
central, **8**–1
choosing an appropriate system, **8**–4
community, **8**–14
comparison of running costs, **10**–3
controls, **9**
district or group, **8**–14
electric underfloor, **8**–13
room, **8**–15
warm air, **8**–11
wet central, **8**–4
Heat loss, **11**
Building Regulations, **11**–6
fabric, **11**–1
factors affecting, **11**–5
U-values, **11**–2
ventilation, **11**–4
Heat pumps, **15**–6
Heat recovery ventilaton, **17**–6
Hobs, **14**–7
Home Energy Conservation Act (HECA), **13**–4
Home Energy Efficiency Scheme (Wales)
contacts, **7**–6
eligibility, **7**–2
Home visit checklist, **2**–2, **2**–7
Hot water
combi boiler, **8**–18
cylinder insulation, **12**–2
cylinder thermostat, **9**–3
immersion heaters, **8**–18
indirect cylinder, **8**–17
linked with central heating, **8**–17
separate systems, **8**–18
solar panels for, **15**–2
Hydroelectricity, **15**–7
Hypothermia, **3**–2

I

Ill health – from cold conditions, **3**–2
Immersion heater
Economy 7, **8**–18
Economy 7 controllers, **9**–11
electric, **8**–18
Incandescent lights, **14**–10
Indirect cylinder, **8**–17
Instantaneous water heaters, **8**–18, **8**–19
Insulation, **12**
cavity wall, **12**–6
costs and savings, **12**–3
external wall, **12**–8
flat roof, **12**–5
floor, **12**–10
grants, **7**–1
hot water cylinder, **12**–2
internal wall, **12**–7
loft, **12**–4
pipe and tank, **12**–4
room within roof, **12**–5
wall, **12**–6

K

Keep Warm Keep Well, **3**–4
Key meter(s) see Prepayment meters

L

Legal position of tenants (condensation), **16**–7
Lighting, **14**–10
Liquid petroleum gas (LPG)
Association, **A**–4
bottled gas heaters, **8**–17
central heating, **8**–2
cost of heating, **10**–2
Living flame gas fire, **8**–15
Local authority grant schemes, **7**–3
Loft insulation
grants, **7**–1
materials, **12**–4
ventilation, **12**–5
Low energy lights, **14**–10

M

Meters, **5**
Economy 7, **5**–2
electricity, **5**–1
gas, **5**–3
prepayment, **5**–3
Methods of payment for fuel, **6**–1
Mineral fibre insulation, **12**–4, **12**–6
Moisture (condensation), **16**
Monitoring fuel costs, **10**–6
Mould
condensation, **16**–4
effect on health, **3**–3
Multiple debt, **6**–7
Multipoint water heater, **8**–18

N

National Energy Action (NEA), **3**–4, **A**–4
National Home Energy Ratings Scheme (NHER), **10**–5, **13**–3

O

Office of Gas and Electricity Markets (Ofgem), **4**–4

Numbers in the index refer to page numbers, not section numbers.

Off-peak
- electricity tariffs, **5**–6
- storage heaters, **8**–12

Ofgem, **4**–4
Oil
- central heating, **8**–2, **8**–5
- cost for heating, **10**–3
- Firing Technical Advisory Service for the Petroleum Industry (OFTEC), **4**–6
- suppliers, **4**–6

Ovens, **14**–7

P

Passive
- solar design, **15**–1
- stack ventilation (PSV), **17**–6

Payback times (insulation), **12**–3
Payment methods for fuel, **6**
Perimeter duct system, **8**–11
Photovoltaics, **15**–3
- grants, **7**–4

Plasterboard laminates, **12**–7
Plumbing defects, **16**–3
Polystyrene
- cavity fill, **12**–6
- slabs for insulation
  - – under floor, **12**–10
  - – room in roof, **12**–5

Polyurethane, cavity fill, **12**–6
Positive
- pressure ventilation, **17**–7

Power, units of, **A**–12
Prepayment meters
- advantages & disadvantages, **5**–5
- electricity, **5**–3
- gas, **5**–4
- paying off arrears, **6**–5

Preserved electricity tariffs, **5**–7
Programmers, central heating and hot water, **9**–6

Q

Quantum meter (gas), **5**–4
Quarterly fuel bills, **5**–7
- payment, **6**–1

R

Radiators, central heating, **8**–10
Rain penetration, **16**–3
Rainwater disposal, **16**–3
Recording fuel costs, **10**–6
Reflective radiator panels, **12**–8
Renewable energy, **15**
- grants, **7**–4
- policy, **15**–1
- types of, **15**

Renewables Obligation, **15**–1
Repayment methods for fuel debt, **6**–5
Rising damp, **16**–1
Roofs
- heat loss, **11**–2
- insulating flat, **12**–5
- room in the roof, **12**–5

Room thermostats, **9**–2
Running costs
- comparative, for heating and hot water, **10**–2
- electrical appliances, **14**–1
- gas appliances, **14**–12
- lighting, **14**–11

S

SALKENT, **10**–2
SAP rating, **13**
Scottish Communities & Homes Renewables Initiative (SCHRI), **7**–4
Seals, draughtproofing, **12**–8
Secondary glazing, **12**–11
SEDBUK, **8**–6
Showers, **8**–19
Smart card meter, **5**–4
Solar
- energy, **15**–1
- hot water heating, **15**–2
- passive design, **15**–1
- photovoltaics (PV), **15**–3

Solid fuel
- Association, **4**–5
- boilers, **8**–8
- central heating (coal and wood), **8**–3
- controls for, **9**–9
- cost of heating and hot water, **10**–2
- room heaters, **8**–8, **9**–9
- suppliers, **4**–5

Solid wall insulation, **12**–7
Standard Assessment Procedure (SAP), **13**–1
Standby, **14**–8
Standing charges, **5**–6
Storage heaters, **8**–12
Suspended floor insulation, **12**–10

T

Tapstat, **9**–3
Tariffs, gas and electricity, **5**–6
Temperatures, **A**–12
- effect on health, **3**–2
- conversion, **A**–12
- recommended hot water, **9**–3
- recommended room, **9**–3

Thermostat
- boiler, **9**–2

Numbers in the index refer to page numbers, not section numbers.

hot water cylinder, **9**–3
room, **9**–2
Thermostatic radiator valves (TRVs), **9**–3
Tile warming, **8**–13
Timber floors, **12**–10
Timeclocks, **9**–5
Timer/programmer, **9**–6
Token meter, see Prepayment meters
Total heat loss, **11**–1
Triple glazing, **12**–11
Tumble dryers, **14**–5
Turbine, wind, **15**–5

U

Under floor heating
electric **8**–13
wet system, **8**–11
Units of temperature, energy and CO_2, **A**–12
Ureaformaldehyde (UF) foam, **12**–6
Useful addresses, **A**–1
Utilities – see Fuel suppliers
U-values, **11**
Building Regulations, **11**–6
examples of typical, **11**–2

V

Valves in wet central heating systems, **9**–5
VAT, **5**–9
Ventilation, **17**
Building Regulations, **17**–3
condensation, **17**–6
energy efficient, **17**–6
flues, **17**–4
fuel burning appliances, **17**–3
heat loss, **11**–1, **11**–4
Vent(s)
types, **17**–4
recommended levels, **17**–4
Visit, home, **2**–2, **2**–7

W

Walls
cavity insulation, **12**–6
external solid wall insulation, **12**–8
heat loss, **11**–2
internal solid wall insulation, **12**–7
recognising types, **12**–6
solid wall insulation, **12**–8
Wall heater gas, **8**–17
Warm
air central heating, **8**–11
Deal, **7**–2
Front, **7**–2
Front Plus, **7**–2
Homes, **7**–2
Washing machines, **14**–5
Water
heating, **8**–17
Wet central heating, **8**–4, **9**–8
Whole house mechanical ventilation, **17**–7
Wind power, **15**–5
Windows
double glazing, **12**–11
draughtproofing, **12**–8
heat loss, **11**–2
secondary glazing, **12**–11
Winter
campaigns, **3**–4
deaths, **3**–1
fuel payments, **7**–4
Wood
stoves/heating, **8**–3
biofuel, renewable energy, **15**–6

ENERGY ADVICE HANDBOOK – FEEDBACK AND COMMENTS

We welcome feedback and comments on this edition of the Energy Advice Handbook so that material is relevant and accurate in future updates. It would be helpful if you complete this sheet, but we also welcome specific comments on parts if preferred.

Please copy this sheet and return it to us by post to:
Energy Inform, 5 Hawkyard, Greenfield, Oldham, OL3 7NP,
or fax to 01457 810682.
You can also email us at handbook@energyinform.co.uk.

1 Please indicate how frequently Sections of the Handbook are used.

Section Title	Often	Occasionally	Rarely	Never
1 Giving Good Energy Advice				
2 How to use the Handbook				
3 Health Risks from Cold, etc.				
4 Fuel Suppliers, etc.				
5 Meters, Tariffs and Fuel Bills				
6 Fuel Payment Methods, etc.				
7 Financial Help, etc.				
8 Basics of Heating, etc.				
9 Controlling Heating, etc.				
10 Comparative Efficiencies, etc.				
11 Heat Loss from Dwellings				
12 Home Insulation				
13 Energy Rating of Homes				
14 Appliances and Lighting, etc.				
15 Renewable Energy, etc.				
16 Condensation and Dampness				
17 Ventilation				
Appendices (Please indicate which Appendix)				

2 Are there any Sections which you would like to see expanded? Please write in.

....

3 Are there any Sections which you think should be omitted?

....

4 Please write in any specific comments, including format/accuracy, etc.

....

....

....

Thank you very much.

Please write in your contact details.

....

....

CREDITS FOR PHOTOGRAPHS AND ILLUSTRATIONS

Illustrations and photographs which appeared in the second edition of the Heating Advice Handbook are not credited here.

Drawings and reproductions by Laura Hughes on pages:
5–3, **7**–2, **8**–6, **8**–8, **8**–16, **9**–3, **9**–5, **11**–2, **11**–3, **11**–7, **12**–4, **12**–5, **12**–11, **14**–7, **14**–11, **15**–2, **15**–6, **17**–4, **17**–7

Page	Description	Credit
1–2	Advice icons	Energy INFORM
3–3	Thermometer card	Energy INFORM
4–4	energywatch logo	energywatch
4–4	Ofgem's logo	Ofgem
4–5	Solid Fuel Assn logo	Solid Fuel Assn
4–6	OFTEC logo	OFTEC
5–4	Smart Card meter	Landis & Gyr
5–4	Key meter	Landis & Gyr
5–4	Quantum meter	British Gas
5–4	Gas prepayment meter	Landis & Gyr
5–7	Fuel bills	Various suppliers
5–8	Also p 5-10,12,13, bills reproduced from actual	Various suppliers
6–2	Pay Point logo	Pay Point
7–5	Web page	EST
8–5	Oil boiler	Worcester Bosch
8–5	Gas boiler	Baxi
8–5	Panel of combi	Worcester Bosch
8–8	Also 8-9 Flues	GPG 284
8–11	Wet underfloor heating	Danfoss
8–14	Community heating	GPG 301
8–15	Electric radiator / fire	Dimplex
8–16	Gas fires (sections)	GPG 301
8–16	Gas fires - drawings	L.Hughes
9–2	Room stat	Honeywell
9–3	Programmable room stat	Invensys
9–3	TRV	Danfoss
9–3	Cylinder stat	Invensys
9–4	Min controls sets	GPG 302
9–5	Control panel of combi	Worcester Bosch
9–7	Digital programmer	Honeywell
9–7	Digital programmer	Invensys
9–7	Digital programmer	Danfoss
9–7	Mechanical programmer	Invensys
9–9	Controls on a solid fuel	Solid Fuel Assn
9–10	Storage heater controls	Dimplex
9–10	Output of storage heater	Dimplex
9–11	Controls on panel heater	Dimplex
9–11	E7 hot water controllers	Horstmann
11–7	U-values – elemental	Building Regs.
12–5	Room in the loft	Knauf redrawn
13–1	Official SAP logo	DEFRA
13–2	SAP Certificate	MVM
13–3	NHER Certificate	NHER
13–3	Logo used for the NHER	NHER
13–5	Rating in Home Info Pack	EST (draft)
14–3	EU Energy Label	EST
14–4	EU Energy Label	DEFRA
14–4	Energy Efficiency Rec. logo	EST
14–5	Small upright freezer	Bosch
14–6	Washing machine	Bosch
14–10	Light bulbs in Table 14.7	GPG171
14–10	Table 14.7	DELight, ECI
15–2	Passive solar design	GIR27 redrawn
15–2	House with 'sunspace'	DETR redrawn
15–2	Solar collectors on roof	NEF
15–3	Solar hot water heating	EST redrawn
15–4	Solar pv panels	Solar Century
15–4	Array of solar pv cells	Proven Eng.
15–5	Wind turbines	BWEA
15–5	Small wind turbine	Energy INFORM
15–6	Ground source heat pump	GIR 72 redrawn
15–7	Biomass pellets	CSE
16–2	Bridging of d.p.c.s	BRE Digest 245
16–4	mould growth (top)	Energy Inform
17–6	Also 17-7,ventilation	GPG 268